Structured Group Psychotherapy for Bipolar Disorder

The Life Goals Program

Second Edition

Mark S. Bauer, MD, is in the Department of Psychiatry and Human Behavior at Brown University and on staff in the Mental Health Service of the Department of Veterans Affairs Medical Center in Providence, RI. Dr. Bauer's career-long focus has been on improving outcome in serious mental illness, particularly manic-depressive disorder. He has contributed advances by developing new assessment tools and new treatment modalities such as the use of high-dose thyroid hormone for rapid cycling. For the past decade, his main focus has been on studying interventions that take efficacious treatments and improve their effectiveness in actual practice. He has been recognized with awards for his research, clinical expertise, teaching, and administrative skills. He served for 11 years on the Scientific Advisory Board for the Depression and Bipolar Support Alliance (formerly National Depressive and Manic-Depressive Association) and has twice been named Exemplary Psychiatrist by the National Alliance for the Mentally Ill.

Linda McBride, CS, MSN, is a Clinical Nurse Specialist in the Mental Health and Behavioral Sciences Service of the Department of Veterans Affairs Medical Center in Providence, RI. During her tenure as an Advanced Practice Nurse she has become recognized for her innovative program development for people with severe mental illnesses. Nurse McBride contributed to the development of a "Collaborative Practice Model" for the treatment of manic-depressive disorder. This innovative model served as a pilot program that has been implemented in mental health services across the country. Nurse McBride has consulted in the United States and abroad. Because of her clinical, research, and patient-education acumen, she has been recognized and presented with multiple awards including the Administrator's Excellence in Nursing Award by the Department of Veterans Affairs.

Structured Group Psychotherapy
for Bipolar Disorder

The Life Goals Program
Second Edition

Mark S. Bauer, MD
Linda McBride, MSN

 Springer Publishing Company

Springer Publishing Company, Inc.
536 Broadway
New York, NY 10012-3955

Acquisitions Editor: Sheri W. Sussman
Production Editor: Pamela Lankas
Cover design by Joanne Honigman

03 04 05 06 07 / 5 4 3 2 1

Library of Congress Cataloging-in-Publication Data

Bauer, Mark S.
    Structured group psychotherapy for bipolar disorder : the life goals program / Mark S. Bauer, Linda McBride — 2nd ed.
      p. cm.
    Includes bibliographical references and index.
    ISBN 0-8261-1694-9
    1. Manic-depressive illness—Treatment. 2. Group psychotherapy.
3. Manic-depressive persons—Life skills guides. I. McBride, Linda.
II. Title.

RC516 .B37 2003
616.89'50651—dc21

                                  2002066813

Printed in the United States of America by Maple-Vail Book Manufacturing Group.

Dr. Bauer: To my pals, Beth, and Nick and Maggie.

*Ms. McBride: For my children, Ryan and Kate,
and for Bud.*

Contents

Foreword

During the last 5 years, a growing body of research has demonstrated the benefits of several specific psychotherapy programs for people with manic-depressive disorder. Although these programs differ in length and format, common elements include structured education regarding manic-depressive disorder and its treatment, use of techniques from cognitive and behavioral psychotherapy, and training in specific self-management skills. This good news regarding structured and specific psychotherapies for manic-depressive disorder, however, has not reached most mental health providers. Bauer and McBride's guide to their Life Goals Program is an effort to spread the word.

Bauer and McBride's program is based on a series of core principles for effective, patient-centered care for manic-depressive disorder. First is the belief that educating and activating people with manic-depressive disorder is the key to long-term management. Effective treatment depends on collaboration between providers and educated, motivated patients. Developing collaborative treatment relationships inside and outside the group is an important focus of therapy. Second is the focus on structured problem-solving techniques. One might view the problem-solving method as a distillation of the essential elements of cognitive-behavioral therapy: breaking problems down into small pieces, identifying specific solutions, focusing on small and specific steps, and evaluating results. The problem-solving methods emphasized in the Life Goals Program are especially appropriate for people struggling with a chronic illness such as manic-depressive disorder. Participants are encouraged to recognize and celebrate positive steps toward long-term goals. Each action plan is seen as a trial or experiment, with the expectation that plans must be continuously revised and refined. The most important principle is that that people with manic-depressive disorder (even those who are severely ill or disabled) are doing their best to manage the symptoms of mood disorder. Even behaviors usually viewed as maladaptive or even criminal (such as suicide attempts or substance use) can be viewed as attempts to manage mood symptoms. The Life Goals Program attempts to support more effective self-management by examining positive and negative consequences

of various coping strategies. For example: rather than immediately con-
demning or forbidding substance use, the group leader asks members to
carefully consider how well it works. Those involved in the care of people
with manic-depressive disorder (both family members and health care
providers) would probably welcome an alternative to scolding and ultima-
tums in the management of disruptive or self-destructive behaviors.

Over the last 2 years, we have used the first edition of *The Life Goals
Program* as part of a population-based effort to improve care for people with
manic-depressive disorder in our health care system. For the majority of
people with manic-depressive disorder (even those in treatment for many
years) Phase 1 of the program was a valuable basic course in effective medical management and self-management. Many of those continuing in the
long-term Phase 2 program described remarkable growth in the skills and
self-confidence needed for effective self-management.

The second edition maintains the philosophy and structure of the first
while incorporating some important improvements. Didactic information
for the initial group sessions includes more specifics regarding types of pharmacotherapy and types of psychotherapy. Information regarding medication
management has been thoroughly updated since the first edition in 1996. The
revised program includes increased attention to stigmatization of psychiatric
disorders and how stigma can affect one's choices for self-management and
collaboration with health care providers. More specific information is included
regarding self-care strategies such as maintenance of regular sleep–wake
cycles. A new session has been added to the Phase 1 portion of the program
to focus on long-term treatment planning (including establishing collaborative
relationships with mental health providers and use of peer support resources
such as the Depression and Bipolar Support Alliance). All participants are
encouraged to create a detailed care plan—to be regularly re-evaluated and
updated during Phase 2 of the program. Group leaders should find the revised
format more user-friendly than that of the first edition.

The second edition of Bauer and McBride's book should serve a variety of
audiences. For mental health providers or systems hoping to establish an
organized psychoeducational group program, this detailed manual will
prove invaluable. In an ideal world, this program or a similar one would be
available through every mental health center or clinic serving people with
manic-depressive disorder. When a full-scale group program is not a realistic option, the Life Goals Program manual should still be a useful resource
for clinicians, patients, and family members.

GREGORY E. SIMON, MD MPH
EVETTE J. LUDMAN, PHD

Acknowledgments

Special thanks to Evette Ludman, PhD for all her guidance, encouragement, and assistance editing Phases 1 and 2 and to the entire nurse therapist team at Group Health: Martha Sharon, RN, Margaret Brooks, RN, and Deborah Ostrovsky, RN. We wish to formally acknowledge the careful review and comments from a number of our other colleagues, including the editorial assistance of Sheri Johnson, PhD, Michel Aubry, MD, Gregory Simon, MD, and Sagar Parikh, MD. Special thanks to Jeffrey Montelo for illustrating the Mood Disorders Spectrum, The Brain, and Neurotransmission exhibits. Special thanks also to Eileen Richardson for her editorial assistance. We also wish to acknowledge the Life Goals Program group members across North America and Europe. They inspired many of the changes we made to the Program.

Introduction

The dual purposes of the Life Goals Program have not changed since the publication of the first edition in 1996. First, the Program assists individuals with bipolar disorder to participate more effectively in the management of their illness. Second, since the substantial social and occupational morbidity caused by manic-depressive disorder does not necessarily, or even regularly, improve once the symptoms of the illness are under control, the Program also addresses directly the functional deficits caused by the illness.

However, since the publication of the first edition of this book in 1996 much has changed in the field of evaluation and treatment of manic-depressive disorder. For the Life Goals therapist to be able to treat individuals effectively, he or she must be current in these areas. Hence the need for updating the "primer" on manic-depressive disorder that comprises the first part of this book.

In addition, there have been substantive changes to the Life Goals procedures themselves. Though not changing either the focus or the content of the program, the additional years of experience at our site and with an increasing number of collaborators in North America and Europe have led us to make changes that improve the delivery of the intervention.

First, what has *not* changed in the area of manic-depressive disorder? It is clear that the disorder has not gone away. The basic diagnostic criteria have not changed. All available information indicates that the morbidity from the disorder has not lessened. There is no evidence that its prevalence is decreasing. In fact, although there is also no firm evidence that the prevalence of the disorder has increased since 1996, the frequency with which it is discussed in the media and socially makes one wonder whether it is being recognized more frequently than in the past.

In addition, we do not yet have breakthrough data on the underlying pathophysiology of the disorder. Although there are intriguing leads, particularly in the fields of genetics and imaging (summarized in chapter 3), we are at the stage of better understanding the complexity of the questions than at the stage of being able to provide sophisticated, definitive answers to the question, "What causes manic-depressive disorder?"

What, then, is sufficiently new to warrant publication of a revised, updated edition of this book? Although there have been no major changes in the diagnosis or outcome of manic-depressive disorder, a new awareness of the role of comorbid, or co-occurring, disorders has developed, as reviewed in chapter 1. In addition, we now have a better, though still evolving, understanding of what characteristics will predict better versus worse outcomes for this disorder. In particular, as outlined in chapter 2, there is an increased sensitivity to the importance of ongoing depressive symptoms, even at low levels, on social and occupational function and conceptually, we continue with regard to specific individuals to ask the unanswerable question "How much of the continued functional deficits are due to ongoing depression, and how much of the continued depression is due to ongoing social and occupational impoverishment?"

In terms of treatment, there has been substantial progress in the development of new interventions for manic-depressive disorder, both pharmacologically and psychotherapeutically. Pharmacologically, as reviewed in detail in chapter 4, we have seen the introduction of several new anticonvulsants that have been applied to treatment of this disorder; among anticonvulsants only carbamazepine and valproate were widely used at the time that the first edition was published. In addition, several new atypical neuroleptics have been introduced; at the time of the first edition, only clozapine and risperidone were available. The application of this expanding group of compounds to symptoms of mania and hypomania holds substantial promise both in terms of different side effect profiles and in terms of efficacy compared to older neuroleptics.

Moreover, we as a field have become more sophisticated in evaluating scientific evidence as the tools of *evidence-based medicine* are applied with increasing reach and sophistication to mental health therapeutics. As a result, in choosing among available interventions for those whom we treat, we can identify and take into account evidence deficits and bias both from scientific sources and from the increasingly virulent marketing strategies to which we all—providers and consumers alike—are subject. This evidence-based mental health approach is apparent in chapters 4 and 5, overviews of biological and psychosocial treatments of manic-depressive disorder, each of which has been completely rewritten for this edition.

Perhaps even more dramatic than the expansion of our pharmacologic armamentarium since 1996 is the explosion of data on psychosocial interventions for bipolar disorder. Although no intervention studies suggest that psychosocial interventions can be successfully used without a pharmacologic component to treatment, it is becoming increasingly obvious that optimal pharmacologic, medical-model treatment requires psychosocial management as well. Chapter 5 takes an evidence-based approach in reviewing these psychosocial interventions, both older studies analyzed together for the first time and many studies published since 1996.

Two aspects that derive from this review of psychosocial interventions deserve particular mention. First, when one compares the methods side by side, it becomes apparent that despite their diverse formats, many share a common core agenda. This agenda focuses on:

- education regarding the illness and options for treatment in general
- recognition of one's own pattern of illness
- identification of symptom triggers
- helpful versus harmful coping responses
- development of a personally tailored plan of action for response to various symptoms.

If it sounds like the Life Goals Program, it is because we and many others have converged on this core agenda. Whether given within an individual, group, or family framework, and whether provided from a predominantly cognitive, educative, or other approach, the consistency of the core agenda across interventions is striking.

Second, we purposely speak of psychosocial rather than psychotherapeutic interventions in chapter 5 because of our recognition that the manner in which care is organized can comprise a major help, or hindrance, to optimal treatment for individuals with serious mental illness, including manic-depressive disorder. Accordingly, there have developed several studies, including two federally funded randomized controlled trials currently under way, that provide information on how systems of care can best facilitate the delivery of treatment for individuals with manic-depressive disorder. These studies are reviewed in chapters 5 and 6 and represent a new dimension of thinking about treatment for such illnesses—and a particularly exciting area of future investigation because it may provide new levers for improving outcome in this difficult, chronic illness.

Although the conceptual bases of the Life Goals Program have not changed since its inception, chapter 6 has been extensively rewritten. This has been done both to simplify and clarify the conceptual sources enumerated in the first edition of this book and to give more explicit acknowledgment to commonalities between the Life Goals Program and the several disease management programs for chronic medical illnesses that have contributed to the current form of this program. The point is made more explicitly throughout the book, but especially in chapters 3 and 6, that manic-depressive disorder is best conceptualized as a *biopsychosocial* disorder (Engel, 1977)—and so therefore must be its treatment.

The major open conceptual issue at this point is the degree to which the success of the Life Goals Program in improving outcome is a function only of the intervention itself versus the degree to which its success depends on the context of care in which it is given. For instance, as outlined in chapter 5, in the Veterans Affairs study all aspects of treatment for manic-depressive illness are brought into an integrated disease management program. In the Group Health Cooperative of Puget Sound study, the individual in treatment collaborates with a registered nurse, who then relays information and guideline-derived management recommendations to various psychiatrists not specially trained in managing the disorder. In a study funded by the Canadian government that is just getting under way at this time in Toronto under the direction of Sagar Parikh, MD, the Life Goals Program is being given as a stand-alone intervention.

In each of these cases, the individuals in treatment are being educated and supported by the Life Goals Program. Will they find their providers to be willing and capable collaborators? Can the Life Goals Program exert some beneficial effect even if they do not? In perhaps the ultimate test of this question, we have recently begun work with a large health maintenance organization to incorporate many of the Life Goals Program components into an Internet-based package for education of individuals with manic-depressive disorder who inhabit that side of the "digital divide." If the principles used by the Life Goals Program and by similar interventions discussed in chapter 5 can exert a beneficial effect in such "supply side" or "pull marketing" interventions, it will provide a truly powerful and widely applicable method to improve outcome and quality of care for this disorder.

Finally, to arm the therapist with current and accurate information about all relevant aspects of manic-depressive disorder, we continue to strive to walk the line between in-depth scholarship and day-to-day utility. Accordingly, we have attempted to make the text of the first part of the book simple and readable, yet have provided an extensive primary source bibliography in the References section for those desiring more in-depth information. As in the first edition, we urge the Life Goals therapist to become familiar with Frederick Goodwin and Kay Redfield Jamison's definitive *Manic-Depressive Illness* (1990), currently being updated, as a comprehensive scholarly text.

In terms of the Life Goals Program procedures themselves, although the focus of the program remains intact, several changes have been made to improve the clarity of the content and ease of delivery. These changes evolve from additional years of personal experience leading groups and the generous suggestions offered by our colleagues and group members, both in the United States and abroad.

The recommended time frame for facilitating Phase 1 and Phase 2 sessions has increased from 60 to 75 minutes, although the pace of each session is determined by therapist judgment and how well group members integrate the session process and content. This time adjustment provides adequate time to deliver Phase 1 Focus Points and Phase 2 behavioral and interpersonal interventions to more impaired group members.

Sessions 1 through 5 have received several minor revisions, as detailed below. Sessions on depression and mania have been reordered based on feedback that commencing the program with sessions on depression was discouraging to group members. The two sessions on mania now precede sessions on depression. A new Session 6, "Treatments for Manic-Depressive Disorder." has been added. A comprehensive Personal Treatment Plan now completes the group psychoeducation component of Phase 1.

In Session 1, the Mood Disorders Spectrum has been reformatted to improve the representation of mood cycling and the intensity of depressive episodes, notably in manic-depressive disorder type II. Additionally, the years have enhanced our insight regarding the range of personal social and intrapsychic manifestations of psychiatric stigma and its tremendous influence on how group members may integrate or reject learning illness management skills. Therefore, psychiatric stigma is more thoroughly processed to increase group member awareness of how tradition and culture may influence their coping responses.

The integration of life events and the impact of stress on mood episode intensity and recurrence has been expanded in the sessions on mania and depression. Personal mania and depression profiles in sessions 2 and 4 now incorporate feedback from family, friends, and coworkers who may offer valuable insights. Many of the session exhibits have been reformatted to facilitate group member use in their everyday lives.

Session 6 provides group members with a summary structure for identifying specific goals of treatment for manic-depressive disorder with an emphasis on self-management and collaboration. Emphasis is placed not only on the medication regime but also on such collaborative and self-management tasks as integration of a structured daily routine, sleep–wake cycle regulation, and the pertinent role of specific psychotherapies to improve mood stability and overall functioning. The session concludes with each group member completing a detailed Personal Care Plan.

Phase 2 retains its behavioral and cognitive orientation to facilitate group member personal goal attainment plans, supplemented with low-intensity interpersonal and psychodynamic therapeutic interventions. An orientation session has been added to the manual to illustrate therapist delivery of the main components in Phase 2. This session fills the gap identified by many of our colleagues during the transition from the completely structured didactic format of Phase 1 to the semi-structured format of Phase 2. The orientation session clarifies strategies to cultivate a supportive group milieu and the ongoing integration of illness management skills learned in Phase 1. It introduces the concepts associated with goal attainment to assist group members as they navigate the identification and development of realistic and meaningful personal life goals.

The stages of goal attainment have been more explicitly operationalized. They now include the Description of the Challenge, overall Goal Identification, Subgoal Development, Construction of Behavioral Steps and Monitoring Progress and Troubleshooting Roadblocks. These changes are intended to facilitate ease of application by the group members, many of whom initially feel overwhelmed by the expectation they will succeed in achieving personal life goals. The term *Challenge* replaces the customary term *problem* at the request of group members working toward improving their self-image.

The section on Therapist Roadblocks and Strategies is revised and includes vignettes to illustrate detailed application of the ideas described. Table 8.4 has been added, offering a quick reference for therapists as they manage the multitude of therapeutic challenges in the Phase 2 process.

Finally, as in the introduction to the first edition, we offer a note on language. We continue our commitment to recognizing the dignity and equality of those who come to us for help with manic-depressive disorder through the language we use. As in the first edition, the words *patient* and *client* appear seldom if at all. As we noted in the Introduction to the first edition:

> When we refer to persons with a mental illness as "patients," we bundle together their illness with their identity. Certainly there is justification for using this shorthand in clinical situations, as we busily try to communicate in concise yet accurate terms during our busy workdays. However, in disorders of mood, behavior, cognition, and perception the distinction between illness and identity becomes easily blurred. This is the rule rather than the exception for the lay public, and frequently a problem with an individual's family and friends. It is an endemic and profoundly demoralizing problem for the individuals we treat, who not infrequently come to consider themselves little more than the product of their bipolar disorder. And it is a temptation for us as providers also to forget that when we treat bipolar disorder that we are treating an individual with a long and unique life history that has nothing to do with the illness—a life history filled with hopes, aspirations, failures, loves, losses, preferences, likes, dislikes, and everything else that makes of us a unique and dignified human being.
>
> Unfortunately many of the individuals we treat have themselves forgotten this, so overwhelmed are they with the burden of their illness and the impact it has had. Part of our job in rehabilitating is to lend hope, and part of lending hope is to reframe their illness: You are a person, and you carry the burden of an illness that you must and can manage.

Therefore, we prefer to speak of persons, individuals, or group members who happen to have this disorder, rather than more clinical—and often distancing and sometimes dehumanizing—terms like *patient*. Perhaps, if culturally we eventually return to the connotation of the original Latin meaning of the word *patient*, "one who suffers," we will then be able to use the term without its less savory baggage.

What of the more obvious change to use of the term *manic-depressive,* rather than *bipolar,* in the text of this edition? We made this decision at a time when the media is becoming more free in the use of the term "bipolar," and when it appears to be entering common usage. In fact, the National Depressive and Manic-Depressive Association has just changed its name to The Depressive and Bipolar Support Alliance, in large part because of feedback from its members who perceived negative annotations to the term "manic-depressive." Why go "backwards"? Why use the old term?

Reexamining the descriptive data on the disorder in chapter 1 makes it clear that mania and hypomania are not typically the polar opposite of depression. In some classic instances, they can be, and in some individuals for a time during their manic or hypomanic episodes they find themselves euphoric, overly optimistic, and without a care in the world. However, this is by no means the rule—and perhaps such euphoric manic periods may be more the exception now than in the past (for reasons that are open to speculation). Hyperactivation, variously defined, appears to be the core symptom of mania and hypomania, and mood and sense of well-being appear to be much more variable and transient. Moreover, additional data reviewed in chapter 2 indicate that subjective quality of life reported by individuals themselves during an episode of mania or hypomania is unequivocally not better, and by some measures worse, than in normal mood. Thus, if we look for, or expect, individuals with manic-depressive illness to regularly have euphoric highs or productive manic periods, we will miss many diagnoses. This perception is also anecdotally shared by many individuals who suffer from the disorder [see, for example, the first-person account of Hartmann, (2002)]. We will also run the risk of underestimating the morbidity and suffering associated with this illness.

Again, language can be a guide to our perceptions. We choose, therefore, to use the more accurate term *manic-depressive* than the more recently introduced yet less accurate term *bipolar* throughout the the book.

PART I

Overview of Manic-Depressive Disorder

Chapter 1

Diagnosis of Manic-Depressive Disorder

CONCEPTUALIZATIONS OF MANIC-DEPRESSIVE DISORDER

Diagnosis is the cornerstone of treatment in psychiatry, as in other areas of medicine. In all fields of mental health, there is increasing awareness of the importance of using specific diagnoses as the basis of developing interventions for persons with mood and behavioral problems.

This is particularly important in the management of manic-depressive disorder, because it can be confused with other conditions that have similar features but vastly different treatments. It is striking, for instance, that a survey of individuals with manic-depressive disorder conducted by the National Depressive and Manic Depressive Association (NDMDA) found that almost half of the sample had had symptoms for at least 5 years but were not diagnosed until after having seen at least three professionals (Lish, Dime-Meenan, Whybrow, Price, & Hirschfeld, 1994). Thus, it is worthwhile to review in some detail the basis for diagnosis of manic-depressive disorder so that the clinician may be comfortable with this critical first step in its treatment.

Diagnosis in psychiatry is based almost exclusively on phenomenology, the descriptive appearance of the syndrome of interest. This is because there are few diagnoses for which the pathophysiology is known or for which valid and reliable diagnostic tests are available.

Over the past several years, as part of the development of the fourth edition of the *Diagnostic and Statistical Manual of Mental Disorders* (DSM-IV; American Psychiatric Association, 1994a, 2000), an extensive effort has been made to review evidence to identify core characteristics and limits of the various psychiatric syndromes, including mood disorders. Of all psychiatric nosological systems, DSM-IV has had perhaps the highest standards for requiring scientific data for additions, deletions, or modifications of the various syndromes. A sample of these data can be found in the multivolume *Sourcebook for DSM-IV,* published as a companion to the manual itself (Widiger & Frances, 1994).

Diagnosis in manic-depressive disorder is made on the basis of two types of descriptive data: *cross-sectional* and *longitudinal.* Cross-sectional data refer to descriptive aspects of a syndrome that occur at a particular point in time, such as the number and type of depressive symptoms that occur during an episode of depression. Longitudinal data refer to the course of symptoms over time, such as the timing, duration, and recurrence of depressive episodes. Both cross-sectional and longitudinal data are essential for the proper diagnosis of manic-depressive disorder. Frequently, diagnostic errors occur when longitudinal data are neglected and the clinician focuses solely on cross-sectional presentation: "This must be manic-depressive disorder because the person appears manic at the present time," or "This cannot be manic-depressive disorder because the person is depressed now."

This longitudinal orientation is not new. Kraepelin's treatise *Manic-Depressive Insanity and Paranoia* (Kraepelin, 1921; see also Berrios & Hauser, 1988) is a classic in large part because of its emphasis on longitudinal as well as cross-sectional data. Kraepelin described two main types of individuals: those whose illness followed a progressive downhill course and those whose illness remitted and recurred frequently with return to their normal baseline. Kraepelin referred to the former as dementia praecox (early dementia), which we now call schizophrenia, the latter as manic-depressive illness. Kraepelin's use of the term *psychosis* differed from our current use. For Kraepelin, psychosis was an indicator of severity rather than of specific paranoid symptoms or hallucinations. This latter group included almost all severe mood disorders, grouping together persons with severe depressive episodes regardless of whether they experienced mania as well. The key point here is that Kraepelin used not only cross-sectional data (the occurrence of mood episodes) but also longitudinal data (the tendency of mood episodes to remit and recur) to separate mood disorders from schizophrenia.

Leonhard (1979) proposed the distinction between manic-depressive, or bipolar disorder and pure depressive disorder, which has come to be called **unipolar depression.** He based this distinction on the occurrence of manic episodes in manic-depression but not in pure depression. He extended evidence of this distinction with the observation that mania tended to occur more frequently in family members of persons with bipolar rather than unipolar disorder. This is an early example of the type of approach used to evaluate evidence in later studies of psychiatric syndromes, (e.g., Robins & Guze, 1970), which eventually served as the basis for evaluating most of the evidence for mood disorder validation for DSM-IV.

Kraepelin's and Leonhard's investigations represent a *categorical approach* to diagnosis, in which manic-depressive disorder is clearly separated from schizophrenia, on the one hand, and unipolar depression, on the other. This approach is most successful when only classic cases are considered. In reality, however, there exist many borderline cases in which features of more than one syndrome exist and clear categorization is not possible. In recognition of this reality, Bleuler's classic *Textbook of Psychiatry* (Bleuler, 1924) proposed that manic-depressive disorder and schizophrenia lie on a continuum that has no sharp border, with persons often exhibiting characteristics of both syndromes and evolving a course midway between the two. This *continuum,* or *dimensional, approach* has led to the identification of *schizoaffective disorder* (Blacker & Tsuang, 1992; Levitt & Tsuang, 1988), which shares characteristics with both schizophrenia and manic-depressive or depressive disorders.

Furthermore, within manic-depressive disorder, levels of severity have been recognized, as outlined in more detail below. The severe end of the spectrum is *type I* manic-depressive disorder, characterized by depressive episodes plus manic episodes. *Type II* manic-depressive disorder is characterized not by manic episodes but by the less severe hypomanic episodes. At the milder end of the spectrum, cyclothymia consists of depressed periods that do not meet criteria for major depression, alternating with hypomania or subsyndromal hypomanic symptoms.

CLINICAL CHARACTERISTICS OF MANIC-DEPRESSIVE DISORDER

CORE CHARACTERISTICS OF MANIC-DEPRESSIVE DISORDER

The phenomenologic approach to diagnosis of the current DSM system is based most recently on the St. Louis, or Feighner, Criteria (Feighner et al., 1972), which specified phenomenologic criteria for the identification of various psychiatric disorders. The St. Louis Criteria, as well as the closely related Research Diagnostic Criteria (RDC) (Spitzer, Endicott, & Bobins, 1978), served as the diagnostic system for most clinical psychiatric research in the 1970s and early 1980s. They provide a common language for disorder description among investigators and increasing comparability of diagnostic samples across various sites. These research tools became the underpinning of clinical practice, with the descriptive approach to clinical diagnosis formally becoming the basis for diagnosis by the third edition of the DSM and its revision (American Psychiatric Association, 1980, 1987). Currently, the DSM-IV and the closely related International Classification of Diseases (ICD-9-CM; World Health Organization, 1977) serve as the basis for the diagnosis of manic-depressive disorder both in clinical practice and in psychiatric research.

The DSM-based definition of manic-depressive *disorder* is built on the identification of individual mood *episodes* (Table 1.1). DSM-IV criteria for individual mood episodes are summarized in Tables 1.2 through 1.5 for *major depressive, manic, mixed,* and *hypomanic episodes.* Criteria for these types of episodes are reviewed in greater detail below. Periods of normal mood are sometimes called *euthymia.*

For the purposes of this portion of the discussion, it is important to understand that *the diagnosis of manic-depressive disorder derives from the occurrence of individual episodes over time.* Persons who experience a manic, hypomanic, or mixed episode, virtually all of whom also have a history of one or more major depressive episodes (Winokur, Clayton, & Reich, 1969), are diagnosed with manic-depressive disorder. Those who experience major depressive and manic episodes are diagnosed with manic-depressive type I disorder, and those with major depressive and hypomanic (milder manic) episodes are diagnosed with manic-depressive type II disorder.

Mood episodes are discrete periods of altered feeling, thought, and behavior. Typically, they have a distinct onset and offset, beginning over days or weeks and eventually ending gradually after several weeks or months. *Major depressive episodes* are defined by discrete periods of depressed or blue mood or loss of interest or pleasure in life that endure over weeks (see Table 1.2). The major symptom of depression is a marked decrease in energy and drive (American Psychiatric Association, 1994a, 2000). Extreme effort may be required to accomplish small tasks and self-care. The depressed person may become completely unable to perform social and occupational roles. Neurovegetative symptoms of depression include disturbances in sleep, appetite, and psychomotor activity. Depressed mood may be experienced as feeling

TABLE 1.1   Summary of Mood Episodes and Mood Disorders

Episode	Disorder
Major depressive episode	Major depressive disorder, single episode
Major depressive episode + major depressive episode	Major depressive disorder, recurrent
Major depressive episode + manic/mixed episode	Manic-depressive (bipolar) disorder, type I
Major depressive episode + hypomanic episode	Manic-depressive (bipolar) disorder, type II
Chronic fluctuations between subsyndromal depression and hypomania	Cyclothymic disorder
Chronic subsyndromal depression	Dysthymic disorder

TABLE 1.2 Criteria for Major Depressive Episode

A. Five (or more) of the following symptoms have been present during the same 2-week period and represent a change from previous functioning; at least one of the symptoms is either (1) depressed mood or (2) loss of interest or pleasure.

   Note: Do not include symptoms that are clearly due to a general medical condition, or mood-incongruent delusions or hallucinations.

   1. Depressed mood most of the day, nearly every day, as indicated by either subjective report (e.g., feels sad or empty) or observation by others (e.g., appears tearful). *Note:* In adolescents, can be irritable mood.
   2. Markedly diminished interest or pleasure in all, or almost all, activities most of the day, nearly every day (as indicated by either subjective account or observation made by others).
   3. Significant weight loss when not dieting or weight gain (e.g., a change of more than 5% of body weight in a month), or decrease or increase in appetite nearly every day. *Note:* In children, consider failure to make weight gains.
   4. Insomnia or hypersomnia nearly every day.
   5. Psychomotor agitation or retardation nearly every day (observable by others, not merely subjective feelings of restlessness or being slowed down).
   6. Fatigue or loss of energy nearly every day.
   7. Feelings of worthlessness or excessive or inappropriate guilt (which may be delusional) nearly every day (not merely self-reproach about being sick).
   8. Diminished ability to think or concentrate, or indecisiveness, nearly every day (either by subjective account or as observed by others).
   9. Recurrent thoughts of death (not just fear of dying), recurrent suicidal ideation without a specific plan, or a suicide attempt or specific plan for committing suicide.

B. The symptoms do not meet criteria for a mixed episode (see Table 1.4).
C. The symptoms cause clinically significant distress or impairment in social, occupational, or other important areas of functioning.
D. The symptoms are not due to the direct physiological effects of a substance (e.g., drug of abuse or medication) or a general medical condition (e.g., hypothyroidism).
E. The symptoms are not better accounted for by bereavement (i.e., after the loss of a loved one, the symptoms persist for longer than 2 months or are characterized by marked functional impairment, morbid preoccupation with worthlessness, suicidal ideation, psychotic symptoms, or psychomotor retardation).

Reprinted with permission from the *Diagnostic and Statistical Manual of Mental Disorders,* Fourth Edition, Text Revision Copyright 2000, American Psychiatric Association.

empty, slowed down, irritable, or angry. Often one's perception of self and others becomes distorted. One may feel inadequate or experience an unwarranted sense of worthlessness or guilt.

Depressive episodes in manic-depressive disorder are indistinguishable from those in major depressive disorder. About half of persons with manic-

TABLE 1.3   Criteria for Manic Episode

A. A distinct period of abnormally and persistently elevated, expansive, or irritable
   mood, lasting at least 1 week (or any duration if hospitalization is necessary).
B. During the period of mood disturbance, three (or more) of the following
   symptoms have persisted (four if the mood is only irritable) and have been
   present to a significant degree:
   1. inflated self-esteem or grandiosity
   2. decreased need for sleep (e.g., feels rested after only 3 hours of sleep)
   3. more talkative than usual or pressure to keep talking
   4. flight of ideas or subjective experience that thoughts are racing
   5. distractibility (i.e., attention too easily drawn to unimportant or irrelevant
      external stimuli)
   6. increase in goal-directed activity (either socially, at work or school, or
      sexually) or psychomotor agitation
   7. excessive involvement in pleasurable activities that have a high potential for
      painful consequences (e.g., engaging in unrestrained buying sprees, sexual
      indiscretions, or foolish business investments)
C. The symptoms do not meet criteria for a mixed episode (see Table 1.4).
D. The mood disturbance is sufficiently severe to cause marked impairment in
   occupational functioning or in usual social activities or relationships with
   others, or to necessitate hospitalization to prevent harm to self or others, or
   there are psychotic features.
E. The symptoms are not due to the direct physiological effects of a substance
   (e.g., a drug of abuse, a medication, or other treatment) or a general medical
   condition (e.g., hyperthyroidism).

Note: Manic-like episodes that are clearly caused by somatic antidepressant
treatment (e.g., medication, electroconvulsive therapy, or light therapy) should not
count toward a diagnosis of bipolar disorder type I.

Reprinted with permission from the *Diagnostic and Statistical Manual of Mental Disorders,*
Fourth Edition, Text Revision Copyright 2000, American Psychiatric Association.

depressive disorder experience depressive episodes characterized by decreased
sleep and appetite, and about half experience more atypical symptoms of
increased sleep and appetite. Recall that the differential diagnosis between
major depressive and manic-depressive disorders is made not by cross-
sectional symptom analysis but by longitudinal course. The diagnostic decision tree for manic-depressive disorder is outlined in Figure 1.1.

   Manic episodes are defined by discrete periods of abnormally elevated,
expansive, or irritable mood accompanied by marked impairment in judgment and social and occupational function. These symptoms are often
accompanied by unrealistic grandiosity, excess energy, and increases in goal-
directed activity that frequently have a high potential for damaging consequences (see Tables 1.3 and 1.5 for a summary of manic and hypomanic

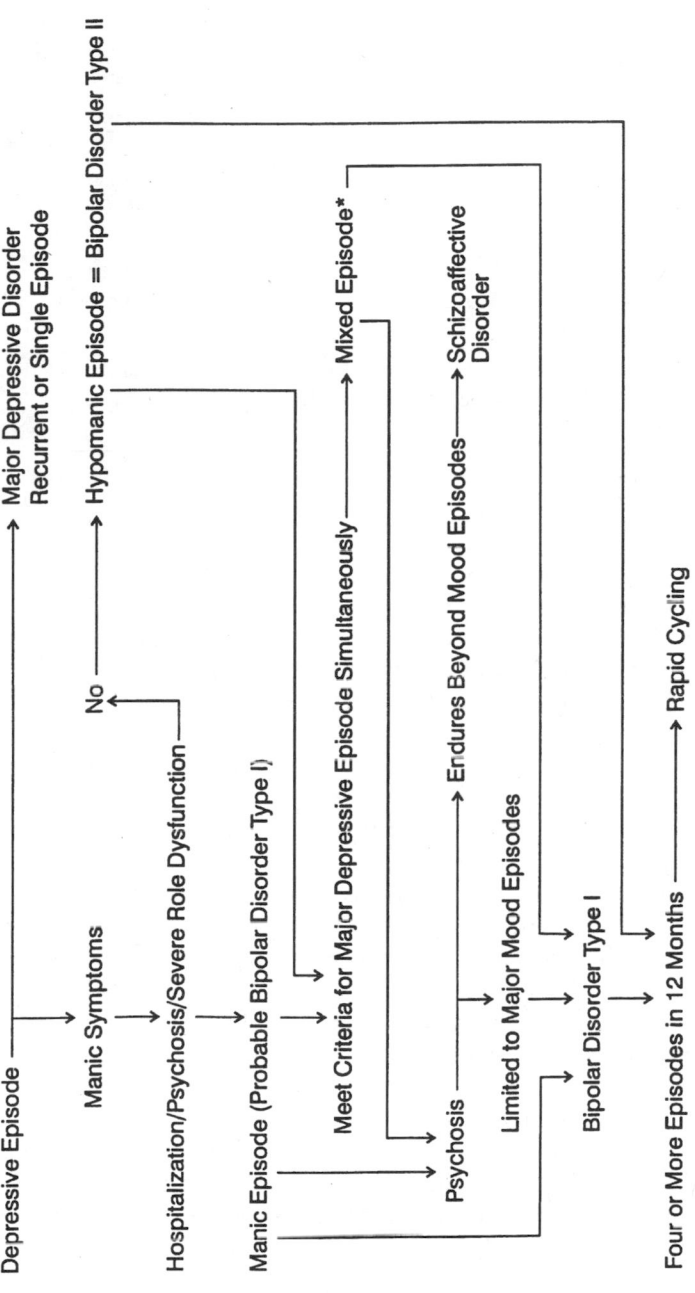

FIGURE 1.1 Decision tree for diagnosis of manic-depressive disorder.

The building blocks for a diagnosis of manic-depressive disorder are individual episodes and their characteristics, as summarized in Table 1.1. This decision tree takes the clinician through the steps that lead to diagnosis of manic-depressive disorder and identification of its subtypes, as well as possible course and episode specifiers.

*Does not apply to hypomanic episode, per DSM-IV, but see McElroy et al, 1992 and Bauer et al, 1994c

TABLE 1.4   Criteria for Mixed Episode

A. The criteria are met both for a manic episode and for a major depressive episode (except for duration) nearly every day during at least a 1-week period.

B. The mood disturbance is sufficiently severe to cause marked impairment in occupational functioning or in usual social activities or relationships with others, or to necessitate hospitalization to prevent harm to self or others, or there are psychotic features.

C. The symptoms are not due to the direct physiological effects of a substance (e.g., a drug of abuse, medication, or other treatment) or a general medical condition (e.g., hyperthyroidism).

Note: Mixed-like episodes that are clearly caused by somatic antidepressant treatment (e.g., medication, electroconvulsive therapy, or light therapy) should not count toward a diagnosis of bipolar disorder type I.

Reprinted with permission from the *Diagnostic and Statistical Manual of Mental Disorders,* Fourth Edition, Text Revision Copyright 2000, American Psychiatric Association.

symptoms, respectively). The mood associated with mania is expansive and labile, often combined with euphoria, irritability, or anger (American Psychiatric Association, 1994a, 2000). Mania is also characterized by increased energy and drive, which classically can lead to impulsive buying, dangerous driving, hypersexuality, substance abuse, and arguments. A person with mania has racing thoughts, a flight of ideas, and pressured speech. These behaviors may incur painful consequences, especially social and functional performance decline (e.g., Romans & McPherson, 1992). Often, the expansive mood associated with mania is accompanied by marked distortions in the reality testing called *psychosis* (see below).

Hypomanic and manic symptoms are identical, but *hypomanic episodes* are less severe. A person is "promoted" from hypomania to mania (type II to type I manic-depressive disorder) by the presence of one of three features: psychosis during the episode, sufficient severity to warrant hospitalization, or marked social role impairment. This is an imperfect set of criteria, however, because psychosis may or may not be an integral part of manic-depressive disorder (see below), because hospitalization may be due to social or personal factors or comorbidities not related to the disorder itself, and because the concept of marked role function impairment is not well operationalized (reviewed in Bauer, Crits-Christoph, & Whybrow, 1993). From time to time individual authors propose subtypes of manic-depressive disorder in addition to type I and type II, but these are not formally or consistently recognized.

Classically, mania and hypomania have been considered to be the opposite of depression: Individuals with mania were said to be cheery, optimistic, and self-confident. Hence the term *bipolar.* However, in most descriptive

TABLE 1.5   Criteria for Hypomanic Episode

A. A distinct period of persistently elevated, expansive, or irritable mood, lasting throughout at least 4 days, that is clearly different from the usual nondepressed mood.

B. During the period of mood disturbance, three (or more) of the following symptoms have persisted (four if the mood is only irritable) and have been present to a significant degree:

1. inflated self-esteem or grandiosity
2. decreased need for sleep (e.g., feels rested after only 3 hours of sleep)
3. more talkative than usual or pressure to keep talking
4. flight of ideas or subjective experience that thoughts are racing
5. distractibility (i.e., attention too easily drawn to unimportant or irrelevant external stimuli)
6. increase in goal-directed activity (either socially, at work or school, or sexually) or psychomotor agitation
7. excessive involvement in pleasurable activities that have a high potential for painful consequences (e.g., the person engages in unrestrained buying sprees, sexual indiscretions, or foolish business investments)

C. The episode is associated with an unequivocal change in functioning that is uncharacteristic of the person when not symptomatic.

D. The disturbance in mood and the change in functioning are observable by others.

E. The episode is not severe enough to cause marked impairment in social or occupational functioning, or to necessitate hospitalization, and there are no psychotic features.

F. The symptoms are not due to the direct physiological effects of a substance (e.g., a drug of abuse, a medication, or other treatment) or a general medical condition (e.g., hyperthyroidism).

Note: Hypomanic-like episodes that are clearly caused by somatic antidepressant treatment (e.g., medication, electroconvulsive therapy, or light therapy) should not count toward a diagnosis of bipolar disorder type II.

Reprinted with permission from the *Diagnostic and Statistical Manual of Mental Disorders,* Fourth Edition, Text Revision Copyright 2000, American Psychiatric Association.

studies, a proportion of individuals with mania actually exhibit substantial dysphoric symptoms (reviewed in Bauer et al., 1991). Furthermore, quality of life in mania is worse, rather than better, than in euthymia (Vojta, Kinosian, Glick, Altshuler, & Bauer, 2001; see also chapter 2). Hence, as noted in the Introduction, our decision to return to the more informative and accurate term *manic-depressive disorder.*

Mixed episodes, defined as the simultaneous occurrence of full-blown manic and depressive episodes (see Table 1.4), are the most prominent example of dysphoria during mania. Although it has been suggested that dysphoric mania may comprise a separate subtype of mania, the addition of this

additional dichotomy may be premature, and it may be of more use scientif-
ically and clinically to consider dysphoric symptoms dimensionally rather
than categorically (Bauer, Gyulai, Yeh, Gonnel, & Whybrow, 1994).

THE MANIC-DEPRESSIVE,
OR BIPOLAR, SPECTRUM

DSM-IV is the first version of the DSM series to recognize formally manic-
depressive disorder type II. Previously, persons with depressive and hypomanic episodes were grouped under the broad category of manic-depressive
disorder "not otherwise specified," which included a variety of unusual
presentations. On the basis of evidence reviewed by Dunner (1993), the disorder was given separate categorical status.

The separation of type II from both type I and major depressive disorder
was supported by several types of evidence. For instance, type II disorder
occurs more frequently in families of persons with type II, compared to families of persons with type I or with major depressive disorder (Coryell, Endicott,
Andreasen, & Keller; Endicott et al., 1985). Study of the course over time of
type II disorder indicated that persons with hypomania tended to have
recurrent hypomanic episodes, but not convert into type I by developing
mania (Coryell et al., 1985). In addition, persons with type II may have more
episodes over time than persons with type I (Goodwin & Jamison, 1990),
indicating that the course of type II differs from that of type I. However,
biological differences between these manic-depressive types have not been
reliably demonstrated (Dunner, 1993).

Nonetheless, as outlined below, it should not be construed that type II
disorder is in all respects milder than type I, although hypomania is by definition less severe than mania. Specifically, the social and occupational function and quality of life for persons with type II are similar to that for persons
with type I disorder, as reviewed in chapter 2.

Persons who experience *subsyndromal* manic-depressive mood fluctuations (i.e., hypomanic and depressive symptoms that do not meet criteria for
a full mood episode) over an extended period of time without major mood
episodes are diagnosed with *cyclothymic disorder* (Table 1.6). Much less is
known about this milder disorder because afflicted persons present for medical attention less frequently than those with full-blown manic-depressive
disorder. Cyclothymia has been considered at various times a temperament,
a personality disorder, and a disorder at the milder end of the manic-depressive
spectrum (Akiskal, 1981). Available data clearly indicate that cyclothymia is
related to the more severe manic-depressive disorders (Akiskal, Djenderedjian,
Rosenthal, & Khani, 1977; Goodwin & Jamison, 1990). Nonetheless, it is not
clear to what degree such categorical disorders may be related to underlying

TABLE 1.6 Diagnostic Criteria for Cyclothymic Disorder

A. For at least 2 years, the presence of numerous periods with hypomanic symptoms and numerous periods with depressive symptoms that do not meet criteria for a major depressive episode. *Note:* In children and adolescents, the duration must be at least 1 year.

B. During the above 2-year period (1 year in children and adolescents), the person has not been without the symptoms in criterion A for more than 2 months at a time.

C. No major depressive episode, manic episode, or mixed episode has been present during the first 2 years of the disturbance.

---

dimensional characteristics, such as temperament (Akiskal & Akiskal, 1988), however vaguely we are able presently to define that construct.

ADDITIONAL ATTRIBUTES OF MANIC-DEPRESSIVE DISORDER

Psychosis (i.e., delusions or hallucinations; American Psychiatric Association, 1994a, 2000) can occur in either "pole" of the disorder. If psychotic symptoms are limited to the major mood episode, persons are considered to have manic-depressive disorder with psychotic features. If psychotic symptoms endure for at least 2 weeks into periods of normal mood, the diagnosis of *schizoaffective disorder* is made (American Psychiatric Association, 1994a, 2000; Spitzer et al., 1978). However, the 2-week cut point is fairly arbitrary, and its validity is not well established (Blacker & Tsuang, 1992; Levitt & Tsuang, 1988). For example, it may be that psychotic symptoms actually represent a separate, comorbid disorder. Or they may be an integral feature of severe manic-depressive disorder that simply takes longer to resolve. Identification of pathophysiologic and genetic bases of psychosis and of manic-depressive disorder will certainly help to resolve these issues. Delusions may be paranoid, persecutory, punishing, or somatic. Auditory and, less commonly, visual hallucinations and other disruptions of thought processes may occur. Hallucinations may have an authoritative or punitive quality. Psychosis makes it difficult for the person to think and concentrate. Thoughts of death or suicide are common and vary in intensity, from wishing one was dead to frightening auditory hallucinations that command the person to take his or her life.

Rapid cycling is defined if four or more mood episodes occur within 12 months. It should be noted that, despite the name, the episodes are not necessarily or even commonly truly cyclic; the diagnosis is based simply on episode counting (see Table 1.7; see also American Psychiatric Association,

TABLE 1.7   Criteria for Rapid-Cycling Specifier

Specify *with rapid cycling* (can be applied to bipolar disorder type I or type II)

At least four episodes of a mood disturbance in the previous 12 months that meet criteria for a major depressive, manic, mixed, or hypomanic episode.

Note: Episodes are demarcated either by partial or full remission for at least 2 months or a switch to an episode of opposite polarity (e.g., major depressive episode to manic episode).

1994a, 2000; Bauer & Whybrow, 1993). This subcategory is of significance because it predicts a relatively poorer outcome and worse response to lithium and other treatments (Bauer & Whybrow, 1993; Bauer, Calabrese, et al., 1994). Although rapid cycling has been considered by some to be an "end stage" of the disorder, empirical evidence indicates that it may have its onset at any time during the disorder (Bauer & Whybrow, 1993) and may come and go over the course of illness (Bauer, Calabrese, et al., 1994; Coryell, Endicott, & Keller, 1992). Several specific risk factors may be associated with rapid cycling, each of which may give clues to its pathophysiology. These include female gender, antidepressant use, and prior or current hypothyroidism (reviewed in Bauer & Whybrow, 1993).

"PSEUDO-" MANIC-DEPRESSIVE DISORDER

It should be noted that a number of medications and medical conditions commonly encountered in medical and mental health practice can mimic manic-depressive disorder. It is important to recognize these, as the individual may not necessarily have true manic-depressive disorder. Moreover, removing the inciting medication (or treating the underlying medical condition) may lead to the remission of the apparent "mood" symptoms. Although either mania or depression has been reported to be caused either by medications or by medical conditions, it is our experience that it is more common to find certain medications as culprits for mania and medical conditions for depression. These most frequent causes are summarized in Tables 1.8 through 1.11.

MANIC-DEPRESSIVE DISORDER AND DEMOGRAPHIC OR CULTURAL CHARACTERISTICS

There are no major differences in the manifestations of manic-depressive disorder across genders, age groups, or cultures. However, women appear to be

TABLE 1.8   Medical Disorders Commonly Associated with Mania

Neurologic disorders
  Stroke
  Head trauma
  Dementia
  Brain tumors
  Infection (including HIV and syphilis)
  Multiple sclerosis
  Huntington's disease

Endocrine disorders
  Hyperthyroidism (in those with preexisting manic-depressive disorder)
  Postpartum status

at higher risk for depressive episodes in manic-depressive disorder (Liebenluft, 1999), rapid cycling (Bauer, Calabrese, et al., 1994), dysphoria during mania (Bauer, Gyulai, Yeh, Gonnel, & Whybrow, 1994; McElroy et al., 1992), and comorbid disorders (Strakowski, Shelton, & Kolbrener, 1993).

Among children and adolescents, the diagnosis of manic-depressive disorder is often complicated by less consistent mood and behavior baseline than occurs in adults (Carlson & Kashani, 1988). Thus, diagnosis is more difficult, particularly determining whether a child has manic-depressive disorder or attention-deficit disorder or both (reviewed in Wozniak & Biederman, 2001). Onset is rare before puberty. Moreover, little is known currently regarding outcome of and optimal treatment for children and adolescents with manic-depressive disorder.

COMORBIDITY: THE CO-OCCURRENCE OF MANIC-DEPRESSIVE DISORDER WITH OTHER PSYCHIATRIC DISORDERS

Comorbidity refers to disorders or conditions that co-occur with a disorder of interest. Alcohol and drug abuse and dependence represent the most consistently described and most clinically important psychiatric comorbidities with manic-depressive disorder. Although rates of alcohol abuse/dependence run from 3% to 13% in the general population, lifetime rates of alcohol dependence from Epidemiologic Catchment Area (ECA) Study data indicate that rates for alcohol dependence in type I disorder are over 30% (Regier et al., 1990). Furthermore, ECA lifetime rates for drug dependence are over 25%, and rates for any substance abuse or dependence are over 60%. Comparable rates for major depressive disorder in ECA data are, respectively, 12%, 11%,

TABLE 1.9   Medical Disorders Commonly Associated with Depression

Neurologic disorders
    Stroke
    Head trauma
    Dementia
    Brain tumors
    Infection (including HIV and syphilis)
    Multiple sclerosis
    Parkinson's disease
    Huntington's disease

Endocrine disorders
    Addison's disease
    Cushing's disease
    Hypothyroidism
    Hyperthyroidism
    Postpartum status

Cancer
    Pancreatic

Metabolic disorders
    B_{12}, folate deficiencies

Any medical disease that causes significant loss of function or self-esteem

and 27%. Thus, manic-depressive disorder represents an enriched sample for substance use disorders, with substantially greater rates than for general population or even unipolar depression.

A more recent study of a clinical population (those requesting treatment, as opposed to a community sample, which the ECA study investigated) was conducted by the Stanley Foundation Bipolar Network investigators (McElroy et al., 2001). They found lifetime substance abuse rates of 42%, including 33% lifetime alcohol dependence. Current rates were much lower: 4% and 2%, respectively. This may reflect the fact that to be able to present for care (or be accepted into a specialty network like the Stanley Foundation's), such substance use disorders had to be in remission. In a sample of veterans with manic-depressive disorder enrolled in a controlled treatment trial (see chapter 5), we are finding higher lifetime rates of comorbid substance abuse and dependence, on the order of 70% (Kilbourne, Bauer, & Williford, submitted for publication).

In addition, the National Comorbidity Study (Kessler et al., 1997) has found that, among individuals with alcohol dependence, 6.2% of men and 6.8% of women have had a history of mania (rates for a major depressive episode are, respectively, 24.3% and 48.5%). Thus, individuals with alcohol

TABLE 1.10   Treatments and Drugs Associated with Mania

Antidepressants	*Dopaminergic agents*
Antidepressant drugs	Levodopa
Bright visible spectrum light treatment	Disulfiram
Electroconvulsant therapy	
	Drugs of abuse
Adrenergic agents	Alcohol
Decongestants	Cocaine
Bronchodilators	Hallucinogens
Stimulants	Amphetamines
	Caffeine
Other agents	
Isoniazid	
Corticosteroids	
Anabolic steroids	

dependence comprise an enriched sample for mood disorders, including manic-depressive disorder type I, and screening this population is likely to identify previously undiagnosed individuals with manic-depressive disorder.

The reasons for the high rates of co-occurrence of manic-depressive and substance use disorders are not clear. One hypothesis for this co-occurrence suggests that persons with manic-depressive disorder self-medicate with drugs or alcohol. According to this hypothesis, persons blunt the painful symptoms of depression with drugs (e.g., McLellan, Childress, & Woody, 1985); similarly, they may heighten the manic energy with stimulants (Weiss, Mirin, Griffin, & Michael, 1988). They may also use substances to decrease manic symptoms, particularly if the symptoms are predominantly irritable or dysphoric. Alternatively, chronic substance use may convert otherwise unipolar depression into manic-depressive disorder by inducing substance-induced manic episodes (in DSM-IV, such persons would not be classified as having manic-depressive disorder, but would be considered to have unipolar depression with substance-induced manic episodes). Furthermore, chronic substance use may cause chronic changes in the brain that in turn alter the course of the illness irreversibly, as Himmelhoch and colleagues have proposed (Himmelhoch, Mullar, Neil, Detre, & Kupfer, 1976).

Finally, it is possible that some common genetic predisposition for mood instability is associated both with manic-depressive mood phenomenology and increased craving for substances, and the predominant expression of the predisposition is then determined by other genetic or environmental factors. According to this hypothesis, some persons possessing the gene develop manic-depressive disorder, some develop substance dependence, and some

TABLE 1.11   Treatments and Drugs Commonly Associated
with Depression

High blood pressure medications	*Hormones*
Alpha-methyldopa	Corticosteroids
Clonidine	Oral contraceptives
	Anabolic steroids
Ulcer medications	
Cimetidine	*Psychotropic agents*
Ranitidine	Benzodiazepines
	Neuroleptics
Drugs of abuse	
Alcohol	
Sedatives	
Amphetamine (withdrawal)	
Cocaine (withdrawal)	
Nicotine (withdrawal)	

develop both. Regardless of the mechanism, comorbid substance dependence represents an important clinical challenge for clinicians treating persons with manic-depressive disorder.

Other psychiatric comorbidities have been described in modest proportions of persons with manic-depressive disorder. Interestingly, recent data indicate that comorbidity may be higher in females with manic-depressive disorder than males (Strakowski et al., 1992), which may contribute to the tendency for females to be associated with more complex forms of manic-depressive disorder such as rapid cycling (Bauer, Calabrese, et al., 1994; Bauer & Whybrow, 1993) and dysphoric mania (Bauer, Kurtz, et al., 1994; McElroy et al., 1992). Interestingly, the recent Stanley Foundation study (McElroy et al., 2001) also found high rates of comorbid anxiety disorders (panic, posttraumatic stress disorder, obsessive compulsive disorder, and phobias), with lifetime diagnoses in 42% and current diagnoses in 30% of cases.

COGNITIVE DISORDERS AND DYSFUNCTION IN MANIC-DEPRESSIVE DISORDER

There has been relatively little investigation of cognitive dysfunction in manic-depressive disorder (reviewed in Martinez-Áran, Vieta, Colom, Reinares, & Benabarre, 2000). There are several reasons for highlighting this issue, however. First, there is an accumulating body of evidence from imaging studies that brain structures may be abnormal in measurable ways that tell us about the pathogenesis of the illness (see chapter 3). Second, and of more direct clinical relevance to treatment, if cognitive function is compromised in subtle ways in individuals with manic-depressive disorder, it may be that their ability to comply with treatment is also subtly compromised.

Martinez-Áran and coworkers (2000) found in reviewing the literature that various types of cognitive dysfunction have been found in individuals with manic-depressive disorder, including problems with memory and executive function (organizing and planning behaviors). Although these deficits tend to improve with remission of symptoms, up to one third of individuals may have deficits that persist in periods of normal mood as well. Consistent with this, Zubieta, Huguelet, O'Neil, and Giordani (2001) found executive dysfunction as well as motor coordination deficits and deficits in verbal learning in individuals with manic-depressive disorder not in mood episodes.

Importantly, data from Savard, Rey, and Post (1980) indicate that older individuals with manic-depressive disorder have greater deficits cognitively than younger individuals. Whether this is a function of increased time ill with manic-depressive disorder or simply the combination of effects of manic-depressive disorder and aging has yet to be elucidated.

Ali and coworkers (2000) found that neuropsychological deficits may be associated with increases in size in the right hippocampus in manic-depressive disorder. However, as with all promising imaging studies that find an association with function, this will require replication.

Overall, then, although manic-depressive disorder does not have the relentless downhill course that Kraepelin (1921) proposed for schizophrenia (and which led him to call that disorder dementia praecox), one cannot rule out the possibility that individuals with manic-depressive disorder may have cognitive compromise to at least a mild degree, even during periods of euthymia. In particular, executive function deficits may interfere with treatment planning and compliance. Clearly, such issues must be taken into consideration when assessing and developing treatment plans for individuals with manic-depressive disorder.

Chapter 2

Impact of Manic-Depressive Disorder

This chapter summarizes the impact of manic-depressive disorder both on the individual and on society. To understand personal impact, one must understand the pattern of onset and the course of the disorder, as well as its associated morbidity, mortality, and personal costs. These sequelae are discussed in terms of **outcome.** To understand the societal impact of manic-depressive disorder, one must understand both its epidemiological characteristics and the costs borne by society for the disorder.

EPIDEMIOLOGIC STUDIES OF MANIC-DEPRESSIVE DISORDER

Epidemiology assesses the *incidence* (onset frequency), *prevalence* (overall population load), and related characteristics of a disorder. Epidemiological studies typically employ large samples of persons who are found in the community but do not necessarily come into clinical care.

These studies are a valuable complement to clinic-based studies. For example, epidemiological studies avoid biases inherent in studying clinic-based samples. For example, clinical populations may underrepresent the milder (or most severe) variants of a disorder; furthermore, willingness to request clinical care may be associated with sample characteristics that bias the sample in unknown ways. In addition, epidemiological studies may be helpful in determining overall population load for a particular disorder, which can be helpful in planning health services. On the other hand, the large sample size and required methodology for most epidemiological studies limit the extent to which any individual subject can be assessed. Smaller higher intensity, clinic-based samples serve as the basis for our most fine-grained phenomenological data and virtually all of our neurobiologic data.

Estimates of the lifetime risk for type I manic-depressive disorder from epidemiological studies have ranged from 0.2% to 0.9% (Fremming, 1951; Helgason, 1979; James & Chapman, 1975; Kessler et al., 1997; Parsons, 1965; Weissman & Myers, 1978). The Epidemiologic Catchment Area (ECA) Study found a lifetime prevalence rate of 1.3% for combined type I or type II variants (Regier et al., 1990; Weissman et al., 1988). This agrees closely with the earlier study of Weissman and Myers (Weissman & Myers, 1978), which found 0.6% prevalence for each of the types individually. These rates are 3- to 10-fold greater than the prevalence rate for schizophrenia and about one fifth that for major depressive disorder. Little is known regarding the prevalence of cyclothymia. The more recent National Comorbidity Study (Kessler et al., 1994) studied a noninstitutionalized population between 15–54 years of age. They found 12-month prevalence of manic episodes of 1.3% and a lifetime prevalence of 1.6%.

Unlike major depressive disorder, manic-depressive disorder has an approximately equal gender distribution (Weissman et al., 1988). Few consistent data are available regarding differences in prevalence across ethnic, cultural, or rural-urban settings. However, one of the more intriguing puzzles regarding the disorder is the tendency of manic-depressive disorder to occur in higher socioeconomic strata than schizophrenia, which tends to aggregate in lower socioeconomic strata. Although many theories have been advanced to explain this phenomenon (reviewed in Goodwin & Jamison, 1990), no certain mechanism has been identified. However, several issues are clear. First, the finding is not likely exclusively the result of diagnostic bias, that is, over-diagnosing persons of lower socioeconomic class with schizophrenia more frequently than manic-depressive disorder and the converse in persons of higher socioeconomic class. Second, the upward socioeconomic "drift" is not due to highly impaired persons being "dragged" upward by higher functioning family members who are normal or who have adaptive subsyndromal manic-depressive spectrum characteristics; rather, persons themselves, at least those with type II disorder, are in many cases themselves highly successful and occupy higher socioeconomic levels (Coryell, Endicott, et al., 1989). Third, the findings are not limited to the United States, but have been replicated in European samples as well (Lenzi et al., 1993).

Among other demographic issues related to diagnosis, recent evidence indicates that African Americans presenting with psychosis are more likely to be diagnosed with schizophrenia than mania compared to Caucasians. However, the sources of this potentially important difference in diagnosis are not yet clear (Strakowski, Shelton, & Kolbrener, 1993).

Of particular interest in regard to epidemiology of manic-depressive disorder is that the incidence of manic-depressive disorder (and that of unipolar depressive disorders) appears to have increased over the past 50 years (Gershon, Hamovit, Guroff, & Nurnberger, 1987). Reasons for this are not clear, although environmental factors, either physiologic or psychosocial, may be responsible. For instance, exposure to increasingly severe social stressors and the breakdown of cultural supports that buffer stresses may contribute to the disorder; increases in exposure to putative environmental toxins may also be considered. In those families afflicted with manic-depressive disorder across generations, those in later generations tend to have earlier onset. This may be due to changes in genetic loading across generations or environmental factors either within the family or in the wider environment (McInnis et al., 1993). Regardless of the cause, the increasing incidence and earlier onset of manic-depressive disorder indicate that this illness is not likely to decrease in importance as a clinical and public health issue.

DEFINING OUTCOME ACROSS THREE DOMAINS

Traditionally, mental health research has focused on *symptoms:* how to quantify them, what causes them, and how to reduce them. This is sensible, because our professional goal is to reduce suffering and because this research orientation grows naturally out of the age-old dyadic, individual-to-clinician relationship.

However, several developments in society at large, in biomedical treatment in general, and in mental health research in particular have led to a purview for mental health research that has expanded beyond simple symptom reduction. Two related intellectual traditions underlie the evolution beyond simple symptom reduction as the target of biomedical treatment: how to understand the impact of illness and its care on a person's overall quality of life, and how to make the best use of available personal and societal resources (e.g., Leaf, 1993; Stewart et al., 1989).

With this orientation, we can therefore conceptualize outcome in manic-depressive disorder according to three separate, but interrelated, domains: *clinical outcome, functional outcome,* and *illness costs.* These domains are summarized in Table 2.1.

Clinical outcome consists of parameters that measure the illness itself, such as symptom severity or type and episode number and duration. This has been the traditional domain of most mental health treatment studies and naturalistic studies of illness course.

Functional outcome consists of social and occupational status and subjective (self-rated) health-related quality of life, areas of growing concern in both medical (Stewart et al., 1989) and mental health research (e.g., Broadhead, Blazer, George, & Tse, 1990; Markowitz, Weissman, Oulette, Lish, & Klerman, 1989; Massion, Warshaw, & Keller, 1993; National Institute of Mental Health [NIMH], 1991). Optimization of functional outcome has recently begun to receive more attention as a goal of management of chronic medical illnesses (e.g., Stewart et al., 1989) as clinicians and policy makers

TABLE 2.1   Outcome Domains for Manic-Depressive Disorder

Domain and parameter	Characteristic typically measured
Clinical outcome	
Symptom duration and intensity	• Symptom severity • Episode number, duration, severity characteristics
Functional outcome	
Social role function	• Quality and extent of marital, parental, social, and leisure by self-report or report of others
Occupational role function	• Employment type, amount of work • Income • Quality of work function by self-report, report of others
Subjective health-related quality of life	• Overall perception of satisfaction with life or lack thereof due to illness, its treatment, or residual disability
Illness costs	
Direct costs	• Costs of treatment including inpatient and outpatient care, medications and studies, and incidental costs incurred as part of treatment (e.g., transportation)
Indirect costs	• Loss of productivity due to illness (e.g., lost wages, need for societal support via disability or welfare payments, death) • Nonmedical societal costs incurred due to illness (e.g., jail, legal costs) • Costs of administering benefits

seek to reduce both direct and indirect treatment costs and to deliver what matters most to afflicted persons and their families. Substantial effort also has been expended in defining and addressing these issues in chronic schizophrenia (see, e.g., Bellack & Musser, 1993; Lehman, 1999). The solutions are likely to be different for a relapsing and remitting illness such as manic-depressive disorder. Unfortunately, development of treatments addressing functional outcome in recurrent mood disorders is quite rudimentary in comparison to that for schizophrenia (NIMH National Advisory Mental Health Council, 1991).

Illness costs consist of both *direct* (treatment) and *indirect* costs. According to the NIMH National Advisory Mental Health Council (1993), direct costs are measured as the estimated dollar expenditures related to illness treatment. They include such factors as institutional care, professional services, medications, and rehabilitation. Indirect costs include those financial losses incurred due to patient and family lost productivity, lost work due to needing and providing care, and losses due to premature death; they also are usually considered to include necessary nontreatment social supports and interventions, such as jail and the legal system.

The interrelationship of the three outcome domains deserves comment here. These domains are not likely to be independent, as discussed below (see "Predictors of Functional Outcome and Illness Costs"); however, functional outcome and illness costs may also not be passively driven by clinical factors. Thus, conceptualizing and measuring outcome in each of these distinct domains are essential if we are to understand the effects of the illness.

CLINICAL OUTCOME

REVIEW OF CLINICAL OUTCOME STUDIES

Manic-depressive disorder has its onset in most persons in adolescence and young adulthood, between the ages of 15 and 30. However, prepubertal mania and first-onset disease in the ninth decade of life are not unheard of. Once developed, multiple episodes are the rule.

A comprehensive review of the literature indicates that the majority of persons with manic-depressive disorder have four or more episodes in a lifetime (Goodwin & Jamison, 1990). Among persons with rapid cycling, four or more episodes in a year is the basis for the diagnosis, with an average of over 50 lifetime episodes (Roy-Byrne, Post, Uhde, Porcu, & Davis, 1985). There is no typical pattern to episode recurrence, with some persons having isolated manic, hypomanic, or depressive episodes, others switching from one pole to the other in linked episodes, and still others switching continually from one pole to the other in quasi-cyclic fashion. However, even persons with rapid "cycling" episodes very rarely have a truly cyclic pattern with stable frequency and period. Rather, the pattern is more accurately described by *chaotic dynamics* in the mathematical sense (Gottschalk, Bauer, & Whybrow, 1995). Specifically, they appear to have clusters of mood episodes at various times that are difficult to predict and have a truly cyclic pattern only for short periods, if at all.

Episode length in manic-depressive disorder typically ranges from 4 to 13 months, with depressive episodes typically longer than manic or hypomanic episodes (Goodwin & Jamison, 1990). Women appear to have more depressive relapses than manic, and men have a more even distribution (Angst, 1978). Recall also that women predominate among persons with rapid cycling, representing 70% to 90% in most studies (Bauer, Calabrese, et al., 1994; Bauer & Whybrow, 1993).

Estimations of outcome in manic-depressive disorder in the early to mid-20th century were by and large optimistic, based on two types of data. First, manic-depressive disorder had been separated from dementia praecox (schizophrenia) by Kraepelin (1921) on the basis of relatively favorable outcome in terms of remitting versus chronic course of psychosis. Subsequent comparative studies, up until the present day, have found manic-depressive disorder to have better outcome than schizophrenia in terms of many parameters, including chronicity of symptoms, severity of impairment, and social and occupational function (Angst, 1978; Lundquist, 1945; O'Connell, Mayo, Flatow, Cuthbertson, & O'Brien, 1991; Petterson, 1977; Tsuang, Woolson, & Fleming, 1979; Williams & McGlashan, 1987).

Second, tremendous optimism accompanied the introduction of lithium treatment for manic-depressive disorder in the 1960s. However, the early very positive experience with lithium derived primarily from experience in controlled clinical trials, which are typically done on highly selected samples of subjects.

More recent data from more naturalistic studies on broader samples over the past three decades contrasts with this earlier optimistic view. Overall, the data indicate that manic-depressive disorder, although with typically better outcome than schizophrenia, is clearly a chronic and relapsing disease that requires lifetime management.

In the early studies, 62% of individuals with manic-depressive disorder described in 1966 had equivocal to poor outcome (Levinstein, Klein, & Pollack, 1966), and 45% of individuals with mania reported in 1969 were chronically ill 6 years after hospitalization (Bratfos & Haug, 1968). One study found only 14.3% to be "well in every way" (Winokur, Clayton, & Reich, 1969), and another found only 24% in "full remission" during follow-up (Tohen, Waternaux, & Tsuang, 1990).

Early studies also indicated, in contrast to the Kraepelinian view, that the intervals between mood episodes may not be periods of return to former levels of functioning. Clayton (1981), Welner, Welner, and Leonard (1977), and Bratfos and Haug (1968) reported that 33% to 45% of study subjects experienced persistent symptoms or social dysfunction that did not resolve between episodes.

Although these studies include data from the prelithium era, more recent studies from the pharmacologic era are not terribly reassuring. Approximately 20% to 40% of persons with manic-depressive disorder do not respond well to lithium (Prien & Gelenberg, 1989), and that proportion may increase to as much as 80% for certain subgroups such as those who experience a rapid cycling pattern (four or more affective episodes per year) (Dunner & Fieve, 1974; Maj, Pirozzi, & Starace, 1989) or mixed manic and depressive episodes (Carlson, Kotin, Davenport, & Adland, 1974).

When assessed 1.5 years after index hospitalization, between 7% and 32% of individuals with manic-depressive disorder remain chronically ill, depending on polarity of index episode (Keller, Lavori, et al., 1986). Only 26% of another sample had good outcome after hospitalization for mania, whereas 40% had moderate and 34% poor outcome (Harrow, Goldberg, Grossman, & Meltzer, 1990). The probability of remaining ill at 1, 2, 3, and 4 years after hospitalization for mania has been estimated at, respectively, 51%, 44%, 33%, and 28% (Tohen et al., 1990). Sixty percent of an ambulatory sample had fair to poor outcome based on global outcome score after 1 year follow-up (O'Connell et al., 1991). Recent 15-year follow-up data from Taiwan support characterizing manic-depressive disorder as a chronic and recurrent disorder (Tsai et al., 2001).

Little is known regarding outcome in persons with type II disorder (Goodwin & Jamison, 1990), although persons with that form of the disorder appear to be at least as impaired in terms of relapse as those with type I. For instance, 70% of persons with type II disorder followed over 5 years experienced multiple relapses, and only 11% were episode-free (Coryell et al., 1989). Recent data from a European private practice indicate that type II compared to unipolar depression has a lower age at onset and more recurrences (Benazzi, 2001a). The disorder may be heterogeneous with individuals with type II who have more than three lifetime episodes of major depression having earlier onset and more chronicity than those with three or fewer episodes (Benazzi, 2001b).

Subsyndromal mood symptoms may remain in 13% to 34% of persons with manic-depressive disorder (Tohen et al., 1990), and substantial inter-episode morbidity may remain despite adequate treatment with lithium (Nilsson & Axelsson, 1989). It is not clear whether such residual symptoms between episodes represent incompletely resolved major affective episodes, medication side effects, demoralization due to functional impairment, or a combination of these factors (Gitlin, Cochran, & Jamison, 1989; Goodwin & Jamison, 1990; Nilsson & Axelsson, 1989; Welner et al., 1977).

THE PARTICULARLY IMPORTANT ISSUE OF DEPRESSIVE SYMPTOMS IN MANIC-DEPRESSIVE DISORDER

In discussing clinical outcome, it is important to highlight in particular the issue of depressive symptoms during manic-depressive disorder. First, depressive symptoms are common, occurring both in depressive episodes and in mixed states. Recall that it has been shown that individuals with a mixed/cycling course in manic-depressive disorder take longer to remit from an episode than do those without mixed/cycling (Keller et al., 1986). However, more recent data indicate that individuals with manic-depressive disorder who experience a depressive episode may remit as slowly as those with a cycling course, despite adequate pharmacotherapy and in some cases psychotherapy (Hlastala et al., 1997). In addition, in a group of outpatients followed prospectively with structured interviews, depressive symptoms were more common than manic symptoms (Bauer, Kirk, Gavin, & Williford, 2001).

Second, depressive symptoms are an important predictor of functional outcome (Bauer et al., 2001). Third, as outlined in the next section, depressive symptoms may be an important determinant of treatment discontinuation. Fourth, as reviewed in Chapter 4, our ability to treat depressive symptoms in manic-depressive disorder lags far behind our ability to treat manic symptoms.

Thus, for all these reasons—prevalence, impact, and difficulty in treatment—we must keep depressive symptoms as a focus of attention. In particular, it may be that psychosocial interventions such as the Life Goals Program can be helpful in addressing this unmet need.

TREATMENT ADHERENCE AND RELATED ISSUES

It is clear that outcome for manic-depressive disorder in general clinical practice is disappointing compared to that which might be expected from clinical trials. Although this is usually multifactorial, one important determinant is likely to be variations in treatment *adherence,* or *compliance.* A review of 12 studies of outpatients treated with lithium found rates of nonadherence ranging from 18% to 53%. Nonadherence rates reached 20% to 50% during the first year of treatment, and nonadherence was greater in lower socioeconomic classes (Goodwin & Jamison, 1990). Nonadherence rates in psychiatric illness are at least as high as in medical illnesses, particularly those that are long term and involve symptom-free periods (Wilcox, Gillan, & Hare, 1965) and may be related to chronicity, complexity, cost of regimen, ease of administration of medication, and physician attitudes (Haynes, Taylor, & Sacket, 1979).

A survey of individuals with manic-depressive disorder indicated that the most common reasons for discontinuation of medications were (1) being bothered that moods were controlled by medications, (2) missing manic symptoms, (3) rejecting the notion of having a chronic illness, and (4) feeling "depressed" (Jamison & Akiskal, 1983; Jamison, Gerner, & Goodwin, 1979). In a subsequent unpublished study by this group, the most common reason for medication discontinuation was side effects.

In assessing treatment outcome we as clinicians tend to focus primarily on measuring symptoms and episodes, and ignore side effects. However, from the perspective of the individual with manic-depressive disorder, side effects can be an important consideration in evaluating subjective outcome and quality of life. There are clearly some situations in which the cure is worse than the disease. If, for example, an atypical neuroleptic prevents manic symptoms but causes significant and disfiguring weight gain, this may also cause the individual subjective symptoms, even secondary depression and functional impairment. The same issue applies to tremor from lithium, hair loss from valproate, and other side effects from various medications.

Thus it is notable that adherence problems are endemic in populations with manic-depressive disorder. Moreover, it is our proposal that some factors that lead to noncompliance are likely to be amenable to psychosocial interventions, such as the Life Goals Program. These include psychoeducational and psychotherapeutic interventions to address knowledge about and attitudes toward the illness and working to simplify and understand treatment regimens. Other aspects may be amenable to other types of psychosocial interventions, such as increasing access to caregivrs in order to deal with side effects and working with providers to address issues of attitude. Several such interventions are currently being studied, as reviewed in chapter 5.

FUNCTIONAL OUTCOME

SOCIAL AND OCCUPATIONAL OUTCOME

Substantial levels of functional impairment are also characteristic of manic-depressive disorder, even when major disease-specific indices have improved.

The book-length study of manic-depressive disorder in the pre–lithium era by Winokur and colleagues (Winokur et al., 1969) documented their sample's functional impairment in detail. For example, 79% of those employed prior to their index episode lost their jobs during that episode. Among those with incomplete remission during follow-up, 73% had long-term decrements in occupational status. Even more striking, 25% of those with complete remissions or only infrequent episodes developed similar occupational decrements. In an early study, 60% had less than satisfactory social recovery (Hastings, 1958).

In a study of persons with manic-depressive disorder treated at the NIMH, only 41% had returned to their jobs at 3 years follow-up, and 15% were totally unemployed. Forty-five percent had normal family and social function, 21% evidenced "complete social withdrawal," and 11% showed "complete family disruption" (Carlson et al., 1974). On global outcome assessment, 57% were judged recovered, 10% had intermittent episodes, and 28% were functionally impaired with moderate to severe affective symptoms. Dion, Tohen, Anthony, & Waternaux (1988) found that although 80% of their sample became symptom-free by 6 months after an index major affective episode, only 43% were employed, and only 21% were employed at pre-episode levels. Harrow and coworkers (Harrow et al., 1990) found at 1.7 years of prospective follow-up after an index manic episode that 23% of persons with such an episode were continuously unemployed, with 36% underemployed compared to pre-episode levels. Occupational function was significantly worse than a comparison group of depressives without history of mania. In addition, 36% showed at least moderate impairment in social function. These deficits were unrelated to the presence of symptoms, with the exception of psychosis, which was associated with profound impairment. Tohen and coworkers (1990) found 28% of subjects unemployed after index hospitalization for mania. Bauwens, Tracy, Pardoen, Vander Elst, and Mendlewicz (1991) found that levels of functional disability were correlated both with number of prior episodes and with residual interepisode psychopathology.

Bellack, Morrison, Mueser, and Wade (1989) reported that manic behavior was found especially correlated with high levels of social disability and that depression mostly affected family and social life. In both cases, poor psychosocial outcomes correlated with poor symptom functioning. This group also found that social competence was substantially impaired in persons with manic-depressive disorder in degrees equivalent to those with schizoaffective disorder and nonnegative symptom schizophrenia. Romans and McPherson (1992) reported that social interaction scores were negatively correlated with age and duration of illness. These data suggest that the longer the illness continues, the greater the impoverishment of the social interactions. O'Connell, Mayo, Eng, Jones, and Gabel (1985) found that social support was the factor most strongly associated with good outcome with persons with manic-depressive disorder on three measures: global assessment scale, social adjustment score, and affective episode score. Social support was defined as the continuously available resources, relationships, and structures that serve as a positive buffer to negative life events and stressors.

Five-year follow-up data from the NIMH Collaborative Program on the Psychobiology of Depression (Coryell, Keller, et al., 1989b) provides evidence of similar levels of impairment in manic-depressive disorder type I and type II. This included similarly fair to very poor work (30% and 42% for types I and II, respectively), marital (30% and 23%), social (45% and 45%), and recreational (45% and 48%) function; sense of satisfaction or contentment (57% and 62%); and overall social adjustment (68% and 62%). Analysis of that data set revealed enduring deficits in educational and occupational status at 5 years of follow-up in a mixed group of individuals with manic-depressive and unipolar depressive disorder, even in those who were recovered for 2 years (Coryell et al., 1993). Additional data also indicate that functional deficits may persist in the absence of major affective episodes (Carlson et al., 1974; Harrow et al., 1990; Keck et al., 1998; O'Connell et al., 1991; Strakowski et al., 1998; Winokur et al., 1969). Subsyndromal levels of depression appear to be strong predictors of ongoing functional deficits (reviewed in Bauer, Kirk, et al., 2001a).

It is likely that these functional deficits result from the illness itself, rather than from preexisting pathology. The premorbid functioning of persons with manic-depressive disorder in social and occupational areas was reported as good (Miklowitz & Goldstein, 1990). Also in support of good premorbid functioning was a survey of persons who attended a self-help group for families of the mentally ill, reporting that 92% of persons with manic-depressive disorder had a high school education and 60% attended post–high school training or college (Plumlee, 1986). Likewise, Bratfos and Haug (1968) earlier reported persons with manic-depressive disorder came from "good" homes and had adjusted well to work and family life before the onset of their illness.

It is common to have the onset of manic-depressive morbidity occur during adolescence and early adulthood. Although there are to date few data specifically on functional deficits in children and adolescents with manic-depressive disorder, data we do have indicate significant deficits (e.g., Geller et al., 2000). Mood symptoms may interfere with the resolution of social, psychological, and cognitive developmental milestones. Therefore, the acquisition of healthy adult living skills, as well as family and other social and occupational achievements, may become impaired initially as a consequence of developmental delays. Also, if incurred during adolescence, lost time or impairment in school or occupation may indicate later occupational and educational underachievement.

HEALTH-RELATED QUALITY OF LIFE

The research community is beginning to increase its recognition and respect for the perspective and value system of the individuals who suffer from mental and medical illnesses. As noted previously, there is in the traditional scheme of clinical assessment no readily available way to determine whether, in the view of the individual with the illness, the cure is worse than the disease. Initially in the field of general medicine and more recently in psychiatry, such assessments have become a matter of greater attention.

In particular, tools have been developed to integrate all aspects of status into a single measurement or set of measurements as determined by the individual, so-called health-related quality of life measures. Non-health-related aspects of quality of life, such as housing, education, and community quality, are, by definition, not measured by such instruments. These instruments are self-reports because the individual must make the integration. Two commonly used instruments are, for example, the Short-Form 36 (SF-36), including the related SF-12 from the Medical Outcomes Study (Ware, Kosinski, & Keller, 1996), and the EuroQol (EuroQol Group, 1990). The former has separate subscales for characterizing physical and mental health, and the latter provides a single summary quantity for health-related quality of life.

Investigating manic-depressive disorder with these instruments can be revealing and sometimes provide surprising data. For example, a recent study determined that, in contrast to the classical conceptualization of mania and hypomania as desirable states, individuals with manic-depressive disorder actually find mania/hypomania less than or at best equal to euthymia in terms of quality of life. Not surprisingly, depression and mixed states were rated worst (Vojta et al., 2001).

ILLNESS COSTS

The overall societal costs of mental illness are substantial. In 1990, costs exceeded $148 billion a year, including $67 billion for direct treatment costs— about 10% of all direct treatment costs nationally (National Advisory Mental Health Council [NAMC], 1993). Worldwide, the Global Burden of Disease studies (Murray & Lopez, 1996, 1997) showed that in established market economies mental disorders account for 43% of the disability and 22% of the global burden (premature death plus life lived with disability) of all disease. Manic-depressive disorder is among the top 10 of all diseases in terms of global burden worldwide, and fifth in terms of self-reported disability (Andrews, Sanderson, & Beard, 1998).

There are as yet few available data regarding direct and indirect illness costs specifically for manic-depressive disorder. The data that are available indicate that direct treatment costs of manic-depressive disorder are substantial. Among the major mental disorders, the rate of hospitalization for manic-depressive disorder is exceeded only by that for schizophrenia (Klerman, Olfson, Leon, & Weissman, 1992). If one can extrapolate to persons with manic-depressive disorder from the data for aggregate mental illness costs (McGuire, 1991), 55% of treatment costs derive from public sector services and 45% from the private sector. It is also clear that substantial loss of productivity, in addition to personal suffering, may occur in manic-depressive disorder. In mental illness in general, functional impairment in 1986 was responsible for 55% of the costs of nonaddictive mental illness in the United States (Rice et al., 1985). In 1955, the figure was 39% (Fein, 1958). Although these figures are derived from very different methodologies and assumptions and may not be directly comparable (McGuire, 1991), both studies indicate that functional impairment accounts for a substantial component of mental illness costs.

With regard specifically to manic-depressive disorder, Greenberg, Stiglin, Finkelstein, and Berndt (1990) used the methodology of Stoudemire, Frank, Hedemark, Kamlet, and Blazer (1986) to estimate societal costs of affective disorders, including manic-depressive disorder. They found that costs in 1990 exceeded $43 billion including over $12 billion in direct treatment costs, over $7 billion due to lost productivity from premature death, and about $23 billion from morbidity. Given the previously cited studies on functional impairment, this last figure is certainly an underestimate, as "only the limited period of the episode itself was assumed to be of concern in calculating morbidity costs" (p. 414). Other researchers estimate that, without adequate treatment, an individual with manic-depressive disorder from age 25 can expect to lose 14 years of effective major activity (e.g., work, school, and family role function) and 9 years of life (Department of Health, Education, and Welfare Medical Practice Project, 1979). Fifteen percent of persons with manic-depressive disorder are unemployed for at least 5 consecutive years, and over 25% of those under age 65 receive disability payments (Klerman et al., 1992).

Moreover, data indicate that there is substantial cost to family and informal caregivers of individuals with manic-depressive disorder as well. Over 90% of caregivers in one study reported moderate or greater distress, and caregiver beliefs and perceptions were a significant predictor of burden (Perlick et al., 1999).

Wyatt and Hentner (1995) estimated that the annual societal costs of manic-depressive disorder alone exceeded $45 billion in 1990, exceeded only by $64 billion spent on schizophrenia. These costs for manic-depressive disorder include over $7 billion in indirect treatment costs and over $38 billion in indirect costs. Of direct treatment costs, $2.4 billion was spent on inpatient treatment, about $300 million on outpatient treatment, $3.0 billion on nursing home and other extended care, and $2.3 billion on the correctional system.

On the positive side, data from Riefman and Wyatt (1980) indicated that treatment innovations can result in societal cost savings. Specifically, they estimated that the introduction of lithium reduced societal expenditures for manic-depressive disorder to 53% of prelithium era levels.

Nonetheless, more recent estimates indicate that at least in one private-sector system, direct treatment costs for individuals with manic-depressive disorder remain significantly higher than for those individuals with depression or diabetes, or for general medical outpatients (Simon & Unutzer, 1999).

Moreover, many individuals with manic-depressive disorder reside in costly institutional settings. In the book-length report of the Epidemiologic Catchment Area Study, Robins and Regier (1990, p. 349) found that 42% of institutionalized manics were in prisons and 58% were in acute or chronic care hospitals.

PREDICTORS OF FUNCTIONAL OUTCOME AND ILLNESS COSTS

In contrast to the numerous studies *describing* functional outcome in manic-depressive disorder, there is relatively little information regarding *predictors* of functional outcome in this illness. Such information is important for at least two reasons. First, knowledge of predictors of poor outcome may help us in identifying high-risk samples for earlier or more intensive intervention, hopefully before functional decline. Second, knowledge of predictors may help us to design better interventions to prevent or reverse functional decline. Very little information exists on predictors of illness costs, and it is needed for the same reasons.

We recently reviewed this area in detail as part of a prospective study of functional outcome in a group of outpatient military veterans with manic-depressive disorder (Bauer, Kirk, et al., 2001). Our review of the 15 studies that had investigated this issue identified several interesting findings. First, many functional measures at intake to these studies (e.g., prior educational or occupational or marital status), which might naturally be expected to predict subsequent outcome, were not significantly related to functional status at follow-up. Second, many characteristics that had been shown in a number of studies to be associated with clinical outcome did not predict functional status. That is, functional outcome did not seem directly related to clinical outcome. Third, ongoing depressive symptoms did appear from the literature to be a common predictor of functional status, even though ongoing manic symptoms did not.

In our prospective study of 43 veterans, the strongest predictor of functional outcome was ongoing depressive symptoms. This was true whether depression was measured as weeks in a full-blown episode or as average symptom score. This latter finding suggests that even low levels of depressive symptoms may be important predictors of functional status.

What is not clear from this or any other correlational study is the direction of the association, that is, whether ongoing depressive symptoms lead to functional impairment or whether functional impairment leads to ongoing depressive symptoms, or both. Both scenarios are conceivable. For example, depression could clearly make work or marital function worse. However, poor work performance or marital relations could also comprise a stress that initiates, maintains, or worsens depression. Doubtless we have all seen both phenomena in our clinical work.

As noted above, there are very few data regarding predictors of illness costs. As we have reviewed elsewhere (Bauer, Kirk, et al., 2001; Bauer, Shea, McBride, & Gavin, 1997), there is indirect evidence regarding predictors of illness costs. For example, Bradley and Zarkin (1996) found that comorbid substance dependence was not associated with increased treatment costs in a sample of the seriously mentally ill that included subjects with manic-depressive disorder. Chart review (Frye, Altshuler, Szuba, Finch, & Mintz, 1996) and modeling (Keck et al., 1996) studies propose that treatment choice may affect hospital stay. Our 1997 study (Bauer, Shea, et al., 1997) found that in a sample of 101 veterans, greater service utilization was predicted by the presence of an affective episode at study intake and, surprisingly, a history of childhood abuse. In our subsequent study (Bauer, Kirk, et al., 2001) that directly measured both clinical symptoms and service utilization, to our knowledge the first such study, we found no significant predictors of illness costs.

Thus, this is clearly an area for further study. What data to date point out, though, is that illness costs or service utilization do not appear to be simply a passive function of severity of illness. That is, illness/treatment behavior is determined by different characteristics. Of specific relevance to the Life Goals Program, it may be that these illness behavior factors are amenable to direct intervention and that services can be used in a more efficient and less costly way.

CAN PSYCHOSOCIAL INTERVENTION IMPACT ACROSS THE THREE OUTCOME DOMAINS?

Several aspects of this review of clinical outcome, functional outcome, and health care costs have particular salience for learning and implementing the Life Goals Program. First, as outlined in Chapter 5, there is reason to believe that psychotherapeutic interventions, as an adjunct to medication management, may directly improve clinical status. Second, adherence to medications has been problematic in manic-depressive disorder, which, as in many other chronic mental and medical illnesses, may improve with more education and related psychosocial support. Third, psychotherapeutic interventions if appropriately structured may address functional deficits and quality of life decrements directly, in addition to acting through improvement in signs and symptoms of the illness. Fourth, appropriate psychosocial interventions, including education of individuals with the illness, may lead to improved and more efficient—and less costly—use of health care resources. The potential for interventions such as the Life Goals Program is therefore to act multimodally to reduce the burden of mental illness by directly reducing symptoms, educating individuals with the illness, addressing their functional deficits, and assisting them in accessing health care services in the most appropriate manner possible.

Chapter 3

Pathological Basis of Manic-Depressive Disorder

APPROACHES TO ETIOLOGY

Dichotomous thinking has characterized the debate over the last decades regarding the causes and pathological bases of manic-depressive disorder and mental disorders in general. At one time, psychological and biological paradigms were consistently presented as mutually exclusive. Similarly, dichotomous thinking based on nature (genes) and nurture (environment) as the cause of manic-depressive disorder has at times shaped the approach to the issues. However, it is clear from current data that no single paradigm can explain the occurrence, variability in course, and severity of manic-depressive disorder. Rather, a more integrative approach to understanding the causes of manic-depressive disorder is needed, one that recognizes the contributions of varying degrees of importance from several sources.

The various hypotheses regarding the basis of manic-depressive disorder are presented below as if they were separate and mutually exclusive proposals, with outline and key references provided in Table 3.1. However, our approach to understanding the likely causes of manic-depressive disorder is not so reductionistic. If the occurrence of manic-depressive disorder could be considered a "dependent variable," there may be multiple "independent variables" that contribute to its occurrence. Some independent variables may have a very strong association (i.e., explain a large percentage of the variance), whereas others may be less important in predicting the dependent variable. Moreover, several independent variables may themselves be associated with one another, rather than being mutually independent. Thus, in understanding studies on a putative cause of manic-depressive disorder, one must keep in mind that there may be other causes that are not addressed in a particular study, but that may contribute nonetheless to the findings.

TABLE 3.1   Major Hypotheses of the Pathophysiological Basis of Manic-Depressive Disorder

Hypothesis	Key reference*
Genetic and congenital evidence	Craddock & Jones, 1999
	Potash & dePaulo, 2000
Neurochemical hypotheses	
Norepinephrine	Bunney et al., 1972a–c
Dopamine	Goodwin & Sack, 1974
Serotonin	Goodwin & Jamison, 1990
Acetylcholine	Janowsky et al., 1973
Phosphatidyl inositol	Lenox & Watson, 1994
	el-Mallakh & Li, 1993
	Sassi & Soares, 2002
Neuroendocrine hypotheses	
Various	Amsterdam et al., 1983
Thyroid	Bauer & Whybrow, 1990
Neuroanatomic hypotheses	
Anatomic evidence	Strakowski et al., 1993a–c
	Jurjus et al., 1993a, b
Functional evidence	Baxter et al., 1985
	Buchsbaum et al., 1986
Physiologic hypotheses	
Membrane, electrolytes	Goodwin & Jamison, 1990
	(pp. 467–481)
Biological rhythms, annual	Faedda et al., 1993
Biological rhythms, circadian	Wehr et al., 1982
	Halaris, 1987
Kindling	Post et al., 1986
Psychosocial hypotheses	
Stress	Johnson & Roberts, 1995
	Johnson & Kizer, 2002
	Ellicott et al., 1990
	Leverich, 1990
Psychoanalytic factors	Fenichel, 1945
	Cooper, 1985
	Kahn, 1993
Integrative biopsychosocial hypotheses	Johnson & Roberts, 1995
	Hume et al., 1988

* The key references are either reviews or well-referenced primary data articles that will provide the reader with an introduction to the area.

Similarly, in trying to understand the source of symptoms at a particular time in a particular person with manic-depressive disorder—which we all do as clinicians trying to treat individuals—we must keep in mind that there may be multiple sources that lead to the symptoms that we are trying to treat. It is also not likely that biological theories will explain all the pathology seen in manic-depressive disorder, although the effectiveness of medications such as lithium renders purely psychosocial theories untenable. An integrative *biopsychosocial* mindset will likely be the most successful approach to treatment.

GENETIC AND CONGENITAL HYPOTHESES

Since the first edition of this book, there has been a multitude of studies on the genetic basis of manic-depressive disorder, particularly those using new molecular biological tools. This research, including both molecular and more traditional studies, is well summarized in two recent, very readable reviews (Craddock & Jones, 1999; Potash & dePaulo, 2000).

Available evidence indicates that familial factors are important determinants of who will develop manic-depressive disorder. Numerous studies have shown that relatives of manic-depressive *probands* (identified cases) have higher rates of manic-depressive disorder than controls or unipolar probands (Table 3.2). Overall, rates of manic-depressive disorder in first-degree relatives (parents, siblings, and children) of probands with manic-depressive disorder are elevated 5 to 10 times over rates found in the general population. In the latter group, the rates are 0.5% to 1.5%; in the former group, 5% to 15%.

Interestingly, rates of unipolar depression in first-degree relatives are about two-fold elevated over those in the general population. Because of the rate of depression in the general population (5% to 20%), this means that a twofold increase is a rate of about 20%. Important for genetic counseling, this in turn means that the probability that a manic-depressive proband will have a child with unipolar depression is greater than the probability that he or she will have a child with manic-depressive disorder (5% to 15% vs. 20%); note that it is most likely that a manic-depressive proband will have neither (100% − 25% to 35%).

Most genetic research has been done on type I disorder. However, type II also appears to have a familial component. Type II probands have more manic-depressive disorder and more manic-depressive type II disorder than unipolar depressives and less type I disorder than type I probands (Endicott et al., 1985; Simpson et al., 1993).

Note that familial occurrence does not differentiate between inborn and environmental factors. Familial aggregation could be due to sharing genetic material, nongenetic congenital factors (e.g., similar inherited or acquired intrauterine factors, or exposure to similar perinatal risk factors), or physiologic or psychological environmental factors.

TABLE 3.2   Rates of Manic-Depressive Disorder in First-Degree Relatives

Study	Proband is:		
	Manic-Depressive	Unipolar	Control
Taylor et al., 1980	4.8	4.1	—
Baron et al., 1982	14.5	3.1	—
Gershon et al., 1982	8.0	2.2	0.5
Coryell et al., 1985	7.0	2.8	—
Tsuang et al., 1985	3.9	2.2	0.2

Data from other types of studies indicate that at least part of this risk is due to biological, and likely genetic, factors. Twin studies indicate that *monozygotic* twins (derived from a single egg and sperm and therefore having an identical genome) have higher concordance rates for manic-depressive disorder than do *dizygotic* twins (derived from fertilization of two eggs) (Bertelsen, 1979). One adoption study showed that rates of manic-depressive disorder in persons adopted away from their biological families are closer to rates in the biological families than the adoptive families (Mendlewicz & Rainer, 1977). Finally, linkage studies, as summarized below, have suggested that in certain families manic-depressive disorder may be linked to specific genes.

Studies of monozygotic twins also indicate that only 40% to 70% are concordant for manic-depressive disorder. Thus, it is impossible (with the possible exception of a few unusual families) that manic-depressive disorder is totally genetically determined. More complex explanations must be sought (reviewed in DePaulo, Simpson, Folstein, & Folstein, 1989).

Several *genetic loci,* or locations on chromosomes, have been proposed (Craddock & Jones, 1999; Potash & dePaulo, 2000), but independent confirmations have been lacking. Overall, the number of families in which a single gene has been associated with manic-depressive disorder is small. Furthermore, no single locus has been replicated in multiple studies. The disparity in these findings may have several explanations. First, of course, is that the findings are falsely positive due to chance or to methodological problems. Alternatively, different genes may produce manic-depressive phenotype in different families. Finally, some studies indicate that manic-depressive disorder is polygenic, rather than being due to a single gene (e.g., Gershon et al., 1982). It is also likely that genes may confer susceptibility to the disorder without actually determining that the disorder occurs. That is, to have the disorder, one must have both the gene and another factor. This other factor may be genetic (polygenic inheritance), another change to the genome (see below), or an environmental (intrauterine, postnatal, physiologic, or psychosocial) stressor.

A related approach to investigating genetic contributions to manic-depressive disorder is to look for differences in genes that code for components of systems thought to be involved in the pathophysiology of the disorder. Chief among such candidate genes have been those responsible for dopamine and serotonin receptors, transporters, and metabolic enzymes (Potash & dePaulo, 2000). A recent study by Mundo and coworkers (Mundo, Walker, Cate, Macciardi, & Kennedy, 2001) is interesting in this regard. It showed that individuals that developed manic symptoms when treated with serotonin-active antidepressants had higher rates of the gene coding for a particular form of the serotonin transporter, compared to those so treated who did not develop manic symptoms. In addition, several studies have indicated that the gene coding for the norepinepinephrine-metabolizing enzyme catechol-O-methyl transferase (COMT) may be associated with the rapid cycling form of manic-depressive disorder (Kirov et al., 1998; Lachman et al., 1996; Papolos et al., 1998).

In addition, recent evidence raises the possibility that the expression of a psychiatric illness that is coded genetically may not be due simply to the presence or absence of specific genes, but rather to modifying pieces of DNA in close proximity to important genes. Specifically, small sections of DNA three base-pairs in length, called *trinucleotide repeats,* appear to be overrepresented in such genetic disorders with prominent psychiatric symptoms, including fragile X syndrome and Huntington's disease. The disproportionate number of trinucleotide repeats are hypothesized to be responsible for over- or underexpression of the candidate gene, ultimately leading to neuropsychiatric symptoms (Petronis & Kennedy, 1995). Recent evidence indicates that this may also be the case for manic-depressive disorder (e.g., Lindblad et al., 1998; Li et al., 1998)

There has been little exploration of nongenetic congenital factors that may be responsible for manic-depressive disorder, although it is reasonable to suppose that perinatal factors that produce brain injury may lead to manic-depressive mood syndromes, just as head trauma in adult life may lead to mood disorders as well as cognitive impairment.

It is intriguing in regard to postnatal factors that trinucleotide repeats may actually change over the post-conception period (i.e., during development), leading to changes in gene expression (Petronis & Kennedy, 1995). This theory is contrary to classical Mendelian genetic theory, which assumes that genetic material is allocated during cell division and conception followed by the playing out of a genetically derived script, impervious to the impact of environmental factors. In contrast, data on these unstable regions of DNA provide the basis for hypothesizing that environment may actually alter genetic expression and perhaps transmission to the next generation.

NEUROTRANSMITTER HYPOTHESES

A variety of hypotheses have been put forward regarding the biological basis of manic-depressive and other mood disorders. The major hypotheses and their supporting evidence have been recounted in great detail in excellent and still reasonably current review by Goodwin and Jamison (1990, pp. 369–596). More recently, Stahl (2000, pp. 135–197) and Sassi and Soares (2002) have reviewed these issues in detail using the methodologies available. Investigators have approached manic-depressive disorder from neurochemical, neuroendocrine, neuroanatomic, and neurophysiologic vantage points, in addition to the genetic and psychosocial orientations outlined above.

Each of these sets of methodologies has provided heuristically powerful conceptual models that have been tested, refined, and tested again. Each has something of value to contribute regarding the pathologic basis of manic-depressive disorder. Nonetheless, we do not yet have data to indicate whether the disorder is basically a disorder of a particular neurotransmitter, a particular neuroanatomic locus, or a particular physiologic system. Integration of these hypotheses awaits development of new methodologies for clinical neurobiologic investigations.

By extension from studies of depression and the actions of antidepressant medications, several neurochemical hypotheses have been proposed. Predominant among these has been the catecholamine hypothesis, articulated with regard to depression by Prange (1964) and by Schildkraut (1965). Deficiency of norepinephrine or its effects was postulated to cause depression. A series of studies by Bunney and coworkers (Bunney, Goodwin, & Murphy, 1972; Bunney, Goodwin, Murphy, House, & Gordon, 1972; Bunney, Murphy, Goodwin, & Borge, 1972) explicitly extended these observations to manic-depressive disorder, proposing that changes in catecholamine function were responsible for the switch to mania.

Dopamine, which has been a prominent focus of schizophrenia research but relatively neglected in affective disorders until recently, has received attention specifically in the study of mania. Dopamine may underlie several of the prominent features of mania, including psychosis (Goodwin & Sack, 1974), alterations in activity level (Goodwin & Sack, 1974), and reward mechanisms (Crow & Deakin, 1981; Kreek & Koob, 1998). More recently, demonstration of prominent dopaminergic effects of the antidepressants nomifensine and bupropion have served to generate more attention for the role of dopamine in mood disorders (reviewed in Kapur & Mann, 1992).

Serotonin has received somewhat more consistent attention as a substrate of mood disorders, particularly in Europe (e.g., Coppen, Prange, Whybrow, & Noguera, 1972). Attention to serotonin in the United States has increased recently when the relatively selective serotonin reuptake inhibitors (SSRIs) were demonstrated to have antidepressant efficacy. A "permissive hypothesis," whereby serotonin alterations permit instability of catecholamine systems, leading to manic and depressive episodes, has been articulated in broad strokes by Goodwin and Jamison (1990, pp. 422–423), although more recent work has focused on norepinephrine-serotonin synergy by multiple mechanisms, including at the level of the gene (reviewed in Stahl, 2000, pp. 245–262). Note, however, that SSRIs alone are not sufficient to treat manic-depressive disorder (see chapter 4).

Janowsky and coworkers (1973) proposed that acetylcholine deficits were associated with mania. As with the serotonin hypothesis, this posits that the cholinergic system also interacts with the catecholaminergic system to produce affective instability. Finally, recent evidence suggests that plasma gamma-aminobutyric acid (GABA) may also be involved in the pathophysiology of manic-depressive disorder (reviewed in Benes & Berretta, 2001; see also Petty, Kramer, Fulton, Moeller, & Rush, 1993; Petty et al., 1996; Post, Leverich, Altshuler, & Mikalauskas, 1992).

SECOND MESSENGER SYSTEM HYPOTHESES

Since the first edition of this book, most of the effort in investigating neurochemical systems involved in manic-depressive disorder has focused on the role of postreceptor intracellular mechanisms, known as second messenger (and sometimes third and fourth messengers). This research is well summarized in reviews by Stahl (2000, pp. 135–197) and Sassi and Soares (2002).

When neurotransmitters bind to postsynaptic neuronal receptors, a series of intracellular events are initiated that are mediated by chemical systems linked to those receptors. So-called G-proteins link the receptors to second messenger systems, which in turn are linked to protein kinases that control the synthesis and operation of cellular components (Sassi & Soares, 2002; Soares, 2000).

The cyclic adenosine monophosphate (AMP) and phosphatidyl inositol systems are the most extensively studied of these second messenger systems. Recent data have generated substantial interest in the phosphatidyl inositol system as a possible mediator of the clinical effects of lithium in manic-depressive disorder, particularly because this second messenger system is linked to subtypes of adrenergic, serotonergic, dopaminergic, and cholinergic neurotransmitter systems. Specifically, lithium at therapeutically relevant concentrations has been demonstrated to inhibit phosphatidyl inositol turnover in cultured cell lines and animal studies (el-Mallakh & Li, 1993; Lenox & Watson, 1994). In clinical studies, persons with manic-depressive disorder have demonstrated alterations in platelet phosphatidyl inositol levels (Brown, Mallinger, & Renbaum, 1993) and responsiveness of neutrophil phosphoinositol accumulation (Greil, Steber, & vanCalker, 1991). Cell lines derived from persons with manic-depressive disorder have been found to exhibit abnormalities of phosphatidyl inositol metabolism (Banks, Aiton,

Cramb, & Naylor, 1990). In a magnetic resonance spectroscopy study of persons with manic-depressive disorder, phosphomonoester levels were found to be higher in the manic state than in remission or in normal controls (Deicken et al., 1995; Kato et al., 1994).

NEUROENDOCRINE HYPOTHESES

Neuroendocrine hypotheses have sought to elucidate important mechanisms in the production and maintenance of symptoms rather than identify a specific etiologic agent in manic-depressive or other mood disorders. These hypotheses developed from the literature on stress response in otherwise normal subjects (Mason, 1975). Typical neuroendocrine studies investigate peripheral or cerebrospinal fluid abnormalities of the particular system in persons with mood disorders and controls and propose that either the neuroendocrine system itself or the neurotransmitter system that controls that hormone is in some way linked to the pathophysiology of the mood disorder of interest. Perhaps the most complete battery of neuroendocrine assessments in manic-depressive disorder was conducted by Amsterdam and colleagues (1983). Taken together, the literature does not identify particular endocrine findings as characteristic of manic-depressive disorder.

Although neuroendocrine research has not been as "hot" an area as some others since the first edition of this book, the thyroid system continues to receive consistent attention from some researchers (reviewed recently by Michael Bauer & Peter Whybrow, 2001). The thyroid axis may be of particular relevance to the pathophysiology of mood disorders. It has been studied as a dependent variable, (as a function of mood) as most neuroendocrine systems have been. However, it has also been studied as an independent variable of some impact. That is, several studies have shown that thyroid hormone administration may actually ameliorate mood disorders in certain paradigms. Specifically, there is evidence that the thyroid hormone triiodothyronine (T3) may speed the response of persons with depression to antidepressant treatment and may convert nonresponders to responders (e.g., Joffe et al., 1993). In the rapid cycling variant of manic-depressive disorder, evidence indicates that supplementation with high doses of the thyroid hormone thyroxine (T4) may induce remission in persons who are refractory to standard pharmacotherapy (e.g., Bauer & Whybrow, 1990; Stancer & Persad, 1982). In both types of studies, response to thyroid supplementation occurs in subjects regardless of whether they had preexisting thyroid disease.

The mechanism for these effects has been the subject of much speculation. One model posits that the brain is functionally hypothyroid either due to changes in hormone synthesis, transport, or metabolism or due to increased demand (Joffe, Singer, Levitt, & MacDonald, 1993). The competing model holds that the brain has an excess of a thyroid-related substance, which administration of exogenous thyroid hormone diminishes (Bauer & Whybrow, 1990).

NEUROANATOMIC HYPOTHESES

Two main types of studies have provided information on the possible neuroanatomic bases of manic-depressive disorder. In the first type, brains of persons with brain injuries who develop a phenomenologically manic-depressive picture have been analyzed, often neuropathologically, to determine sites of injury that may have produced the manic-depressive clinical picture. For example, lesions of the right side of the brain, particularly frontotemporal lesions, may be associated with manic-like syndromes (Starkstein, Boston, & Robinson, 1988).

In the second type of study, persons with manic-depressive disorder who do not have a known organic basis for their illness are studied either with *anatomic* (computerized tomography and magnetic resonance imaging [MRI]) or *functional* imaging (single photon or positron emission tomography, functional MRI, or magnetic resonance spectroscopy [MRS]) to identify regions of abnormality.

Among anatomic studies, abnormalities of computerized tomography (e.g., Nasrallah, Coffman, & Olson, 1989; Strakowski, Shelton, & Kolbrener, 1993; Strakowski, Wilson, et al., 1993; Strakowski, Woods, & Tohen, 1993) and subcortical magnetic resonance imaging (e.g., Jurjus, Nasrallah, Olson, et al., 1993; Strakowski, Woods, & Tohen, 1993) have demonstrated abnormalities in persons with manic-depressive disorder. However, not all findings have been replicated (Jurjus, Nasrallah, Brogan, & Olson, 1993), and the findings may not be specific for manic-depressive disorder. Furthermore, the degree to which anatomic abnormalities reflect pathogenic factors, as opposed to end-organ damage or effects of chronic medication usage, has yet to be established.

MRI studies of manic-depressive disorder have been an area of intense interest over the past several years, with particular interest in the size of the temporal lobes, limbic system, basal ganglia, ventricles, and total brain volume. Unfortunately, no consistent findings have emerged (e.g., Altshuler et al., 2000; Brambilla et al., 2001; Hauser et al., 2000; Sassi & Soares, 2002).

Similarly, there has been substantial interest in quantitating and localizing so-called T2 hyperintensities found in MRI studies of individuals with manic-depressive disorder. These phenomena, thought to represent increased water content of micro-regions of the brain, also occur in chronic medical illnesses such as hypertension and diabetes. Unfortunately, no consistency regarding prevalence or distribution in manic-depressive disorder has yet been demonstrated (Altshuler et al., 1995; Yildiz, Sachs, Dorer, & Renshaw, 2001).

Among functional imaging studies of manic-depressive disorder, blood flow, glucose metabolism, and, more recently, functional MRI/MRS and neurotransmitter binding have been the major variables of interest. In studies using blood flow methodologies, frontal (Buchsbaum et al., 1986) and temporal (Post et al., 1987) cortical structures have been the site of abnormalities in manic-depressive disorder, while among subcortical areas, the caudate has received the most attention (Baxter et al., 1985). Although no consistent evidence has emerged regarding a single neurotransmitter system or a single brain region, some promising results have recently emerged regarding serotonin 5HT-1a receptor levels in several brain regions (Drevets et al., 1999).

CELL DEGENERATION AND NEUROPROTECTIVE EFFECTS OF MEDICATIONS

One of the most exciting areas of recent research focuses on the possibility that lithium and perhaps certain anticonvulsants such as valproate may actually exert a *neuroprotective* effect in manic-depressive disorder. Evidence indicates that these agents may protect nerve cells by stimulating production of protective proteins or by stimulating nerve growth (reviewed in Manji & Lenox, 2000). Interestingly, there is some clinical evidence from MRI that lithium treatment may actually increase total brain gray matter, although this will, of course, require replication (Manji & Lenox, 2000). Thus, it is possible that cellular degeneration, albeit not as virulent as in Alzheimer's disease, may play a role in manic-depressive disorder.

HYPOTHESES REGARDING COMPLEX PHYSIOLOGIC SYSTEMS

Several complex systems, which for want of a better term are grouped together in this section as "physiologic" systems, have been postulated to play a pathogenic role in manic-depressive disorder. Classic theories of membrane and electrolyte balance abnormalities (reviewed in Goodwin & Jamison, 1990, pp. 467–481) have been investigated extensively in the past but appear, for the time being, to have passed out of favor. Two other hypotheses regarding complex systems have been of greater interest in recent years: the biological rhythms and kindling theories.

Complex Physiological Systems: Biological Rhythms

Two types of data indicate that biological rhythms may play a role in the pathogenesis of manic-depressive disorder. First, a number of observational studies have demonstrated seasonal peaks in the onset of affective episodes or hospitalizations for mood disorders. For manic-depressive disorder, the predominant seasons appear to be spring and fall (e.g., Goodwin & Jamison,

1990, Table 7.11; Kamo et al., 1993), although other patterns may occur with some consistency across the years (Faedda et al., 1993). Seasonal affective disorder, in which persons become depressed and remit at specific, regular times of the year, has been codified in the *Diagnostic and Statistical Manual of Mental Disorders* (4th ed.) (American Psychiatric Association, 1994a, 2000) by applying the course modifier "seasonal pattern" to recurrent mood disorders (Bauer & Dunner, 1993). Although the relationship of seasonal affective disorder, particularly the winter depression variant, to manic-depressive disorder is not yet clear, there does appear to be some overlap. For example, in most studies, a large percentage of persons with seasonal affective disorder have manic-depressive disorder, typically type II. In addition, the clinical picture of winter depression is similar to the hypersomnolent, anergic, hyperphagic depression common in manic-depressive disorder (reviewed in Bauer & Dunner, 1993). Treatment with bright light has been shown to be efficacious in winter depression (reviewed in Terman et al., 1989), and also appears to be an effective antidepressant in nonseasonal individuals with manic-depressive disorder treated in the winter (Deltito, Moline, Pollak, Martin, & Maremmami, 1991) and perhaps in the summer (Bauer, 1993); bright light also appears to be capable of inducing manic symptoms, as do other antidepressants (Bauer, Kurtz, et al., 1994).

The second type of data, which may provide a mechanism for the pattern of seasonal recurrence, is that persons with manic-depressive disorder often exhibit abnormalities of circadian, or daily, rhythms. Many rhythmic parameters have been studied in persons with manic-depressive and other mood disorders, with various abnormalities found regarding the *amplitude* (height of the rhythm) and *phase* (timing of the rhythm). Among the most promising findings is that light sensitivity to suppression of the rhythmic hormone melatonin may be altered in persons with manic-depressive disorder (Lewy et al., 1985; Lewy, Wehr, Goodwin, Newsome, & Markey, 1980) and their relatives (Nurnberger et al., 1989).

One of the most prominent biological rhythms, sleep, has also been implicated in the pathogenesis of manic-depressive disorder. However, it should be noted that it is not clear whether it is the rhythmic aspects of sleep or its nonrhythmic, restorative components that are most relevant. One of the most striking findings in mania is the lack of need for sleep, and there is evidence that sleep deprivation may be both antidepressant and pro-manic (Liebenluft & Suppes, 1999; Wehr et al., 1982). Thus, further exploration of sleep disturbance in manic-depressive disorder, as both a dependent and an independent variable, is warranted.

Complex Physiologic Systems: Kindling Models

The second major hypothesis involving complex physiologic systems proposes an analogy between the occurrence of episodes in manic-depressive disorder and seizures in animal models of epilepsy. Post and coworkers (Post, Rubinow, & Ballenger, 1985; Post, Uhde, Rubinow, & Weiss, 1986) have proposed that an autonomous pattern of affective episodes in manic-depressive disorder may develop from increasing sensitization of an individual to stressors. This process was proposed to be similar to kindling in animals and humans, in which subthreshold convulsant stimuli can decrease the threshold for seizures and eventually lead to spontaneous seizures. An analogy was also drawn between mood episodes in manic-depressive disorder and behavioral sensitization in animals, in which repeated exposure to pharmacological stimuli can decrease the threshold for specific behavioral responses.

There are several attractive aspects to this hypothesis. It is supported by the increased frequency of episodes over the course of manic-depressive disorder (e.g., Angst, 1981) and the response of many persons with manic-depressive disorder to treatment with the anticonvulsants carbamazepine and valproate. However, the clinical data in support of this heuristically powerful conceptual paradigm are, at this point, quite limited (reviewed in Bauer & Whybrow, 1991). It remains to be seen whether the kindling phenomenon—which may be stated simply as "Those who have had more episodes will continue to have more episodes than those who have had fewer episodes"—is due to (a) damage caused by those earlier episodes or (b) simply the continued expression of what was bad illness in the first place.

STRESS AND MANIC-DEPRESSIVE DISORDER

The possible association of stressful life events and the onset of depression has generated substantial interest among researchers from various theoretical backgrounds (e.g., Beck et al., 1979; Brown, 1989; Brown, Harris, & Copeland, 1977; Johnson & Roberts, 1995; Klerman, Weissman, Rounsavillen, & Chevron, 1984; Paykel & Cooper, 1992; Perris, 1984a, 1984b). Most of the literature regarding analysis of the relationship between stressful life events and manic-depressive disorder has focused on the precipitation of episodes in established manic-depressive disorder, rather than the onset of the disorder *de novo*.

In a prospective study of persons with type I disorder, Hall, Dunner, Zeller, and Fieve (1977) found no difference in life events among those who became manic, those who became depressed, and those who remained well; the only exception was a somewhat increased incidence of work difficulties in those who developed manic symptoms. In a prospective study, Sclare and Creed (1990) found no difference in events prior to and subsequent to admission for mania. In contrast, a retrospective study by Kennedy and coworkers (Kennedy, Thompson, Stancer, Roy, & Persad, 1983) reported an increased rate in adverse life events not directly related to illness in the 4 months preceding admission to the hospital for mania compared to 4 months after. In a prospective study, Hunt, Bruce-Jones, and Silverstone (1992) found a several-fold increase in adverse life events the month prior to manic or depressive relapse, compared to baseline, without difference between manic and depressive relapses. Ellicott and coworkers (Ellicott, Hammer, Gitlin, Brown, & Jamison, 1990) found that there were subgroups of persons with manic-depressive disorder who had varying thresholds of sensitivity to stress, and identified a significant association between stressful life events and the onset of mood disturbance. Of interest was that medication levels and compliance with treatment regimes did not account for any of the variance in outcome. Leverich (1990) also identified several factors, including stressful life events, associated with mood disturbance during the maintenance medication prophylaxis of mood disorders in general.

Thus, there are several studies that demonstrate a relationship between stressful life events and the onset of affective episodes in already established manic-depressive disorder. However, several studies have failed to find meaningful associations. There are also several types of methodological problems that may make interpretation of the studies difficult, and comparison across studies impossible. Examples of such problems include recall bias in retrospective design, and in both retrospective and prospective studies sample heterogeneity, length of time window for identification of relevant events, definition of onset of mood episode, and choice of signal event (e.g., hospitalization vs. onset of episode). Within prospective studies, differences in attribution and recall can be significantly different, depending on whether a person is interviewed for life events prior to or after the episode in question has commenced.

It is likely, then, that adverse life events are associated with mood episodes, particularly those episodes that are sufficiently severe to warrant hospitalization. In this respect, such life events need to be attended to for clinical purposes. However, from a theoretical point of view, it is not clear whether such events actually play a pathogenic role.

PSYCHOSOCIAL HYPOTHESES

The psychological theories of mood disorders—psychoanalytic, interpersonal, and cognitive-behavioral—are broad in scope. These theories propose that the symptoms of mood disorders are produced by psychological factors, with biological components playing at most a secondary role in the expression of symptoms. Unfortunately, the bulk of theory regarding the psychological basis of mood disorders concerns depression, with little attention paid as yet to mania or manic-depressive disorder.

Cognitive theory tenets regard depression as an affective response to negative beliefs (Beck et al., 1979; Rush & Hollon, 1991). Attributions regarding events are based on unrealistically negative assumptions: that when bad things happen, they happen because of one's inadequacy, they will always happen, and similar bad things will happen in other situations. Relatively stable patterns of attribution develop relatively early in life, and misinterpretations of events and maladaptive responses are triggered by proximate events (reviewed in Abramson, Seligman, & Tensdale, 1978; Seligman, Abramson, Semmel, & von Baeyer, 1979). These aspects of cognitive theory of mood disorders are discussed in more detail in chapter 6.

Comparatively, behavior theory views depression as a consequence of a low rate of response-contingent positive reinforcement. The goal of behavior therapy is to increase positive reinforcement by participation in pleasant activities or building assertive skills needed to elicit social rewards. The learned helplessness model (Seligman, 1975) and behavioral therapy for depression (Lewinsohn, 1974) testify to the merit of these theoretical strategies. Interestingly, there is recent evidence indicating that in cognitive-behavioral therapy, it may be as much the behavioral aspects of treatment as its cognitive aspects that are responsible for therapeutic effects (Jacobsen et al., 1996).

The interpersonal theory of depression, which serves as the theoretical basis for interpersonal psychotherapy (Klerman et al., 1984; Weissman & Klerman, 1991), builds on the work of Adolph Meyer and Harry Stack Sullivan, both of whom considered an individual's environment to play an important role in symptom development and protection from illness. Interpersonal theory proposes that depression develops most often in the context of adverse events, particularly interpersonal loss. Interpersonal psychotherapy then seeks to reduce symptoms by psychoeducation and subsequently by addressing problems in interpersonal relationships, primarily focusing on grief, role disputes, role transitions, and interpersonal deficits.

Psychoanalytic theories regarding depression are wide ranging, with perhaps their most concise and elegant formulation in Sigmund Freud's classic *Mourning and Melancholia* (Freud, 1924). Further development of Freud's theories of depression are found throughout his *New Introductory Lectures in Psychoanalysis* (Freud, 1933). For subsequent development of psychoanalytic theories of depression, the reader is referred in particular to Abraham (1927) and Fenichel (1945).

As with other theories, psychoanalytic theory regarding mania has been much more limited than for depression. Theories focus on mania as a defense against underlying depression that is only partially successful. For example, Dooley (1921) proposed that mania was a mechanism whereby one could ward off painful depressive thoughts. Schwartz (1961) suggested that mania, particularly its hyperactive and grandiose components, functioned as a defense against underlying emptiness and deprivation.

Fenichel (1945) also considered mania to be a response to depression. He proposed that, in depression, symptoms were caused by a battering superego punishing the self, whereas "the triumphant character of mania arises from the release of energy hitherto bound in the depressive struggle and now seeking discharge" (p. 408). Nonetheless, he remarks succinctly later in a discussion of cyclicity in manic-depressive and other mood disorders: "[y]et it is impossible to get rid of the impression that additional purely biological factors are involved."

More recent psychoanalytic theorists have emphasized the need for revision of traditional psychoanalytic theories in the face of accumulating evidence of a biological component to major mental illnesses, including manic-depressive disorder. It is also important to note that there is no consistent evidence that manic-depressive disorder is caused by or associated with personality disorders, as defined by the DSM system (Goodwin & Jamison, 1990, pp. 281–317). However, some recent psychoanalytic clinicians have proposed that analytic treatment may be helpful in reducing stresses that may precipitate episodes (e.g., Kahn, 1993). These issues are discussed in greater detail in chapter 5.

It is worth quoting Cooper (1985) at length with regard to revisions in psychoanalytic thinking necessitated by the recognition of substantial biological components to the major mental illnesses:

> Most analytic treatment carries with it a strong implication that it is a major analytic task of the individual to accept responsibility for his actions. In the psychoanalytic view, this responsibility is nearly total. . . . However, it now seems likely that there are individuals with depressive, anxious, and dysphoric states for whom the usual psychodynamic view of responsibility seems inappropriate. . . . There is a group of chronically depressed and anxious individuals . . . whose mood regulation is vastly changed by antidepressant medication. The entry of these new molecules into their metabolism alters, tending to normalize, the way they see the world, the way they do battle with their superegos, the way they respond to object separation. It may be that we have been co-conspirators with these individuals in their need to construct a rational-seeming world in which they hold themselves unconsciously responsible for events. (p. 1399)

BIOPSYCHOSOCIAL HYPOTHESES

Successful treatment of manic-depressive disorder with medications has made the biological basis of manic-depressive disorder incontrovertible. Nonetheless, psychosocial factors may play prominent roles in the development of manic-depressive disorder and, once established, impact on its course. Several models that integrate psychological factors and biological mechanisms have been developed. These have been well reviewed by Johnson and colleagues (Johnson & Kizer, 2002; Johnson & Roberts, 1995).

Several examples illustrate the diversity of these proposals. As described previously, the kindling model proposes that discrete environmental stressors may be translated into enduring neurobiological changes that are responsible for mood episodes in manic-depressive disorder. Ehlers, Frank, and Kupfer (1988) proposed that the regulation of biological rhythms in persons with manic-depressive disorder may be disrupted by changes in psychosocial events. Specifically, they propose that mood episodes cause disruptions in social rhythms (e.g., eating, sleeping, and other aspects of one's daily routine). They propose that these social rhythms are important regulators of biological circadian rhythms; without these regulators, abnormalities of circadian rhythms develop, leading to the onset, worsening, or perpetuation of mood symptoms. Depue and colleagues (Depue & Iacono, 1989; Depue, Kleinman, Davis, Hutchinson, & Kraus, 1985) have proposed that mood disordered individuals, including those with manic-depressive spectrum disorders, have deficits in the regulation of biological responses to stress. Thus, environmental stressors may cause disruptions of biological systems that cause mood symptoms in vulnerable individuals, even though similar stressors may not cause disruptions in persons without mood disorders.

Hume and colleagues (Hume, Barker, Robertson, & Swan, 1988) proposed another stress-vulnerability model specifically for manic-depressive disorder in which the threshold for commencement of mood symptoms, particularly in manic-depressive disorder, is influenced by a combination of the "perception" one has of stressful life events and a vulnerable biochemical mood regulatory system. Thus, adverse life events, coupled with both psychological and biological vulnerability, are required to produce both the mood and the somatic symptoms of depression. Similar to cognitive theorists, Hume described attributions regarding the cause of adverse events, particularly one's control over events (after Rotter, 1966), as particularly important in producing the psychological vulnerability to depression and manic-depressive disorder. However, they do not describe specific mechanisms by which manic, as opposed to depressive, symptoms may be produced.

Nonetheless, one may recall the biopsychosocial model developed by George L. Engel in the 1970s (Engel, 1977) that proposed that all illness—medical, surgical, as well as mental—can best be understood in a unified biopsychosical context, and that treatment must consider all these aspects to be successful. This model and its treatment corollary are particularly compelling for chronic illness. Its applicability specifically to manic-depressive disorder is likely, and is being tested indirectly in several of the treatment studies discussed in the following chapters.

CONCLUSIONS

Numerous family genetic studies indicate that there is a hereditary biological component to manic-depressive disorder, yet the fact that only 40% to 70% of monozygotic twins are concordant for manic-depressive disorder indicates that genetics is not destiny. Anatomic studies of the body's most complex organ, the brain, may have abnormalities in individuals with manic-depressive disorder, yet it is not clear how consistent these findings are, or how specific for manic-depressive disorder. Most neurotransmitter septems and most neuroendocrine axes studied to date have shown some abnormalities in manic-depressive disorder, yet it is not clear to what degree these are individual in the pathogenesis of symptoms, and to what degree these findings reflect "downstream," or secondary, changes. Each of the complex physiologic and psychosocial hypotheses are attractive heuristically, yet they have, in most cases, little supporting data and are notoriously difficult to test.

Absent certainty, we in our roles as treating clinicians and educators of individuals and families who suffer with manic-depressive disorder are best advised to take a nonreductionistic and biopsychosocial view of this illness. There are many promising biological leads, though many in the past turned cold. We know for certain that the illness is not fully genetically determined and is not likely to be explained solely by biological mechanisms. However, it is also beyond doubt, based on treatment studies reviewed in chapter 4, that there is a biological component to the illness. Attention to the role of environmental, particularly psychosocial factors is also important in modulating the course of the disease, as summarized in chapter 5. This was, in fact, the basis for developing the Life Goals Program in the first place. Let us therefore turn to the biological and psychosocial interventions used in manic-depressive disorder, then to the Life Goals Program itself.

Chapter 4

Overview of Biological Treatments for Manic-Depressive Disorder

The goal of treatment is to improve outcome. As discussed in chapter 2, it is useful to consider outcomes according to three conceptually distinct domains: (a) improving *clinical outcome* (episodes and symptoms); (b) improving *functional outcome* (social and occupational function and health-related quality of life); and (c) reducing *illness costs,* including both *direct costs* (costs of treatment for the disorder) and *indirect costs* (lost productivity and societal costs not reflected in treatment costs, such as disability payments and legal costs).

Recall that these domains of outcome are only loosely related, so that all the functional disability due to manic-depressive disorder should not be expected to resolve simply with pharmacologic treatment. However, we also know that ongoing depressive symptoms, even at low levels, are associated with substantial functional disability, and it is likely that this disability may actually be due to the depressive symptoms. As pointed out in chapter 2, it is not clear whether the ongoing depressive symptoms cause ongoing functional disability, or whether the functional disability (e.g., marital stress and occupational compromise) produces ongoing depression. Either mechanism is plausible, and a combination of both directions of causality is most likely. Therefore, to maximize therapeutic impact for the individual, it is important to provide optimal pharmacologic treatment of the core manic and depressive symptoms of this disorder in the hope of minimizing both clinical and functional compromise.

We consider medical model treatment—that is, with pharmacologic and related interventions—to be the cornerstone of treatment for manic-depressive disorder because of the reams of efficacy data indicating that medications are beneficial for this illness. Moreover, all the psychotherapy studies since the advent of medication treatment have used psychotherapy in addition to, not instead of, medications.

That said, the thrust of our work since the early 1990s in developing the Life Goals Program and related interventions stems from recognition of the fact that medication administration alone is not likely to result in adequate outcome for manic-depressive disorder. Rather, collaboration between an educated individual with the illness and his or her treating clinicians is essential. In support of an effective collaborative practice model, individuals and clinicians should understand the data that support various treatment modalities as well as its limitations.

This chapter reviews what is known about the various classes of pharmacologic agents typically encountered in the treatment of individuals with manic-depressive disorder in order to assist the Life Goals Program therapist in guiding individuals toward better self-management and collaboration with their prescribing clinician (and if applicable other members of their clinical team). This chapter is not meant to replace more comprehensive reviews, but it does summarize information in sufficient detail to allow the therapist to understand the various treatments he or she will encounter and to answer many individual questions about pharmacologic treatment.

The chapter is divided into two main sections. The first is a review of efficacy data concerning the major medications used to treat manic and depressive symptoms in manic-depressive disorder. The second section reviews basic issues in use of the various classes of agents that are likely to be encountered in clinical practice. This latter section contains a brief review of various classes of agents including putative mechanisms of action, dosage ranges, and side effect profiles.

This last area is particularly important to therapists who are leading psychoeducational programs for manic-depressive disorder, because it is side effects that frequently lead individuals to discontinue medications. The successful psychoeducational program will help individuals to recognize these side effects and advocate for action by their providers that will help to minimize them. Those wishing more detailed guidance on the use of these medications, including indications, doses, and side effects, may wish to consult the *Field Guide to Psychiatric Assessment and Treatment* (Bauer, 2003).

EFFICACY DATA ON AGENTS TO TREAT AND PREVENT MANIC AND DEPRESSIVE SYMPTOMS IN MANIC-DEPRESSIVE DISORDER

CLASSIFYING THE EVIDENCE

Hundreds of formal studies and thousands of other clinical reports contain information on the treatment of manic-depressive disorder. How is one to approach this massive amount of information?

Several techniques have been developed to improve the ability to review and summarize scientific literature and draw overall conclusions from often divergent types of data. For example, quantitative techniques such as meta-analysis provide numeric conclusions with regard to significance of similar interventions in diverse studies (e.g., Irwig et al., 1994). More qualitative techniques of "evidence-based medicine" (American College of Cardiology/ American Heart Association, 1996; Chalmers, 1993; Evidence-Based Working Group, 1992) have been used in reviewing and summarizing treatment interventions in medicine and more recently in mental health. Briefly, these techniques consist of comprehensively identifying relevant data-based articles, summarizing their methods and conclusions, then in a standardized fashion rating the scientific quality of the evidence based on the rigor of their methodology. In the 1980s, the U.S. Agency for Healthcare Research and Quality (formerly the Agency for Health Care Policy and Research, AHRQ/AHCPR), developed guidelines for the identification and treatment of depression in primary care using techniques of evidence-based medicine (AHCPR, 1993). This basic system was adapted by the U.S. Department of Veterans Affairs for developing their treatment guidelines for a wide variety of medical, surgical, and psychiatric disorders (e.g., Bauer et al., 1999; Veterans Health Administration, 1997). Several other sets of clinical practice guidelines for manic-depressive disorder have also used evidence-based medicine techniques, including practice guidelines from the American Psychiatric Association (1994b), the Texas Department of Mental Health and Mental Retardation (Gilbert et al., 1998; Rush et al., 1999), and the Canadian Psychiatric Association (Haslam et al., 1997), although not all clinical practice guidelines do (e.g., Kahn, Docherty, Carpenter, & Frances, 1997; Sachs, Printz, Kahn, Carpenter, & Docherty, 2000). We have found the evidence-based medicine approach useful to classify studies by quality of data in doing our reviews both of pharmacologic (this chapter) and psychotherapeutic (chapter 5) interventions for manic-depressive disorder.

The AHRQ/AHCPR classification scheme used for classifying studies by rigor is summarized in Table 4.1. This chapter summarizes the studies that we have reviewed to date that are classified as Class A (controlled trials) or Class B (formal investigations with a priori methodologic structure and quantitative outcome analyses). To locate these studies our review sought to locate all studies on pharmacologic treatment for manic-depressive disorder that filled the following criteria:

- Published in peer-reviewed journals
- Investigated an intervention in a sample of individuals with manic-depressive disorder or reported separately results for bipolar subsamples from a diagnostically heterogeneous group
- Specified quantitative outcome variables
- Written in English (limitation of the author)

TABLE 4.1   AHRQ/AHCPR Evidence Classification System

Class A: Randomized or other controlled trials
   Examples: Randomized controlled trials of drug versus placebo control or
   alternative active agent; other controlled trials with treatment assignment
   independent of subject characteristic, time of presentation, etc. May be parallel
   group or "A–B–A" within-subjects design

Class B: Well-designed clinical studies
   Examples: Open studies with a priori design and follow-up period of designated
   endpoint; pre- or post-mirror-image studies with "post-" period designed a priori

Class C: Case series, case reports, retrospective chart reviews
   Examples: Prospectively gathered data on a series of individuals followed in
   treatment; retrospective chart review after implementation of an intervention

In addition, though our primary interest was in monotherapy studies, as these tell most about an agent's efficacy, much clinical treatment includes combination treatment strategies. Therefore, we have also included Class A studies (i.e., controlled trials) of various combination treatment studies that have been published.

Thus we summarize in the following text monotherapy studies with Class A or Class B evidence, and combination therapy studies with Class A or Class B evidence. If an agent had at least two positive Class A studies, we did not include the lower level Class B studies (e.g., Class B studies of lithium or lamotrigine as prophylactic agents).

This would exclude studies of some agents that are gaining wide usage in clinical practice because they are not yet published studies with either Class A or B monotherapy evidence, or Class A combination therapy evidence. An example is the new anticonvulsant topiramate, for which such evidence is in the pipeline but not yet published. The reader is referred to the useful review of Yatham et al. (2002) for an extensive review of published and unpublished data on the newer anticonvulsants.

Literature databases including MEDLINE, PsychLit, and the Cochrane Collaboration were searched. Articles were reviewed by title, abstract, and text as relevant. Authors known to be actively working in the field in the United States and Europe were contacted regarding further work in print or in press. Review of the bibliography of each located article was scanned for additional articles. This step was repeated iteratively until no further references were found. Over 500 articles and abstracts were reviewed in this process, in which we were aided by the energetic and careful scholarly efforts of Landis Mitchner, MD, who was at the time a resident in the Brown University Psychiatry Training Program.

The search is not, and will never be, complete. Nonetheless, we present data on studies reviewed by December 2001, in hopes that this will answer accurately most of the questions that will come up in discussing pharmacologic treatment with group members.

ORGANIZING THE EVIDENCE

Manic-depressive disorder is a multifaceted illness. The optimal treatment for this illness would be a single agent that treated all facets—one that truly was a *mood stabilizer*. This ideal agent would have four actions:

- Treat acute manic symptoms (considering hypomania and mania as milder and more severe aspects of the same continuum of symptoms, as discussed in chapter 1)
- Treat acute depressive symptoms
- Prevent future manic symptoms
- Prevent future depressive symptoms

Such an agent—or, in the real world, often combination of agents—would provide necessary pharmacologic intervention for manic-depressive disorder (leaving aside at this point the issue of psychotic symptoms, which, as we discuss below, are treated with the neuroleptic, or antipsychotic, family of medications).

This approach to understanding treatment for manic-depressive disorder leads conceptually to a 2-by-2 table to understand mood stabilizer effects. This is illustrated in Table 4.2. The columns reflect activity against manic and/or depressive symptoms. The rows reflect activity in the acute phase of the illness (i.e., leading to the reduction of symptoms that are there) and prophylaxis (i.e., preventing the recurrence of symptoms once they are gone). Another term used for this latter function is *maintenance* treatment.

If an agent is shown to have efficacy in all four of the actions listed above—that is, to "hit" in all four cells of the 2-by-2 table by both treating and preventing both manic and depressive symptoms—it might be considered a gold standard mood stabilizer. Even if not, this categorization scheme will provide a method by which to organize the evidence for which agents have which actions in manic-depressive disorder.

Therefore we have classified relevant studies according to their aim of assessing an agent's impact on (a) acute mania, (b) acute depression, or (c) prophylaxis of episodes. Most studies did not differentiate prophylaxis of mania versus depressive episodes, so these studies are summarized as a single group.

TREATMENT OF ACUTE MANIC SYMPTOMS

There are several types of pharmacologic intervention that have been used to treat acute manic symptoms. These include primarily lithium, various

TABLE 4.2   Organizing Efficacy Evidence: The Mood Stabilizer 2-by-2 Table

	Mania	Depression
Acute		
Prophylaxis		

neuroleptics, and several (though not all) anticonvulsants. Several other agents have also been studied, including in particular the calcium channel blocker verapamil and the benzodiazepines clonazepam and lorazepam.

Table 4.3 summarizes positive Class A and Table 4.4 (p. 60) summarizes some interesting Class B studies reviewed to date concerning acute treatment of manic symptoms. As can be seen, Class A studies support the antimanic efficacy of lithium, carbamazepine, valproate, olanzapine, verapamil, and the benzodiazepines clonazepam and lorazepam. At least two placebo-controlled trials support the efficacy of lithium, valproate, olanzapine, and verapamil. A variety of less frequently used agents are also supported by Class A studies. Several combination strategies are also supported by positive, placebo-controlled Class A evidence, although to a lesser degree and with less uniformity of approach (Table 4.5, p. 61).

TREATMENT OF ACUTE DEPRESSIVE SYMPTOMS

In contrast to evidence regarding acute mania, evidence is scarce concerning efficacy of specific agents for depression in manic-depressive disorder (reviewed in Zornberg & Pope, 1993). Most treatment is undertaken empirically, that is, primarily by extension from treatment experience in unipolar depression. Although a comprehensive discussion of evidence for efficacy of various antidepressants in unipolar depression is clearly beyond the scope of this book, it has been amply reviewed in several references (e.g., Gareri, Falconi, DeFazio, & DeSarro, 2000; Keller & Boland, 1997; see also Thase & Sachs, 2000).

Table 4.6 (p. 62) summarizes the positive Class A and Table 4.7 (p. 63), summarizes some interesting Class B studies reviewed to date concerning acute treatment of acute depressive symptoms. As can be seen, many fewer agents have proven efficacy for depression than for mania. Positive Class A data exist for lithium, imipramine, fluoxetine, lamotrigine, tranylcypromine,

TABLE 4.3　Acute Mania: Monotherapy, Positive Class A Studies of Major Agents

Agent Placebo control	Study
Lithium	Maggs (1963) Stokes (1971) Bowden (1994)
CBZ	Ballenger (1978)
VPA	Emrich (1980) Pope (1991) Bowden (1994)
Olanzapine	Tohen (1999) Tohen (2000)
Clonazepam	Edwards (1991)
Verapamil (calcium channel blocker)	Giannini (1984) Dubovsky (1986)

Agent Active agent control	Study
Lithium	Johnson (1968) Spring (1970) Platman (1970) Johnson (1971) Prien (1972) Takahashi (1975) Shopsin (1975)
CBZ	Okuma (1979) Lerer (1987) Luznat (1988) Brown (1989 Okuma (1990) Small (1991)
VPA	Freeman (1992) Vasudev (2000)
LMT	Ichim (2000)

TABLE 4.3 *(Continued)*

Agent	
Active agent control	Study
Clonazepam	Chouinard (1983)
Lorazepam	Bradwejn (1990)
Verapamil	Hoschl (1989) Garza-Trevino (1992) Walton (1996)

Key: Abbreviations for Tables 4.3–4.8
- BL   Baseline
- CBZ   Carbamazepine
- CPZ   Chlorpromazine
- ECT   Electroconvulsive Therapy
- GBP   Gabapentin
- HAL   Haloperidol
- IMI   Imipramine
- Li   Lithium
- LMT   Lamotrigine
- Nlpt Neuroleptic
- RC   Rapid Cycling
- T_3, T_4 Thyroid Hormones: Triiodothyronine (T3), Thyroxine (T4)
- TCP   Tranylcypromine
- TAU   Treatment as usual
- VPA   Valproate

TABLE 4.4   Acute Mania: Monotherapy, Some Interesting Class B Studies

Agent	Study
Clozapine	Kimmel (1994)
	Calabrese (1996)
	Green (2000)
ECT	Schnur (1992)
Gabapentin	Erfurth (1998)
Low Vanadium Diet	Naylor (1981)
Nimodipine (Calcium Channel Blocker)	Brunet (1990)
Tiagabine	Grunze (1999)

and ECT. Efficacy data from two or more placebo-controlled Class A studies exist only for lithium. In contrast to acute mania, for acute depression no combination strategies have been supported by positive placebo-controlled Class A studies (Table 4.8, p. 64).

PROPHYLAXIS OF MANIC AND DEPRESSIVE SYMPTOMS

As noted previously, most prophylaxis studies reported recurrence rates without distinguishing between manic and depressive symptoms. For example, some studies reported such statistics as time to first episode without specifying whether the first episode was manic or depressed. Other studies reported summary statistics for affective symptoms without separating manic or depressive symptoms. We found that when studies did report specific polarity of symptoms during recurrence, they only infrequently reported impact of treatment on recurrence of depressive symptoms.

Studies of single agents in prophylaxis (Table 4.9, p. 65) show that far and away the most support for any prophylactic agent comes from studies of lithium, with lesser support for carbamazepine and lamotrigine. The one prophylactic study of valproate showed no difference from placebo (lithium was also found to be no different from placebo in this study, although the study was underpowered to make definitive conclusions about this comparison). A Class B open trial supports its use as monotherapy (Table 4.10, p. 66). As can be seen from Table 4.11 (p. 67), various combination therapies have also been studied with Class A or Class B studies.

It may be surprising that there is such a paucity of data on treatment of acute depression and prophylaxis of manic-depressive disorder, with the clear exception of lithium. Yet we frequently encounter many other medications used chronically in this illness, such as valproate and the neuroleptics, for which there is good acute antimanic evidence but little evidence for

TABLE 4.5   Acute Mania: Combination Therapy, Placebo, and Some Interesting Active Control Class A Studies

Agent[a]	
Positive placebo-controlled trials	Study
HAL → Lithium	Garfinkle (1980)
CBZ → Lithium	Kramlinger (1989)
Phenytoin → HAL	Mishory (2000)
VPA → Nlpt	Muller-Oerlinghausen (2000)

Agent	
Active agent control	Study
Thiothixene + Li vs.CPZ + Li	Janicak (1988)
Lorazepam + Li vs. HAL + Li	Lenox (1992)
Zuclothixol + Clonazepam vs. Li + Clonazepam	Gouliaev (1996)
Clozapine + Li vs. CPZ + Li	Barbini (1997)

prophylaxis. This is because these agents typically are started during the course of an acute manic episode and because clinicians are loathe to stop them and switch to a different agent such as lithium. In addition, many individuals have failed or been intolerant of treatment with lithium. However, alternative agents are not necessarily suboptimal treatment. It is important that clinicians recognize that data on long-term prophylactic efficacy are scant for these agents, as for many other agents used in psychiatric practice.

SUMMARY OF EFFICACY DATA FOR TREATMENT OF MOOD SYMPTOMS IN MANIC-DEPRESSIVE DISORDER

Several patterns are evident from this review. First, there are many more agents of proven efficacy in the treatment of mania than depression or prophylaxis. Second, if we apply criteria for efficacy similar to those used by the U.S. Food and Drug Administration (FDA)—specifically, at least two positive

TABLE 4.6   Acute Depression: Monotherapy, Class A Studies

Agent Placebo control	Study
Lithium	Goodwin (1972)
	Baron (1975)
	Mendels (1976)
Imipramine	Cohn (1989)
Fluoxetine	Cohn (1989)
LMT	Calabrese (1999)

Agent Active agent control	Study
Tranylcypromine vs. IMI	Himmelhoch (1991)
	Thase (1992)
ECT	Sackheim (1987)
	Sackheim (1993)
	Sackheim (2000)

placebo-controlled trials—the list of proven agents shrinks substantially. For mania, the list includes the agents listed in Table 4.3; for depression, in Table 4.6; and for prophylaxis, Table 4.9. Also, inspection of individual prophylaxis studies of lithium indicates that fewer studies have assessed the impact of an agent on prevention of depressive symptoms than manic, and the data indicate much less robust effects in the prevention of depression (data not shown). This recapitulates the findings in treating acute episodes: The data are much less strong for treatment and prevention of depression than of mania.

To summarize, Table 4.12 (p. 68) returns to the 2-by-2 format and lists agents that meet the FDA-like criteria of at least two positive placebo-controlled trials to establish efficacy. Lithium is the only agent to "hit" in all four cells of the table. As such, it remains the only agent to fulfill the gold standard criteria for mood stabilizer according to the proposed definition.

TABLE 4.7   Acute Depression: Monotherapy, Some Interesting Class B Studies

Agent	Study	Results
Imipramine, Tranylcypromine, Phenelzine, ECT	Greenblatt (1964)	ECT 80% improved vs. drugs 40% improved
Benzerazide + 5HTP + deprenil	Mendlewicz (1980)	Pos.
Dexamethasone intravenous	Arana (1981)	Pos.
Bright Light	Deltito (1991)	Pos.
VPA	Winsberg (2001)	Pos.

ISSUES IN USAGE: OVERVIEW

Providing detailed prescribing information regarding all the agents used in manic-depressive disorder is both beyond the scope of this psychotherapy manual and well covered in other existing texts. The reader is referred to the following guides for information on prescribing specifics:

- Hyman, Arana, and Rosenbaum (1995)
- Schatzberg, Cole, and DeBattista (1997)
- Ellsworth, Witt, Dugdale, and Oliver (2001)
- www.Medscape.com
- www.ePocrates.com (for handheld devices)

Basic information on dose- and serum-level ranges for lithium and commonly used anticonvulsants is found in Table 4.13 (p. 69). Although we do not include specific dosing guidelines for each neuroleptic and antidepressant agent, it will be helpful to have a rough guide to dosage equivalents for these classes. Tables 4.14 (p. 70), 4.15 (p. 71), 4.16 (p. 72), and 4.17 (p. 73) provide this information for, respectively, neuroleptics (both typical and atypical), antidepressants, and benzodiazepines.

Some information specifically on side effects of medications is essential for clinicians involved in the psychotherapy of individuals with manic-depressive disorder, because side effects may lead to medication discontinuation in 18% to 53%, a figure that is greater in lower socioeconomic classes (Goodwin & Jamison, 1990, p. 755). Clinicians responsible for psychoeducation do not need to manage the side effects directly—and, in fact, to have clinicians other than the prescriber managing the medication regimen is a recipe for chaos. However, they can play an important role in supporting the individual's illness management skills. In some cases, the clinician may find himself or herself contacting the prescriber directly regarding troublesome

TABLE 4.8   Acute Depression: Combination Therapy, Some Interesting Class A Studies of Major Agents

Agent Placebo control	Study
IMI or Paroxetine → Lithium	Nemeroff (2001)[a]
Inositol → Mood Stablilizer	Chengappa (2001)[a]

Agent Active agent control	Study
Sulpride + Li vs. Amitriptyline + Li	Bochetta (1993)
Bupropion + Mood Stabilizer vs. Desipramine + Mood Stabilizer	Sachs (1994)
Paroxetine + Li or VPA vs. Li + VPA or VPA + Li	Young (2000)
Moclobemide + Mood Stabilizer vs. Imipramine + Mood Stabilizer	Silverstone (2001)

[a] Primary analyses were not statisticaly significant in these studies.

or dangerous side effects that the person may be experiencing. More often, clinicians will play the role of educating individuals regarding potential side effects, validating them in their concern about troublesome symptoms that may or may not be side effects, coaching them in the often anxiety-producing task of discussing possible side effects with the prescriber, and supporting them during periods of medication adjustment, which can often be frustrating and difficult for the individual.

ISSUES IN USAGE: LITHIUM AND COMMONLY USED ANTICONVULSANTS

Prior to the 1970s, manic-depressive disorder was managed with treatment targeted only toward resolution of individual episodes: antidepressants and electroconvulsive therapy (ECT) for depressive episodes, and neuroleptics and occasionally ECT for mania (DeCarolis, Gilberti, Roccatagliata, Rossi, & Venutti, 1964; Lehman & Hanrahan, 1954). Lithium's efficacy in the treatment of acute mania, acute depression, and prophylaxis in the studies summarized in the sections above, many of which were conducted in the Department of Veterans Affairs under the direction of Robert Prien, MD, established that

TABLE 4.9   Prophylaxis: Monotherapy, Class A Studies

Agent Placebo control	Study
Lithium	Baastrup (1970)
	Coppen (1971)
	Cundall (1972)
	Prien (1973a)
	Prien (1973b)
	Stallone (1973)
	Dunner (1976)
	Fieve (1976)
	Kane (1982)
LMT	Calabrese (2000)
	Frye (2000)

Agent Some interesting active agent studies	Study
Lithium	Prien (1984)
	Gelenberg (1989)
CBZ	Coxhead (1992)
	Simhandl (1993)
LMT vs. Li	Schaerer (2000)

agent as the gold standard in treatment of manic-depressive disorder. It also changed the perspective of psychiatrists who began to consider that a single agent may be efficacious in treating both of the very different acute symptoms, and that long-term monotherapy may have the potential of stabilizing individuals with the disorder and allow their return to maximal function.

However, lithium was far from being the panacea for manic-depressive disorder. Certain factors predict relatively poorer response to lithium, including mixed mania and depression (Swann et al., 1986), rapid cycling (Maj et al., 1989), and substance abuse (Himmelhoch et al., 1976a). As discussed in chapter 1, these are relatively common concomitants of manic-depressive disorder, encountered frequently in the real world of general clinical practice, more so than in controlled treatment trials in relatively highly selected populations. The implications of the differences between effects of treatments in general clinical practice and in controlled trials are important both to treatment and to the genesis of this manual, and are reviewed in more detail in chapter 6.

TABLE 4.10 Prophylaxis: Monotherapy, Some Interesting Class B Studies

Agent	Study	Results
VPA	Calabrese (1993)	Pos. (in RC)
LMT	Calabrese (1999)	Pos. (in RC)

Subsequently, encouraging results have been found with other agents, including the anticonvulsants carbamazepine and sodium valproate, and more recently lamotrigine. However, as detailed in the previous sections, these agents have been shown to date to have efficacy primarily for acute manic episodes, and in the case of lamotrigine, for acute depressive episodes. At this time, data are scant with regard to their efficacy in long-term prophylaxis.

No one knows how lithium or the anticonvulsants exert their effects in manic-depressive disorder. For lithium, it is fairly certain that it does not exert its effects by binding to any specific membrane-bound receptors in pre- or postsynaptic neurons. As summarized in chapter 3, it is more likely that lithium acts by affecting the second messenger systems within the neuron, such as the phosphatidyl inositol system, or by modulating the enzyme protein kinase C (Stahl, 2000, pp. 267ff). Similarly, the mechanisms of action of the newer anticonvulsants are unclear. Likely they involve modulation of ion channels, the inhibitory neurotransmitter gamma-aminobutyric acid (GABA), or excitatory neurotransmitter systems such as the glutamate system. All these systems that are potential targets for lithium and anticonvulsants are widely distributed in the brain. Even if the specific target system for drug action is identified, it will likely be several more years before animal and human imaging studies identify the key anatomic locale(s) of action.

Side effects for these agents can be considered to be of three types. First, potentially life-threatening side effects are rare but must be recognized promptly; these are enumerated in Table 4.18 (p. 74). Second, side effects that we consider clinically relevant are those that cause some discomfort or morbidity to the individual; these are summarized in Table 4.19 (p. 75). These are much more common than life-threatening side effects, and few people take any of these psychotropic agents without at least some recognizable side effects. We stress that their detection and discussion are important because they can be a prime cause for medication discontinuation. Third, several types of medication effects are detected only on laboratory screening; these are listed in Table 4.20 (p. 76). They do not, in and of themselves, require treatment. Some, such as increased thyroid-stimulating hormone (TSH) due to lithium, warrant continued monitoring to ensure that the clinical syndrome of hypothyroidism (Table 4.19) does not develop. Others, such as the mild electrocardiogram or white blood cell changes associated with lithium, are benign.

TABLE 4.11 Prophylaxis: Combination Therapy, Positive Class A Studies

Agent	
Placebo control	Study
Imipramine → Lithium	Quitkin (1981)
	Kane (1982)
Fluphenthixol → Lithium	Esparon (1986)
High-Dose T4 → TAU	Bauer (1990)
VPA → Li	Solomon (1997)
Omega-3 Fatty Acids → TAU	Stoll (1999)
Magnesium → Verapamil	Giannini (2000)
Agent	
Some interesting active agent studies	Study
Methylene Blue High vs.Low Dose + Li	Naylor (1986)
TAU plus: CBZ vs. Li vs. Li + CBZ	Denicoff (1997)

Extensive reviews of side effects of lithium can be found in several sources (e.g., Gitlin et al., 1989; Goodwin & Jamison, 1990 pp. 701–709), as well as in the general handbooks listed above. Similarly, focused reviews of the side effects of various anticonvulsants (Swann, 2001), including carbamazepine (Ketter & Post, 1994) and sodium valproate (Keck, McElroy, & Bennett, 1994), and lamotrigine (Botts & Raskind, 1999), are also readily available.

Issues in Usage: Neuroleptics

Prior to the advent of lithium treatment, neuroleptics were the mainstay of antimanic therapy. They have undergone a renaissance since the development of what have come to be known as atypical neuroleptics because of the relatively more benign neurologic side effect profile of these agents.

Although clearly both the older, typical or conventional neuroleptics and the newer atypicals have acute antimanic efficacy, they have yet to be shown to have efficacy in acute depression or in prophylaxis. Nonetheless, neuroleptics are widely used in manic-depressive disorder, with up to two thirds of individuals with the disorder receiving chronic treatment (Keck et al., 1996), at least some of which is likely warranted for continued antimanic effect.

TABLE 4.12 Summary of Class A Efficacy Data for Treating the Various Phases of Manic-Depressive Disorder (At Least Two Placebo-Controlled Trials)

	Mania	Depression
Acute	Lithium VPA Olanzapine Verapamil	Lithium
Prophylaxis	Lithium LMT	

It is likely that atypical neuroleptics will be even more widely used than typicals, because their side effect profile is *erroneously* presumed to be benign. Their use must be justified no less than for the typicals, as they too have problematic side effects, as outlined below.

The primary action of neuroleptics is to block neuronal membrane dopamine receptors of the D2 subclass (Stahl, 2000, pp. 402ff). It is likely that they exert their antipsychotic effects through blocking D2 receptors in the mesolimbic pathway, although site of their overall sedative and antimanic effects are not known. Side effects are primarily due to D2 blockade in the mesocortical and nigrostriatal pathways, with the former responsible for the cognitive side effects and the latter responsible for the movement side effects including both parkinsonian symptoms and tardive dyskinesia.

Atypical antipsychotics differ from typicals in having, in addition, the ability to block serotonin (5HT) receptors, particularly of the 5HT2A subtype. Serotonin inhibits dopamine release in the nigrostriatal pathway. Thus, atypical agents that block the 5HT2A receptor and prevent serotonin from inhibiting dopamine release in this area may be expected to have fewer movement-related side effects than the pure D2-blocking typicals, and indeed they do. By the same mechanism in the mesocortical pathway, they may be expected to have fewer cognitive side effects than the typicals. This also appears to be the case, although whether they truly are effective in treating the "negative" symptoms of schizophrenia is still open to question.

It is not likely that the atypicals are more effective than the typicals in treating the positive, psychotic symptoms in schizophrenia or manic-depressive disorder. In fact, it is our clinical experience that a number of severely manic individuals who do not respond to the atypical antipsychotics may respond to the typical agents. This may be because the atypicals' blockade of 5HT2A receptors and resultant increase in dopamine release, helpful in minimizing

TABLE 4.13 Typical Dosages and Serum Levels for Lithium and Commonly Used Anticonvulsants

Drug	Therapeutic levels	Typical doses (mg/day)
Lithium	0.5–1.5 IU/L Goal: > 0.8	1,200–2,400
Carbamazepine	4–12 mcg/ml Goal: > 8.0	400–1,200
Valproate	45–125 mcg/ml Goal: > 80	1,500–4,500
Lamotrigine	2–20 mcg/ml	50–500

side effects, may actually "undo" some of the dopamine blockade at the D2 receptors, which appears necessary for the resolution of psychotic symptoms. The sole exception to this is clozapine, which has been shown to have efficacy in the positive, psychotic symptoms of schizophrenia where other agents have failed (Kane, Hongfeld, Singer, & Meltzer, 1988).

As noted previously, dosage equivalents for most typical and atypical neuroleptics can be found in Tables 4.14 and 4.15. A summary of most common neuroleptic side effects is found in Table 4.21 (p. 77). Reviews of side effects of the typicals and atypicals can be found in the general references cited above, as well as more specific references (e.g., Arana, 1988 (typicals); Malhotra, Litman, & Pickar, 1993; Stanniland & Taylor, 2000; Strip, 2000 (atypicals); Taylor & McAskill, 2000; Zarate, 2000). Understanding two basic principles of neuroleptics classification will allow understanding of the most important of their side effects: atypical versus typical and high potency versus low potency.

As noted above, atypical neuroleptics appear to have fewer cognitive blunting side effects than do typical neuroleptics, possibly because of a better balance between D2 receptor blockade and dopamine release. Importantly, atypical neuroleptics also appear to have lower rates of tardive dyskinesia, the often irreversible movement disorder that comes after prolonged exposure to neuroleptics, perhaps particularly in individuals with affective disorders (Casey, 1984). However, the rates of tardive dyskinesia are not negligible, and we have many fewer years of exposure to the atypicals than the typicals, because the latter have been studied since the 1950s and the former only since the 1990s. We will likely have to wait another decade or two before we have definitive comparative rates for long-term usage.

Because of the relatively lower incidence of tardive dyskinesia with the atypicals, these agents have taken psychiatry by storm and are prescribed widely not only for psychosis but also in other diagnoses for agitation, irritability, anxiety, and the like, with relatively more or less justification.

TABLE 4.14 Typical Neuroleptic Dose Equivalencies

Generic	Brand	Dose
Chlorpromazine	Thorazine	100 mg
Acetophenazine	Tindal	20
Chlorprothixene	Taractan	100
Droperidol	Inapsine	2
Fluphenazine	Prolixin/Permitil	2
Haloperidol	Haldol	2
Loxapine	Loxitane/Daxolin	10
Mesoridazine	Serentil	50
Molindone	Moban	10
Perphenazine	Trilafon	10
Pimozide	Orap	2
Thioridazine	Mellaril	100
Thiothixene	Navane	4
Trifluoperazine	Stelazine	5
Fluphenazine depot	1cc (25 mg) q 3 weeks = 1,000 mg Chlorpromazine	
Haloperidol depot	1cc (100 mg) q 4 weeks = 500 mg Chlorpromazine	

However, a major—though silent, compared to tardive dyskinesia—problem with the atypicals is their propensity to cause weight gain, elevations of triglycerides to clinically significant levels, and diabetes mellitus. This is of particular concern with olanzapine, but it also occurs to a lesser extent with other atypicals. In addition, concern regarding cardiac arrhythmia that may be responsible for sudden death (prolongation of the QT interval on EKG) has surfaced in association with the older typical neuroleptic, thioridazine, and also with the atypical ziprasidone.

As this is being written, mental health prescribers are in the midst of a ruthless marketing war between the makers of the various atypicals, with each company, indirectly and veiled in the guise of public service and continuing medical education, pointing out the flaws in the others' products. Despite all this hype and rhetoric, it will pay off simply to be knowledgeable of side effects and to work in a careful, collaborative manner with the individuals being treated.

The second way of categorizing neuroleptics is as high- and low-potency agents. A simple rule of thumb is that the lower potency agents will be relatively sedating and also high in anticholinergic (dry mouth, blurry vision,

TABLE 4.15 Atypical Neuroleptic Dose Equivalencies

Generic	Brand	Dose
Risperidone	Risperdal	2 mg
Clozapine	Clozaril	100
Olanzapine	Zyprexa	2
Quetiapine	Seroquel	100
Ziprazadone	Geodon	25

and urinary hesitancy) and antiadrenergic (hypotension) side effects. In contrast, they are relatively low in extrapyramidal motor side effects (parkinsonian symptoms, dystonic reactions, and akathisia). The reverse is true for the high-potency agents. In Table 4.14, agents with chlorpromazine equivalencies of 50 mg or more are usually considered low potency, those with equivalencies of 2 to 4 mg high potency, and the others intermediate potency.

This knowledge is useful because agents can be chosen based on those side effects one wants to avoid (e.g., hypotension in the elderly; dystonic reactions in the young). Conversely, choice may be made based on desired side effects (e.g., sedation in the highly agitated manic). In our experience, for instance, polypharmacy with a high-potency or atypical neuroleptic plus a benzodiazepine can be avoided simply by using a sedating, low-potency typical such as chlorpromazine.

The high/low-potency categorization does not work quite as nicely in atypicals. For example, risperidone behaves as a classic high-potency typical at higher doses and has a relatively low dose range, as expected (see Table 4.15). However, olanzapine is one of the most sedating agents, used in similarly low doses. Quetiapine and ziprazidone have higher dose ranges, whereas clozapine shares characteristics of low-potency typicals. Thus, it is probably easiest to consider risperidone and clozapine as, respectively, high- and low-potency agents, and the other three agents as relatively sedating, with mild to moderate hypotensive effects.

ISSUES IN USAGE: BENZODIAZEPINES

Benzodiazepines (see Table 4.17) will be reviewed only briefly here, as their use is only adjunctive to the core agents in manic-depressive disorder. As outlined above, some studies have documented efficacy for clonazepam and lorazepam in the treatment of acute mania, although they are not likely to be of equal efficacy to lithium, neuroleptics, or anticonvulsants. They are

TABLE 4.16   Antidepressant Dose Equivalencies

| Drug name | | | | |
Generic	Brand	Dose		
Imipramine	Tofranil	100 mg	200 mg	300 mg
Tricyclic				
Amitriptyline	Elavil	100–199	200–299	300+
Amoxapine	Asendin	100–149	150–449	450+
Clomipramine	Anafranil	75–99	100–249	250+
Desipramine	Norpramine	50–124	125–249	250+
Doxepin	Sinequan	100–149	150–299	300+
Nortriptyline	Aventyl	50–74	75–149	150+
Protriptyline	Vivactil	10–24	25–49	50+
Trimipramine	Surmontil	50–74	75–299	300+
Selective serotonin reuptake inhibitors				
Citalopram	Cylexa	10–19	20–59	60+
Fluoxetine	Prozac	10–19	20–59	60+
Paroxetine	Paxil	10–19	20–59	60+
Sertraline	Zoloft	25–49	50–199	200+
Monoamine oxidase inhibitors				
Phenelzine	Nardil	15–29	30–89	90+
Tranylcypromine	Parnate	10–19	20–59	60+
Serotonin-norepinephrine reuptake inhibitors				
Venlafaxine	Effexor	75–149	150–299	300+
Mirtazepine	Remeron	15–29	30–44	45+
Other agents				
Trazodone	Deseryl	100–149	150–449	450+
Nefazodone	Serzone	100–299	300–599	600+
Bupropion	Wellbutrin	100–199	200–399	400+

also sometimes used for treatment of comorbid anxiety, frequently for detoxification from comorbid alcohol dependence, and probably too frequently for insomnia.

These agents likely exert their effect by virtue of effects on the GABA system. Major side effects include physiologic or behavioral addiction, oversedation, and, in the elderly, confusion and falls leading to hip fracture or cerebral bleeding. Because of the high prevalence of comorbid alcohol and drug dependence in manic-depressive disorder (see chapter 1), use of benzodiazepines is relatively or absolutely contraindicated in many individuals. Nonetheless, we have safely treated a number of individuals who have comorbid anxiety disorders with low doses of slow-onset benzodiazepines such as

TABLE 4.17   Benzodiazepine Dose Equivalencies

Generic	Brand	Dose
Diazepam	Valium	10 mg
Alprazolam	Xanax	1
Chlordiazepoxide	Librium	50
Clonazepam	Klonopin	0.5
Clorazepate	Tranxene	15
Flurazepam	Dalmane	60
Halazepam	Paxipam	40
Lorazepam	Ativan	2
Oxazepam	Serax	30
Prazepam	Centrax	20
Temazepan	Restoril	60
Triazolam	Halcion	0.5

oxazepam, despite their having histories of substance dependence. Such treatment requires a strong treatment alliance and good illness management skills on the part of the individual being treated, as well as a flexible attitude on the part of the prescriber.

ISSUES IN USAGE: ANTIDEPRESSANTS

A relatively nontechnical summary of the basic neuropharmacology of antidepressants can be found in the reviews by Richelson (1993), Bauer and Frazer (1994), and Stahl (2000). To review briefly, antidepressant agents of several types have been established as efficacious treatments for major depressive episodes (Table 4.16). Tricyclic antidepressants, so-called because their chemical structure contains three rings, were first demonstrated to have antidepressant efficacy in the 1950s (Kuhn, 1958). Their mechanism of action is thought to involve increasing the amount of norepinephrine and perhaps serotonin at synaptic receptors (reviewed in Heninger & Charney, 1987), although these mechanisms clearly do not completely explain their antidepressant effects.

The monoamine oxidase inhibitors (MAOIs) were also discovered to have antidepressant effects (Crane, 1957; Loomer, Saunders, & Kline, 1957) and are considered to exert their effects by increasing available norepinephrine and serotonin. They achieve this effect by decreasing the metabolism (breakdown) of norepinephrine and serotonin by inactivating the enzyme monoamine oxidase. They are effective antidepressants, although they have

TABLE 4.18   Side Effects of Lithium and Commonly Used Anticonvulsants: Life-Threatening

	Therapeutic levels		Toxic levels
	Idiopathic	Dose related	Dose related
Lithium			Renal failure Encephalopathy
CBZ	Agranulocytosis* Aplastic anemia* Stevens-Johnson*		
VPA	Hepatic necrosis (children)	Thrombocytopenia	Thrombocytopenia
LMT	Stevens-Johnson*		

* Typically during first 1 to 6 months of treatment.
CBZ = carbamazepine
LMT = lamotrigine
VPA = valproate

been relatively underutilized because of the dietary restrictions necessary for their safe use. As amply documented elsewhere, ingestion of the dietary substance tyramine or coadministration with certain other prescription or over-the-counter medications can result in life-threatening elevations in blood pressure (Shulman, Walker, MacKenzie, & Knowles, 1989). Some of the more common sources of dietary tyramine and frequently encountered medications that interact adversely with MAOIs are summarized in Table 4.22 (p. 78).

Over the past several years relatively selective serotonin reuptake inhibitors (SSRIs), which, as the name implies, increase the amount of serotonin in the synapse by blocking its reuptake into presynaptic nerve terminals, have been established as efficacious treatments for major depression (e.g., Sussman, 1994). Their side effect profile differs from that of the tricyclic antidepressants, and they are often well tolerated by persons with depression (Rudorfer, Manji, & Potter, 1994). Importantly, toxicity in overdose situations is relatively less than tricyclic antidepressants.

Two compounds, venlafaxine and mirtazapine, belong to the promising "new" class of serotonin-norepinephrine reuptake inhibitors (SNRIs). Although their structures are novel, recall that the old tricyclic antidepressants inhibit reuptake of both these compounds as well.

Three additional agents that are not classified in the above groups include trazodone, nefazodone, and bupropion. Trazodone and the closely related nefazodone are multicyclic (four-ring) antidepressants with prominent serotonin-blocking effects. In contrast to reuptake inhibiting effects, these agents

TABLE 4.19 Side Effects of Lithium and Commonly Used Anticonvulsants: Clinically Significant Side Effects

Side effects	Lithium	CBZ	VPA	LMT
Neurologic/muscular	Lethargy Memory Tremor* Myoclonus	Lethargy Blurred vision Ataxia*	Lethargy Depression Tremor* Ataxia	Lethargy Ataxia Blurred vision Headache
Endocrine/metabolic	Weight gain* Hypothyroidism		Weight gain*	
Cardiopulmonary				
Hematologic			Thrombocytopenia	
Renal	Nephrogenic diabetes insipidus			
Hepatic		Jaundice	Jaundice	
Gastrointestinal	Nausea* Diarrhea*	Nausea*	Nausea* Diarrhea*	Nausea*
Dermatologic	Maculopapular rash Psoriasis Acne	Maculopapular rash Alopecia	Maculopapular rash	Maculopapular rash
Other			Back pain	

* Most common reasons in our experience for noncompliance.
CBZ = carbamazepine; LMT = lamotrigine; VPA = valproate.

TABLE 4.20 Side Effects of Lithium and Commonly Used Anticonvulsants: Subclinical Laboratory Abnormalities

Side effects	Lithium	CBZ	VPA	LMT
Neurologic/Muscular				
Endocrine/Metabolic	Increased TSH	Decreased FTI		
Cardiopulmonary	EKG T-wave depression			
Hematologic	Leukocytosis (to 20,000)	Leukopenia	Thrombocytopenia (OK > 20,000)	
Renal	Decreased urine-specific gravity, GFR			
Hepatic		Increased LFTs	Increased LFTs	

CBZ = carbamazepine; EKG = electrocardiogram; FTI = free thyroxine index; GFR = glomerular filtration rate; LFT = liver function test; LMT = lamotrigine; VPA = valproate; TSH = thyroid-stimulating hormone.

TABLE 4.21 Common or Important Side Effects of Neuroleptics at Therapeutic Dosages*

Side effects	Higher potency	Lower potency	Clozapine	Risperidone	Olanzapine	Quetiapine	Ziprasidone
Clinically significant side effects							
Allergic reactions/rash	x	x	x	x	x	x	x
Weight gain	x	x	x	x	xx	x	x
Sedation		xx	xx		xx		
Low blood pressure		xx	xx	x	x	x	x
Breast enlargement	x	x		x			
Light sensitivity (vision)		x					
Retinal damage		Thioridazine (x)					
Light sensitivity (skin)	x	x					
Parkinson's disease	xx	x		x			
Dystonic reactions (muscle spasms)	xx			x			
Motor restlessness (akathisia)	xx			x			
Increased seizures (in epilepsy)	x	x	xx				
Mania (paradoxical)				x			
Potentially life-threatening or irreversible							
Bone marrow suppression			xx				
Tardive dyskinesia	xx	xx		??	??	??	??
QT interval prolongation on EKG		Thio/mesoridazine (xx)					x

* xx = frequently encountered; x = encountered infrequently or with only some of the drugs of this class. See selected references for more details.
EKG = electrocardiogram.

TABLE 4.22 Dietary and Pharmacologic Substances Causing Adverse Interactions with Monoamine Oxidase Inhibitor Antidepressants

Foodstuffs high in tyramine
  Beverages
    Dark beer
    Red wine
  Cheese
    Almost all except cream cheese,
    cottage cheese, and ricotta
  Meats
    Organ meats (e.g., liver, sweetbreads)
    Fermented meats (e.g., sausages)
    Smoked meats
  Other
    Soups containing forbidden foods
    Soy sauce
  Foods with any signs of spoilage

  Fruits
    Raspberries

  Vegetables
    Broad beans

  Fish
    Any pickled.fish

Most commonly encountered medications*
  Over-the-counter
    Phenylpropanolamine
    Pseudoephedrine
  Prescription-only
    Amphetamines
    Epinephrine
    Local anesthetics that contain epinephrine
    Isoproterenol
    Levodopa
    Meperidine
    Methylphenidate

* No medications should be taken without the express permission of the prescribing physician. Note that over-the-counter remedies often include forbidden medications. Great care must be taken in reading ingredient labels to avoid adverse interactions. This is especially true of cold medications.

decrease serotonin effects at selected groups of postsynaptic serotonin receptors. Trazodone is highly sedative, which can be useful in treating depressive episodes in which insomnia predominates; however, this property often precludes increasing the dose sufficiently high to reach antidepressant levels. This "unwanted" side effect, on the other hand, has led to its frequent administration for insomnia as an alternative to benzodiazepines. Nefazodone is less sedating but typically must be given twice a day.

Bupropion is chemically quite different from other antidepressants and strongly blocks the reuptake of dopamine in the synapse. Although dopamine is typically considered more involved in mechanisms of psychosis rather than depression, there is undoubtedly a role for dopamine in mood disorders as well (see chapter 3). Furthermore, it is likely that bupropion has additional nondopaminergic effects that are relevant to its antidepressant properties. Bupropion also has been proposed to induce mania less frequently than other antidepressants and to have mood-stabilizing effects in manic-depressive disorder (e.g., Haykal & Akiskal, 1990; Sachs, Lafer, Truman, Noeth, & Thibault, 1994; Shopsin, 1983), but other data indicate that bupropion has the same ability to induce mania or rapid cycling as other antidepressants (Fogelson et al., 1992).

Major side effects of antidepressants are summarized in Table 4.23. In addition, comprehensive reviews of antidepressant side effects can be found in the general references noted earlier in the chapter or in several more specific reviews (e.g., Depression Guideline Panel, 1993; Ferguson, 2001; Montgomery, 1998; Rudorfer et al., 1994; Settle, 1998).

Among nonpharmacologic somatic treatments for depression in manic-depressive disorder, electroconvulsive therapy has clearly been established as an effective agent both for acute mania and for depression. As for other treatments, data specifically on manic-depressive disorder lag behind that for unipolar depression. Two reports describe beneficial effects of high-intensity visible spectrum light of the type used to treat seasonal affective disorder in persons with depressive episodes during manic-depressive disorder. Deltito and colleagues (Deltito, Moline, Pollak, Martin, & Maremmami, 1991) found light effects in persons with nonseasonal manic-depressive disorder superior to effects in nonseasonal unipolar depressives treated in winter. Bauer (1993) reported a small case series of persons with manic-depressive disorder who had a good response to light treatment for depressive episodes occurring in the summer. Though preliminary, each of these reports suggests that further exploration of potential effects of light treatment in manic-depressive disorder, apart from seasonal factors, is warranted.

SPECIAL ASPECTS IN THE TREATMENT OF DEPRESSIVE EPISODES IN MANIC-DEPRESSIVE DISORDER

Several special aspects that differentiate treatment of depressive episodes during manic-depressive disorder should be noted. First, lithium appears to be an effective antidepressant in depressive episodes during manic-depressive disorder (see Tables 4.5 and 4.9), whereas the evidence is equivocal for its efficacy in unipolar depression (Fieve, Platman, & Plutchik, 1968; Goodwin et al., 1972).

Second, it should be kept in mind that all somatic antidepressant treatments are potentially pro-manic, with the probable exception of lithium. These two facts indicate that lithium should be the first-line treatment for unmedicated persons with manic-depressive disorder in the depressed phase.

TABLE 4.23 Common or Important Side Effects of Antidepressants at the Therapeutic Dosages

Side effects	Tricyclics	Heterocyclics	MAOIs	SSRIs	SNRIs
Clinically significant side effects					
Allergic reactions	x	x	x	x	x
Sedation	x	x	x		x
Insomnia		Bupropion	x	x	
Nervousness		Bupropion		x	
Dry mouth	x				
Gastrointestinal distress				xx	x
Constipation	x				x
Weight gain	xx	x	xx		Mirtazepine
Appetite suppression				Fluoxetine	
Sexual dysfunction	x		x	xx	
Heart rhythm disruption	x				
Low blood pressure	xx		xx		
High blood pressure					Venlafaxine
Potentially life-threatening complications					
High blood pressure (life-threatening)			x		
Priapism		Trazodone			
Hepatic failure		Nefazodone			
Overdose toxicity	+3	+2	+2	+1 Citalopram +2	??

xx = frequently encountered; x = encountered infrequently or with only some of the drugs of this class. See selected references for more details. Overdose toxicity is rated 0 to +3 based on frequency of mortality or severe morbidity after overdose. MAOIs = monoamine oxidase inhibitors; SNRIs = serotonin-norepinephrine reuptake inhibitors; SSRI = selective serotonin reuptake inhibitors.

Third, although there are few data indicating that depression during manic-depressive disorder responds preferentially to any particular drug, there is evidence as noted above that persons with manic-depressive disorder who have hypersomnolent, anergic depressive episodes may respond to monoamine oxidase inhibitors better than to tricyclics (Himmelhoch, Thase, Mallinger, & Fuchs, 1991; Thase, Mallinger, McKnight, & Himmelhoch, 1992). In this regard, it should also be noted that ECT may be more effective than tricyclic antidepressants in depressed individuals with manic-depressive disorder (reviewed in Zornberg & Pope, 1993). Thus, these modalities cannot be ignored as potential agents in treating manic-depressive disorder and should not be relegated to "last chance" status. Increasing education and comonitoring during group psychotherapy can improve compliance and make MAOIs more practically useful and ECT more acceptable when indicated.

SPECIAL ISSUES IN PROPHYLAXIS OF MANIC-DEPRESSIVE DISORDER

Several currently controversial issues in prophylaxis of manic-depressive disorder with lithium deserve comment. First, when is lifetime, or at least long-term, prophylaxis warranted? After one manic episode? One hypomanic episode? One depressive episode with a strong family history of manic-depressive disorder? There is insufficient empirical evidence with which to make strong recommendations, although a creative study by Zarin and Pass (1987) using computer-based modeling investigated trade-offs of treatment versus observation based on costs and benefits of recurrence risks and drug side effects under several strategies. In clinical practice without clear guidelines, such decisions need to take into account individual and family capability in reporting symptoms, rapidity of onset of episodes, episode severity, and associated morbidity. Clearly, the risks of a wait-and-see strategy would be different in a person who had a psychotic manic episode than in a person who had mild hypomania.

Second, can lithium ever be discontinued? Again, there are no solid data on which to base this decision. However, if lithium discontinuation is contemplated, there is evidence that rapid discontinuation (in less than 2 weeks) is more likely to result in relapse than slow taper (2 to 4 weeks), with relapse rates higher in persons with type I compared to type II disorder (Faedda, Tondo, Baldessarni, Suppes, & Tohen, 1993; Suppes, Baldessarni, Faedda, Tondo, & Tohen, 1993). In those with type I disorder, relapse rates were, respectively, 96% and 73%, whereas in those with type II disorder, relapse rates were 91% and 33% (Faedda et al., 1993). There is some theoretical concern, based on a report of four individuals, that those in whom lithium has been discontinued may not be recaptured by resumption of lithium (Post et al., 1992), but these are preliminary observations on a sample from the National Institute of Mental Health that may not be representative of persons with manic-depressive disorder seen in general clinical practice.

Third, treatment options for refractory manic-depressive disorder, particularly rapid cycling, have yet to be established. Persons with rapid cycling represent a treatment dilemma (Bauer, 1994). Withdrawal of antidepressants, which may induce rapid cycling, often leaves the person in a protracted, severe depression. Switching agents often results in resumption of cycling. Complex treatment strategies may be required, such as anticonvulsants plus lithium, combinations of anticonvulsants, or adjuvant treatment with high doses of the thyroid hormone thyroxine.

CRITICAL THINKING ABOUT TREATMENT SIDE EFFECTS

All psychotropic medications have side effects. Some are actually desirable (e.g., sedation with antidepressants in persons with prominent insomnia), and specific antidepressants are often chosen on the basis of desired side effects. However, side effects usually represent factors that decrease a person's quality of life and compromise compliance.

Identification of some side effects and attribution to a particular agent are sometimes easy: An antidepressant is started, and within 2 weeks the person develops impotence; a neuroleptic is begun, and within 2 days the person develops akathisia, an uncomfortable motor restlessness. In these cases, doses can be reduced, medications changed, or agents added to manage the side effects.

However, in other cases, the nature of the problem and the solution may not be so straightforward. For instance, it is not uncommon that a person whose manic episode has resolved with lithium treatment will complain of lethargy and a loss of zest for life, without meeting full criteria for a major depressive episode; such symptoms can often markedly compromise social and occupational function, decrease quality of life, and even lead to noncompliance with treatment. Thus, understanding the source of these subsyndromal yet clinically significant symptoms can be critical in managing treatment. Several possible sources are commonly encountered in clinical practice, and the astute clinician will consider these types of issues:

- Does this represent a swing into depression as part of the course of illness? In this case, increasing the lithium dose or treating with an antidepressant may be indicated.
- Is this one of the subtle cognitive side effects of lithium? In this case, it may be prudent to decrease the lithium dose or change to another medication.
- Could the symptoms be lithium-induced hypothyroidism? In this case, thyroid supplementation would be required.
- Could the person be suffering primarily from a substantial blow to his or her self-esteem, conscious or unconscious, because of behavior during the manic episode?

- Could the person be under actual real-world stress due to that behavior (e.g., financial crisis, marital conflicts, or legal difficulties)?
- Could the symptoms be due to the demoralization expected with any significant, relapsing illness that disrupts the individual's life?
- Could the person, who may have organized his or her self-concept, social function, and even occupation around high-energy hypomanic behavior, be experiencing for the first time life with relatively normal mood and energy and simply not recognize normalcy?

Note that, in this last case, regardless of which state is best considered "normal" for an individual, the adjustment to living without hypomanic-level energy and optimism can be difficult, more difficult in some cases than adjusting to having this serious, relapsing disorder itself.

Facing these symptoms is not an uncommon occurrence individuals and their clinicians in general clinical practice. Published data are of limited help in identifying the source of these more subtle changes, because there is evidence to support several causes (Gitlin et al., 1989; Goodwin & Jamison, 1990, p. 150; Nilsson & Axelsson, 1989; Welner et al., 1977). In these situations, the psychotherapist plays an important role both in supporting the investigation of medical sources for the difficulties and in helping the person to develop strategies to cope with the temporary or permanent changes in his or her life.

Several conceptual issues are worth reviewing at this point. First, side effects may be encountered at any serum level of the drug, even within the therapeutic range. Some side effects may be dose-related even within that range and may respond to dosage reduction. Other side effects that occur within the therapeutic range are more idiosyncratic and may require discontinuation of the offending medication. Side effects or serious toxicity is more likely to occur when dosages exceed the established therapeutic range, but susceptibility varies widely among individuals. Recall that not all laboratory abnormalities encountered during treatment are clinically significant; however, judgment of the significance of abnormal laboratory values is best left to the prescribing clinician.

A second issue of note is that the elderly may be more susceptible to side effects, even within the therapeutic range. Metabolism of many drugs slows during aging, necessitating use of lower dosages. In addition, older persons are more frequently treated with more drugs than younger persons, thus increasing the likelihood that they will experience toxicity due to drug-drug interactions.

Third, as noted in chapter 1, symptoms of manic-depressive disorder, particularly mania and depression, may themselves represent side effects of medications. In such substance-induced mood episodes, the first line of treatment is to reduce or remove the offending substance if at all possible. Note that these substances do not necessarily cause mood episodes in every exposed person, even those with preexisting manic-depressive disorder. However, the new onset of mood symptoms within days of exposure to a new drug casts suspicion on that substance as an etiologic agent. Data from an NIMH sample indicate that about 40% of manic episodes occur during antidepressant treatment, and estimates are that about half of these, or 20% of manic episodes overall, may be caused by antidepressants (Altshuler et al., 1995), although rates may not be as high in other populations (e.g., Altshuler et al., 2001).

Fourth, some side effects are particularly relevant to manic-depressive disorder. For example, among neuroleptics it is important to keep in mind that the frequency of tardive dyskinesia, an irreversible movement disorder associated with neuroleptic use, appears to be higher in persons with mood disorders than in those with schizophrenia (Casey, 1984). It is not clear whether this is caused by some particular susceptibility of persons with mood disorders or by the on–off patterns of prescribing that are more common in treating mood disorders (mania leads to neuroleptic treatment; resolution of mania leads to neuroleptic discontinuation; recurrence of mania leads to neuroleptic treatment, etc.). Regardless, neuroleptics must be used judiciously in persons with manic-depressive disorder in view of the risk of this irreversible side effect.

As another example, it should be kept in mind that all somatic antidepressant treatments, including medications, ECT, and light, may cause switches from depression into mania or hypomania. Rapid cycling can also result. Thus, initiation of these agents in treatment of the depressed phase of bipolar disorder requires careful monitoring for these effects.

SIDE EFFECTS DUE TO DRUG INTERACTIONS

An important, but often overlooked, cause of side effects is the interaction of multiple medications that an individual may be taking. Common drug interactions with mood stabilizers and their potential clinical impact are summarized in Tables 4.24, 4.25, and 4.26. For more comprehensive reviews of psychotropic drug interactions, the reader is referred to work by Callahan and coworkers (Callahan, Fava, & Rosenbaum, 1993) and Cozza and Armstrong (2001). It is not uncommon for a person, who had been treated for a long duration without problems, to develop side effects following prescription of a seemingly innocuous medication that is the source of the toxicity. For example, thiazide diuretics (a type of "water pill") and nonsteroidal antiinflammatory agents such as ibuprofen can increase the lithium level and produce side effects or even serious toxicity.

However, not all drug interactions are associated with increases in serum levels of the drug of interest. Most drugs circulate in the bloodstream highly bound to plasma proteins; for many drugs, 99% of the circulating drug is

TABLE 4.24   Lithium Drug Interactions

Agent	Impact	Frequency	Potential severity
Thiazide diuretics*	Increase lithium	+++	+++
NSAIDs**	Increase lithium	+++	+++
ACE inhibitors***	Increase lithium Renal insufficiency	++	+
Calcium channel blockers	Decrease lithium Ataxia	++	+
Haloperidol	Encephalopathy	+	++
Furosemide	Dehydration	+	+
Neuromuscular blockade agents	Potentiate neuromuscular blockade	+	+

* Thiazide diuretics are occasionally planfully used with lithium to reduce urine volume due to diabetes insipidus.
** Nonsteroidal antiinflammatory agents (NSAIDs) such as ibuprofen; sulindac may be safest.
*** Angiotensin-converting enzyme (ACE) inhibitors, such as lisinopril.

TABLE 4.25   Carbamazepine Drug Interactions

Agent	Impact	Frequency	Potential severity
Carbamazepine (CBZ) itself*	Decrease CBZ autoinduction of P450 enzymes	+++	+
Warfarin	Decrease warfarin	++	+++
Calcium channel blockers	Increase CBZ	++	++
Oral contraceptives (OCs)	Decrease OCs	++	+++
Valproate (VPA)	Decrease VPA	++	+
Erythromycin	Increase CBZ	++	++
Lamotrigine (LMT)	Decrease LMT	++	+
Fluoxetine	Increase CBZ	+	+
Haloperidol	Decrease haloperidol	+	+
Theophylline	Decrease theophylline, CBZ	+	+
Doxycycline	Increase doxycycline	+	+
MAOIs	Do not interact*	—	—

* There have been theoretical concerns because CBZ is a "tricyclic" compound, but CBZ can be safely given with monoamine oxidase inhibitors (MAOIs) because it does not have the same chemical effects as tricyclic antidepressants, which are contraindicated with MAOIs.

TABLE 4.26   Valproate Drug Interactions

Agent	Impact	Frequency	Potential severity
Anticoagulants (aspirin and warfarin)	Increase bleeding time	++	+++
Diazepam	Displace diazepam	++	++
CBZ	Decrease VPA	++	+
Felbamate	Increase felbamate	+	+
Phenobarbital	Increase phenobarbital	+	+
Phenytoin	Increase/decrease phenytoin	+	+
Zidovudine	Increase zidovudine	+	+

CBS = carbamazepine; VPA = valproate.

protein-bound. A bound drug is unavailable to cause either therapeutic or toxic effects. Thus, the 1% of the drug that is freely circulating is responsible for its effects. The addition of a second drug that competes for binding sites can thus substantially increase the amount of free drug without meaningful changes in the total serum level. For example, a second drug may decrease the protein-bound fraction of a drug from 99% to 98% by competing for common binding sites. This seemingly small change actually represents a doubling of the amount of free, and active, drug (from 1% to 2%).

PREGNANCY AND BIOLOGICAL TREATMENT OF MANIC-DEPRESSIVE DISORDER

Finally, in terms of side effects, consideration of the teratogenic (propensity to induce birth defects) and perinatal effects of mood stabilizers must be kept in mind when treating women of childbearing age. Such considerations are summarized for lithium, carbamazepine, and valproate in Table 4.27, and can be found for antidepressants and other psychotropics in various specific reviews (e.g., Altshuler et al., 1996; Iqbal, 1999). Lithium has been thought to increase the risk of cardiovascular defects (Schou, Goldfield, Weinstein, & Villeneuve, 1973). However, reexamination of this issue has suggested that the risk is less than previously supposed (Cohen, Friedman, Jefferson, Johnson, & Weiner, 1994). The anticonvulsants, particularly valproic acid, may be associated with neural tube defects (Delgado-Escueta & Janz, 1992); folic acid should always be administered to females of childbearing age during treatment with anticonvulsants. There is less certainty regarding teratogenicity of neuroleptics or antidepressants.

TABLE 4.27 Teratogenetic and Perinatal Effects of Lithium and Commonly Used Anticonvulsants

Drug	Associated birth defects	Max risk trimester	Risk increase (x-Fold)	Breast milk transfer?
Lithium	Ebstein's anomaly	First	10–20	Yes
	"Floppy baby" syndrome	Perinatal	—	
CBZ	Neural tube defects	First	5	Yes
VPA	Neural tube defects	First	5–15	Yes
	Orofacial malformations	First	<	

CBZ = carbamazepine; VPA = valproate.

Overall, it is clear that the less fetal drug exposure, the better—for any prescription or nonprescription medication—from a purely pharmacologic point of view. Furthermore, the first trimester appears to be the most sensitive stage of fetal development for most malformations, so avoidance of drug exposure during that period is particularly important. In addition, if the mother is taking medication around the time of birth, the newborn may actually be born with clinically relevant levels of medication in his or her blood.

However, there are few absolutes in clinical treatment, including in dealing with the potential for teratogenicity when treating a pregnant woman with manic-depressive illness. Many factors must be considered, including the seriousness of the illness and alternate available treatments, including ECT. For example, Edlund and Craig (1984), despite finding an increased risk of birth defects in women exposed to neuroleptics during pregnancy, pointed out that these risks must be weighed in light of the increased rates of fetal death in pregnant psychotic women.

Clearly, the risk of teratogenicity must also be balanced against the potential mortality and morbidity of untreated manic-depressive disorder due to the potential for suicide, risk-taking behavior, and drug and alcohol use. Thus, clinicians, particularly the prescribing clinician, must support the individual by providing accurate information and support through the decision-making process. But decisions regarding such profound matters of life, death, and serious morbidity are ultimately borne by the individual and his or her family.

Chapter 5

Psychosocial Treatments for Manic-Depressive Disorder

WHY CONSIDER PSYCHOSOCIAL TREATMENTS FOR MANIC-DEPRESSIVE DISORDER?

As we enter the fourth decade of predominantly medically based treatment for manic-depressive disorder, there are several reasons to increase attention to psychosocial treatments as adjuncts to medical model treatment. In doing so, we do not move away from the medical model, but actually move in concert with cutting-edge thinking in the management of chronic medical illnesses, which includes a key role for psychosocial as well as medical treatment (e.g., Ciechanowski, Katon, Russo, & Walker, 2001; Kaplan, Greenfield, & Ware, 1989; Lorig et al., 1994; Von Korff, Gruman, Schaefer, Curry, & Wagner, 1997; Wagner, Austin, & Von Korff, 1996).

With regard specifically to manic-depressive disorder, there are five main reasons for attention to psychosocial adjunctive treatments, which are covered in detail in chapter 2. First, lack of treatment adherence makes delivery of efficacious medications difficult. Current evidence indicates that as much as 20% to 55% of individuals with manic-depressive disorder have major lapses in adherence (e.g., Gitlin et al., 1989; Harvey & Peet, 1991; Keck, McElroy, Strakowski, Bourne, & West, 1997; Lee, Wing, & Wong, 1992). Second, despite the substantial efficacy of available somatic treatments for manic-depressive disorder, nonresponse and breakthrough episodes remain a major problem. Thus, other modalities—specifically, combining medication with psychotherapy—may improve clinical outcome where predominantly medical management alone may not. Third, evidence indicates that both life stressors (e.g., Ellicott et al., 1990; Johnson et al., 1995) and social support (e.g., Johnson, Greenhouse, & Bauer, 1999) may impact the course of manic-depressive disorder. Thus, modulation of these factors, not directly amenable to medication treatment may improve outcome (reviewed in Johnson et al., 1999). Fourth, social, family, and occupational dysfunctions are the rule rather than the exception. Such functional deficits may persist in the absence of major affective episodes, and even subsyndromal levels of depression appear to be a strong predictor of ongoing functional deficits. Finally, manic-depressive disorder is a costly illness, and it is possible that psychosocial interventions in addition to medical model treatment may reduce costs.

In this chapter, we will consider two broad groups of psychosocial interventions, psychotherapy and what the U.S. National Institute of Mental Health has called the context of care (National Advisory Mental Health Council, 1993). *Psychotherapy* refers to verbal and behavioral interaction between a clinician and an individual (or group of individuals or the individual with his or her support system) to relieve the individual's suffering or dysfunction (after Beahrs & Gutheil, 2001). This chapter covers a wide range of psychotherapies, including several that are highly structured and supported by manuals that specify explicitly how the therapy is to be implemented, as well as interventions that are more free-form. It is important to keep this distinction in mind as one contemplates using a particular approach for clinical or research purposes or evaluates study data.

By *contexts of care*, we mean the organization of clinical resources to deliver care to individuals with manic-depressive disorder who present for treatment. These can be considered along a continuum of intensity (Figure 5.1). There are multiple determinants of the context of care, including, for example, available clinical resources, legislative constraints and incentives, insurance, other financial concerns, and an individual's resources. In many cases these determinants are fixed and only minimally amenable to manipulation by the individual or his or her caregivers (e.g., reimbursement systems). Notably, these reimbursement systems under the rubric of "managed care" tend to push services down the continuum toward lower levels of intensity and cost wherever possible. Thus, it is important both to optimize and to study the impact of various contexts of care along the continuum on clinical and economic outcome. Despite the complexities of this area of study, several contexts of care interventions for manic-depressive disorder have been meticulously described, and a few are being subjected to controlled clinical trials. It is therefore important to review these contexts of care—psychosocial interventions in their own right—in particular with regard to their impact on outcome.

This chapter is divided into several sections. A brief overview of the various types of psychotherapeutic approaches is first presented. Quantitative studies of the various modalities are then reviewed in detail. Next, a series of "how to" references are enumerated for clinicians and researchers looking

TABLE 5.1   AHCPR/AHRQ Evidence Classification System

Class A: Randomized or other controlled trials
Examples: Randomized controlled trials of intervention versus waiting list control or no added treatment; other controlled trials with treatment assignment independent of subject characteristic, time of presentation, etc.

Class B: Well-designed clinical studies
Examples: Open studies with a priori design and follow-up period of designated endpoint; pre-/post-mirror-image studies with "post-" period designed a priori

Class C: Case series, case reports, retrospective chart reviews
Examples: Prospectively gathered data on a series of individuals followed in treatment; retrospective chart review after implementation of an intervention

for references to learn more about particular approaches. Context of care interventions are reviewed next, including both early qualitative descriptions of lithium clinics and recent state-of-the-art controlled trials. Finally, trends in available evidence are summarized, and common themes across various psychosocial modalities, including in particular the Life Goals Program, are identified.

REVIEW OF PSYCHOTHERAPY INTERVENTIONS

RATIONALE FOR DEVELOPMENT OF SPECIFIC MODALITIES

Several psychotherapeutic approaches to manic-depressive disorder have been used, including (in historical order of development) psychoanalytic, family, interpersonal, cognitive-behavioral, and illness management/psychoeducational. The rationales for each of these are summarized below.

Psychoanalysis and Psychodynamic Psychotherapy

Manic-depressive disorder has attracted the attention of psychoanalysts since the early days of the treatment. Perhaps the most comprehensive review of psychoanalytic thought on manic-depressive disorder was summarized by Frieda Fromm-Reichmann's group, which undertook extensive study of several cases in an ongoing long-term case supervision seminar (Cohen, Baker, Cohen, Fromm-Reichmann, & Weigert, 1954; Fromm-Reichmann, 1949), as well as by the more recent work of Jackson (1993). The common threads through much of psychoanalytic thought about manic-depressive disorder are the contrast of manic-depressive disorder with schizophrenia and the conceptualization of mania as an alternate expression of the basic conflicts that produce depression under other circumstances. As with much psychoanalytic thought, the emphasis is placed on mechanisms related to unconscious conflicts that have their origin in early childhood development, the resolution of which will ameliorate present-day affective symptoms.

Family Interventions

Family treatment was another early focus of psychosocial treatment for manic-depressive disorder (e.g., Davenport, Ebert, Adland, & Goodwin, 1977; Fitzgerald, 1972; Greene, Lee, & Lustig, 1975), as it was readily apparent that the illness often caused substantial stress in the marriage (an anecdotal impression that has been borne out quantitatively in studies of functional outcome, as summarized in chapter 2). More recently, quantitative research has also identified family interactions as predictor of course in manic-depressive disorder. In particular, levels of "expressed emotion" (EE) in their interactions have been shown to be associated with relapse in schizophrenia (e.g., Vaughan & Leff, 1976). Miklowitz and coworkers have extended these findings, demonstrating that high EE predicts relapse after hospitalization for manic-depressive disorder (e.g., Miklowitz & Goldstein, 1988; Simoneau, Miklowitz, Richardson, & Saleem, 1998).

Interpersonal Interventions

With regard to intrafamily stress as a potential modulator of manic-depressive disorder, several investigators have focused more broadly on interpersonal interactions from one of two perspectives. Frank and coworkers (e.g., Frank, Swartz, & Kupfer, 2000) have written extensively on interpersonal interactions as a key stressor and/or remediating factor in manic-depressive disorder. Accordingly, they took the approach of adapting interpersonal therapy (IPT; Klerman et al., 1984) for depression to manic-depressive disorder and adding elements to stabilize the pattern or rhythm of social interactions.

The second interpersonal approach has focused on the potential therapeutic impact of interpersonal group therapy interventions for individuals with manic-depressive disorder. Although some authors have cautioned about the negative impact of group interventions on such individuals (e.g., Kufferle, 1988) or about the negative impact of individuals with manic-depressive disorder on groups (e.g., Yalom, 1975), others have utilized primarily interpersonal here-and-now approaches in group format to address interpersonal difficulties (e.g., Pollack, 1990; Shakir, Volkmar, Bacon, & Pfefferbaum, 1979; van Gent, Vida, & Zwart, 1988). In addition, others have addressed interpersonal issues of stigma and social isolation by incorporating interpersonal elements into psychoeducational groups such as the Life Goals Program and other interventions (e.g., Kripke & Robinson, 1985).

Cognitive-Behavioral Techniques

Cognitive-behavioral techniques, originally outlined by Beck and coworkers (e.g., Beck et al., 1979), have been elaborated by a number of clinicians and investigators, as summarized below. Principally, the cognitive-behavioral conceptualization and treatment of depressive episodes in manic-depressive disorder are very similar to that for unipolar disorder (Basco & Rush, 1996; Scott, 1996a, 1996b). There is less certainty and few data regarding how to conceptualize mania, although in some respects mania may share the same attributional style regarding negative events as is found in depression (Reilly-Harrington, Alloy, Fresco, & Whitehouse, 1999). Furthermore, because it appears that life stressors play a modulatory role in the course of manic-depressive disorder (see chapter 3), benefit may derive from helping the individual to deal with cognitive distortions that could worsen the impact of such stressors. Thus, the basic cognitive-behavioral approach and techniques of addressing dysfunctional attitudes and cognitive schemata in depression have been applied to manic-depressive disorder. As Scott (1996a) pointed out, educational techniques often draw on cognitive-behavior therapy's "collaborative, educational style, the use of a step by step approach and of guided discovery" (p. 199).

Psychoeducation

Finally, the need for better education regarding manic-depressive disorder and its treatment (often called psychoeducation when applied to psychiatric disorders) has been evident as long as compliance and stigma have been recognized as problems in this illness. These techniques were incorporated into various aspects of lithium clinics as early as the 1970s, as described below. In addition, aspects of education have been incorporated more or less explicitly into most psychotherapeutic modalities (except perhaps the classic psychoanalytic). Recently, psychoeducation techniques have received growing attention, leading to the development of formal manual-based interventions, such as the Life Goals Program, and the cognitive-behavioral intervention of Lam and coworkers (2000). As noted above, much of this attention has been stimulated by the increasing recognition of the individual as comanager of his or her illness in both psychiatric (e.g., Hastings, 1989) and medical (e.g., Ciechanowski et al., 2001; Kaplan et al., 1989; Lorig et al., 1994; von Korff et al., 1997; Wagner et al., 1996) settings.

AN EVIDENCE-BASED REVIEW OF PSYCHOTHERAPY STUDIES

Summarizing the Literature

The same review methodology used for biological treatment studies in chapter 4 was used for psychotherapy studies. Peer-reviewed, quantitative English-language studies were located and categorized using the Agency for Healthcare Research and Quality/U.S. Agency for Health Care Policy and Research (AHRQ/AHCPR) criteria. These criteria, with psychosocial study examples, are outlined in Table 5.1.

The results of the literature search are reviewed below and summarized in Table 5.2. Studies are categorized as Class A, B, or C. In Table 5.2 outcomes are categorized as positive (+), negative (–), or equivocal (+/–) based on results reported in each study. A result is reported as (+) if at least some parameters in the group of outcome variables were positive (e.g., improvement of manic but not depressive symptoms; improvement of some but not all measures of substance abuse). If no statistical analyses are presented (e.g., for Class C and some Class B studies), then the author's qualitative conclusions serve as the basis for the rating.

In all studies located, psychotherapy interventions were used as adjuncts to standard medication management rather than as alternatives to psychopharmacologic agents. Studies are presented chronologically below.

Quantitative Studies of Psychotherapy for Manic-Depressive Disorder

In the early days of lithium treatment, Benson (1975) reported a retrospective series of 31 individuals with manic-depressive disorder treated in his private practice with individual, group, or couples group interventions. Individuals were in almost all cases seen at least bimonthly, and several were seen multiple times per week. Benson followed individuals for 3 to 41 months and defined treatment "failure" as "emotional and/or social deterioration or dropping out of the study." He did not consider symptomatic worsening because he felt that when this occurred in this series, it was associated with a drop in the lithium level, and symptoms remitted with increase of lithium dose. Benson reported a failure rate of 14%, "markedly lower than lithium prophylaxis alone," and made the point that psychotherapy should not be neglected in the context of medication treatment.

Davenport and colleagues (Davenport, Ebert, Adland, & Goodwin, 1977) reported on a retrospective analysis of follow-up data on a cohort of individuals with manic-depressive disorder 2 to 10 years after discharge from the U.S. National Institute of Mental Health (NIMH). Sixty-five individuals were assigned at discharge to attend a weekly couples group based on geographic availability and space in couples group. Individuals living at a geographic

TABLE 5.2 Evidence Table for Psychotherapy Interventions for Manic-Depressive Disorder

Study	N	Intervention	Study duration	Outcome variables	Study type	Evidence class
Benson (1975)	31 outpatients	Various modalities including individual, group, or couples	3–41 (avg 13) months	Emotional or social deterioration (+) or treatment dropout (+)	Retrospective review	C
Davenport (1977)	65 former inpatients	Couples group postdischarge	2–10 (avg 3.9) years	Occupational (+/–), social (+), family (+), clinical (+) function	Retrospective review	C
Volkmar et al., (1981)	20 outpatients	Interpersonal group	2 years	Weeks in hospital (+), occupational status (+)	Retrospective review	C
Cochran (1984)	28 outpatients	Individual cognitive-behavioral intervention focusing on adherence	6 months	Medication adherence (+/–)	Randomized controlled trial vs. no added treatment	A
Kripke & Robinson (1985)	14 outpatients	Group focusing on education and problem solving	10 years	Clinical (+) and occupational (+) status	Retrospective review	C
Van Gent et al. (1988), Van Gent & Zwat (1993)	26 outpatients	Group using combination of psychoeducation, interpersonal, and behavioral techniques	5 years	SCL-90 scores (+), admissions (+), lithium discontinuation (+)	Pre-/post-therapy	C

TABLE 5.2 (*Continued*)

Study	N	Intervention	Study duration	Outcome variables	Study type	Evidence class
Clarkin et al. (1990)	21 inpatients	Inpatient family intervention (IFI), a family treatment emphasizing education and reduction in stress including maladaptive family interactions; manual-based	18 months	Global status (+), symptoms (+), social role function (+), family attitudes (+)	Randomized controlled trial vs. no added intervention with blinded assessments	A
Van Gent & Zwart (1991)	39 partners of subjects	Psychoeducational group emphasizing diagnosis, treatment, genetics, social interactions, and partner function	6 months	Knowledge about illness and treatment (+), subject and partner interaction ratings (−), subject mood (−), compliance (−)	Randomized controlled trial vs. no added intervention	A
Peet & Harvey (1991)	60 outpatients	Videotape/handout of lithium information followed by in-home visit for further information	24 weeks	Knowledge about (+) and attitudes toward (−) lithium	Randomized controlled trial vs. waiting list control	A
Retzer et al., (1991)	20 outpatients	Family therapy focusing on seven domains of system function	6 sessions (avg) over 14.4 months (avg)	Hospitalization rates (+)	Retrospective review of records pre-/post-therapy; some interviews	C

(*continued*)

TABLE 5.2 Evidence Table for Psychotherapy Interventions for Manic-Depressive Disorder (*Continued*)

Study	N	Intervention	Study duration	Outcome variables	Study type	Evidence class
Cerbone et al. (1992)	43 outpatients	Group interpersonal, focusing on "here-and-now" and "counseling, education, and support"	1 year retrospective, 1 year prospective	Affective episodes (+), hospital days (+), medication adherence (–), neuroleptic use (–), social and interpersonal function (+)	Pre-/post-therapy	C
Palmer & Will (1995)	4 outpatients	Group cognitive-behavioral	9 months	Clinical outcome, social function (+/–)	Prospective open trial	B
Honig et al. (1997)	52 outpatient couples	Multicouple psychoeducational group	12 weeks	Expressed emotion (+)	Controlled trial vs. waiting list control	A/B
Hlastala et al. (1997)	42 outpatients	Interpersonal plus social rhythms therapy (IPSRT), individual therapy focusing on stabilizing social rhythms and interpersonal stress in an acute mood episode; manual-based	1 year	Clinical symptoms (–)	Randomized controlled trial vs. no added intervention	A
Clarkin et al. (1998)	33 in- and outpatients	Couples psychoeducation; manual-based	11 months	Clinical (–) and functional (+) outcome, medication adherence (–)	Randomized controlled trial vs. no added intervention	A

TABLE 5.2 (Continued)

Study	N	Intervention	Study duration	Outcome variables	Study type	Evidence class
Bauer, McBride, et al. (1998)	29 outpatients, 4 therapists	Life Goals Program, a psychoeducation and behavioral-cognitive group; manual-based	18 months (avg.)	Therapist adherence (+), subject knowledge base (+), functional goal attainment (+)	Open trial	B
Perry et al. (1999)	69 outpatients	Psychoeducation to teach subjects to identify early warning signs of relapse and implement action plan for treatment	18 months	Time to relapse (+), social function (+)	Randomized controlled trial vs. no added intervention	A
Frank et al. (1999)	82 outpatients	Relapse-prevention application of IPSRT (see Hlastala et al., 1997)	1 year	Clinical symptoms (−)	Randomized controlled trial vs. no added intervention	A
Zaretsky et al. (1999)	11 outpatients	Cognitive-behavior with Basco-Rush adaptation for manic-depressive disorder; manual-based	20 weeks	Clinical symptoms (+), automatic thoughts (+), dysfunctional attitudes (−)	Open trial	B

(continued)

TABLE 5.2 Evidence Table for Psychotherapy Interventions for Manic-Depressive Disorder (*Continued*)

Study	N	Intervention	Study duration	Outcome variables	Study type	Evidence class
Lam et al. (2000)	25 outpatients	Cognitive-behavioral and psychoeducation; manual-based	1 year	Episodes (+), social function (+)	Randomized controlled trial vs. no added intervention	A
Miklowitz et al. (2000)	101 in- and outpatients	Family-focused treatment (FFT), family/couples in-home sessions focused on psychoeducation, response to symptoms, adherence; manual-based	1 year	Clinical outcome (+), medication compliance (–), expressed emotion (+)	Randomized controlled trial vs. no added intervention	A
Weiss et al. (2000)	45 outpatients with comorbid substance dependence	Integrated group therapy (IGT), relapse-prevention strategies for both disorders utilizing cognitive-behavioral techniques; manual-based	9 months	Substance use and impact (+), mood symptoms (+), compliance (–), hospitalization rates (–)	Open trial with subjects assigned to IGT or none in sequential blocks	B

Refer to Table 5.1 specifics on class designations.

Outcomes are categorized as positive (+), negative (–), or equivocal (+/–) based on results reported in each study. A result is reported as (+) if at least some parameters in the group of outcome variables were positive (e.g., improvement of manic but not depressive symptoms; improvement of some but not all measures of substance abuse). If no statistical analyses are presented (e.g., for Class C and some Class B studies), then the author's qualitative conclusions serve as the basis for the rating.

distance were referred to community care. Those who lived near the NIMH but for whom there was no room in couples group were referred to a lithium maintenance group. The couples group content was not well described in their report, but it appears that Davenport and colleagues emphasized optimizing marital interactions plus addressing issues around fear of episode recurrence. They assessed outcome with a questionnaire covering social, occupational, and clinical function and marital interactions. It appears from responses that the individuals in the couples group did better than the community care group in terms of social function and family interaction and better than the lithium group in terms of family interaction. No note is made of differences in occupational function. The couples group suffered no marital failures or rehospitalizations, despite recurrence of substantial symptoms, whereas several occurred in each of the other groups.

Volkmar and coworkers (Vokmar, Shakir, Bacon, & Pfefferbaum, 1981) retrospectively summarized experience with an interpersonal group based on the approach of Yalom (1975). Twenty individuals with manic-depressive disorder, highly screened for motivation for group therapy, met weekly with two therapists in 75-minute sessions. Compared to the 2 years prior to group, hospital days during 2 years of group treatment reduced from 17 to 4 weeks on average. The authors also noted that the number of members fully employed or full-time students increased from 6 to 16. Shakir and colleagues (Shakir, Volkmar, Bacon, & Pfefferbaum, 1979) published preliminary data on this cohort. It is unclear whether individuals had been prescribed lithium during the baseline period, although the data indicate that individuals did better with the combination of lithium plus group treatment than prior to the study.

Cochran (1984) studied an individual cognitive-behavioral intervention of six weekly groups aimed at improving compliance. Twenty-eight individuals with manic-depressive disorder newly admitted to an outpatient lithium clinic were randomized to receive either the intervention or no added treatment and were assessed posttreatment, at 3 months, and at 6 months on several indices of medication adherence. Immediately posttreatment, those who received the intervention scored better than controls on some but not all adherence measures. However, these differences disappeared by 3 months. By 6 months, those who received the intervention again scored better than controls on several indices of compliance. Additionally, controls were more likely to have had an affective episode precipitated by lithium nonadherence. Although those who received the intervention did not differ from controls in terms of any form of nonadherence, they did have a lower incidence of breaches of treatment that were judged to be major.

Kripke and Robinson (1985) summarized retrospectively 10 years of experience with a group of 14 outpatients with manic-depressive disorder treated in a group that initially focused on medication issues during lithium treatment. The group eventually included psychoeducation around medications and impending symptoms, feedback on status from group members, and problem solving. The authors reported that hospitalization rates were lower than before group treatment and that 5 of 14 improved employment status during treatment.

Van Gent and Zwart (1993) studied an initial 10-session group psychotherapy intervention in individuals taking lithium for manic-depressive disorder, followed by a 5-year ongoing maintenance protocol. Their intervention consisted of an eclectic group led by a social worker and a psychiatrist that met weekly for 90 minutes over 10 to 13 sessions. The group combined psychoeducation with interpersonal and behavioral interventions. The authors' pre-/post-analysis found initially that the group reduced "insufficiency in thinking and behaving" according to the SCL-90, and this was confirmed in their longer term study, although no other subscale scores changed. They also found that, compared to lithium treatment without group intervention, admissions per year reduced as did the number of lithium discontinuations.

Clarkin and coworkers (1990) conducted a study of intensive family intervention (IFI) in a mixed group of inpatients with mood or schizophrenic spectrum disorders, including 21 with manic-depressive disorder, in a randomized controlled trial of IFI versus no added intervention. This intervention is an individual family intervention that seeks to educate treated individuals and their families about the illness, identify and resolve current and future stresses, and minimize stressful family interactions characterized by high EE. Individuals received at least 6 sessions during their hospital admission. They measured symptoms, social role function, global function, and family attitudes using blinded ratings at 6 and 18 months. The analysis in this report also included results for individuals with major depression. Although individuals with unipolar depression did worse with the intervention by 18 months, those with manic-depressive disorder were better with IFI in terms of global ratings, symptoms, social role function, and family attitudes. Interestingly, the beneficial effects in manic-depressive individuals were solely due to improvement in females, although differences were seen across treatments among males.

Van Gent and Zwart (1991) also conducted a randomized controlled trial of a psychoeducation group for 39 partners of individuals with manic-depressive versus no added treatment controls. Their intervention consisted of five educational sessions covering the disorder, medications, genetics, interpersonal interactions, and the partner's own functioning. They found that knowledge about several aspects of the illness improved in the intervention group compared to controls, although there was no change in measures of interactions in either partner or the treated individual, no change in treated individual's mood, and no change in compliance.

Peet and Harvey (1991) studied a videotaped lecture, handout, and home visit to convey information regarding lithium to individuals with manic-depressive disorder attending a lithium clinic. Thirty were randomly assigned to the videotape/handout intervention followed by a home visit to answer questions. Thirty served as waiting list controls, then received the videotape/handout but no home visit. Pretest using standardized questionnaires to measure lithium knowledge was followed by posttest 6 weeks after the intervention. At 6 weeks, the intervention group had greater improvement in scores than the waiting list control group, and their gains in knowledge were maintained until the end of the 24-week study. The waiting list control group later received the videotape/handout intervention (without home visit); their scores then significantly improved and remained high and indistinguishable from the earlier intervention group. Although there were overall improvements in attitude toward lithium, there were no effects of the intervention.

Retzer and coworkers (Retzer, Simon, Weber, Stierlin, & Schmidt, 1991) reported on the impact of family therapy intervention aimed at seven aspects of systemic function: flexibility of world/family view (relational reality), ability to simultaneously consider opposing aspects of reality (softening/hardening of relational reality), tendency toward "either/or" thinking (system logic), "individuation in the family" among all members' roles, attempts at relational monitoring among family members, interview atmosphere during assessment, and degree to which the index patient was seen as a "victim" versus an "agent" (the latter taking more responsibility for their own actions). Individuals with manic-depressive disorder received a mean of 6 sessions (range 1–14) over a mean of 14 months (range 0–35). The authors retrospectively reviewed records of 20 individuals with manic-depressive disorder as well as 10 with schizoaffective disorder, and supplemented where possible with follow-up interviews a mean of 3 years posttherapy. Their quantitative analyses focused on rehospitalization rates compared pre- versus posttherapy, and they found significant improvements in both groups. Qualitatively, they also investigated changes in the above seven dimensions across high- and low-relapse groups. They found that movement away from "either/or" toward "both/and" logic was characteristic of both groups. However, the low-relapse group was distinguished by more movement away from seeing the individual as "victim" and more as "agent." Description of medication prescription indicated that individuals had a tendency to receive fewer medications after family therapy. It is impossible in such uncontrolled studies to determine whether the view of the individual less as "victim" and more as "agent" was due to actual clinical improvement (i.e., in reality, being less of a victim of the illness and more able to take responsibility), or due to a change in willingness to take responsibility, leading to or supporting clinical improvement, or both.

Cerbone and coworkers (Cerbone, Mayo, Cuthbertsone, & O'Connell, 1992) conducted an open trial of open-ended group treatment emphasizing "here and now" techniques focusing on counseling, education, and support. They reviewed charts for 1 year prior to group and 1 year during group treatment and extracted scores for rating affective episodes and measuring social and interpersonal adjustment. Although ratings were not blinded, they included extraneous chart notes to reduce bias. Compared to the baseline year, individuals with manic-depressive disorder had shorter or less severe affective episodes during group, shorter hospital stays among those admitted, and higher social and interpersonal adjustment scores. There were no differences in medication adherence or need for neuroleptics.

Palmer and Williams (1995) conducted an open trial feasibility study of cognitive-behavioral techniques adapted for group treatment of manic-depressive disorder, entering six and studying four individuals over 9 months. Their closed-group intervention consisted of seventeen 90-minute weekly sessions and six monthly follow-up sessions. The intervention focuses on psychoeducation and development of an "action plan" (i.e., an individual's specific cognitive-behavioral plan for illness management). Results of this pilot study indicated that the treatment package was effective for at least some participants, with two or three participants improving on several clinical and/or functional measures.

Honig and coworkers (Honig, Hofman, Rozendaal, & Dingemans, 1997) investigated the impact of a multicouple psychoeducational group in individuals with manic-depressive disorder, with a particular focus on its impact on EE. Their intervention consisted of six 2-hour sessions with the individual and one or more significant other given biweekly. The authors conducted a controlled trial investigating 29 couples in the intervention group and 23 on a waiting list, although it is not clear whether the couples were assigned randomly or through some other method (e.g., a posthoc control group). They investigated EE and symptom status at baseline, then report on EE, but did not mention symptom status at 12-week follow-up. Honig and colleagues found more changes from high EE to low EE in the intervention than in the control group. However, they also found that EE was relatively stable over the course of the study, with more than 75% of ratings unchanged. Consistent with the hypothesis that high EE is associated with worse course in manic-depressive disorder, they found that those with consistently low EE during the study, compared to those with consistently high EE, had had fewer admissions prior to the study.

Hlastala and coworkers (1997) reported initial results with an eclectic intervention developed by Frank and coworkers (2000). Their multimodal manual-based intervention aimed at minimizing the impact of interpersonal and chronobiological stressors on the course of manic-depressive disorder.

Some data indicate that psychosocial stressors can be associated with affective relapse in established manic-depressive disorder (reviewed in Johnson & Roberts, 1995). Additional theoretical (Goodwin & Jamison, 1990) and empirical (e.g., Carney, Fitzgerald, & Monaghan, 1988; Gottschalk, Bauer, & Whybrow, 1995; Wehr, Sack, & Rosenthal, 1987) work indicates that chronobiologic factors may play a role in the course of manic-depressive disorder. Thus, this group's manual-based intervention employs techniques that analyze and stabilize the daily routine of individuals with manic-depressive disorder (social rhythms therapy, SRT) while directly addressing interpersonal stressors using interpersonal therapy (IPT), which had been shown to be efficacious in treating and preventing episodes in major depressive disorder (e.g., Klerman, Dimascio, Weissman, Prusott, & Paykel, 1974). The weekly, IPSRT intervention consists of four phases. An initial phase of weekly sessions lasting several weeks to months focuses on assessment of illness and social rhythms, as well as on psychoeducation. A several-month intermediate phase then includes weekly sessions that focus on developing SRT- and IPT-based strategies to deal with stressors. A preventive phase of monthly sessions continues for at least 2 years, and a termination phase concludes treatment with 4 to 6 monthly sessions. An initial report on a randomized controlled trial of interpersonal/social rhythms therapy (IPSRT) versus no added intervention on 42 subjects (Hlastala et al., 1997) that there was no effect of treatment compared to control. However, it indicated that individuals in a manic episode were likely to reach remission more quickly than those who were depressed or cycling, who were similar in time to remission.

Clarkin and coworkers (Clarkin, Carpenter, Hull, Wilner, & Glick, 1998) conducted a randomized controlled trial of a 25-session psychoeducational intervention for individuals with manic-depressive disorder and their spouses versus no added treatment in a sample of 33 in- or outpatients. Treatments were given weekly or biweekly to individual couples by experienced social workers using a formalized manual. Clinical outcome, functional outcome, and medication adherence were measured at baseline and after 11 months. Symptom ratings did not change over time between the groups, whereas functional outcome showed significant improvement for the sample treated with the group intervention. Adherence levels were high in both groups but were rated higher in the sample treated with the group intervention.

Our group (Bauer, McBride, et al., 1998) conducted an open trial of the Life Goals Program and found that the program could be effectively taught to therapists ($n = 4$) across two sites with good adherence to the manual. Group members ($n = 29$) significantly increased their knowledge base in Phase 1, and 69% successfully completed Phase 1. During a mean treatment time of 18 months in Phase 2, 70% reached their first self-identified goal and did so by a mean of 7 months (range 2–17 months). Clinical symptoms were not measured.

A follow-up analysis of IPSRT (Frank et al., 1999) investigated time to relapse in 82 remitted subjects who entered the preventive phase. They found no difference in recurrence rate with IPSRT over 1 year of follow-up, although there may be a reduced likelihood of developing new episodes at 24 months. Interestingly, however, they found that subjects who changed treatment between the initial and preventive phases (either IPSRT to control or vice versa) did worse in a number of analyses than those who remained either in IPSRT or the control condition. Of further interest is that these findings are true both for relapses close to the time of potential change and for relapses more than 12 weeks after the time of potential change, and that only the treatment modality and not the therapist changed. The authors also reported that changing therapist due to job change or maternity leave did not appear to be associated with relapse. They hypothesize that changing from any treatment that worked (by definition the individuals in the preventive phase had remitted) is a stress that can negatively impact the course of their illness.

Perry and coworkers (Perry, Tarrier, Morriss, McCarthy, & Limb, 1999) conducted a randomized controlled trial of a psychoeducation program versus no added intervention in a group of 69 outpatients with manic-depressive disorder. Their intervention consists of two stages: training the individual to identify prodromal symptoms of an affective episode and developing an action plan for response. The intervention was given individually by a psychologist, and a median of 9 sessions was delivered (range 0–12). They assessed symptomatic relapses and social function at 3, 6, and 18 months. Time to manic relapse and overall days manic, but not time to depressive relapse or overall days depressed, was significantly better in the experimental group. The experimental group also had better social and occupational function at 18 months, but not earlier.

Zaretsky, Segal, and Gemar (1999) applied the cognitive-behavioral techniques outlined in the manual by Basco and Rush (1996) in an open trial of 11 individuals with manic-depressive disorder who were currently depressed. They delivered 20 weekly individual sessions and tracked symptom levels and dysfunctional attitudes. Three of 11 dropped out, and their data were deleted from the analysis rather than using the more typical last-value-carried-forward method. They report significant reductions compared to baseline in several measures of depression and automatic thoughts, but not in dysfunctional attitudes. In a case-control posthoc comparison, a sample of individuals with unipolar depression showed both symptomatic and attitudinal improvement compared to baseline.

Lam and coworkers (2000) implemented a randomized controlled trial of cognitive therapy adapted for manic-depressive disorder to 25 outpatients who received either the intervention or no added treatment. Their manual-based intervention consisted of 12 to 20 individual sessions over 6 months focusing on standard cognitive approaches plus psychoeducation specifically about manic-depressive disorder, behavioral skills to cope with prodromal symptoms, and coping with functional sequelae of the illness. They found that compared to the control group, those treated with cognitive therapy had fewer total and hypomanic episodes without difference in depressive episodes, as well as higher social function. The intervention group also showed better scores at coping with prodromal manic symptoms at 6 and 12 months and with prodromal depressive symptoms by 12 months.

Miklowitz and coworkers (2000) report a randomized controlled trial of Family-Focused Therapy (FFT) versus no additional treatment in 101 in- or outpatients with manic-depressive disorder. FFT is manual-based and consists of three modules of 1-hour family or couples sessions given weekly to monthly in the individual's home over 9 months, and is an outgrowth of Behavioral Family Management developed by Miklowitz and Goldstein (1990). The first module consists of psychoeducation about the disorder, including identification and management of prodromal symptoms and development of a management plan. The second module focuses on improving intrafamilial communication to reduce stress. The third module focuses on continued problem solving during ongoing treatment. The authors found that over 1 year FFT individuals had fewer relapses and greater time to relapse than controls, as well as greater improvement of depressive but not manic symptoms. There was no effect on medication adherence. Although high EE did not in itself predict relapse or symptoms scores over time, individuals with high-EE families showed the greatest improvement in symptom scores under FFT, consistent with the theoretical underpinnings of the treatment. Furthermore, additional analyses (Simoneau, Miklowitz, Richards, Saleem, & George, 2000) indicated that families of individuals treated with FFT showed more positive nonverbal interactions than did control families, although no reduction in negative nonverbal interactions was seen. It is also notable that individuals treated with FFT did not show an improvement vs. control until 6 months (Miklowitz, et al., 2000).

Weiss and colleagues (2000) developed Integrated Group Treatment (IGT) to address the needs of individuals with manic-depressive disorder and comorbid substance dependence. IGT focuses on the commonalities in recovery and relapse across the two disorders and implements a set of cognitive-behavioral relapse prevention strategies. The intervention is manual-based and is given in 12 and subsequently 20 weekly hour-long sessions. They conducted an open study that enrolled sequential blocks of individuals either in IGT ($n = 21$) or no added treatment ($n = 24$) and investigated effects on substance use and its impact, mood symptoms, and compliance. They measured outcome over 6 months and then 3 months posttreatment. In terms of substance use outcome, participants showed improvement in most (but not all) formal ratings of drug and alcohol use, including months abstinent. In terms of mood symptoms, they found improvement in mania ratings but not depression ratings. Reported medication compliance was high but not different across the groups. Hospitalization rates did not differ across the groups.

One additional study, not published at the time of this writing, but may be by the time of publication, deserves specific mention. In a recent randomized controlled trial of family therapy developed by I. W. Miller and colleagues, presented in scientific meetings, as summarized by Craighead and Miklowitz (2000), single- and multifamily group interventions produced better recovery rates than no added intervention, and the two family treatments did not differ. Individuals with poor family function prior to treatment were reported to benefit from the family interventions, whereas those with good function showed no difference in outcome.

ADDITIONAL PSYCHOTHERAPY STUDIES AND "HOW TO" PSYCHOTHERAPY RESOURCES

To complement the above quantitative studies, a wealth of anecdotal or qualitative literature exists on the psychotherapy of manic-depressive disorder. These studies are often valuable for the detailed descriptions and case vignettes they contain of particular types of interventions. As such, they may serve as "how to" references to aid to investigators and clinicians seeking to learn more about the specifics of a particular modality. Table 5.3 includes a select list of references that seem particularly valuable in this regard. Some of these refer to interventions reviewed above, and others are chosen as examples that illustrate application of a particular general approach (e.g., psychodynamic, psychoeducational) in manic-depressive disorder.

REVIEW OF CONTEXT OF CARE STUDIES

LITHIUM CLINICS

As noted above, psychotherapeutic interventions primarily use individual or team therapists to address issues with individuals or groups who receive care together. An additional type of psychosocial intervention is the organization of the caregiving system itself. The recent burgeoning of interest in manipulating contexts of care to optimize treatment for manic-depressive disorder actually has its roots as far back as the 1970s.

With the dissemination of lithium for the treatment of manic-depressive disorder in that decade, the conceptual approach to treatment shifted from a predominantly psychotherapeutic to a medical model approach. The impact of this shift can be seen from contrasting some of the prelithium psychoanalytic references cited (e.g., Cohen et al., 1954; Fromm-Reichmann, 1949) to

TABLE 5.3 "How to" References for Psychosocial Interventions in Manic-Depressive Disorder

Area	Suggested references
Psychotherapy	
Psychodynamic-psychoanalytic	Cohen et al., 1954; Jackson, 1993; Kahn, 1993; Teixeira, 1992
Marital	Fitzgerald, 1972; Greene et al., 1975; Lesser, 1983; Van Gent & Zwart, 1991
Family	Miklowitz & Goldstein, 1997; Weber et al., 1988
Cognitive-behavioral	Basco & Rush, 1996; Lam et al., 1999; Scott, 1996a, 1996b
Interpersonal (IPT, individual)	Frank et al., 1994
Interpersonal (interactive group)	Graves, 1993; Pollack, 1990; Volkmar et al., 1981; Wuslin et al., 1988
Psychoeducation	Bauer & McBride, 1996; Foelker et al., 1986; Kripke & Robinson, 185; Powell et al., 1977
Education for chronic medical conditions	Lorig et al., 1994
Useful psychotherapy reviews	Colom et al., 1998; Craighead & Miklowitz, 2000; Goodwin & Jamison, 1990; Huxley et al., 2000; Swartz & Frank, 2001
Contexts of care	
Lithium clinics	Fieve, 1975; Gitlin & Jamison, 1984; Seeger et al., 1989
Multimodal care delivery systems	Bauer, Williford, et al., 2001b; Shea, McBride, et al., 1997

traditional psychotherapeutic references from early in the lithium era (e.g., Fitzgerald, 1972; Greene et al., 1975). The earlier references treated manic-depressive disorder as psychological in origin and in need of solely psychological treatment. The latter psychoanalytic references, although employing a strong psychotherapeutic emphasis, work from a perspective that assumes that integrated psychotherapeutic and medical model treatment is necessary. Thus, virtually all psychotherapeutic interventions for manic-depressive disorder, even psychoanalytic (e.g., Kahn, 1993), embrace to some degree a bio- as well as a psychosocial model for treatment.

The issue of how to organize medical model treatment was explored by clinicians treating large numbers of individuals with manic-depressive disorder. There seemed to be potential efficiencies and opportunities for standardization of care if individuals were treated in specialty clinics staffed by physicians and support staff who were comfortable with dealing with the disorder. In turn, concentration of individuals with the same staff allowed development of further expertise. Additionally, in community mental health systems, financial limitations made it advantageous for psychiatrists to work in teams with nonphysician providers to implement care for this group (e.g., Shelley & Fieve, 1974).

Information about lithium clinics comes both from early description of programs (e.g., Fieve, 1975; Foelker, Molinari, Marmion, & Chacko, 1986; Seeger et al., 1989; Shelley & Fieve, 1974) and from a survey of programs by Gitlin and Jamison (1984). Typically, lithium clinics use a team approach including psychiatrist, nurse or other medical paraprofessional, and sometimes social worker or other counselor. Standardized individual and family information comprised part of the assessment for all individuals in most clinics. Important for quality of care, a standardized battery of baseline and follow-up labs are implemented. Follow-up appointments are provided at regular intervals. All of the standardizations support not only high-quality care but also the conduct of research as a common database evolved on all individuals. Unfortunately, there are to our knowledge no quantitative data on the impact of lithium clinics.

This emphasis on medical model efficiency did not, however, mean that psychotherapy was neglected. On the contrary, it was recognized from the earliest days of these clinics that psychotherapeutic interventions were necessary to optimize medical model management. Most notable is that several types of psychotherapeutic interventions (e.g., psychoeducation, interpersonal process groups) evolved as part of lithium clinics (e.g., Ellenberg, Salamon, & Meaney, 1980; Foelker et al., 1986; Kripke & Robinson, 1985; Powell et al., 1977).

MORE RECENTLY DEVELOPED CONTEXTS OF CARE: MANUAL-BASED INTERVENTIONS AND CONTROLLED CLINICAL TRIALS

Neither lithium nor the plethora of more recently developed medications have proven to be the panacea for manic-depressive disorder. As the availability of treatment of proven efficacy for manic-depressive disorder has grown, so has the complexity of treatment. Further, the problems of adherence and knowledge deficit continue, and provider knowledge deficit regarding the ever-widening range of available treatments also becomes an issue. All these contribute to what has been called the *efficacy-effectiveness gap* for manic-depressive disorder (Bauer et al., 2001b), as has been recognized for other illnesses as well (IOM, 1985). This term refers to the difference between the performance of an intervention in highly controlled trials *(efficacy)* and its performance in real-world clinical practice *(effectiveness)*. At least two randomized controlled trials are under way currently that investigate care organization interventions specifically designed to improve effectiveness—that is, improved delivery and acceptance of optimal medication management—of treatment for manic-depressive disorder.

The first such intervention is a randomized controlled trial of a tripartite intervention for individuals treated in the U.S. Department of Veterans Affairs (VA) health care system. This study randomly assigns individuals hospitalized for manic-depressive disorder at the point of discharge either to continue usual care or to enter the Bipolar Disorders Program (BDP; study described in detail in Bauer, Williford, et al., 2001). The BDP addresses three aspects of treatment for the individual being treated: education, provider support, and access and continuity to a consistent team of caregivers. Education for the individual with the illness is administered through the Life Goals Program Phase 1. Provider education is provided through an adaptation of the VA treatment guidelines for manic-depressive disorder (reviewed in Bauer et al., 1999). Access and continuity are provided by a primary mental health nurse who implements manual-based procedures to ensure timely access to care for the treated individual (described in Bauer, Williford, et al., 2001; Shea, McBride, et al., 1997).

Preliminary data from an open pre/post design indicated reductions in service utilization and cost of almost 50% with the BDP compared to pre-BDP, as well as improvement in several process measures thought to be markers for quality of care (Bauer, McBride, et al., 1997). Of additional relevance to the issue of psychotherapy for manic-depressive disorder, one of the major predictors of service utilization in this cohort was a history of childhood abuse (Bauer, Shea, McBride, & Gavin, 1997). This suggests that psychotherapeutic interventions aimed at these issues may improve outcome and reduce costs for manic-depressive disorder. The current randomized controlled trial of the BDP versus usual VA care is tracking clinical outcome, functional outcome, and health care costs over 3 years of prospective follow-up in 330 subjects across 11 hospitals coast to coast. It is due to finish in 2003.

Similarly, in another staff model health care organization, the Group Health Cooperative (GHC) of Puget Sound, Washington, Simon and coworkers (2001) are funded by the NIMH to test a similar program designed to provide education for the individual being treated, case-specific feedback to providers, and improve access to care for individuals with manic-depressive disorder. This program has enrolled 441 outpatients with manic-depressive disorder in various phases of their illness and randomized them either to receive a multimodal program to optimize treatment or to no added care.

Their program, implemented across three sites in the greater Seattle area, consists of both Phase 1 and Phase 2 of the Life Goals Program to address both psychoeducational and functional needs of participants, plus computer-guided medication treatment algorithm recommendations that are provided for treating psychiatrists. A nurse-clinician provides telephone outreach to the individual being treated and liaison for the treating psychiatrists involved. Clinical and functional outcome and health care costs are being tracked over 2 years. Preliminary 1-year analyses indicate significant reduction in manic symptoms and a trend toward reduction in depressive symptoms with the intervention (Simon et al., 2002b).

The GHC intervention provides an interesting comparison with the VA BDP in several respects. Both interventions are being tested in samples designed to reflect the populations from which they are being drawn, rather than using highly selected participants. Both interventions address the same triad of aspects of care: access, education, and provider guidance. Both approach individuals being treated as important collaborators in the management of their illness.

On the other hand, there are several ways in which the GHC study will be complementary to the VA study. First, it studies outpatients rather than individuals who are sufficiently ill as to require acute hospitalization. Second, there are several demographic differences between the samples, with the GHC sample being of generally higher socioeconomic status and of fairly even gender distribution. Third, the GHC intervention does not control all aspects of treatment, but rather provides information and feedback to treating psychiatrists who are not trained in the research intervention. To do so, it uses sophisticated computer technology to convey algorithm recommendations through nurse-facilitators to treating psychiatrists. In contrast, the VA BDP takes over responsibility for outpatient treatment of manic-depressive disorder, but emphasizes collaboration with other clinicians on an as-needed basis for management of medical and psychiatric comorbidities.

PATTERNS IN THE PSYCHOSOCIAL INTERVENTION DATA TO DATE

OVERVIEW OF EFFICACY RESULTS

Table 5.4 reorganizes data from Table 5.2 by grouping studies according to type of intervention and results across three outcome domains: clinical outcome, functional outcome, and the intermediate outcome variable of disease management skills. Unfortunately, to date no studies of psychotherapies have investigated impact on costs. However, such economic evaluations are an integral part of the VA and GHC intervention trials.

TABLE 5.4 Patterns of Efficacy across Psychotherapy Type and Outcome Domain*

Intervention	Clinical outcome	Functional outcome	Disease management skills
Couples/partners	+ Davenport (1977) (C) - Clarkin et al. (1998) (A)	+ Davenport (1977) (C) + Honig (1977) (A/B) + Clarkin et al. (1998) (A)	+ Van Gent & Zwart (1991) (A) - Clarkin et al. (1998) (A)
Group, interpersonal, and psychoeducational	+ Volkmar et al. (1981) (C) + Kripke & Robinson (1985) (C) + Van Gent et al. (1988); Van Gent & Zwart (1993) (C) + Cerbone et al., (1992) (C) + Weiss et al. (2000) (B)	+ Volkmar et al. (1981) (C) + Kripke & Robinson (1985) (C) + Cerbone et al. (1992) (C) + Bauer et al. (1998) (B)	+ Van Gent et al. (1988); Van Gent & Zwart (1993) (C) + Cerbone et al. (1992) (C) + Bauer et al. (1998) (B) - Weiss et al. (2000) (B)
Cognitive-behavioral	+/- Palmer & Williams (1995) (B) + Zaretsky et al. (1999) (B) + Lam et al. (2000) (A)	+/- Palmer & Will (1995) (B) + Lam et al. (2000) (A)	+/- Cochran (1984) (A)
Family	+ Clarkin et al. (1990) (A) + Retzer et al. (1991) (C) + Miklowitz et al. (2000) (A)	+ Clarkin et al. (1990) (A)	- Miklowitz et al. (2000) (A)
Interpersonal/social rhythms	- Hlastala et al. (1997) (A) - Frank et al. (1999) (A)		
Individual psychoeducation	+ Perry et al. (1999) (A)	+ Perry et al. (1999) (A)	+ Peet & Harvey (1991) (A)
Other/eclectic	+ Benson (1975) (C)		

* Studies from Table 5.2, reanalyzed by type of intervention, positive (+), negative (-), or equivocal (+/-) impact on the outcome domain noted, and quality of evidence (A, B, or C). See text for details.

It is clear from inspection of Tables 5.2 and 5.4 that several types of psychotherapy have efficacy in improving at least some aspects of outcome in manic-depressive disorder. Specifically, Class A data exist for some types of couples/partners, cognitive-behavioral, family, and individual psychoeducation. Class B/C data exist for each of these and for group interpersonal/psychoeducational therapy as well. Class A data for the VA and GHC psychosocial interventions must await the outcome of those clinical trials, although Class B data do exist for the VA intervention (Bauer, McBride, et al., 1997).

Perhaps due to the small number of psychotherapy studies to date, there is no type of psychotherapeutic intervention that appears more typically positive than others. The most surprising exception to overall positive results across interventions is the case of IPSRT, studied in a Class A trial, which showed no difference between the intervention and the control arm of no intervention added to clinical management either acutely (Hlastala et al., 1997) or in terms of relapse prevention (Frank et al., 1999). This may say as much about the efficacy of the control arm's good clinical management than it does about the lack of utility of IPSRT in improving outcome of the disorder. Specifically, standard management at such centers of expertise may encompass a similar core agenda to that of active treatment, even though the outward form is different, as outlined below.

COMMON THEMES ACROSS MODALITIES

COLLABORATIVE PRACTICE AND SUPPORT SYSTEMS

Qualitative inspection of the studies reviewed reveals certain themes and consistencies that appear in multiple interventions. First, and by definition, psychotherapy presupposes a collaborative practice approach to managing manic-depressive disorder. This collaboration includes the individual being treated, provider, and, where possible, partner or family members. Rather than a paternalistic, order-following approach to treatment, all interventions expect the individual and, where possible, significant others to become educated regarding the illness and to become partners in managing it. Although the specific methods and priorities may differ somewhat (e.g., work with couples vs. group work only with those in treatment vs. individual cognitive interventions), this theme is perhaps most evident across all modalities. The care organization interventions of Bauer, Williford, and coworkers (2001) and Simon and coworkers (2001) also build upon this basic collaborative approach.

Second, few interventions manage the individual in isolation. Family or couples interventions have been tested in those whose social network has not unraveled. In those interventions that work with a less select group, the individual is often seen as part of a group to enhance social support, reinforce teaching, and combat stigma and demoralization.

THE CORE PSYCHOSOCIAL AGENDA

The third and most important for the purposes of this manual is the impressive degree of convergent validity regarding agenda for disease management information and skills to be imparted by these diverse interventions. Specifically, imparting education, focusing on early warning symptoms and triggers of episodes, and developing detailed and person-specific action plans—which form the core of the Life Goals Program—are found across most of the other interventions as well. This core agenda is also an important part of such diverse approaches as the cognitive-behavioral interventions of Palmer and Williams (1995) and Lam and coworkers (2000), the psychoeducational intervention of Perry and coworkers (1999) and Weiss and coworkers (Weiss, Griffin, et al., 2000), the IPSRT intervention of Frank and coworkers (2000), and the family intervention of Miklowitz and coworkers (Miklowitz & Goldstein, 1997; Miklowitz et al., 2000). Whether or not the developers of these interventions came to this common agenda in isolation or as part of ongoing collaborations and discussions is less important than the impressive fact that the agenda has been identified and incorporated into each of these interventions.

Thus, given the positive results most of these interventions with explicit disease management components—education, collaborative management strategies with the individual being treated, inclusion of as wide a social support system as is available—have produced, it is likely that this basic approach will be critical. It will, perhaps, be more critical even than the specific type of intervention in which these disease management components are embedded.

DIRECTIONS FOR FUTURE RESEARCH

It is of foremost important that interventions with Class B/C data be moved forward to Class A studies. Focus should be on impact on functional outcome and costs as well as the more traditional clinical outcome measures.

In addition, it may be most useful in terms of reducing the public health burden to focus on designs that test the core agenda outlined above—generic education about the illness, identifying personal symptom pattern and triggers, developing individualized action plan—than to conduct "horse races" among the various specific modalities. It will be interesting to see whether the NIMH's Systematic Treatment Enhancement Program (STEP; principal investigator: Gary Sachs), which is studying various types of psychotherapies in conjunction with various types of medications, is able to address these issues.

Moreover, the drive to isolate and test the active components of psychosocial interventions should always look toward issues of parsimony, because the most cost-effective interventions are likely to be the most widely disseminated. This is one of the major reasons that the Life Goals Program is delivered in group format. In addition, one needs to recognize that benefits from psychosocial interventions may not be evident until some months into treatment (Bauer et al., 1998; Miklowitz et al., 2000). Thus, research designs—not to mention clinical programs and insurance benefit packages—should take this long-lead time into account.

A further challenge will be to develop interventions that not only are able to be widely disseminated but that are sustainable in general clinical practice settings. This will require that interventions be

- applicable to the majority of individuals encountered in such settings,
- implementable by clinical staff likely to be available in those settings, and
- acceptable cost-wise from the perspective of the payor, who will make the decision regarding whether or not to implement a specific type of treatment.

These issues of sustainability are not specific to psychosocial treatments, but they have been a focus of debate around increasingly expensive medications for other psychiatric and medical disorders as well. However, the payoff for manic-depressive disorder is potentially great in terms of reduced morbidity if researchers can develop psychosocial interventions that are indeed able to be disseminated and sustained in general clinical practice. We will now turn in detail to the conceptual background and structure of the Life Goals Program, which was designed with such issues as dissemination and sustainability in mind.

Chapter 6

The Conceptual Framework for the Life Goals Program

GOALS OF THE LIFE GOALS PROGRAM

We take as the goal of any treatment, most simply stated, to improve outcome. Recall from chapter 2 that outcome can be conceptualized across three domains: clinical outcome, functional outcome, and illness costs. The specific goals of the Life Goals Program are therefore twofold:

- The first goal is *to improve clinical outcome by improving disease management skills,* which facilitates the group member's participation in medical model treatment; improved disease-specific outcome is anticipated to have beneficial effects on both functional outcome and direct and indirect illness costs (Phase 1).
- Because improvements in disease outcome alone do not necessarily lead to improvements in functional outcome, the second goal is *to improve functional outcome directly by assisting individuals in achieving social, occupational, and quality of life goals* that they have identified and that they have not been able to attain due to illness (Phase 2).

In attempting to understand how the Life Goals Program addresses these two goals, it is useful to summarize its conceptual bases. The underpinnings of Phase 1 and Phase 2 are similar in that they each seek to assist individuals in better management of their lives. Phase 1 derives from efforts to improve participation in medical model treatment. Phase 2 derives from efforts to improve management of an individual's function in everyday life, or their functional outcome as detailed in chapter 2.

A BRIEF OUTLINE OF THE TWO PHASES
OF THE LIFE GOALS PROGRAM

The conceptual basis of the Life Goals Program is diverse, drawing on both established theories applied to the development and treatment of mood disorders and on several concepts not typically associated with that area. These phases, each reviewed in turn below, are summarized in Table 6.1.

As outlined above, the goals of the Life Goals Program are twofold: to improve disease-specific outcome by increasing illness self-management skills, and to improve functional outcome by assisting individuals in achieving functional goals they have identified that they have not been able to attain due to illness. Accordingly, the program is separated into two sequential stages, or phases.

Phase 1 is a highly structured psychoeducational program designed to improve the person's ability to manage collaboratively his or her own care by improving self-management skills. Basic features of manic-depressive disorder are introduced to the group members. This general, "nonpersonalized" knowledge is then elaborated by moving into a more "personalized," or person-specific, conceptualization of each individual's experience of the illness. With this as the basic approach, group members are assisted in identifying their own specific symptom pattern, early warning symptoms, and triggers.

The concept of the *personal cost-benefit analysis* is introduced in developing coping strategies for symptoms and in understanding lack of fit between prescribed medication and behavior and what the individual person chooses to do in treatment. Throughout both Phase 1 and Phase 2, the group member is assumed to act always in his or her perceived best self-interest,

TABLE 6.1   Summary of the Conceptual Framework of Specific Elements of the Life Goals Program

Phase 1
> *Host factor improvement*
>> Psychoeducation
>> Development of disease management skills using personal cost-benefit analysis

Phase 2
> *The main treatment paradigm*
>> Select goals
>> Devise goal-attainment strategies using
>>> Personal cost-benefit analysis
>>> Behavioral strategies

> *To address roadblocks*
>> Cognitive techniques
>> Interpersonal group techniques

which is clarified and modified through this type of application of personal cost-benefit analyses. As part of this process, group members develop their own personalized *Action Plans* with which to respond to symptom emergence, involving clinical personnel and their own support network if available.

Phase 2 focuses on assisting the group member to identify one, and subsequently several, goals in his or her life that have not been reached due to the disruption of having manic-depressive disorder. The therapist and group member subsequently develop realistic step-wise plans with attainable behavioral steps to address these goals. The plans are structured with the therapist to maximize the probability of success. Progress is outlined in behaviorally measurable terms. The member's goals may be as apparently simple and mundane as getting a driver's license or beginning a hobby, or as lofty as getting a job or getting married.

For any goal, particularly the more complex, the therapist helps the member to reformat goals according to four key principles:

- The goals must be chosen by the individual and be important to his or her quality of life.
- The goals must be specifically measurable.
- The goals must be formulated to depend primarily on the actions of the individual himself or herself and not depend on the cooperation of another person.
- The goals must be broken down into a series of small, realistically attainable steps.

Clearly, such complex goals as getting a job or getting married, and indeed most goals that involve social interaction, appear to violate the third principle. Suffice it to say at this point that the focus of the treatment in the Life Goals Program is on the member's actions and their effect on his or her role function and subjective quality of life, including self-esteem. The finer points of behavioral rule development are outlined in chapter 8 of this manual.

However, there are always roadblocks to success, due to cognitive distortions or to factors responsive to interpersonal group interventions, such as demoralization, stigma, and lack of opportunity for learning from peers. Cognitive and interpersonal techniques are used to address and minimize these respective types of roadblocks.

Phase 2 does not have the same degree of a priori structure to its agenda as does Phase 1. Rather, duration of treatment and pace of progress are member-specific and dictated by progress toward specific goals. In Phase 2, a group member identifies an overall goal, breaks it down into component subgoals, then formulates plans to meet them and monitors progress with the therapist in the group context. Roadblocks to goal attainment are addressed by group member and therapist to facilitate progress. As identified goals are reached, the member either terminates group or cycles back through another round of goal identification, subgoal construction, and work/monitoring. Thus, Phase 1 is typically structured as a closed group, and Phase 2 is open-ended and can accommodate individuals joining at various stages.

ADAPTIVE COPING AND THE COST-BENEFIT ANALYSIS APPROACH TO AN INDIVIDUAL'S DECISION MAKING

If there is a single most important concept underlying the development of the Life Goals Program in both Phase 1 and Phase 2, it is this: *Individuals will act in their own perceived self-interest.* This is particularly true in trying to adapt to stressors in life, including having a chronic illness such as manic-depressive disorder. Whether or not an individual's perception of his or her own best interest matches the clinician's, one can assume that the individual will tend to act in a manner that, as best as the individual can tell, helps him or her adapt successfully. It is in reality often the case that individuals with the illness and their treating clinicians will indeed differ in what they see as adaptive. One of the critical components of successful treatment, of, in particular, establishing a successful treatment alliance, is to come to a consensus on what are more versus less adaptive coping strategies. To accomplish this, the clinician must understand how an individual chooses and discards various options both in managing his or her disease and in managing his or her life with the disorder. We refer to this process as a personal cost-benefit analysis.

The term *cost-benefit analysis* derives from health care economics. A variety of economic techniques, including cost-benefit, cost-effectiveness, and cost-utility analysis, have been applied to health care decision making, primarily on the system level (reviewed in, e.g., Carr-Hill, 1989; Collen & Goodman, 1985; Gold, Siegel, Russell, & Weinstein, 1996; Maynard, 1990; Torrance, 1987; Weinstein & Stason, 1977). The basic concept behind each of those technically different calculations is the same. If a system makes a particular decision on how to allocate its resources, that decision will cost a certain amount of resources, and in return will generate a certain amount of payoff. This payoff may be quantitated in terms of dollars, health care effects, or well-being, or in terms of some other metric. Something is spent, something is gained. The rubrics of cost benefit, cost effectiveness, and cost utility analyze these payoffs somewhat differently, but the concept is the same. Similar principles have been applied to decisions that individuals make as well, for example, trading side effects and costs of a particular intervention against projected time until well, level of function, or other outcome (reviewed in Gold et al., 1996).

We have chosen the term "cost-benefit analysis" to describe the internal metric that individuals use in making treatment decisions, with the "bottom line" always being their own perceived optimal adaptation. We have chosen this specific term rather than cost effectiveness or cost utility simply because that term is in common parlance and is the one we wished to use with group members, rather than having chosen it for technical reasons.

The basic concept of a cost-benefit trade-off can be applied easily to an individual's decision making in manic-depressive disorder. Each decision a person makes with regard to his or her disease management is based on a similar process of evaluating the costs and benefits of various options. Individuals are acutely aware of both the costs and benefits of various treatment options—usually much more so than the providers, because it is the individuals themselves who must bear the cost.

An example can illustrate this metric. Lithium is an efficacious treatment for acute depression, for acute mania, and for prevention of future episodes. This much both provider and the person in treatment can agree on (although the individual usually takes the provider's word for it). But what of the cost? Who decides the value of increased urinary frequency, of tremor, of acne, of weight gain? It is the individual who identifies these as significant, and who puts a value on them for his or her own life.

Furthermore, it is clear that there is no common value scale for all people (see, e.g., Gold et al., 1996, chapter 4). We have treated persons who easily tolerate tremors that are visible at rest. We have also treated surgeons and violinists who cannot tolerate the mildest tremor, not even objectively visible on provocative testing. The basis for such an individual's metric has obvious logic: "If I develop this side effect, I cannot do my work well." If identified, this is usually well understood and appreciated by clinicians.

More subtle factors may contribute to individual decision making. Personal preferences, memories, powerful associations, social needs, and founded or unfounded fears may also dictate that, for example, lithium-induced urinary frequency is intolerable to an individual, despite the ability of lithium to keep him or her out of the hospital and at work for extended periods of time. This type of personal cost-benefit analysis, though often partially conscious at best, may not be evident to the clinician. Yet it is driven by the individual's sense of his or her own optimal adaptation.

Another, not uncommon, example of personal cost-benefit analysis in managing illness is self-induced social isolation as a response to irritable mood. Although not completely adaptive as a singular response, social isolation may actually be a reasonable response for the person with irritable hypomania or depression. The person from past experience knows that he or she is at high risk for verbal or even physical aggressiveness. This could lead to alienation of loved ones, coworkers, or important others. There could be legal implications for serious outbursts. A series of less adaptive responses to these impulses may also be set in motion, such as using alcohol or drugs to blunt the irritability.

Thus, it is easy to see that there is a logic to noncompliance, and the goal of improved disease management skills is not served by convincing the person in treatment that taking a particular medication is the best option for him or her, but rather to understand with the person the underlying cost-benefit analysis that he or she is doing and to search for acceptable treatment alternatives. This aspect of cost-benefit analysis is the basis for much of psychoeducational component of the Life Goals Program that seeks to improve disease management skills in Phase 1, and functional goal attainment in Phase 2.

Personal cost-benefit analysis is also quite applicable to the task of helping individuals to improve functional status in Phase 2. The choice of social isolation as a coping response to irritable mood may also have undesirable functional impacts. These include alienation of significant others, decreased work time, decreased leisure activities, and ultimately less exposure to activities and interactions that maintain or increase self-esteem. The group member in Phase 2 requires assistance in identifying these negative consequences and in making informed decisions regarding coping strategies.

Thus, the person's choice of strategies both for disease management and for coping behavior in functional goal attainment can be considered to be a function of individual cost-benefit analyses by the individual himself or herself. Key concepts to be aware of are the following:

- There are always both positive and negative aspects (costs and benefits) to each strategy.
- These calculations reduce diverse aspects of the decision to a common metric to produce a yes or no decision.
- The individual is the one who creates and implements this metric.
- The analyses are often only partially conscious to the individual, but they are always made on the basis of his or her attempt to adapt with the greatest benefit, or least harm to self.

The task of the therapist in the Life Goals Program is therefore to help the person recognize the components of the process and to identify the unrecognized costs and benefits associated with the decision. In doing this task, the therapist starts from the individual's own metric and works as an expert in helping the individual reach a decision. Note that the cost-benefit approach in the Life Goals Program, as with its other aspects, is geared to the individual rather than to the family. Clearly, though, these techniques can be adapted for use outside the formal group setting to include family members where indicated.

THE SPECIFIC CONCEPTUAL BASES OF PHASE 1

THE EFFICACY–EFFECTIVENESS GAP IN MANIC-DEPRESSIVE DISORDER

As reviewed in chapter 4, there are numerous medications of proven efficacy in the treatment of various phases of manic-depressive disorder. These data, particularly for lithium, strongly support the concept that manic-depressive disorder is in large degree a medication-responsive illness. However, data from real-world clinical practice indicate that high rates of residual symptoms and substantial morbidity remain (e.g., Markar & Mander, 1989; also reviewed in Bauer, 2001 and Bauer, Williford et al., 2001a). It is likely that some individuals, or some aspects of the illness, may simply not respond to medications. However, it is also clear that even if medications do have clear and proven efficacy in formal clinical trials, typically, they have much less effectiveness in general clinical practice.

This efficacy–effectiveness gap is likely due to several factors relevant to the Life Goals Program, including the fact that individuals are less complex and "better behaved" in clinical trials than in real-world practice, and the fact that the average provider in clinical practice may not be as adept at using particular interventions as are providers involved with clinical trials. We have been particularly interested in the potentially remediable contributors to the efficacy–effectiveness gap as it relates to manic-depressive disorder (e.g., Bauer, Williford, et al., 2001b).

THE COLLABORATIVE PRACTICE MODEL FOR MANIC-DEPRESSIVE DISORDER

The development of the Life Goals Program was in part an effort to address the efficacy–effectiveness gap by assisting individuals in improving their disease management skills. This approach is not a unique effort but has been attempted in several areas both in mental health and in medicine. Frequently such educational efforts are part of an approach to treatment we have come to call the *collaborative practice model.*

We define the collaborative practice model as an organization of care that (1) emphasizes development in the individual of disease management skills and (2) supports the provider capability and availability in order to (3) engage individuals in timely, joint decision making regarding their illness (Bauer, 2001). The collaborative practice model is an organization of care, and as such has elements in addition to education of individuals with illness (i.e., provider support). However, improving an individual's disease management skills is clearly a critical aspect of any type of collaborative practice, because its overall goal is improved joint decision making between a provider and an individual with an illness.

It will be helpful to describe briefly the development of the collaborative practice model, particularly as it applies to manic-depressive disorder,
because the conceptual bases of the model overlap so extensively with
those from which our specific intervention developed. There are three main
sources: development of lithium clinics in the early 1970s, mental health
nursing practice since the 1960s, and disease management models for
chronic medical illnesses such as diabetes and hypertension over the past 10
to 15 years.

As outlined in chapter 5, with the development of lithium as a treatment
for manic-depressive disorder in the 1970s, the conceptual approach to
treatment for this illness shifted dramatically from a predominantly psychotherapeutic to a medical-model approach—that is, one that assumed that
this behavioral disorder was at least partly biological in origin and was
amenable to medication treatment. To support medical-model treatment,
lithium clinics were established in many centers that treated substantial numbers of individuals with manic-depressive disorder (see descriptions of these
early clinics in Fieve, 1975; Foelker et al., 1986; Gitlin & Jamison, 1984; Seeger
et al., 1989; Shelley & Fieve, 1974; reviewed in Bauer, 2001b). Despite their
emphasis on medical-model efficiency, many lithium clinics also included
some type of psychotherapeutic intervention. These psychotherapeutic
interventions were predominantly educative, aimed at improving understanding and management of the illness. They also included efforts at destigmatization and the use of process groups to address issues of demoralization and
isolation. In fact, much of the current burgeoning of interest in adjunctive
psychotherapy for manic-depressive disorder (reviewed chapter 5) can be
traced back to these early lithium clinic efforts at psychoeducation. Thus, the
roots of augmented medical-model treatment for manic-depressive disorder
run back over three decades.

In parallel, there has been a long tradition in nursing practice of emphasizing education and collaboration with individuals with specific illnesses to
achieve jointly identified goals. For example, Orlando (1961) emphasized
using the nurse's relationship to the individual to elucidate perceived needs
and implement joint evaluation of interventions. Payton and Ivy (1981)
described the objective of the psychoeducational model as providing people
with the abilities required to manage their lives according to their own preferences. Wilkinson (1991) applied the nursing collaborative practice model
to medical-model psychiatric care, focusing on three-way collaboration
among nurse, psychiatrist, and individual with the illness in order to maximize self-management.

The psychiatric nursing literature offers several specific psychoeducation
models relevant to the care of other major mental illnesses such as schizophrenia (e.g., Ascher-Svanum, 1989; Harmon & Tratnack, 1992; McCay, 1984;
Moller & Wer, 1989). In terms of manic-depressive disorder specifically, the

literature about psychoeducation for persons with this disorder has been a focus of attention as well (Hume et al., 1988; Hutchinson, 1992; Pollack, 1990, 1993).

A specific contribution of the nursing literature to the Life Goals Program comes from the Nebraska Model (Moller & Wer, 1989). This educational approach offers a six-session program of psychoeducation that lasts 3 hours each. The goals of each session are established on the program schedule. As a structured education program, the Nebraska Model focuses on disease management, symptom recognition, causes of relapse, participation in decisions about the plan of care, and medical information to facilitate knowledgeable choices for responsible self-management.

The third stream of influence on development of the collaborative practice approach to treating manic-depressive and other serious mental illnesses derives from the treatment of chronic medical diseases such as hypertension and diabetes. Von Korff and colleagues (1997) identified several behavioral principles from social learning and self-regulation theories that underlie this collaborative practice approach:

- Illness management behavior is learned.
- Self-efficacy (motivation and self-confidence) is important to success in self-management.
- The social environment can support or impede self-care.
- Monitoring and responding to changes in status improve adaptation.

These elements address system and provider characteristics as well as characteristics of the individual with the chronic illness. The authors reviewed the extensive literature on collaborative practice model application to chronic medical illness and outlined four key elements to the collaborative practice model, including

- Collaborative definition of problems
- Joint goal setting and planning
- Provision of a continuum of self-management and support services
- Active and sustained follow-up

They also proposed that for successful chronic disease management, the individual must engage in four types of self-management tasks (Wagner et al., 1996):

- Health promotion activities
- Appropriate interaction with providers and health care systems
- Monitoring of the individual's status
- Management of the individual's illness impact on functional status

They also pointed out that medical care is not well organized to support these functions by virtue of training, culture, and structure. From a review of several successful programs, they proposed that the reorganization of care that includes four components can support these self-management tasks and improve outcome:

- Practice redesign
- Education of individuals with an illness
- Support by expert systems (e.g., provider education, consultation)
- Information systems (e.g., feedback and reminders to providers)

It is apparent that several aspects of the collaborative practice model as articulated by Wagner and colleagues (1996) and Von Korff and colleagues (1997) are relevant to our efforts to develop interventions that improve an individual's disease management skills. Each of the behavioral principles indicates that disease management skills can improve, and that both internal individual factors and clinician response factors will determine how well those skills are learned. The self-management task provides an agenda that overlaps extensively both with that of Phase 1 (the first three tasks) and with that of Phase 2 (the fourth task). The elements of the collaborative practice model all emphasize self-management, and all require adequate disease management skills.

Finally, although the practice redesign elements are, by their nature, system-oriented, provision of education for individuals with the illness is clearly an integral part of this map for the reorganization of care. The basic elements of education to improve disease management skills are summarized in Table 6.2.

HOST FACTORS IN THE MODULATION OF DISEASE OUTCOME

In our focus on helping individuals improve disease management skills, we have found it useful to consider the characteristics of individuals that support and impede good disease management. It has been particularly striking to us to treat individuals with severe forms of the illness, such as those with rapid cycling or psychosis who seem to manage their lives and illness quite well. On the other hand, there are also individuals whose lives and illness are far more impaired than would be predicted by the severity of their illness alone. Some of these persons have easily identifiable comorbid medical or psychiatric disorders. The most obvious among psychiatric disorders are comorbid substance use disorders and brain injuries.

However, others' lives and behavior in treatment are quite impaired even in the absence of comorbid disorders. These individuals are not necessarily or even typically malingerers or have personality disorders, although their

TABLE 6.2 Basics of Education to Improve Disease Management Skills

1. *Principles*
   A. Gear education to educational, cultural, motivational factors.
   B. Include both knowledge about the disorder in general and exploration of the individual's specific form of illness and how it affects his or her life.
   C. Pay close attention to opportunities for destigmatization and demystification.
   D. Emphasize the role of the person in treatment and his or her family as comanagers of the illness, including judging costs and benefits of specific treatment options according to the individual's priorities.
2. *Components of Psychoeducation*
   A. The disorder
      a. Biological basis
         i. Genetic factors (especially for persons of childbearing age)
         ii. Possible brain mechanisms
      b. Environmental components
         i. Psychosocial factors
         ii. Physical environmental factors
      c. Course and outcome
         i. Prevalence
         ii. Episode types and patterns
         iii. Potential triggers for episodes
         iv. Comorbidities and complications
   B. Treatment
      a. Somatic therapies: somatic and psychosocial
         i. Goals
         ii. Side effect recognition and management
         iii. Costs and benefits of individual treatment options
      b. Coping skills
         i. Recognition of early warning signs of relapse
         ii. Avoidance/management of triggers for episodes
         iii. Activation of adaptive coping behaviors and avoidance of maladaptive responses

social behavior and behavior in treatment frequently lead to either of these labels. Rather, there appear to be individual characteristics that affect disease management capabilities. Sometimes these individual characteristics may affect participation in treatment as well, leading to suboptimal treatment and outcome. Recall also from chapter 2 the related quantitative observation that illness-severity characteristics do not predict functional deficits.

It has been useful to us to conceptualize these additional factors separately from the basic illness process, because they may explain variability outcome that is not readily predicted from the severity of the illness itself. This is not conceptually novel in understanding biomedical illnesses. It is most simply and obviously articulated in the study of infectious diseases, in which the outcome of infection is a function not only of the severity of the infecting agent but also of the capability of the individual to fight off the infection. Persons treated with cancer chemotherapy, those with acquired immune deficiency syndrome (AIDS), and persons with other types of immune system disorders are considered "compromised hosts," and are unable to handle the externally imposed infectious stress.

We conceptualize outcome in manic-depressive disorder not only as a function of the disease process but also as a function of *host factors.* Host factors may be broadly defined as those characteristics of the person that can be separately measured from her or his genetic or biologically determined manic-depressive disorder. These host factors are proposed to consist of two categories, *comorbid disorders,* which are reasonably easily identified and characterized, and *disease management skills,* which are much less well defined and measured (Figure 6.1). Comorbid disorders will not be discussed further here because they are operationalized in standard fashions and are summarized briefly above and in chapter 2. Note that both medical and psychiatric comorbidity comprise relevant host factors.

Disease management skills can be defined as the ability of a person to cope with his or her illness and to participate actively in treatment. These are more difficult to identify and to measure in pure form, yet are of critical importance in general clinical practice: It is these types of factors that to a large extent determine where and how a person with a disorder will present for treatment, and indeed whether the person will present for treatment at all. In fact, it is not fanciful to propose that a provider never treats manic-depressive disorder directly. Rather, the clinician provides treatment only via the disease management skills of the individual being treated (Figure 6.2). This is true of medical illnesses as well, even those as simple as strep throat: If the individual does not seek treatment, then the illness does not get treated.

There is little consensus on how to conceptualize these disease management skills, let alone how to identify and measure them. Certainly, there is much literature on compliance, or adherence, to treatment for medical (e.g., Cramer & Spilker, 1994) and psychiatric (e.g., Blackwell, 1995) illnesses. There is equally extensive literature on cultural determinants of illness attitudes (e.g., Kelly, Mamos, & Scott, 1987), as well as overlapping literature on the impact of social and socioeconomic factors on treatment accessibility and participation and illness outcome (e.g., Adler, Boyce, Chesney, Folkman, & Syme, 1993). To some extent, cognitive (e.g., Beck et al., 1979, pp. 371–385) and psychoanalytic (e.g., Fromm-Reichmann, 1950; Scanlon, 1982) studies have addressed the role of psychopathology in participation in treatment. Other conceptualizations, such as the application of locus of control theory (Rotter, 1966), have been applied to disease management skills, specifically in manic-depressive disorder (Hastings, 1989).

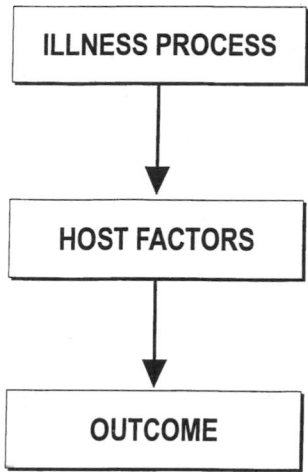

FIGURE 6.1   Host factors are characteristics of the individual that are conceptually separate from the underlying illness process itself. The most important of these host factors are disease management skills and comorbid illnesses, including both medical and psychiatric illnesses. Among disease management skills are included simple cognitive skills and experience and attitudes toward the illness and its treatment. Illness attitudes are derived from both personal factors and social or cultural factors.

In the most simple conceptualization, host factors modulate illness outcome, given a particular severity of illness. For instance, a person may have severe, rapid cycling manic-depressive disorder, or psychotic features during manic or depressive episodes, yet still have reasonable levels of outcome across the three domains of disease-specific outcome, functional outcome, and illness costs. Despite a severe form of illness, management skills are intact, and there are no comorbid disorders. A person with fairly straightforward manic-depressive disorder may have a much worse outcome due to poor disease management skills or comorbid substance use disorders.

Moreover, a broad spectrum of theories has been applied to various aspects of health behavior, including how individuals engage in treatment (see, for example, Glanz et al., 1997). A number of aspects of the Life Goals Program resemble those found in widely disseminated health behavior interventions; for instance, the personal cost-benefit approach to understanding and improving treatment decisions resembles the "decisional balance" approach found in motivational interviewing (e.g., Miller & Rollnick, 2002). Similarities also exist between the approach to functional goals in Phase 2 and the approach used in problem-solving therapy for depression (e.g., Dowrick et al., 2000; Mynors-Wallis et al., 2000).

Each of the many theoretical and methodological approaches leads to different conceptualizations as to why individuals manage their illnesses in a

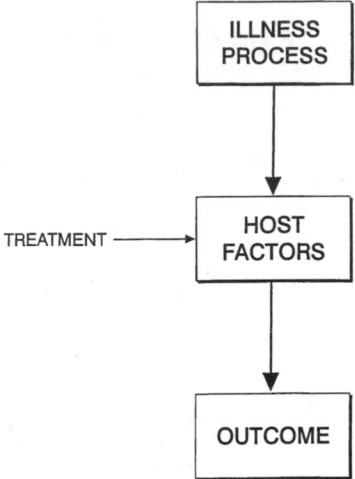

FIGURE 6.2   Figure 6.1 is revised to make the point that, despite our usual assumptions, a clinician never treats an illness process directly. We would like to believe that the antibiotic or mood stabilizer that we give is targeted directly at a bacterial infection or a chemical imbalance. However, this is not the case. In reality, all treatment is modulated by host factors, specifically illness management skills. If a person with an illness does not show up for appointments, or does not take prescribed medication, or does not do cognitive or behavioral homework, then little treatment is delivered. Thus, recognition of host factors and attention to their role in treatment is of critical importance to improving outcome.

particular manner. For example, in assessing the unwillingness of a person with manic-depressive disorder to accept lithium treatment, a cultural approach might focus on the role of the individual's religious orientation that leads the individual to cast his or her abnormal thoughts, feelings, and behavior as a moral issue to be addressed by dint of will or grace rather than succumb to the weakness of taking a pill. A psychoanalytic approach might understand this unwillingness as a narcissistic defense against the realization that the individual has a defect for which he or she must rely on outside assistance. An economic approach might emphasize the reluctance to assume the cost of lithium treatment in terms of both monetary and personal time. Each of these approaches to treatment behavior in treatment derives from a particular set of theories, methodologic tools, or disciplines. Yet these facets of understanding treatment behavior in treatment are neither mutually exclusive nor explicitly related; in some ways, they may be usefully complementary.

We have chosen to group these factors together under the multidimensional rubric of disease management skills, rather than address behavior in treatment as a function of an individual methodological or theoretical approach (e.g., socioeconomic determinants or psychodynamic mechanisms). We have taken this "lumping" rather than "splitting" approach in recognition of the fact that no one theoretical or methodological approach has yet addressed all the determinants of disease management skills or has produced a conceptual schema to reconcile the various approaches. Furthermore, we have found it useful conceptually to approach these factors as including not only those behaviors that deal with an individual's behavior in the clinical setting strictly defined, as in the compliance or adherence literature, but also all those self-management skills that go on day to day as an individual lives with the illness. Thus, issues such as "Shall I go to work today?" and "How shall I deal with the fact that I want to scream at my spouse?" are conceptualized as being as important to outcome as the more commonly addressed issue "Shall I take my medication today?"

In view of the relative lack of unanimity in conceptual grounding, we have worked from our clinical and scientific experience with persons who have manic-depressive disorder and attempted to identify those disease management skills that could potentially be improved by treatment in the group psychotherapy modality. The major components of disease management skills that we propose are summarized in Table 6.3.

Two aspects of the relationship of disease management skills to illness outcome deserve specific mention. First, disease management skills must be better defined and their effects must be empirically determined, because they may affect outcome in counterintuitive ways. For example, in a multisite

TABLE 6.3 Examples of Determinants of Disease Management Skills

Knowledge base

Cultural factors
   Religious background
   Ethnic background

Socioeconomic factors
   Family support
   Other social supports
   Financial resources
   Competing time and resource demands

Individual attitudes and preferences

Individual functional capabilities
   Cognitive capacity and style
   Cognitive set
   Psychodynamic factors
   Locus of control

study of rapid cycling manic-depressive disorder (Bauer et al., 1994), we found that persons with manic-depressive disorder who have a history of rapid cycling were of significantly higher socioeconomic status than those without rapid cycling. This finding was surprising, because one would expect that this more severe form of the illness would be associated with greater socioeconomic impairment and lower socioeconomic status. On further analysis, we found that the difference was accounted for by individuals whose rapid cycling was exclusively associated with antidepressants, which may be a risk factor for rapid cycling (Bauer & Whybrow, 1993; Wehr & Goodwin, 1979; Wehr et al., 1993). We proposed that higher socioeconomic status led to more intensive treatment, and specifically greater exposure to antidepressants, which in turn led to a higher prevalence of rapid cycling. Thus, data on the impact of specific aspects of illness management skills on outcome, and the interrelationship of these skills, are important.

Second, although life would be simple if the causal relationship of disease management skills to outcome were simply unidirectional, as illustrated in Figure 6.2, this is in reality not likely the case. Outcomes themselves, particularly clinical and functional outcome, affect host factors, which in turn affect treatment (Figure 6.3). Let us look at examples of feedback from each of these two outcome domains to illustrate this relationship.

For clinical outcome, uncontrolled mania or depression can decrease insight and compliance with treatment for both mood disorders and comorbid illnesses. In addition, in some unfortunate circumstances, the mood disorder can lead to morbidity through suicide attempts or accidents. For example, impaired renal function after overdose can preclude the use of lithium for mood stabilization, or brain damage after coma from overdose can impair cognitive skills. Thus, an intervention to improve disease management skills, such as the Life Goals Program, must be conceptualized as breaking a cycle rather than reducing a simple, unidirectional risk factor for poor outcome.

Several aspects of functional outcome can play an important role in determining disease management skills and can affect comorbid disorders. Impaired occupational function compromises insurance and financial status, which has a clear impact on accessibility of treatment. Social relationships, particularly supportive family relationships and friendships, can be significant factors in forming illness attitudes and in providing for the mundane but important management needs related to stable housing and transportation to clinical appointments. Aspects of subjective health-related quality of life can be powerful determinants of attitude toward illness, particularly those aspects addressed by proposed curative interpersonal group treatment factors such as demoralization and lack of hope.

In summary, to have maximal control on the symptoms of manic-depressive disorder and optimal functional outcome, the individual with the illness needs to be adept at participating in medical model treatment and in managing his

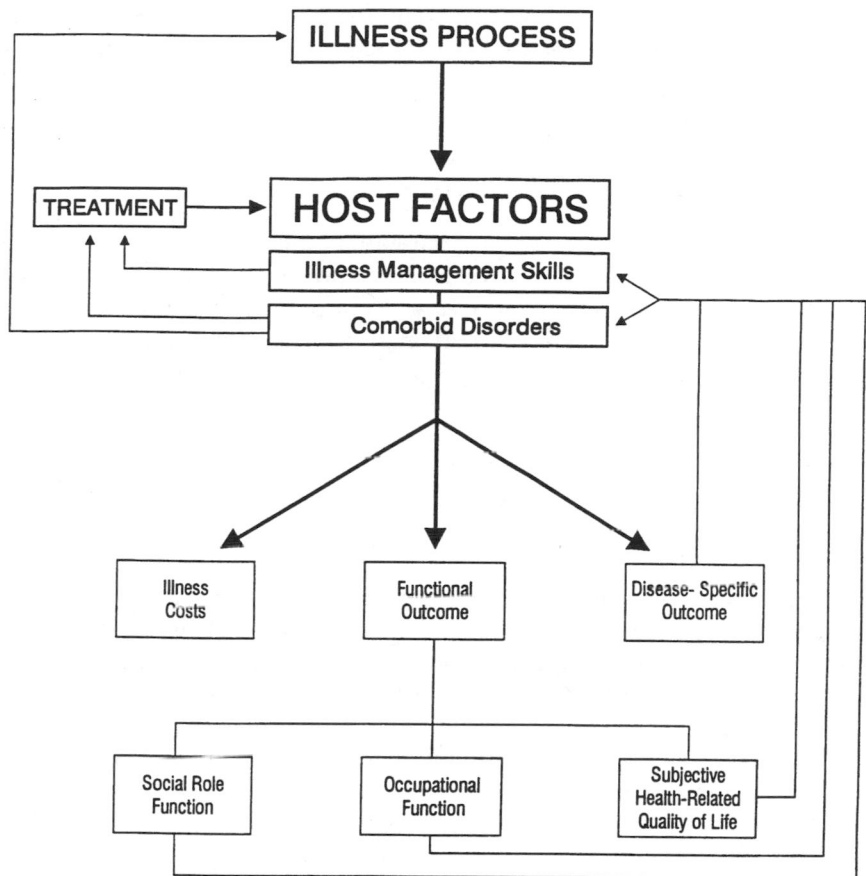

FIGURE 6.3 In a more realistic conceptualization, it should be noted that there is not a simple one-way flow from disease process to outcome. As described in the text, host factors modulate illness processes to impact outcome; however, various aspects of outcome feed back to impact host factors. For example, poor occupational outcome compromises ability to finance treatment. Furthermore, if poor outcome leads to worsening of comorbid disorders (e.g., increased drug or alcohol intake), such physiologic insults may actually worsen neurobiologic illness process themselves.

or her life with the illness. Not all individuals are naturally adept at disease management (note that part of the efficacy–effectiveness gap is likely due to the fact that only those individuals who are most adept at disease management enter and can tolerate completing controlled efficacy trials). Sometimes poor disease management is the result of relatively obvious factors, such as comorbid psychiatric or medical disorders. Developmental or cultural factors or simply lack of experience and modeling may be responsible. Less identifiable factors may also be involved. In any event, the Life Goals Program, particularly Phase 1, seeks to improve disease management skills so that individuals may be better collaborators in their treatment and improve their clinical, and eventually functional, outcome.

INTERPERSONAL GROUP TECHNIQUES

Interpersonal group techniques are dealt with in some detail in the section on conceptual bases of Phase 2. However, it should be noted that interpersonal group techniques support Phase 1 as well. In particular, the therapist uses these techniques to work toward destigmatization, and the creation of a supportive social group can be an important contributor to improved disease management skills.

THE SPECIFIC CONCEPTUAL BASES OF PHASE 2

One of the initial premises of the Life Goals Program (Bauer & McBride, 1996, Section 2) was that medical-model treatment alone is not sufficient to ensure optimal outcome for manic-depressive disorder. This is not surprising, because functional outcome does not appear to be simply driven by clinical outcome (see chapter 2). Optimal medication management, or even psychotherapy, aimed at reducing symptoms in no way guarantees an impact on functional outcome. These findings are predicted by Engel's biopsychosocial model of illness and its treatment (Engel, 1977) as noted in that chapter. Rather, if improved functional outcome is a goal, then therapeutic interventions must be targeted directly at that goal.

As is apparent from chapter 5, the Life Goals Program differs from many forms of psychotherapy for manic-depressive disorder in explicitly recognizing this and gearing its treatment accordingly to specific functional goals. Thus, because one goal of the Life Goals Program is to improve functional outcome, it was necessary to develop a component to address those deficits directly. This is the goal of Phase 2. The major conceptual bases for Phase 2 derive from

- Behavioral therapy
- Cognitive therapy
- Interpersonal group therapy

BEHAVIORAL ELEMENTS OF THE LIFE GOALS PROGRAM

Several theorists have utilized behavioral concepts to attempt to understand and to treat depression. Rehm (1981) proposed that goal-directed behavior consists of a cycle of self-monitoring, self-evaluation, and self-reinforcement.

It was proposed that depression is characterized by selective attention to negative events, an increase in self-punishment, and a decrease in positive reinforcement. This dynamic provides the vulnerability to depression, which is unmasked by untoward environmental events.

In addition, Ferster (1974) proposed that depression was characterized by a reduced frequency of positively reinforced events and high rates of avoidant activity. Thus, lack of positive reinforcement led to depressive symptoms.

In contrast, Lewinsohn (1974) determined that individuals with depression did not have reduced rates of positive reinforcement, but suggested that depressives had lower rates of positive reinforcement that was dependent on their own actions; such reduced rates of "response-contingent reinforcement" lead to depressive symptoms, including depressed mood and cognitive changes.

Seligman (Peterson & Seligman, 1984) proposed that the key mechanism for the production of depression was not the reduction of positive reinforcement but rather the loss of control over negative events. This theory was developed from the animal model of learned helplessness and received support in studies of normal and clinically depressed human samples.

As can be seen from this selective and brief encapsulation of behavioral theories of depression, the common theme among them appears to be that depression is characterized by a perceived reduction in positive reinforcement for which individuals perceive themselves to be responsible. This may be due to an actual decrease in positive reinforcement in the environment, or simply an impaired ability to recognize the positive reinforcement that does exist and one's own role in it. It follows that, whatever the source of this perception of decreased positive reinforcement, therapeutic interventions that increase the awareness of successful events and one's own role in them would address the behavioral sources of depression.

To do this, the Life Goals Program focuses on identifying potential sources of positive reinforcement that are meaningful to group members—the goals—and has the therapist work with members to develop strategies that will maximize the chance of success in pursuing their goals. Strategies are developed to assess realistically the sources of success and failure so that the members can learn to assess their own role in the process accurately and to evolve more successful strategies when necessary.

Phase 2 takes what appears to be very complex, and to the group member overwhelming, goals and break them down into manageable steps. The goal of doing so is to increase the probability of success at each step. Consistent with this approach, Phase 2 relies in its formal behavioral elements almost exclusively on positive reinforcement for goals achieved, rather than negative reinforcement. Overall, then, the approach is to *develop strategies that make goals attainable and increase the probability of success, thus maximizing positive reinforcement* in this group in which demoralization and failure are endemic.

Cognitive Elements of the Life Goals Program

Cognitive theory (Beck et al., 1979) states that depression is the result of erroneous appraisals about oneself and of the external world, characterized by a depressogenic *cognitive triad*. The depressed person sees himself or herself as unilaterally responsible for the adverse events in his or her life. In addition, individual negative events are seen by the person as part of a general characteristic of his or her world. Furthermore, the depressed person has a negative, pessimistic view of the future: Things are bad now, and they will never change. Thus, the depressed individual makes *internal, global,* and *stable* negative attributions about events in his or her life. In plain terms, the depressogenic cognitive triad leads a person to believe that everything in his or her life is negative, that it always will be negative, and that it is that person's fault.

Cognitive theory postulates that these negative views of one's self and life, which lead to depressed mood, are maintained by a *cognitive schema,* or pattern of interpreting events negatively, that is highly conserved over development. This set of mental index cards are pulled out when the person is confronted by a negative event, the characteristics of the event matched to the dysfunctional attitude on the index card, and the new experience frequently added to the file box as a match—yet another event in evidence of one's internally, globally, and stably negative life.

In addition, cognitive theory proposes that negatively slanted information processing maintains this cognitive set, leading the person actually to extract information from each experience in a negatively biased manner. One sees the world, as it were, through gray-colored glasses.

Finally, Beck and colleagues (1979) point out that the person is not the generator of negative cognitions in a world that is not evenhanded. They posit that there are reciprocal interactions between the depressed person and his or her world such that more negative events may indeed occur to the depressed person, thereby reinforcing with the negative cognitive set to maintain the depressive symptoms. For example, friends may indeed leave, jobs may indeed be terminated, family members may indeed be accusatory regarding the depressed person's failings. In this regard, Coyne and Gotlib (1986) stated as part of a lively debate (see also Segal & Shaw, 1986) regarding the relationship of cognitive schemata to actual negative events:

> It is likely that future theorists and researchers will think it exceedingly odd that anyone attempted to explore and explain the cognitive process of depressed persons without reference to these factors (actual negative events in the real world). The emphasis of the cognitive model on the depressed person's distorted thinking processes may be unnecessary or at least overstated, and great attention to the social context of the depression may be warranted. (p. 703)

Cognitive theory has not been explored extensively in manic-depressive disorder, although it has served as the basis for several interventions (see chapter 5). It is possible that the same cognitive processes accompany depression during manic-depressive disorder as accompany unipolar depression. That is, the depressogenic cognitive triad may be characteristic of depressive episodes during manic-depressive disorder. However, it is not clear whether the triad would normalize during euthymic or manic phases of the illness, or even become globally, internally, and stably positive during the manic phase. This latter possibility is not likely in view of the high prevalence of depressive symptoms during manic and hypomanic episodes (e.g., Bauer et al., 1993; Bauer, Gyulai, et al., 1994).

Cognitive theory may play a role in another important aspect of manic-depressive disorder: The possibility that a negative cognitive set is an enduring feature of manic-depressive disorder suggested to us that cognitive theory might be particularly relevant to understanding and clarifying long-term coping strategies, rather than primarily to improving depressive symptoms. Support for this conceptualization comes from evidence that dysfunctional attitudes are likely not limited to depressive disorders, but may be an important part of coping strategies for persons in many walks of life faced with demands. The coping strategies people in general choose have been hypothesized to be determined in large part by their cognitive set. Consistent with this, cognitive set may have an effect on such diverse outcomes as physical health, health service utilization, and perhaps longevity (Carver & Scheier, 2001; Colligan, Offord, Malinchoc, Schulman, & Seligman, 1994; Kamen-Seigel, Rodin, Seligman, & Dwyer, 1991; Peterson & Seligman, 1987), as well as function in distinctly nonmedical areas of life (e.g., Carver & Scheier, 2001; Seligman, Nolen-Hoeksema, Thornton, & Thornton, 1990; Zulow, Oettingen, Peterson, & Seligman, 1988; Zullow & Seligman, 1990;). Thus, in individuals with manic-depressive disorder, dysfunctional coping strategies that lead to functional disabilities may be due to a skewed cognitive triad by virtue of their chronic or recurrent illness, rather than specifically because of their being in an acute mood episode.

In formal cognitive therapy, the ultimate goal is cognitive restructuring, or normalizing the underlying cognitive schema that produces the depressogenic cognitive triad when activated by negative events. The Life Goals Program does not attempt cognitive restructuring but rather uses cognitive techniques to challenge maladaptive cognitions and test negative attributions about events, specifically outcomes of an individual's goal attainment strategies. In this manner, the program seeks both to reduce maladaptive strategies driven by erroneous cognitions and to render more accurate the member's attributions about his or her successes and, in particular, failures.

INTERPERSONAL GROUP ELEMENTS OF THE LIFE GOALS PROGRAM

The above therapeutic orientations comprise the backbone or skeleton of the Life Goals Program, particularly Phase 2. However, to run an effective group, there must be a significant amount of interpersonal group "meat" on those bones. Interpersonal group theory and techniques are less explicitly defined and less well operationalized than behavioral or cognitive techniques. [Note that we speak here of interpersonal *group* techniques and theories, and not those of Klerman's IPT (Klerman et al., 1984)]. However, attention to such seemingly subjective yet critical aspects of the person's subjective experience as stigma and isolation can be of great importance in achieving therapeutic gains in an expressly behavioral program. It is primarily the interpersonal, rather than the behavioral, aspects of the group that address these issues.

How can this inclusion of interpersonal group factors as important aspects of group treatment for manic-depressive disorder be reconciled with the remark by one of the most influential interpersonal theorists who considered the presence of manic-depressive disorder no less than "one of the worst calamities that can befall a therapy group" (Yalom, 1975, p. 393)? Specifically, how can these factors conceptually and technically be incorporated into behaviorally oriented group treatment? How can one incorporate these techniques if it has been reported that individuals with manic-depressive disorder may be liable to decompensate clinically in interpersonally oriented group work (e.g., Kufferle, 1988)?

Yalom identified several specific curative factors associated with interpersonal group therapy, which are listed in Table 6.4. They are similar to the therapeutic factors identified empirically by Hogue and McLoughlin (1991) for interpersonal group work. Curative factors specific to homogeneous groups such as for manic-depressive disorder have also been identified. Homogeneous groups have specific value for increasing ego strength, cohesiveness, altruism, and hopefulness in a nonconfrontive and supportive way (Yalom, 1975).

The key adaptation that differentiates the Life Goals Program from traditional interpersonal groups is that the therapist advocates the *selective modulation* of intensive interpersonal stimulation and changes the role of interpersonal techniques in treatment. These techniques are not seen as the major curative factors, but rather as adjuncts to the main task of behavioral change. They specifically target the demoralization, isolation, stigmatization, shame, and simple lack of peer behavior modeling that are commonly perceived by individuals with manic-depressive disorder. This leads to judicious and limited use of the interpersonal techniques, primarily in Phase 2, that address these issues. This is in clear distinction to their wholesale application as the primary therapeutic modality, as they would be used in primarily

TABLE 6.4   Proposed Curative Elements of Interpersonal Group Therapy

From Yalom (1975)
   Instillation of hope
   Universality
   Imparting of information
   Altruism
   Corrective recapitulation of the primary family group
   Development of socializing techniques
   Imitative behavior
   Interpersonal learning

From Hogue and McLoughlin (1991)
   Self-responsibility
   Self-understanding
   Instillation of hope
   Group cohesiveness
   Catharsis
   Altruism
   Universality
   Interpersonal input
   Advice
   Interpersonal output

interpersonal groups. In distinction to traditional interpersonal group practice, the therapist facilitates the group's exploration of ways of working together while avoiding precipitous exposure of sensitive personal material and interpersonal overstimulation. Such interpersonal overstimulation may occur through unwarranted conflict resolution or even on occasion through friendships between group members. Although these factors may serve an important curative function for some members, their context and pace of their development must be modulated carefully by the therapist. As collaborators in the development of group norms and culture, group members are encouraged to set limits on their participation in a way that minimizes stress and maximizes their existing resources and positive qualities.

Overall, the stance of the therapist is that group members are never coerced or cajoled or confronted into participation in group process. Each member sets his or her own level of participation, which is not to be overstepped by the therapist or other members. Rather, as a member's participation develops in appropriate ways, it is rewarded. When the level of participation is too intimate, too intense, or too transferential, the therapist modulates the level of intensity, where appropriate clarifying, mediating, and setting limits.

Because it is a characteristic of all but the most structured psychotherapy groups to develop their own system of interpersonal dynamics, the role of the therapist is twofold. First, he or she must recognize when interpersonal interventions are useful in supporting behavioral change. Second, however, he or she must protect the group members from processing insight-focused issues that derive from group interpersonal dynamics that may lead to unsupported emotional turmoil. For example, uncovering and processing of transference material regarding the therapist or other group members is virtually always to be avoided. The Phase 2 section of the manual contains guidelines that assist the therapist through these and other group management issues that relate to the modulated use of interpersonal group techniques.

A NOTE ON PROVIDER FACTORS

In closing this transitional chapter of the manual, it is important to note explicitly that outcome, including the effects of the Life Goals Program, will not depend solely on member and therapist factors. Recall that the Life Goals Program is implemented in a setting that consists in its most simple form of a three-way collaboration among the individual with the illness, the therapist, and the prescribing clinician and perhaps other team members. In our clinical experience, the prescriber and caregiving system play a substantial role in determining the success that an individual has in implementing the disease management capabilities that he or she has developed in the Life Goals Program. Specific clinician factors of importance include treatment capabilities and especially the provider's accessibility and attitudes toward collaboratively including the individual being treated in decision making about his or her treatment.

It stands to reason that a collaborative attitude on the part of the prescriber would prove important in several key aspects of treatment plan development. These include defining target symptoms for treatment, choosing medication and psychotherapeutic treatments, and establishing the treatment alliance and parameters with individuals in treatment. These considerations were anticipated by Jamison and coworkers (1974), who conceived of compliance with lithium treatment during manic-depressive disorder as a function of several factors, including illness, personal, drug, and physician characteristics.

The National Depressive and Manic Depressive Association (NDMDA) member survey provides an informative look at treatment from the perspective of the person being treated (Lish et al., 1994). There is to our knowledge only one published study on provider attitudes toward treatment of manic-depressive disorder. Ludman and colleagues (2002), at the Group Health Cooperative of Puget Sound, have adapted an instrument to assess provider attitudes toward collaborative treatment. Their report provides psychometric assessment of the instrument, and also shows clear variability in provider attitudes toward collaboration. An unpublished pilot study that we conducted indicates that there is a wide variability in provider attitudes and also in resource accessibility. We developed and piloted a provider questionnaire (Bauer & Fogel, questionnaire, 1994) for both psychiatrists and nonphysician mental health providers to assess perceived resources and attitudes in the treatment of manic-depressive disorder, which we gave to 38 providers representing physician, nursing, and social work disciplines in several public and private treatment settings in Rhode Island.

Most striking among our pilot results was the great variability of provider attitudes reported. A sample of item responses will illustrate this. We found that only 14% of practitioners give reading material about manic-depressive disorder to the majority of persons with manic-depressive disorder whom they treat, and 60% of practitioners give reading material to less than 10%. When asked to identify "virtually automatic" reasons for hospitalization for mania from among six possible reasons (e.g., psychosis, endangerment to self/others, comorbid substance abuse), 29% identified only one reason, and 24% identified four or more, indicating a wide spectrum in willingness to consider individual (patient) factors in the decision. On another item, we found that 24% of practitioners agreed or strongly agreed that most persons with nonmanic manic-depressive spectrum disorders (type II and cyclothymia) actually have primary personality disorders. Thus, it is likely that attitudes toward persons with manic-depressive disorder and their management will vary substantially among providers.

To date, the Life Goals Program has been tested in several settings in which prescriber controls vary. As summarized in chapter 5, the intervention in the Department of Veterans Affairs study takes all manic-depressive management into a single program with a nurse and a psychiatrist who is trained in the collaborative practice model (Bauer, Williford, et al., 2001). The Group Health Cooperative Intervention (Simon et. al., 2001) uses the Life Goals Program in conjunction with the nurse facilitation, but the individual may be treated by one of a number of psychiatrists in the system who may or may not be oriented toward collaborative practice. A number of interventions are being studied in which there is even less control over, or input into, physician practice style. It remains to be seen how much the impact of the Life Goals Program depends on the attitudes, capabilities, and availabilities of treating clinicians; how much depends on system factors, such as clinician availability and access; and how much can be achieved solely through attention to the individual seeking optional treatment for the illness. The issue, however, is eminently researchable.

PART **II**

The Life Goals Program

Chapter 7

Phase 1:
Illness Management Skills

OVERVIEW OF THE PROGRAM
THERAPIST PREPARATION

The psychotherapist conducting the group therapy for individuals with manic-depressive disorder should be a trained professional therapist with a background in group psychotherapy, familiarity with the concepts and practices of cognitive and behavioral therapy, and a comprehensive understanding of the issues relevant to manic-depressive disorder. Review of this manual serves as a guide to facilitate the processing of specific agenda considered relevant for persons learning to cope with manic-depressive disorder. Although this manual is highly structured, much of the flow of the individual session will be determined by the characteristics of the group members and style of the therapist.

THERAPIST GUIDELINES

THE GROUP CLIMATE

The Life Goals Program provides a psychoeducational and problem-solving approach to the psychosocial treatment of manic-depressive disorder using cognitive, behavioral, and low-intensity interpersonal strategies. The therapist's role is to provide group members with information and facilitate group member integration of new concepts and behaviors. Group members learn how to develop accurate perceptions of themselves, their illness, and their environment, set realistic goals, and cope with problems more effectively

(Beck et al., 1979). Solutions to current everyday problems associated with living with manic-depressive disorder and its chronic and episodic sequelae provide the focus. Interactional dynamics are not emphasized but are evident in the generic curative functions of group therapy (Yalom, 1975). Interpretations of unconscious functions and interpersonal stimulation are avoided in favor of discussing the impact of specific behaviors on current life situations.

Consistent with Goodwin and Jamison's orientation (1990), this group therapy program takes the "long-lead" approach. It is characterized by a low-intensity style that views confrontation as intrusive and potentially relapsogenic (Kufferle, 1988). Similar to motivational interviewing techniques (Miller & Rollnick, 2002), behavior change is viewed as an individually determined process that must be experienced as personally motivated on the part of the group member. *In other words, the group member changes as he or she recognizes and compares the costs and benefits of particular behavior patterns.*

The therapist's role in this regard is to support the group member's effort to cope with the illness and facilitate processes that may activate development of more effective coping strategies when coping is ineffective. It is important that the individual is self-determined and integrates the processes associated with behavior change; otherwise, it is likely the group member will resist or drop out (Prochaska & DiClemente, 1984; Miller & Rollmack, 2002). For example, the processes of change described by Prochaska and DiClemente are (1) precontemplation—not thinking about making a behavior change, (2) contemplation—thinking about making a change in behavior, (3) action—taking action to change a behavior, and (4) maintenance—the behavior is changed. However, with a chronic illness, it is more accurate to view the process as one in which the group member may progress through the change cycle, yet revert back to the more familiar but ineffective behavior, and then address the same issues once again. This is considered the natural course of behavior change in managing a chronic illness. Thus, a member may make multiple attempts to implement a more effective coping strategy before it becomes stable.

THE THERAPIST'S TECHNICAL APPROACH

The group milieu is a nonthreatening climate of acceptance that encourages participation in self-directed learning and behavior change. Group members are encouraged to question and explore both their own ideas and those of others, as well as to share relevant experiences. A collaborative therapist–group member style is advocated to maximize each group member's sense of autonomy and responsibility over his or her behavior change.

The therapist is the expert regarding clinical and treatment issues, but recognizes and capitalizes on the variability of the group members' personal experiences. This approach supports the group member's self-esteem and sense of control over specific aspects of his or her illness and treatment. Each group member is indeed an expert in his or her own illness.

The didactic and process components of the group therapy program employ questioning and individual group member contributions in place of dry lectures and therapist-originated interpretations. Through questioning, the therapist elicits the group member's thinking, values, perceptions, and ultimately personally generated methods for solving problems (Beck et al., 1979).

The underlying approach to psychoeducation and development of illness management skills, which will appear throughout this manual, is to begin by stimulating group member contributions with *nonpersonalized* discussions of various aspects of the illness (e.g., by generating group discussion about the symptoms of mania). The therapist then moves each group member toward focusing on relevant aspects of *his or her* own illness (e.g., by notebook tasks, such as generating a personalized list of early warning signs of mania).

It has been our experience that group member ability to tolerate the stimulation of group interaction and self-revelation varies. Similarly, certain topics such as suicide and psychosis may be difficult for some group members to tolerate. It is strongly recommended that the therapist modulate group member (non)participation and offer support based on observation of verbal and nonverbal cues. Similarly, "process" issues (e.g., interpersonal style differences among group members or group members and the therapist) should be acknowledged but not allowed to disrupt the content agenda of the group session.

We are often asked about inclusion of members with schizoaffective disorder. Members with schizoaffective disorder have been involved in the group program since its inception. Typically, these members successfully learn illness management skills, benefit from the supportive culture, and tolerate the low-intensity cognitive, behavioral, and interpersonal techniques. Specific members with severe thought disorders have had difficulty tolerating the program milieu. It is suggested that the therapist meets and assesses all potential group members prior to commencing the program and establishes goals based on individual member attributes and symptom profiles.

It is important for the therapist to keep in mind that manic-depressive disorder has a variable and unpredictable course. Therapist flexibility is necessary to compensate for such variability in mood, cognition, behavior, and dependency characteristics of persons with manic-depressive disorder. The therapist places limits on extraneous issues, yet is ready to deal with the inevitable crises, which are presented to the group. Such crises should be handled as clinically appropriate in conjunction with the other treating clinicians.

If a group member gets off track in a noncrisis situation, the therapist lets him or her know that the issue is an important one, then identifies a time and place where it can be processed further. When possible, agenda relevant to the group can be extracted and reformulated for the appropriate session goal. Frequently, themes that group members bring up several times represent issues that can be reformatted into behaviorally driven goals in Phase 2.

Even the most compliant individuals may never achieve complete illness control. They are often vulnerable to some level of mood instability either spontaneously or due to psychosocial stressors. Additionally, change is typically a gradual process. Realistic expectations on the part of both group member and therapist will limit frustration, disappointment, denial, and resentment for both. Helping group members to deal constructively with limitations due to the illness is one of the overall goals of the program.

Retention of members in group therapy with chronic relapsing mental disorders such as manic-depressive disorder may be difficult. It requires that the therapist maintain an active outreach program that is committed to the group as a specific vehicle to promote, develop, and restore the optimal functioning of persons affected with manic-depressive disorder. The therapist should maintain an active membership outreach system to help absent members to overcome roadblocks that may affect their participation. Typically, members who adhere to the ground rules of the group program are always welcome to rejoin their cohort (described in Session 1).

OVERVIEW OF THE PHASES

SUMMARY AND IMPLEMENTATION

The program is structured into two sequential components: Phase 1 and Phase 2. The manual contains sections for each of the six sessions for Phase 1 and an outline of techniques for Phase 2. Phase 1 is agenda-driven, with each session divided into *focus points*. Phase 2 is content-driven rather than agenda-driven, and duration is individualized for each group member based on his or her needs and goals, as described below. An outline has been provided for the first session of Phase 2 for the therapist who would like guidelines for introducing group members to the ideas and concepts inherent in Phase 2 processes. Group sessions in each component meet once weekly for 75 minutes.

Groups consist of 5 to 7 group members for Phase 1 and 5 to 7 group members for Phase 2, each with one therapist. Groups are designed to have stable membership, but there will be times Phase 2 groups will be consolidated from multiple cohorts who have completed Phase 1. Coverage of all Phase 1 sessions is required prior to entry into Phase 2.

The level of content and language for both Phase 1 and Phase 2 is appropriate for those who are able to read and write at the sixth- to eighth-grade level. The structure is easily implemented in groups of more highly educated persons (e.g., in a university student health service). However, it is conceivable that the group procedures could be implemented with semiliterate members if additional assistance is given in the writing tasks. A French version (Aubrey, 2000) and a Spanish version (contact the authors) of the first edition are available. A Spanish version of this edition is under development.

It is probably best to begin Phase 1 when the person is not acutely distressed or disorganized, although by no means does he or she need to be symptom-free. Hypomanic and certainly manic or psychotic symptoms that lead to diminished insight and that occur early in establishment of the group may disrupt the group member's treatment alliance and group affiliation. However, such symptoms occurring once the treatment alliance and group cohesion have developed can usually be managed within the group context. It may be appropriate to begin group membership toward the end of hospitalization for a manic or depressive episode. In this situation, the group may serve to support the transition from inpatient to outpatient status by beginning the rehabilitative process and strengthening the group member's social network. Current substance dependence is not a contraindication to participation (Bauer et al., 1998), but current intoxication certainly is.

Effort has been taken to minimize cultural bias beyond the obvious necessity of depending on verbal and writing skills. Though structured, the manual is written so that content relevant to each group's specific background and needs can be covered. It is expected that each group's cultural background will be expressed as this content is developed.

The group meetings can be held in a small room, either with a conference table or without, if clipboards are provided, because some writing is required. Other equipment needed includes a flip chart, a whiteboard, and a means to hang up exhibits for display to the group. The exhibits consist of individual pages in the manual, which should be both enlarged for display and copied for distribution to the group members at the beginning of each session. Two exhibits in Phase 1 are to be made into wallet-sized cards. Once these are completed by the group members, they can be folded and laminated for durability.

We suggest making up a folder or notebook for handouts for each group member and keeping the folders at the clinic or hospital in a secure and confidential place. This is because the worksheets may be used throughout both phases, and it is easy to forget to bring them back if they go home. Often, the staff can provide a safer and more secure repository than the group members could at home. However, it is necessary to emphasize that the notebooks are their property and will be kept completely confidential.

PHASE 1

Phase 1 lasts 6 weeks and focuses on identifying early warning signs and triggers of impending episodes and developing coping skills to limit the recurrence and progression of episodes. Each session consists of several focus points to be covered. New members attend an orientation group that includes basic information on group structure and on manic-depressive disorder. Two weeks are then spent on mania and 2 weeks on depression. The sequence of the sessions was changed from the first edition of this manual based on feedback from multiple groups and colleagues who implemented the program. Starting with sessions about depression early in the group series was discouraging to the members, so we decided to address mania first. A sixth session has been added that consolidates self-management strategies into a comprehensive treatment plan that includes strategies for effective collaboration between the individual in treatment and his/her provider, daily activity and sleep pattern regulation, and making informed treatment decisions.

In the first session on mania and the first session on depression, group members work on identifying symptoms of the relevant affective episode, with the goal of ultimately generating a list of their own symptoms. In the second session on each type of mood episode, general discussion focuses on identification of ineffective and effective coping strategies, with the group member ultimately developing a list of his or her own patterns of response and incorporating ideas from other group members.

Each Phase 1 session begins with a *session rationale* and is followed by *session goals* and a summary of the *focus points.* The session rationale provides the reason(s) for the session goals. The session goals are behavioral outcomes for the group members that the therapist is attempting to facilitate. Each *focus point* contains a distinct idea and, basically, a smaller unit of the session goal. The therapist is provided with standardized guides for delivering various focus point ideas. These are the *therapist didactics.* They include the therapist's verbal presentation and questions intended to facilitate group discussion and elicit information from the group member about his or her values, ideas, and affect about relevant issues.

We recommend that the therapist use the therapist didactic verbatim. However, at certain times, group member needs may dictate changes in the manner of presentation. If so, the content of each should be covered with language as close as possible as specified in the manual. The *focus points* are designed to be delivered in the order written. However, in some cases, the flow of the group session may make it desirable to reorder certain focus points. For example, in Session 5, Depression Part 2, the therapist may decide to cover substance abuse and suicidality (Focus Point 3) before the group has fully completed Focus Point 2 because group members have brought up the topics early while generating the group list of responses to depression. In this case, it may make sense to dwell on substance abuse and suicidal behavior in depth at the time the issue arises. It is still necessary for the therapist to cover each focus point completely within its given session, ensuring that each session's content is entirely covered before going on to the next session.

The pace of the session should be determined by a combination of therapist judgment about how well the group members are integrating the group process and maintenance of the protocol. Naturally, the higher functioning group member will progress more quickly than the affective or thought-disordered group member.

It is likely that, at times, the group members will challenge the therapist with alternative ways of thinking about the disorder and coping strategies. The approach taken should be matter-of-fact inquiry that explores the group members' logic and thought, focusing on the costs and benefits of the specific approaches presented.

Each session should begin with a brief 1- or 2-minute review of the preceding session. That way, issues can be clarified and the session content reinforced. Part of the review should focus on the task of the preceding session. This gives time to complete assignments to the more severely ill group members, as well as a message about the value of the assignment to the group at large.

Completion of the Phase 1 component is a prerequisite to advancing to Phase 2. The skills developed in Phase 2 presuppose some facility with the skills developed in Phase 1. In addition, this sequential format delivers the message that one must first learn to manage the illness before addressing meaningful life goals effectively.

PHASE 2

The focus of Phase 2 is to address the psychological, social, and occupational aspects of manic-depressive disorder as they affect the individual's life. Whereas group sessions for Phase 1 are designed to impart specific information and generate specific group member responses, Phase 2 employs a semistructured format to address goals identified by the individual group member. The therapist assists the group member to develop a specific goal in the realm of illness management, social, occupational, or leisure function that is of importance to him or her. The goal is then articulated and reformulated into specific terms by which the group member and therapist can measure progress. Goals may include such tasks as improving medication adherence, sleep hygiene, dating, entering vocational training, job seeking, or increasing social contacts or avocations during leisure time.

Regardless of the goal identified, it is to be formulated in terms *that make the group member the main agent,* with minimal dependence on others' behavior for the success of the task. For example, "getting married" depends on another person, as well as on the group member's own behavior; in contrast, "asking someone out on a date" is formulated as being a task more under the group member's control.

The duration of participation in Phase 2 is not based on a specific number of sessions, but is determined by successful completion of goals. When a group member's goal has been achieved, either planned termination is initiated or the group member formulates a second goal, or a further iteration of the first goal, which may occur with an individual who is practicing strategies for effective (hypo)manic or depressive episode management, and continues the process.

In formulating and working toward these goals, a wide range of issues in coping with illness may emerge and need to be worked through to accomplish the task at hand. Examples include problems with the collaborative relationship between the member and his/her provider, a lack of self-esteem, hopelessness, denial/acceptance of the illness, feelings about previous treatment and episode experiences, concerns about the impact of the illness on family and relationships, concerns about genetic transmission, and side effects of medication (see, e.g., Goodwin & Jamison, 1990, pp. 725–740). In addition, group members may address ambivalence about the diagnosis and the need for medication, as well as the impact of social stigma in the context of a supportive peer group.

Group members are assisted in this process through therapist and peer feedback. In this manner, the various curative functions of interpersonal group therapy (see chapter 6) contribute to the curative functions of the treatment itself. These include imparting information, instilling hope, establishing the universality of the group member's experience, and building morale through group cohesiveness. In conjunction with this, cognitive and behavioral strategies are used to help group members overcome roadblocks to successful problem-solving strategies, such as addressing self-defeating beliefs and values.

Entrance into the Phase 2 group may also be an ongoing occurrence, because when some group members finish Phase 2, others who have completed Phase 1 will join to take their place, providing for heterogeneity with regard to functional adaption to the illness and problem-solving sophistication. This may be considered an advantage, because the more experienced group members can begin to function as resource persons for those less experienced. This principle has provided an underlying strategy for self-help groups for affective illness, such as those sponsored by the National Depressive and Manic-Depressive Association (NDMDA; now Depression and Bipolar Support Alliance, DBSA), and in sponsorship relationships developed in 12-step programs for substance abuse.

PHASE 1 AND PHASE 2 MATERIALS LISTS

Therapist monitors for Phase 1 (to be completed by supervisor or alternate).

PHASE 1

SESSION 1 ORIENTATION

Therapist:
Life Goals Program Progress Note
Black- or whiteboard with marker
Overhead or poster-sized exhibits:
    The Mood Disorder Spectrum
    Brain
    Neurotransmission
    Psychiatric Stigma
    Strategies to Cope with Psychiatric Stigma

Group members:
Group meeting schedule and locations
Pad and pencils
Handouts or notebooks:
    The Mood Disorder Spectrum
    Brain
    Neurotransmission
    Psychiatric Stigma
    Strategies to Cope with Psychiatric Stigma

SESSION 2, MANIA PART 1

Therapist:
Life Goals Program Progress Note
Black- or whiteboard with marker
Overhead or poster-sized exhibits:
    Personal Mania Profile
    Personal Triggers of a Manic Episode

Group members:
Group meeting schedule and locations
Pad and pencils
Handouts or notebooks:
    Personal Mania Profile
    Personal Triggers of a Manic Episode

SESSION 3, MANIA PART 2

Therapist:
Life Goals Program Progress Note
Black- or whiteboard with marker
Overhead or poster-sized exhibits:
    Responses to Manic Episode/Stress That May Trigger a Manic Episode—1:
        Costs and Benefits
    Responses to Manic Episode/Stress 2: Costs and Benefits
    Action Plan: Outline of Coping Strategies for Mania/Stress That May
        Trigger a Manic Episode
    Action Plan for Mania

Group members:
Group meeting schedule and locations
Pad and pencils
Handouts or notebooks:
    Responses to Manic Episode/Stress That May Trigger a Manic Episode—1:
        Costs and Benefits
    Responses to Manic Episode/Stress 2: Costs and Benefits
    Action Plan: Outline of Coping Strategies for Mania/Stress That May
        Trigger a Manic Episode
    Action Plan for Mania

SESSION 4, DEPRESSION PART 1

Therapist:
Life Goals Program Progress Note
Black- or whiteboard with marker
Overhead or poster-sized exhibits:
    Personal Depression Profile
    Personal Triggers of a Depressive Episode

Group members:
Group meeting schedule and locations
Pad and pencils
Handouts or notebooks:
    Personal Depression Profile
    Personal Triggers of a Depressive Episode

SESSION 5, DEPRESSION PART 2

Therapist:
Life Goals Program Progress Note
Black- or whiteboard with marker

Overhead or poster-sized exhibits:

Responses to Depressive Episode/Stress That May Trigger a Manic Episode—1: Costs and Benefits

Responses to Depression Episode/Stress 2: Costs and Benefits

Action Plan: Outline of Coping Strategies for Depression/Stress That May Trigger a Depressive Episode

Action Plan for Depression

Group members:

Group meeting schedule and locations

Pad and pencils

Handouts or notebooks:

Responses to Depressive Episode/Stress That May Trigger a Depressive Episode—1: Costs and Benefits

Responses to Depression Episode/Stress 2: Costs and Benefits

Action Plan: Outline of Coping Strategies for Depression/Stress That May Lead to a Depressive Episode

Action Plan for Depression

SESSION 6, TREATMENTS FOR MANIC-DEPRESSIVE DISORDER

Therapist:

Life Goals Program Progress Note

Black- or whiteboard with marker

Overhead or poster-sized exhibits:

Goals of Treatment for Manic-Depressive Disorder

Personal Care Plan

- Personal Daily Activity and Sleep Schedule
- Current Medications
- Costs and Benefits of Treatment
- Self-help and Pychotherapy

Essentials of a Collaborative Relationship

Good Sleep Habits

Major Medication Classes Used to Treat Manic-Depressive Disorder

Making Informed Decisions and Evaluating Treatment

Psychotherapies for Manic-Depressive Disorder

Group members:

Group meeting schedule and locations

Pad and pencils

Handouts or notebooks:

Goals of Treatment For Manic-Depressive Disorder

Personal Care Plan

- Personal Daily Activity and Sleep Schedule

- Current Medications
- Costs and Benefits of Treatment
- Self-help and Psychotherapy

Essentials of a Collaborative Relationship
Good Sleep Habits
Major Medication Classes Used to Treat Manic-Depressive Disorder
Making Informed Decisions and Evaluating Treatment
Psychotherapies for Manic-Depressive Disorder
List of local NDMDA and NAMI chapters

PHASE 2

Therapist:
Life Goals Program Progress Notes
Life Goals Worksheets
Black- or whiteboard with marker
Overhead or poster-sized exhibits for Sessions 1–6

Group members:
Group meeting schedule and locations
Pad and pencils
Handouts or notebooks containing sessions 1–6 worksheets
Life Goals worksheets

SESSION 1: ORIENTATION

SESSION RATIONALE

This session is designed to orient the group members to the group therapy environment, to begin to establish the therapeutic relationship, to provide an objective description of manic-depressive disorder, and to explore the impact of psychiatric stigma on treatment for manic-depressive disorder.

SESSION GOALS

1. Group members will be acclimated to the group therapy treatment program, including guidelines for interaction among members.
2. Group members will learn that manic-depressive disorder is a biologically based mental illness.
3. Group members will learn that manic-depressive disorder has a relapsing and remitting course and a widely variable pattern of symptoms and symptom severity.
4. Group members will begin to identify stigma issues relevant to their illness that will facilitate insight regarding their active participation in their treatment and self-care/monitoring activities.

FOCUS POINTS

Focus Point 1: Establish the therapeutic relationship/environment.

Establishing the therapeutic relationship and the group therapy norms are of primary importance in the initial sessions. The therapist's explanation of the program goals and modeling of a supportive relationship will enhance an environment for the development of trust and rapport.

Focus Point 2: The Mood Disorder Spectrum: Disorder severity and patterns.

Symptoms of manic-depressive disorder represent exaggerations of normal mood fluctuations and occur in multiple degrees of severity ranging from cyclothymic disorder to manic-depressive disorder type II, to manic-depressive disorder type I. The Mood Disorder Spectrum is a descriptive tool meant to provide a way to understand the range of variability of mood disorders.

Focus Point 3: Normalize symptoms of psychosis.

Mood episodes may be accompanied by psychosis. Psychosis may be experienced as delusions, hallucinations, paranoia, and other perceptual disturbances.

Focus Point 4: Provide accurate information about the causes of manic-depressive disorder.

Manic-depressive disorder is a chronic illness that results from biologic dysfunction, probably best understood as an impairment in the brain's ability to regulate activity in the neurons (brain cells) involved in mood regulation. Genetic vulnerability, psychosocial, and other environmental factors influence the degree of illness severity, episode recurrence, and each individual's response to the illness.

Focus Point 5: Recognize the high prevalence of manic-depressive symptoms and the stigma attached to manic-depressive disorder.

Manic-depressive disorder is a mental illness beset with psychiatric stigma. Psychiatric stigma influences group members' beliefs. It may lead to a sense of being different, a sense of shame, denial, and impaired illness management skills. Increasing member awareness about the influence of psychiatric stigma may enhance group members' positive self-perception and promote the development of effective illness management skills.

SCRIPT

FOCUS POINT 1: Establish the therapeutic relationship/environment.

> **Therapist Directions**
> Ask group members to fill out name tags. Begin the group by welcoming participants and introducing yourself and your coleader. Ask group members to go around and say their names.

Therapist Didactic.   Welcome to the Life Goals group. You may know of manic-depressive disorder by its other name, bipolar disorder. We sometimes use the term *bipolar* to emphasize the opposite "poles" or extremes of mood swings that can occur. We use the term *manic-depressive* because we think it describes the disorder more accurately since mania and depression are not always opposite. However, either term is okay—use whichever one you are most comfortable with. This program has two parts: Phase 1 and Phase 2. Phase 1 meets six times. During these meetings, we will be discussing things like what manic-depressive disorder is, the impact of psychiatric stigma and how it may influence your treatment, treatments for manic-depression, the signs and symptoms of depression and mania, triggers that can bring about an episode of depression or mania, and ways that you can effectively cope with this condition. Some of the topics that we cover in this group may be new to you, and some may be a review. We think that it is important for you to have an opportunity to focus on how to best manage your manic-depressive disorder, whether or not the topics we will be discussing are new to you. You will also have the opportunity to ask questions. Today we will be talking about what manic-depressive disorder is, its causes, and how psychiatric stigma may affect your treatment.

This program covers multiple topics. Their complexity may be challenging. We do not want you to think in six sessions we expect you will have all that is needed to manage this condition. These groups are a beginning. In fact, we will often review this information during Phase 2.

- I wonder what people thought we would be talking about in this group?
- Does anyone have any particular concerns about being here?
- I wonder what other people have told you about group treatment?
- Has anyone been in a group such as this before? What was that experience like?
- Any other thoughts about being here?

There are some very important guidelines for being a member of a group such as this. Most important, we promise to keep what people say here confidential and never talk about the group members and what they say to people outside the group. There is one exception—that is, if a group member is in need of urgent care, I will discuss it with a member of the treatment team. For example, if a person is high risk for suicide or in other ways a danger to him or herself or others. Tell us what you want or if you are having a problem. We are here to help you plan a way to cope with problems, should they come up. Should something go wrong, we ask that you touch base with us before you leave for the day. If you are going to miss an appointment, let us know. Everyone in this group should feel free to participate, saying as much or as little as he or she feels comfortable. We ask that you not show up to group under the influence of alcohol or drugs.

- Does anyone want to comment or have any questions?
- How do these guidelines sound to you? Are there other guidelines you want to talk about?

We will be working here as a group for weeks or longer. During that time, you'll be working on issues and problems common to many of you. At times you may be of help to others in the group, and at times others may be helpful to you. Part of group building is giving and getting feedback or advice from your associates here. It is our experience that feedback and advice can be helpful if it is wanted by the other person, and not so helpful if it's not wanted. So we ask that you find out first if your advice is wanted before giving it. That way, people will be able to decide for themselves if they are able to hear advice and feedback at that time. Something else we learned is that feedback is most helpful if it is offered as a suggestion or through an example of a personal experience, but not as a criticism.

- What do you think about this?
- Is everyone comfortable with this?

Therapist Directions
In some cases, it may be helpful to have the group write out a statement, or contract, agreeing to abstain from alcohol and drugs, as well as guidelines for giving feedback, then have all group members sign the agreement.

FOCUS POINT 2: The Mood Disorder Spectrum: Disorder severity and patterns.

Therapist Didactic.   Normal moods fluctuate in response to the things that happen in everyday life. In manic-depressive disorder, moods go beyond the everyday ups and downs. The "downs" consist of sad or blue moods, sometimes with a sense that things are bad and will never get better. The "ups" are harder to describe. Many times the ups in manic-depressive disorder are happy and optimistic. Other times they are mostly irritable. Often the main feeling is one of "speediness" or "raciness"—as though a person has too much energy and cannot turn off his or her motor. Sometimes the ups are just plain racy and irritable.

Mood swings vary in degree of severity. This chart can help us to see the degrees of mood extremes, ranging from normal to depression and mania. This is called the "Mood Disorder Spectrum."

Therapist Directions
Display Exhibit 1, "The Mood Disorder Spectrum." Point out each mood type during the discussion.

Normal moods are a feeling response to everyday occurrences or events. There is some normal mood variability, so that every day we go through minor ups and downs, even without bad stress or good things happening to us. In some mood disorders, people have a consistently depressed mood. Even when good things happen, they remain depressed. Examples are dysthymic disorder and major depression.

EXHIBIT 1   The Mood Disorder Spectrum

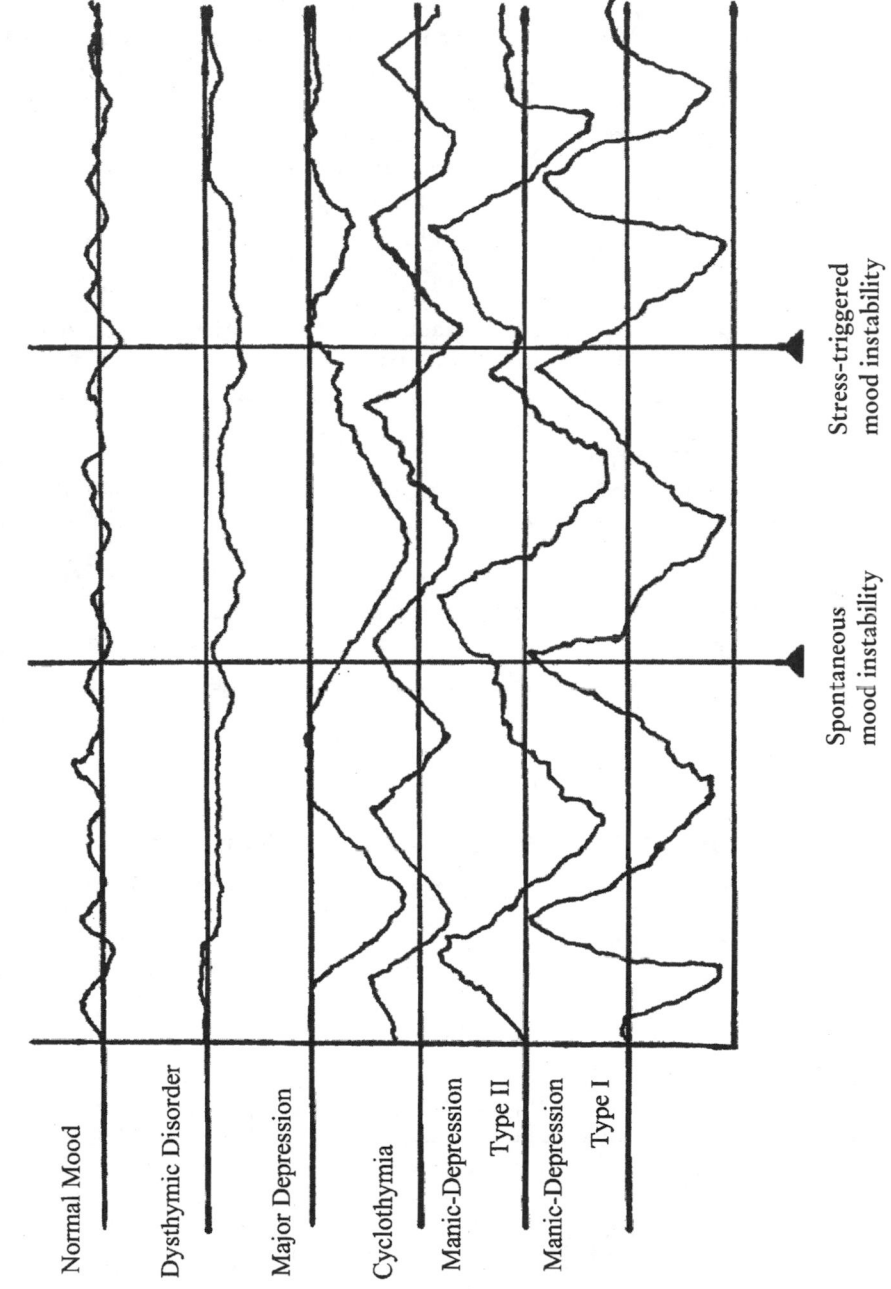

Normal Mood

Dysthymic Disorder

Major Depression

Cyclothymia

Manic-Depression
Type II

Manic-Depression
Type I

Spontaneous
mood instability

Stress-triggered
mood instability

In cyclothymia and the manic-depressive disorders, type I and type II, up and down mood swings are more severe than normal. Sometimes they may be triggered by stress. Stress may be any change in our routine, good or bad. However, major mood swings can occur even when there are no good or bad things happening. So, in manic-depressive disorder, major mood swings can happen spontaneously or in response to stress.

In manic-depressive type I, the manic period is more severe than in type II. We call the milder up periods in type II hypomania, which means "mild mania." In both manic-depressive types I and II, the periods of depression are equally severe.

- Do any of these patterns seem familiar to you? Perhaps they have happened to you or to someone you know.

Therapist Directions
Referring to Exhibit 1 ("The Mood Disorder Spectrum"), point out examples of episodes that are induced by stress and episodes that occur spontaneously.

- What has your experience been like? Has anyone had an experience with depression or mania that seemed to happen out of the blue, without any cause?
- Can anyone recall an episode being triggered by stress?

FOCUS POINT 3: Normalize symptoms of psychosis.

Therapist Directions
When discussing psychosis, it is important to be general at first. Group members may be very defensive about their psychotic experiences. It is usually not helpful to say to group members that these experiences are not real, because often they are quite vivid to the group member; for example, they may be considered as a spiritual experience, or be related to cultural or intrapsychic factors. Therefore, it is important to take a nonjudgmental approach, while at the same time not colluding with the group member by supporting his or her interpretation of reality as accurate.

Therapist Didactic.   Often, extremes in mood, either up or down, will mean an altered sense of reality. This is sometimes experienced as what professionals call "psychosis." *Psychosis* is a medical term. It may be experienced as hallucinations, that is, seeing or hearing things that others cannot. Or a person may have delusions, or unusual beliefs, such as believing that special messages are being delivered to you. Paranoia is an example of a delusion. Paranoia means extreme suspiciousness, such as believing others are colluding against you. It is more than just the supersensitivity that depressed people get when they are with other people. These experiences can be confusing, frightening, or embarrassing. For some people, at some times, particular hallucinations and delusions may be comforting.

- Can you think of experiences that you've heard about or others had during high or low moods that were confusing, frightening, or comforting?

FOCUS POINT 4: Provide accurate information about the causes of manic-depressive disorder.

Therapist Directions
Refer to Exhibit 2 ("Brain"), and Exhibit 3 ("Neurotransmission") and discuss neural transmission and the organization of the brain as it pertains to mood regulation. Provide details about the biochemical basis of the disorder based on the level of sophistication of the group members. The depth of exposition will depend greatly on the educational and cultural background of the group members. Clearly, a presentation geared toward college or graduate students and professionals will be at a different level from one for group members who have not finished high school. For any level of presentation, the most important message to get across is that manic-depressive disorder has a biological basis and that the disordered organ is the brain. A sample presentation is provided below.

Therapist Didactic. The brain is where all thought, feeling, and behavior originates. It is made up of billions of cells. Let's look together at Exhibit 2. Here we see the cortex and the cerebellum. Each section of the brain has a specific function. For example, the cerebellum is where centers are located that help us to balance while walking upright. In the cross-sectional view of the brain we can see several more areas. The outer layer labeled "frontal lobe" is where thoughts are produced. The shaded section below the outer layer of the brain is called the "limbic system." The limbic system is where many centers for mood regulation are located. The bottom portion of the brain that is shaped like a knob is the medulla. This is where basic bodily

EXHIBIT 2   Brain: Surface View from the Side

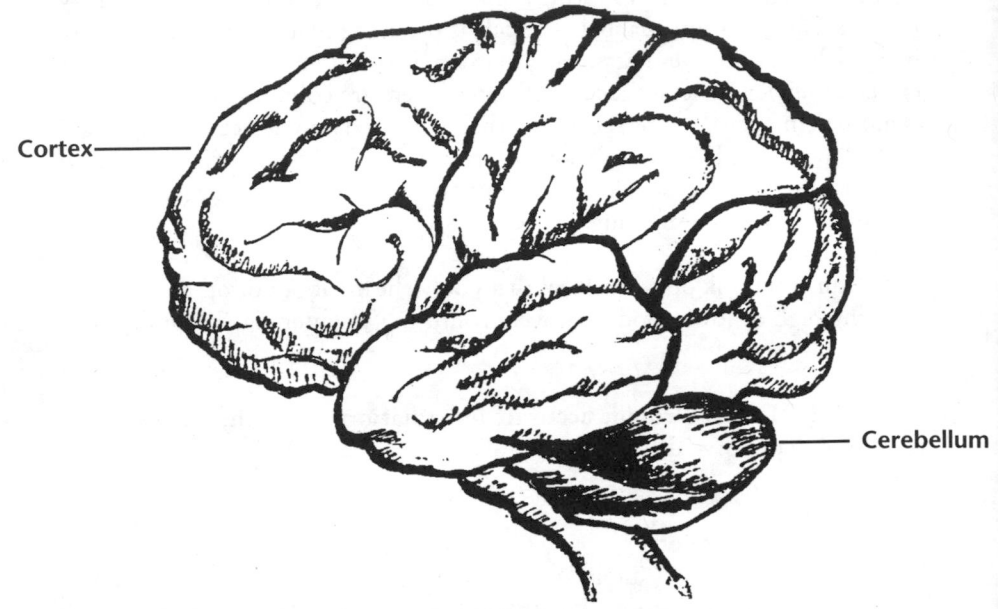

Cortex

Cerebellum

Brain: Cross-section view at the midpoint.

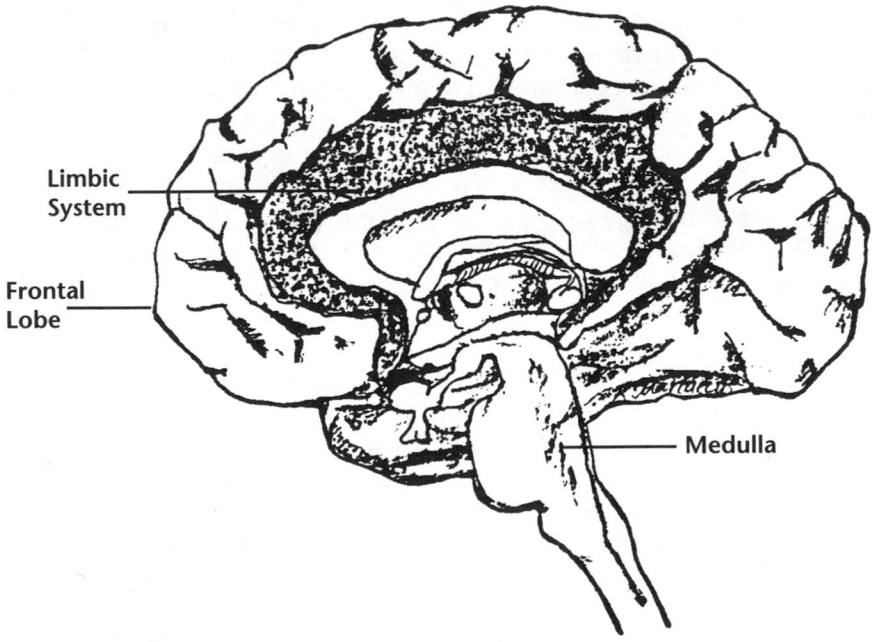

Limbic
System

Frontal
Lobe

Medulla

EXHIBIT 3 Neurotransmission

Manic-depressive disorder may be caused by changes in:

1. Electric impulses in the nerve cell

2. Neurotransmitter supply in the nerve cell

3. Neurotransmitter release from the nerve cell

4. Neurotransmitter binding to the target nerve cell

5. Effect of neurotransmitter binding on electrical impulses in the target nerve cell

Electrical impulses release chemicals called neurotransmitters.
Neurotransmitters send messages to the target nerve cell.
Chemical changes in the target nerve cell trigger new electrical impulses.

Note that each of these is a place where medications that treat manic-depressive disorder may act.

functions are regulated, for example, appetite and sex drive. Notice that although there are many parts of the brain, they are interconnected. This explains how changes in mood affect how we think and behave.

- Any questions?

Next let's take a look at Exhibit 3, Neurotransmission. Neurotransmission is the delivery of nerve impulses across a synapse. The synapse is the space between nerve cells. Neurotransmission is facilitated by neurotransmitters. A neurotransmitter is a chemical substance in brain cells. These chemicals regulate brain cell activity. You may have heard of several neurotransmitters such as GABA, serotonin, epinephrine, and dopamine. When neurotransmitters from one brain cell are released into the synapse, they attach to an adjacent brain cell in places called receptor sites. This activity creates an electric impulse that activates cellular activity. The numbered items on Exhibit 3 explain more about brain cells and neurotransmission. Manic-depressive disorder occurs when there is an imbalance in this system. Medications used to treat manic-depression may act to stabilize this condition at one or more of the areas numbered on the diagram.

FOCUS POINT 5: Recognize the high prevalence of manic-depressive symptoms and the stigma attached to manic-depression.

Therapist Didactic. Manic-depressive disorder affects 1 in 100 people in the United States. It affects people from all walks of life. Even some famous people have this. Sometimes having a condition like this can make a person feel alone because, as with other problems, people do not generally talk about it openly. Discussing having manic-depressive disorder is not usually part of common conversation. People may fear the discrimination associated with psychiatric stigma. Basically, lots of people have it, most do not discuss it, and lots of people are living okay with it.

- Have you met other people with this condition before coming here?
- How was their life?
- Have you heard of famous people with this condition?
- Do you think people with manic-depressive disorder share problems similar to people who do not have it?

Therapist Directions
During this discussion, generate two lists of group member contributions, one about *sources* of information about manic-depressive disorder, the second, the *causes* of manic-depressive disorder they heard about. Review each list. Highlight the accurate causes of manic-depression.

Therapist Didactic.   Our ideas about manic-depressive disorder come from our learning from other people, such as family, friends, neighbors, and health care providers. As a culture, we are also greatly influenced by the media— movies, TV, books, newspapers, and magazines.

- Where did you learn about manic-depressive disorder?
- What were the causes of manic-depressive disorder you heard about?

Some of the ideas about manic-depressive disorder people have are accurate, and others inaccurate. Our personal feelings and knowledge about manic-depressive disorder are influenced by our learning from other people. Psychiatric stigma is caused by the inaccurate beliefs people have about manic-depressive disorder. It may be recognized as negative attitudes, restrictions, and discrimination. Psychiatric stigma is fueled by stereotypes, myths, and misconceptions. It influences the way people think and feel about having manic-depressive disorder and the way other people act toward a person who has it. Psychiatric stigma is an experience people with manic-depressive disorder live with every day. It can have a powerful impact on the way a person with manic-depressive disorder thinks, feels, and manages his/her condition.

Therapist Directions
The following discussion is meant to facilitate group member insight about how psychiatric stigma affects their lives and the decisions they make managing their illness. List group member ideas, thoughts, and beliefs under the heading "Thoughts." Facilitate this discussion with an emphasis on eliciting general versus personal information from the group members. Next, generate a list of "Feelings" from specific information listed under the heading "Thoughts." In a third column, under the heading "Behavior," list the reactions a person may have to the thoughts and feelings listed. The main point of this exercise is to elicit the negative effects psychiatric stigma has on the way group members think, feel, and react in response to having manic-depression. Display Exhibit 4A if needed to seed the discussion.

- What are some of the negative comments about manic-depressive disorder you heard about before coming to this group?
- How might these comments influence the way a person feels about having a diagnosis of manic-depression?
- How might these ideas and feelings influence the way a person reacts to having a diagnosis of manic-depression?

Therapist Didactic.   It is clear that psychiatric stigma influences the way we think, feel, and react in response to having or knowing someone who has manic-depression or other mental illness. When faced with a challenge, whether psychiatric stigma or something else, people have typical responses to help ease the pain or keep things going as well as possible. These responses are called coping responses or adaptations. Basically, people make an effort to adjust to what is happening to them the best way they know how.

• What are some of the things people can do to cope with psychiatric stigma?

Therapist Directions
Generate a list of group member contributions about coping strategies to manage psychiatric stigma. Reinforce all participation.

Therapist Didactic.   How a person copes with psychiatric stigma depends on the specific individual, group, or social situation. Different coping strategies may be helpful for different people at different times.

Therapist Directions
Display Exhibit 4B, "Strategies to Cope with Psychiatric Stigma." Discuss items listed and point out commonalities with the group list. Do not challenge the reactions of group members.

Therapist Didactic.   So far today we talked about manic-depressive disorder as a condition that affects 1 in 100 people. It is caused by a chemical imbalance in the part of the brain that regulates mood. Stress, either good or bad, and any change in routine can bring about a mood swing, but this can also happen without an apparent cause. Sometimes the symptoms can be frightening because changes in thought and perception can accompany a mood swing. For example, a person may mistakenly hear voices or believe someone is out to get him or her. These changes in mood and perception affect behavior, and a person can have problems at home and at work. We also discussed psychiatric stigma and learned that it may affect the way a person thinks, feels, and reacts to having manic-depressive disorder. Some strategies to cope with stigma were discussed. Most important, stigma is tied closely to the way an individual perceives himself or herself, and learns to manage manic-depressive disorder.

EXHIBIT 4A   Psychiatric Stigma

Thoughts	Feelings	Behaviors
Examples		
• Less value or worth	• Shame	• Rejecting the diagnosis
• Changed identity	• Suffering	• Not taking meds
	• Doubt	• Not reporting symptoms
	• Fear	
	• Demoralization	

EXHIBIT 4B   Strategies to Cope with Psychiatric Stigma

1. Identify and secure places in life with people who do not stigmatize and get support:
   • Friends and understanding family members
   • Therapy (group, individual, family)
   • Community support, self-help groups

2. Learn illness management techniques and coping skills.
   • If available, work with a partner

3. Education: Tell trusted others about the illness in order to prevent misunderstandings.

4. Do not share the illness with potential "stigmatizers" in order to avoid potential discriminatory behaviors.

In the following weeks, we will be talking about the manic and depressive phases of manic-depression and working on learning ways to effectively cope with mood episodes. Many of the coping skills we will be discussing have been found to be useful for many people. In Session 6, we will discuss the treatments for manic-depressive disorder, and each of you will complete a personal care plan.

- Do you have any questions?

Therapist Directions
Thank group members for their attendance and participation. Discuss parking arrangements. Tell group members you will hold on to their notebooks for safe keeping if they would like. Say good-bye. Remind the group of the next meeting time and place.

SESSION 2: MANIA PART 1

SESSION RATIONALE

This session is designed to facilitate group member self-awareness of signs, symptoms, and triggers of a (hypo)manic episode that will enable him or her to participate in illness monitoring and effective coping behaviors.

SESSION GOALS

1. Group members will develop a personal list of signs and symptoms of (hypo)mania.
2. Group members will identify the variability of their episode patterns.
3. Group members will develop a personal list of actual and potential triggers of (hypo)mania.

FOCUS POINTS

Focus Point 1: Identify session goals of developing self-monitoring skills for recognizing (hypo)mania and its triggers.

Manic-depressive disorder is characterized by extremes in mood and related changes in behavior and cognition. Symptom recognition is the first step, leading to a coping strategy intervention that can prevent, limit, or help the group member to cope with a (hypo)manic episode.

Focus Point 2: Identify the pattern of episode recurrence, and the personal signs and symptoms of mania. Construct a Personal Mania Profile.

A manic episode can occur in different ways. The symptoms may come on slowly, gradually worsening, or they may come on quickly, sometimes directly switching from another mood state (e.g., to or from depression), or the symptoms of mania and depression may be intermixed. To efficiently monitor their illness, group members need to be aware of their specific pattern. Individual patterns are variable in length and frequency. Validate each group member's illness pattern through discussion of the variability in symptoms and patterns of occurrence. Encourage group members to become aware of symptoms of mania recognized by family, friends, and coworkers.

Focus Point 3: Identify personal triggers of (hypo)mania. Complete a list of Personal Triggers of a manic episode.

A manic episode can be precipitated by stressful life events, mental or physical changes, or nonadherence to the plan of care (medication, sleep, hygiene).

Helping group members to recognize potential triggers can be a valuable illness management and prevention strategy. However, the illness can recur spontaneously despite good medical and self-management.

SCRIPT

FOCUS POINT 1: Identify session goals of developing self-monitoring skills for recognizing (hypo)mania and its triggers.

Therapist Directions
Welcome group members back, and distribute workbooks to those who left them behind following the prior session. Distribute worksheets for this session to anyone who left his or her workbook at home.

Therapist Didactic.   Last week we discussed the guidelines for being a member of this group, the basic biology associated with manic-depression and how symptoms vary in severity and may include psychosis. We also discussed psychiatric stigma. It affects how people with manic-depression think, feel, and react to having this condition. It can cause problems taking care of yourself and collaborating with your health care providers.

Today, and next week, we will be talking about the manic phase of manic-depressive disorder. You will recall that it is a characteristic of manic-depressive disorder to have mood swings, both highs and lows. It is the "highs" that we refer to as mania. Discussions about mania may stimulate difficult memories and feelings. Please be assured we are sensitive to these issues and want to make sure that everyone is comfortable. We do not expect group members to unwillingly share personal information,

- Does anyone have any questions?

Some people with manic-depression experience only mild high symptoms and don't need hospitalization. This milder form of mania is called hypomania. To simplify our discussions here, I'll often refer to the "highs" in both type 1 and type 2 manic-depression as mania, although mania and hypomania are not exactly the same. There is a lot of variation in how people experience mania. Even though there are symptoms common to many people, mania is a very personal experience. By the end of today's session, you will make a list of your own personal signs and symptoms of mania, describe the pattern of how your manias occur, and identify personal stressors we refer to as "triggers" that may cause or worsen mania. The purpose of knowing your personal symptoms of mania is to be aware of when an episode begins so you may respond to the early symptoms with a well-thought-out plan to prevent, limit, or help you to cope with a manic episode.

- We will begin by looking at the symptoms of mania that are common to a lot of people. Then we will identify any symptoms that you think we may have left out. Does anyone have any questions so far?
- What are some other words people use to refer to mania besides *high?*
- Some people feel good during a manic episode. Others feel racy, irritable, and depressed. What is it like for you?

Therapist Directions

In conducting the following discussion, special attention should be paid to the issue of guilt and remorse over things done during a manic episode. Often, group members will find these experiences so embarrassing or shameful that they will be hesitant to talk about them. Watch for both verbal and nonverbal cues and emphasize toleration and nonjudgmental feedback among group members. On the other hand, sometimes group members aggrandize their manic experiences. This may be minimized by redirecting group members to focus on the full range of manic symptoms and their negative impact.

FOCUS POINT 2: Identify the pattern of episode recurrence and the personal signs and symptoms of mania. Construct a Personal Mania Profile.

Let's talk about the signs and symptoms of mania. Mania is experienced as the way a person thinks, feels, and acts. So, in talking about mania, it can help to think about it in this way. A person's thoughts, feelings, and actions are actually his or her signs and symptoms. At this point we will focus on the full range of manic symptoms. Later, you will have the opportunity to more fully describe your individual experiences if you'd like to.

Therapist Directions

Display three headings on the board: **Thoughts, Feelings, Behaviors.** Query group members, and write each of their contributions as stated under the appropriate heading. Once the group members generate a list, display Exhibit 5 ("Personal Mania Profile"). Because of the quality of perceptual and cognitive impairment that often accompanies mania, as well as amnesia about the symptoms of an active episode, recall of mania can be difficult.

- What are some examples of thoughts, feelings, and actions or behaviors that a person might have when he or she is manic?
- Sometimes it helps to think about your most recent or severe episode in order to remember the signs and symptoms of mania.
- During mania, many people do things that they later regret. Mania may have been a painful and embarrassing experience. It may also be difficult to remember. Many people experience amnesia about their manic episodes.

Please open your notebooks to Exhibit 5 ("Personal Mania Profile"). Please take the next few minutes to check off the symptoms on this list that represent your experience of mania. Although some of the symptoms on this list are common to many people's experience of mania, your list is a **"cluster"** of symptoms that is personal to you. So fill in your personal symptoms that are not already listed in the blank spaces provided. Your personal symptoms may be subtle or distinct changes in your way of thinking, feeling, or behaving that are unique to you. Sometimes people close to you may recognize symptoms of mania that you overlook. For that reason, we have spaces on the worksheets for you to include the feedback of family, friends, or coworkers. If you are working on managing this condition with someone close to you, you might think about asking him or her about this and include his or her responses on your worksheet later. Mark an *F* in the space provided for those symptoms people close to you recognize.

Next, mark with an *E* the signs and symptoms that you recognize as the earliest to emerge in the box provided under the "E" column. If you can recognize the early symptoms, you can begin to cope earlier, before the mania gets out of hand.

- Any questions?

The thoughts, feelings, and behaviors on your Personal Mania Profile are the core symptoms of your manic or hypomanic episode. Manic signs and symptoms can occur in a variety of ways:

1. They can come on slowly and gradually increase in severity over time.
2. They can come on quite quickly and directly switch from one mood state to another.
3. A person can have both manic and depressive symptoms intermixed.

EXHIBIT 5   Personal Mania Profile

1. Place a check mark next to symptoms that you experience.
2. Mark an *E* next to those that are particular early warning signs.
3. Mark an *X* next to those that come on quickly without warning.
4. Mark an *F* next to those symptoms that are recognized by family, friends, and coworkers.
5. Add other symptoms not included on the list in the blank spaces provided.

√   E   X   F   **Thoughts**

Difficulty with concentration and memory

More religious thoughts

Thoughts about having special powers

Racing or sped up thoughts

The rest of the world is in slow motion

Thoughts jump from one idea to another quickly

Paranoia: that people are plotting against you

Unreal concerns that you are worthless or evil

Hallucinations: unreal voices or visions

Thoughts of suicide

_____

_____

√   E   X   F   **Feelings**

Feeling "high," completely optimistic, euphoric

Feeling depressed

More energy

Feeling impatient, irritable

Feelings change quickly

Feeling unusually self-confident or invulnerable

Know-it-all attitude

_____

_____

√   E   X   F   **Behavior**

Speech loud, rapid, ranging

Less sleep

Overly sociable, giving more advice

More sex drive

Doing more projects

Setting goals that are not realistic

Spending more money impulsively, shopping sprees

Involvement in dangerous activities

_____

_____

Think about what the pattern has been for you.

- Has anyone had mania come on very quickly and without warning? Mark an *X* next to the symptoms that come on quickly and without warning in the box provided.
- Has anyone noticed that mania has come on gradually and increased in severity over time?
- Has anyone had mania and lost the ability to realize its potential for painful consequences or know the difference between what was real or not real?

FOCUS POINT 3: Identify personal triggers of (hypo)mania. Complete a list of Personal Triggers of a Manic Episode.

We can compare manic-depression to diabetes. They are both medical illnesses. In diabetes, it is the blood sugar levels that go too high or too low. In manic-depression, it is the person's moods that can go too high or too low. Both of these conditions are caused by chemical imbalances in the body. Both conditions can worsen spontaneously, that is, without an apparent cause. In addition, we know that there are certain things that can trigger a manic episode. For some people, these include changes in the environment, such as changes in the seasons, and stressful personal experiences, such as needing surgery or other medical problem.

Stress can be thought of as any change in routine and either good or bad life events—anything that can stimulate your feelings and upset your pattern of daily life. It is normal to react to a good or bad experience with a good or bad mood. People with manic-depression may be very sensitive to stress. Also, if stress triggers a mood episode, the mood episode can last long after the stress itself is gone.

Therapist Directions
List the examples provided by the group members. Once the group member list is completed, discuss Exhibit 6 ("Personal Triggers of a Manic Episode"). Query group members about whether they have experienced mania following or concurrent with the triggers on the generic list. Point out items on the board list not on the generic list, recognizing group member individuality.

EXHIBIT 6   Personal Triggers of a Manic Episode

Check all those that have triggered manic episodes for you. Fill in the
blank spaces with specific experiences.

_____ Bad life events _____

_____

_____

_____ Good life events _____

_____

_____

_____ Change in medication (psychiatric or medical, prescription or
over-the-counter)

Which medications? _____

_____ Physical illness _____

Which illness? _____

_____ Drug or alcohol use _____

_____ Changes in smoking habits _____

_____ Change in seasons _____

What seasons? _____

_____ Change in routine _____

_____

_____

- What types of stresses in daily life do you think might bring about a manic episode?
- If you think about your own most recent or most severe manic episode, can you recall if there was a crisis, stress, or change in routine that seemed to occur just before it began? How about a good event? What was it?
- Has anyone here had the experience of having an episode of mania despite having no triggers even though they were maintaining their treatment plan and medications?

I'd like for you to take a look at your worksheet (Exhibit 6: "Personal Triggers of a Manic Episode"). Please take the next few minutes to check off the items that triggered a manic episode in your past. Then fill in the *specific* changes in your daily life and bad or good life events that triggered manic episodes for you on the lines provided. Make sure you add other triggers that you may have experienced—ones that you contributed to our board list.

Now, each of you has a personal profile of your mania that includes your signs and symptoms, which we refer to as your "Personal Mania Profile." You also completed a list of actual and potential stressors that may trigger a manic episode. Next week we will take this information a step further and identify strategies for coping with symptoms and triggers of mania.

- Are there any questions of comments before we finish today?

Therapist Directions
Close the session, and mention next week's topic. Note day, date, and time of the next session. Thank members for their participation.

SESSION 3: MANIA, PART 2

SESSION RATIONALE

This session is designed to help group members to begin the process of associating the early signs, symptoms, and triggers of a manic episode with the initiation of effective coping behavior.

SESSION GOALS

1. Group members will identify ineffective personal strategies for coping with (hypo)mania.
2. Group members will identify effective personal coping strategies to respond to the early signs and symptoms of (hypo)mania.
3. Group members will identify coping strategies to manage the triggers that may contribute to the emergence of a (hypo)manic episode.
4. Group members will review the high rates of comorbidity of drug and alcohol abuse with manic-depressive disorder.
5. Group members will develop insight about the negative consequences associated with medication nonadherence and other strategies to enhance a manic episode.

FOCUS POINTS

Focus Point 1: Provide the rationale for identification of early signs and symptoms of mania and stress that may lead to mania as signals to initiate effective coping responses.

In the past, group members may have used various response strategies to cope with the emergence of manic signs and symptoms and the stressors that trigger episodes. Their methods may have been effective, partially effective, ineffective, or damaging. An initial step toward becoming an effective illness manager is to learn to recognize the stressors that may lead to (hypo)mania and the signs and symptoms of mania signals to cope. Recognizing and responding effectively to stress and the early signs and symptoms of mania may limit the episode intensity, impact of the stressor, and severe family, social, and occupational consequences.

Focus Point 2: Learn to recognize adaptive and maladaptive coping responses to the signs and symptoms of (hypo)mania and stress that may trigger a manic episode. Understand these responses in terms of "costs and benefits."

An important element of behavior change is to learn to recognize adaptive and maladaptive coping responses. Coping strategies may reduce, neutralize, contribute to, perpetuate, or worsen the manic episode and the stress that may trigger mania. Ineffective coping behavior can serve to validate faulty cognitions and self-appraisals. This negative thinking can sabotage new learning skills. Effective coping behavior can be protective of both the group member and those around him or her. Often, coping responses will have both adaptive and maladaptive aspects. Focus Point 3 deals with substance abuse and medication noncompliance as coping strategies. This focus point may flow directly from the content of Focus Point 2, or may need to be prompted by the therapist as outlined below.

Focus Point 3: Recognize the role of substance abuse, medication noncompliance, and other ineffective coping behaviors that perpetuate the "high" of mania and stress that may trigger a manic episode in terms of "costs and benefits."

The early signs and symptoms of mania may be valued by some group members. Mania and hypomania may be enjoyable and a welcome relief from depression. Some people describe it as like being on a drug. Substance abuse and medication noncompliance may be strategies used to cope that have significant negative consequences on a person's quality of life and treatment response.

Focus Point 4: Develop a Personal Action Plan for (Hypo)Mania.

Concentration, memory, and judgment are usually impaired in (hypo)mania. A predetermined action plan may improve effective coping and overall illness management.

SCRIPT

FOCUS POINT 1: Provide the rationale for identification of stress that may lead to mania and the early signs and symptoms of mania as signals to initiate effective coping responses.

Therapist Directions
Welcome the group back; distribute workbooks to those who left them behind with you. Distribute copies of the session's exhibits to those who left their workbooks at home.

Therapist Didactic.   In the last week's group, we learned that manic signs and symptoms can recur, and that each of you has a personal cluster of symptoms that emerges in a pattern we called your "Personal Mania Profile." We also discussed and each of you developed a list of actual and potential stressors that may trigger a manic episode. By getting familiar with these stressors and your Personal Mania Profile, you can learn to manage your condition more effectively by catching an episode as early as possible and responding with a well thought out Action Plan.

Today, we will briefly review the Personal Mania Profile you developed last week. Then we will discuss some ways people have attempted to cope in the past with mania and the stress that may have triggered mania. We will analyze these coping strategies using a "cost-benefit" analysis. Finally, each of you will formulate a Mania Action Plan, which will help you prevent, limit, or cope more effectively with a manic episode.

- Look over your Personal Mania Profile. This is the list of your signs and symptoms illustrated as "Thoughts," "Feelings," and "Behaviors." Have you added any more information since last week? Recall that family, friends, and coworkers may notice changes in your behavior indicating early signs of mania. If you've had the opportunity to discuss this and have information to add to your list, please do it now. Be sure to indicate which of these signs and symptoms emerge *early,* and mark them with an *E.* Mark an *X* next to signs and symptoms that emerge *quickly.*
- We now want to look at how you attempted to cope in the past with mania and the stressors that triggered mania. Recall that people with manic-depression may be very sensitive to stress and rather than stimulate minor mood variations, stress may stimulate a manic episode.

FOCUS POINT 2: Learn to recognize adaptive and maladaptive coping responses to the signs and symptoms of (hypo)mania and stress that may trigger a manic episode. Understand these responses in terms of "costs and benefits."

Therapist Didactic. We believe when people face stress or begin to feel the early warning signs of mania, they do the best they can to ease the pain, or to keep things like work and relationships going as well as possible. We call these things people do in response to stress and manic symptoms "coping responses." In general, people make an effort to do the best they can to adjust to what is happening to them the best way they know how. Some of the things people do to cope with manic symptoms and stress may be helpful, others neutral, and some may actually be harmful.

Therapist Directions
Begin a list on the board using a column labeled "Coping Responses."
At this point, focus only on the responses themselves, not the costs
and benefits. Assessing costs and benefits prematurely can sometimes seem judgmental and can inhibit group member participation. If group members seem resistant to contributing to the discussion, it may be because memories of manic experiences stimulate
denial, shame, and embarrassment. Once the group members have
contributed to the list, refer to the generic list, Exhibit 7 ("Responses
to a Manic Episode/Stress That May Trigger a manic Episode—1: Costs
and Benefits"), focusing at this point only on the upper section that
lists specific responses.

- Now, take a moment to look in your notebooks at your worksheet of
  Personal Triggers of a Manic Episode.
- What are some things people may do to cope with stress that may lead
  to mania?
- What are the things people may do when they begin to have manic
  symptoms?

Now that we have a list of some of the things people may do in response
to a manic episode and the stress that may trigger a manic episode, let's take
the next step and consider the "costs and benefits" of these responses. The
term *cost-benefit analysis* is common language in financial matters. When
you think about it, it is something we do informally whenever we make a
decision or a choice. The costs and benefits are the disadvantages and advantages. When we make decisions, we generally weigh the good and bad effects
of that decision with the other choices we have thought about. All decisions
and things people do to cope have some good points and some bad points—
some benefits and some costs. There are no perfect decisions. The point is to
make decisions to cope that have more benefits than costs.

- Are there any questions so far?

Sometimes we make decisions to do things to cope because it is the way
we've always responded. For example, when people experience pleasurable
mania, they may think about the benefits but not the costs associated with
letting the episode continue. At the time, they simply feel that they are in fine
shape, and there is something wrong with the world around them.
Sometimes these feelings are a welcome change from depression. However,
even mild mania has its costs. Usually some personal or social difficulties or
catastrophes are just around the corner. Understanding the costs and benefits of mania are personal, and it is the person experiencing it who will conclude how the costs and benefits will balance out.

EXHIBIT 7   Responses to a Manic Episode/Stress That May Trigger a Manic Episode—1: Costs and Benefits

Examples

- Spend money, use charge cards
- Maintain sleep schedule
- Drive fast
- Lots of projects (working, writing)
- Don't use alcohol or street drugs
- Make up for lost time from depression
- Gamble
- Maintain routine daily activities
- Participate in arguments
- More impulsive relationships and sexual activity
- Continue medication
- Drop out of treatment
- Call MD/Nurse/therapist
- Stop listening to people's feedback
- Retreat to a tranquil environment

Response:	
Good Effects: (Pro health, good for you)	**Bad Effects:** (More problems caused)

Response:	
Good Effects:	**Bad Effects:**

In the first session, we mentioned that some famous people had manic-depressive disorder. It is probable that, in some ways, their illness may have actually helped them in terms of productivity, although most aspects of the illness were crippling. In your own lives, each of you may have also felt that mild manic symptoms were helpful in some way.

Therapist Directions
Facilitate a cost-benefit analysis of mania on the board, or use Exhibit 7 "Responses to a Manic Episode/Stress That May Trigger a Manic Episode—1: Costs and Benefits." Be careful not to be nonjudgmental. Taking a position for or against mania may stifle the group from actively participating. Effecting change is internally driven and not directed from an outside source.

- What sort of benefits have you gotten from being manic?
- What are some of the disadvantages of mania?
- Are there things you have done to enhance a manic episode? We can think of this as a coping response. Let's look at the costs and benefits of _____ (behaviors to enhance a manic episode).

Therapist Directions
This is an opportunity to discuss medication noncompliance and substance abuse as strategies to cope if initiated by the group. Otherwise, the therapist should proceed with a cost-benefit analysis of at least one or two responses from the group list of coping strategies to manage stress that may trigger a manic episode or symptoms of mania. Again, the therapist should be careful to be nonjudgmental when doing the cost-benefit analysis of ineffective coping responses. Therapeutic techniques that may further put the group members at ease during this activity include empathy, establishing a sense of universality, and humor. If medication noncompliance and substance abuse are not processed here, go on to Focus Point 3.

FOCUS POINT 3: Recognize the role of substance abuse, medication noncompliance, and other behaviors that perpetuate the stressors and "high" of mania in terms of "costs and benefits."

Therapist Directions
Substance abuse and medication noncompliance worsen the course of manic-depressive episodes. They require special attention and discussion. The use of alcohol and drugs is common in the depressed phase and the manic phase. However, the issues may be somewhat different in the two phases. For persons in the depressed phase, substances are often used to blunt the bad feelings. For persons in the manic phase, substances may be used either to decrease or to increase the symptoms. Mania may also increase appetite for substances without apparent connection to increasing or decreasing symptoms. Facilitate a cost-benefit analysis of substance abuse, then medication noncompliance, using Exhibit 8 ("Responses to a Manic Episode/Stress That May Trigger a Manic Episode—2: Costs and Benefits"). Contributions from the group members should be listed on the board and acknowledged in a nonjudgmental way. The therapist should maintain a nonpersonalized way of addressing substance abuse and medication noncompliance, especially in view of the defensiveness a directed approach can engender. Generate ideas from the group about why substance abuse and medication noncompliance are often used to cope with stress and the emergence of manic signs and symptoms.

Therapist Didactic.   There are high rates of substance abuse and dependence associated with manic-depressive disorder. The lifetime prevalence of alcohol and drug abuse is about 70%, and currently active substance use disorders are as high as 30%–35%. Substance use is an important issue in mania and coping with stress that may lead to mania. Alcohol or drugs may be used during mania for many reasons, sometimes to increase and sometimes to decrease symptoms.

- What happens when people use alcohol or drugs when they are manic or in response to stress that may lead to mania?
- What are the reasons that a person would use alcohol or drugs during mania?
- What would be good points/advantages/benefits of using drugs or alcohol during mania?

EXHIBIT 8   Responses to a Manic Episode/Stress That May Trigger a
Manic Episode—2: Costs and Benefits.

Response:	
Good Effects:	**Bad Effects:**

Response:	
Good Effects:	**Bad Effects:**

Response:	
Good Effects:	**Bad Effects:**

- What are the costs or bad points of using drugs or alcohol during mania?
- Another common response to becoming manic is to decrease or stop prescribed medication. What leads to this?
- What happens when people stop prescribed medication when they are manic?
- What are the good points? What are the disadvantages?

Therapist Directions
Refer to Exhibit 8 ("Responses to a Manic Episode/Stress That May Trigger a Manic Episode—2: Costs and Benefits"). Have group members construct a cost-benefit analysis to at least two personal coping responses for stress and/or mania. One response should, on balance, be beneficial, and one response should, on balance, be maladaptive. Additional worksheets may be provided for further examples, which the group member can complete in the group or at home.

Therapist Didactic. Turn to Exhibit 8 ("Responses to a Manic Episode/ Stress That May Trigger a Manic Episode—2: Costs and Benefits") in your notebooks. Please take the next few minutes to go through a cost-benefit analysis of at least one of your major coping responses when you get manic. In other words, choose one way you typically respond to being manic, and make a list of the good effects and the bad effects of these responses.

Next, refer to your list of Personal Triggers of a Manic Episode. Identify one or two coping strategies for specific stressors, and list the costs and benefits associated with each response.

FOCUS POINT 4: Develop a Personal Action Plan for Mania.

So far, you have developed your Personal Mania Profile and Personal Triggers of a Manic Episode and listed some of the coping responses you tried in the past to cope with mania and stress that may trigger mania. We carefully analyzed several of these coping responses to mania and stress that may trigger mania using a cost-benefit analysis. Now you are going to develop a personal Action Plan to cope with mania. This is a plan that you will write on a worksheet and a card. You can keep the card in your purse or wallet, and take along with you when you leave today.

- What do you think would be important to include in an action plan for coping with mania?
- What do you think would be important to include in an action plan for coping with stress that may trigger mania?
- What has helped in the past?

Therapist Directions
Write the group member contributions on the board, and discuss the rationale behind each of their ideas. Once the group member contributions have been exhausted, display Exhibit 9 ("Action Plan: Outline of Coping Strategies for Mania/Stress That May Trigger a Manic Episode"). Review the list and discuss items with the group. Provide positive statements about the group-generated board lists; especially contributions that are "personal" and not included on the generic list. Then have each group member fill out Exhibit 9 "Action Plan: Outline of Coping Strategies for Mania/Stress That May Trigger a Manic Episode." Once completed direct the group to complete the wallet card (Exhibit 10, "Action Plan for Mania"). Recall that group members who are more impaired cognitively or in a mood episode may require assistance. Discuss generic items on the cards to stimulate completion.

Each of you by now has begun to get more familiar with the early signs and symptoms of mania, stressors that may lead to the initiation of a manic episode, and develop an action plan to cope with early manic symptoms and the stress that may lead to an episode. This knowledge will make it possible for you to manage your condition better and to prevent or limit future manic episodes: Be patient with this. Learning to cope with stress and manic symptoms effectively takes time and practice. You also completed a card: Action Plan for Mania. Keep this in your wallet or purse to use as a quick reference. Next week, we will begin to discuss the depression part of manic-depressive disorder.

Therapist Directions
Close the session, and mention the day, date, time, and place of next session. Collect workbooks from those group members agreeable to storing them on site.

**EXHIBIT 9   Action Plan: Outline of Coping Strategies
for Mania/Stress That May Trigger a Manic Episode**

1. Alert health care provider of early manic symptoms and stress that may lead to mania.

2. Discuss medication changes for medical illness with health care provider.

3. Get early assessment and treatment of physical illness.

4. Avoid alcohol and drugs. (Note: Even increasing tobacco can undo the effects of prescribed medication.)

5. Maintain daily routine.

6. Minimize sleep loss.

7. Activate support persons: _____   _____

8. Know your personal coping responses. List specific things to do:

   •

   •

9. Know your personal coping responses. List specific things *not* to do:

   •

   •

EXHIBIT 10   Action Plan for Mania

Action Plan for Mania

1. Check meds
2. Check: alcohol/drugs/
   nicotine
3. Recognize stress triggers:
   - Physical
   - Emotional
4. Maintain daily activities and sleep
5. Activate support persons:

6. Coping skills/to do:
   _____
   _____
7. Coping skills/not to do:
   _____
8. Contact provider
   Phone: _____
9. Support group
   Phone: _____

Action Plan for Mania

1. Check meds
2. Check: alcohol/drugs/
   nicotine
3. Recognize stress triggers:
   - Physical
   - Emotional
4. Maintain daily activities and sleep
5. Activate support persons:

6. Coping skills/to do:
   _____
   _____
7. Coping skills/not to do:
   _____
8. Contact provider
   Phone: _____
9. Support group
   Phone: _____

Action Plan for Mania

1. Check meds
2. Check: alcohol/drugs/
   nicotine
3. Recognize stress triggers:
   - Physical
   - Emotional
4. Maintain daily activities and sleep
5. Activate support persons:

6. Coping skills/to do:
   _____
   _____
7. Coping skills/not to do:
   _____
8. Contact provider
   Phone: _____
9. Support group
   Phone: _____

SESSION 4: DEPRESSION, PART 1

SESSION RATIONALE

This session is designed to facilitate group member self-awareness of signs, symptoms, and triggers of a depressive episode that will enable him or her to participate in illness management and effective coping behaviors.

SESSION GOALS

1. Group members will develop a personal list of signs and symptoms of depression.
2. Group members will identify the variability of their depressive episode patterns.
3. Group members will develop a personal list of actual and potential triggers of depression.

FOCUS POINTS

Focus Point 1: Identify session goals of developing self-monitoring skills for recognizing depression and its triggers.

Manic-depressive disorder is characterized by extremes in mood and related changes in behavior and cognition. Symptom recognition is the first step leading to a coping strategy intervention that can prevent, limit, or help the group member to cope with a depressive episode.

Focus Point 2: Identify the pattern of episode recurrence and the personal signs and symptoms of depression. Construct a Personal Depression Profile.

A depressive episode may be characterized by a progressive or abrupt change in mood, behavior, and cognition. The symptoms may come on slowly, with gradual worsening, or they may come on quickly, sometimes directly switching from one mood state to another. In order to efficiently monitor their illness, group members need to be aware of their own specific pattern. Individual patterns are variable in length and frequency. Validate the group member's illness pattern through discussion of the variability in symptoms and patterns of occurrence. Encourage group members to become aware of symptoms of depression recognized by family, friends, and coworkers.

Focus Point 3: Identify personal triggers of depression. Complete a list of Personal Triggers of a Depressive Episode.

Illness instability can be precipitated by a change in one's personal routine, stressful life events, mental, or physical changes or nonadherence to the plan of care (medication, sleep, hygiene). However, it is important to recognize that it is a quality of the disorder to relapse and remit spontaneously. This complexity can confuse and demoralize the group member. Helping group members to recognize potential triggers can be valuable in illness management and prevention.

SCRIPT

FOCUS POINT 1: Identify session goals of developing self-monitoring skills for recognizing depression and its triggers.

> **Therapist Directions**
> Welcome group members back, and distribute workbooks and worksheets as appropriate.

Therapist Didactic. During the past several weeks we have discussed the guidelines for being a member of this group, the biological basis of manic-depression that makes it a treatable condition, and the various symptoms that may include psychosis. We also discussed psychiatric stigma and its potential harmful role as a barrier to learning how to effectively manage this condition. For the past 2 weeks we have been discussing your personal profiles for mania and triggers that may lead to a manic episode. Each of you has developed plans for coping with mania and stress that may trigger a manic episode and has practiced making decisions for effective coping based on carefully thought out cost-benefit analyses.

Today and next week we are going to talk about the depressive phase of manic-depressive disorder. By the end of today's session, you will be able to identify a list of your own personal signs and symptoms of depression, describe the patterns of how your depressions occur, and identify triggers that may cause or worsen depression.

Recall that there are signs and symptoms of manic-depression that are common, but every individual's episodes are a little bit different. What we are going to do is first look at the symptoms of depression that are common to a lot of people. Next, we will identify any symptoms that you think we may have left out. Then each of you will be asked to complete your Personal Depression Profile. Once your Personal Depression Profiles are completed, we will develop a List of Personal Triggers of a Depressive Episode.

- Does anyone have any questions so far?

FOCUS POINT 2: Identify the pattern of episode recurrence and the personal signs and symptoms of depression. Construct a Personal Depression Profile.

Let's talk about the signs and symptoms of depression. Like mania, depression is experienced as the way a person thinks, feels, and acts. So, in talking about depression, it can help to think about it in this way: A person's thoughts, feelings, and behaviors are his or her signs and symptoms.

- What are some examples of thoughts, feelings, and behaviors that a person may have when he or she is depressed?
- Sometimes it helps to recall depressive signs and symptoms by thinking about your most recent or severe episode of depression.

Therapist Directions
- Display three headings on the board: **Thoughts, Feelings, Behavior.** Query group members, and write each of their contributions *as stated* under the appropriate heading.
- Once group members generate a reasonable list, display Exhibit 11 ("Personal Depression Profile"). The exhibit may also be used to stimulate discussion if the group is not contributing. Highlight group member contributions while reviewing the list.

Please open your notebooks to Exhibit 11 ("Personal Depression Profile"). In each of your notebooks, please take the next few minutes to check off the symptoms on this list that represent *your* experience of depression. Although some of the symptoms on this list are common to many people's experience of depression, your list is a **"cluster"** of symptoms that are personal to you. Most important is that you identify the symptoms of depression that are personal to you in the blank spaces provided and not included in the common symptom list. These symptoms are unique, and awareness of them may improve your ability to recognize that a depression is imminent. Sometimes family, friends, and coworkers may recognize depressive symptoms that you are not aware of. For this reason, we have included spaces on the worksheets for those symptoms others in your life may report to you. Place an *F* in the space provided next to symptoms others notice when you are becoming depressed.

EXHIBIT 11   Personal Depression Profile

1. Place a check mark next to symptoms that you experience.
2. Mark an *E* next to those that are particular early warning signs.
3. Mark an *X* next to those that come on quickly without warning.
4. Mark an *F* next to those symptoms that are recognized by family, friends, and coworkers.
5. Add other symptoms not included on the list in the blank spaces provided.

√   E   X   F   **Thoughts**

Difficulty with concentration and memory

Things are bad and are not going to get better

Difficulty making decisions

Thoughts that others do not care when they really might

Frequent thoughts about dying or suicide

Paranoia: that people are plotting against you

Unreal concerns that you are worthless or evil

Hallucinations: unreal voices or visions

Thoughts about problems that depression caused in the past

_____

_____

√   E   X   F   **Feelings**

Feeling worthless

Feeling guilty without cause

Feeling sad without cause

Easily irritable

Not feeling good even though good things happen

Less energy

Changes in appetite

_____

_____

√   E   X   F   **Behavior**

Restlessness and pacing

Trouble sleeping or too much sleep

Trouble starting or finishing projects

Keeping away from people

Stopping work or usual activities

Fighting without good reason

Frequently crying with little or no reason

Preparing a suicide plan

_____

_____

Note: It is common explicitly or implicitly to comment on the social appropriateness of certain types of symptoms. For example, it is difficult not to respond subtly to "I beat my wife" as a socially unacceptable symptom, whereas "I isolate" might be handled with equanimity. It is essential to establish and maintain a therapeutic atmosphere of tolerance. Keep in mind, however, that imminent danger to self or others requires a clinically appropriate response.

- Look over the signs and symptoms on your Personal Depression Profile. Does your profile look accurate? Are there other things to add to your list?

These thoughts, feelings, and behaviors are the core symptoms of your depression. Some of them come earlier than others. Mark with an *E* in the space provided those that are likely to be the first to emerge. If you can recognize the early signs, you can begin coping early, before the depression gets out of hand. These may be considered "early warning signs."

- Any questions?

Therapist Didactic. A return of depressive signs and symptoms can occur in several ways.

1. Symptoms can return slowly and gradually, increasing in severity over time.
2. Symptoms can return quickly, sometimes directly switching from one mood state to another. Mark an *X* in the box provided next to symptoms that come on quickly and without warning.
3. A person can have both manic and depressive symptoms intermixed—that is, a depressed or irritable mood with manic energy. During a depressive episode without manic symptoms, a person has no energy or interest.

- What has it been like for people here?

FOCUS POINT 3: Identify personal triggers of depression. Complete a list of Personal Triggers of a Depressive Episode.

Therapist Didactic. Now we are going to discuss actual and potential triggers of depression. Recall that manic-depressive disorder can be compared to diabetes. In the case of diabetes, blood sugar levels can go too high or too low because the body cannot regulate them. In manic-depressive disorder, it is the person's moods that go too high or too low. Both conditions have periods of stability when the person is okay and times when they are not. In both diabetes and manic-depressive disorder, the condition may become unstable either because of stress or spontaneously because instability is a characteristic of the disorder.

Recall that stress can be thought of as either good or bad life events or any change in routine—anything that can stimulate your feelings or upset your pattern of daily life. It is normal to react to a change and good or bad events, with a change in how you feel. People with manic-depressive disorder are more sensitive than others to stress and change: Research on manic-depressive disorder has shown a relationship between stress and mood instability. Also, if stress triggers a mood episode, the mood episode can last long after the stress itself is gone.

- What types of stresses in daily life do you think might bring about, or contribute to, a depressive episode?

Therapist Directions
List on the board the examples contributed by the group members.

- If you think about your own most recent or severe depressive episode, can you recall if there was a crisis, a minor stress, or change in routine that seemed to occur just before you became depressed?
- How about something good that happened? What was it?
- Has anyone here had the experience of having an episode of depression despite having no triggers and maintaining the treatment plan?
- Has anyone ever had a manic episode trigger the depressive phase?

If you recall, we reviewed a common list of depressive signs and symptoms, then each of you added to that list symptoms unique to you. We are going to do a similar exercise with the triggers of depression.

Therapist Directions
Display Exhibit 12 ("Personal Triggers of a Depressive Episode").
Point out the similarities between the group list and the generic list.
Recognize group member individuality: Items on the group list not on generic list.

I'd like you to take a look at your worksheet (Exhibit 12). Please take the next few minutes to check off the items that triggered a depressive episode in your past. Then fill in any change in routine and *specific* bad or good life

EXHIBIT 12   Personal Triggers of a Depressive Episode

Check all those that have triggered depressive episodes for you. Fill in the
blank spaces with specific experiences.

_____ Bad life events _____

_____

_____

_____ Good life events _____

_____

_____

_____ Change in medication (psychiatric or medical, prescription or
over-the-counter)
Which medications? _____

_____ Physical illness _____
Which illness? _____

_____ Drug or alcohol use _____

_____ Changes in smoking habits _____

_____ Change in seasons _____
What seasons? _____

_____ Change in routine _____

_____

_____

events that triggered a depressive episode in the past or you think could trigger a depressive phase in the future. Make sure you add personal triggers that you may have experienced—ones that you contributed to our board list.

- Now that you have identified your personal list of potential triggers of a depressive episode, can you add anything that we overlooked?

Today we learned that depressive signs and symptoms are common to a lot of people, but that each of you has a cluster of symptoms that emerge in a pattern, which we call your Personal Depression Profile. You also developed a list of changes in your routine and the stressors that you think might bring about or contribute to a depressive episode for you. Next week, we will take this a step further and identify strategies for coping with depressive symptoms and stress that may lead to a depressive episode.

Therapist Directions
Close the session. Note day, date, time, and place of next session. Provide positive statements about the work the group accomplished during the session.

SESSION 5: DEPRESSION, PART 2

SESSION RATIONALE

This session is designed to help group members begin the process of associating signs, symptoms, and triggers of a depressive episode with the initiation of effective coping behavior.

SESSION GOALS

1. Group members will identify ineffective personal strategies for coping with depression.
2. Group members will identify effective personal coping strategies to respond to the early signs and symptoms of depression.
3. Group members will identify coping strategies that minimize the triggers that may contribute to the emergence of a depressive episode.
4. Group members will become aware of the high rates of comorbidity of drug and alcohol abuse with manic-depression.
5. Group members will become aware of the high rates of suicidal behavior in manic-depression.

FOCUS POINTS

Focus Point 1: Provide the rationale for identification of early signs and symptoms of depression and stress that may lead to depression as signals to initiate effective coping responses.

In the past, the group member may have used various response strategies to cope with the emergence of depressive signs and symptoms and the stressors that trigger episodes. These methods may have been effective, partially effective, ineffective, or damaging. An initial step toward becoming an effective illness manager is to learn to recognize the stressors that may lead to depression and the emergence of signs and symptoms of depression as signals to cope. In the past, group members may have responded to the emergence of symptoms with fear, hopelessness, passivity, and other ineffective coping responses. Recognizing and responding effectively to stress and the early signs and symptoms of depression may limit the episode intensity, impact of the stressor, and the family, social, and occupational functional impairment.

Focus Point 2: Learn to recognize adaptive and maladaptive coping responses to the signs and symptoms of depression and stress that may trigger a depressive episode. Understand these responses in terms of "costs and benefits."

An important element of behavior change is to learn to recognize adaptive and maladaptive coping responses that perpetuate or worsen the depressive episode and stress that may trigger depression. Ineffective coping behavior can serve to validate faulty thinking and self-appraisals. This negative thinking can sabotage new learning skills. Effective coping behavior can be protective, both of the group member and of people around him or her. Often, coping responses will have both adaptive and maladaptive aspects. There is a high rate of substance abuse and suicidal behavior in people with manic-depression. This session points directly to these topics with specific exercises intended for the group to conclude the serious costs associated with these behaviors. Focus Point 3 may flow directly from group input in Focus Point 2, or it may need to be prompted by the therapist, as outlined below.

Focus Point 3: Recognize substance abuse and suicidal behavior as ineffective coping strategies for managing depression and stress that may trigger or perpetuate a depressive episode. Begin to understand their high rates of comorbidity with manic-depressive disorder.

Many people drink alcohol or use drugs to cope with depressed feelings. Particular focus on drug and alcohol use is needed, in view of the high rates of comorbidity of drug and alcohol use disorders with manic-depressive disorder. The lifetime prevalence rate of alcoholism and alcohol abuse is 35% to 45%. The lifetime drug abuse/dependence prevalence rate is equally high. The combined lifetime prevalence rate for alcohol and drug abuse/dependence is over 70%, with rates of current substance use disorders as high as 30%–35%. That is, well over half of all persons with manic-depressive disorder have had clinically significant problems with substance use.

Group members with manic-depressive disorder are also at extremely high risk for suicide. The emergence of suicidal ideation, with or without intent or plan, often accompanies severe depression. Group members may not raise this topic during the discussion of coping responses that were used earlier in this and other sessions for several reasons. First, they may not recognize suicide as an effort to relieve the pain of depression, even though it is a form of adaptation to the illness. Second, group members may be embarrassed to admit to suicidal feelings or behaviors, because they are generally the least acceptable in terms of social standards of acceptable behavior.

Focus Point 4: Develop a Personal Action Plan for Depression.

When experiencing depression, concentration, memory, and logical flow of thought may become impaired. Therefore, the formulation of a predetermined action plan for coping with the emergence of depressive signs and symptoms is more likely to improve effective illness management.

SCRIPT

FOCUS POINT 1: Provide the rationale for identification of early signs and symptoms of depression and stress that may lead to depression as signals to initiate effective coping responses.

> **Therapist Directions**
> Welcome the group, pass out the workbooks, or if group members have brought them home and someone is without theirs, provide copies of the sessions' worksheets.

Therapist Didactic.   In the group last week, we learned depressive signs and symptoms can recur, and that each of you has a personal cluster of symptoms that emerge in a pattern that we called your Personal Depression Profile. By getting familiar with your personal profile, you can manage your depression by responding to those signs and symptoms as early as possible and respond ing with a well-thought-out action plan.

We also discussed and each of you generated a list of stressors that may trigger or perpetuate a depressive episode. Today we will begin discussing coping strategies intended to minimize these stressors as a strategy to limit future depressive episodes.

- Does anyone have any questions?

FOCUS POINT 2: Learn to recognize adaptive and maladaptive coping responses to the signs and symptoms of depression and stress that may trigger a depressive episode. Understand these responses in terms of "costs and benefits."

To begin, we are going to discuss some ways you have attempted to cope in the past with depression and the stressors that may lead to depression. Then we will discuss the possible costs and benefits of these coping strategies. Finally, each of you will formulate your own personal action plan to respond to depression and stress, which will help you to prevent or cope with a major depressive episode.

Look over your Personal Depression Profile. Recall that this is your list of signs and symptoms labeled "Thoughts," "Feelings," and "Behaviors."

- Have you thought of any more personal signs and symptoms since meeting last week? Please take a moment and add them to your list.

If you've had the opportunity to discuss symptoms family, friends, or coworkers may observe, add them to your list and mark them with an *F.* Be sure to mark symptoms that emerge *early* with an *E*, and mark an *X* next to symptoms that emerge *quickly*. Next, take a moment to review your Personal Triggers of a Depressive Episode.

- Can you add anything more to the list?

Let's briefly review the concept of "coping responses" and the process of a cost-benefit analysis. We believe that when people are depressed or face stress in their lives, they take action to help ease the pain or to keep things going as well as possible. We referred to these actions or behaviors as *coping responses* or *adaptations*. Basically, people make an effort to adjust to what is happening to them the best way they know how. Some of the things people do to cope with depression and stress are helpful; others may be neutral and some actually harmful. What we are going to do now is to generate a list on the board of coping responses (things people do) that people use when they get depressed or face stress. Later, we will look carefully at the advantages and disadvantages of these responses.

- What are some things people may do when they get depressed?
- What are some things people may do when they experience stress that may lead to a depressive episode?

Therapist Directions
Begin a list on the board using a column titled "Coping Responses." At this point focus only on responses without assessing costs or benefits. Assessing costs and benefits prematurely can sometimes seem judgmental and can inhibit group member participation. If group members seem resistant to contributing to the discussion, it may be that recall of past experiences coping with depression stimulates dread, shame, and embarrassment. Once the group members have contributed to the list, refer to the generic list, Exhibit 13 ("Responses to a Depressive Episode/Stress That May Trigger a Depressive Episode—1: Costs and Benefits"), focusing only on the upper section which lists specific responses.

Now that we have a list of things people may do to cope with depression and stress that may lead to depression, we will take the next step in this exercise and consider the costs and benefits. Recall that all decisions and things people do to cope have some good points and some bad points—some benefits and some costs. There are no perfect decisions or solutions to a problem. The point is to make decisions and choose solutions that have more benefits than costs. For example, the fact that you are here today tells me that

EXHIBIT 13   Responses to a Depressive Episode/Stress That May Trigger a Depressive Episode—1: Costs and Benefits

Examples

- Avoid friends
- Stop activities and exercise
- Try to maintain daily routine
- Get support from a trusted friend
- Pray
- Drop out of treatment

- Make therapist/doctor appointment
- Stop working
- Stop medications
- Share family/work duties
- Use alcohol and drugs
- Plan suicide

Response:	
Good Effects: (Pro health, good for you)	**Bad Effects:** (More problems caused)

Response:	
Good Effects: (Pro health, good for you)	**Bad Effects:** (More problems caused)

you weighed the "costs" associated with taking the drive to get here, finding a parking space, dealing with whoever and what other obstacles were in your path once here and before leaving home. You also identified specific "benefits," things about coming that were meaningful to you.

The fact that you are here tells me you decided the "benefits" of coming to group today outweigh the "costs." The way we cope and make decisions involves thinking carefully about costs and benefits, but sometimes we respond or make a decision to "cope" in a way we are accustomed to. We develop habits. Sometimes if we give more thought to it, we may find our response is not always in our best interests.

Therapist Directions
Use the board or Exhibit 13 to demonstrate the following example, listing items in the cost-benefit columns.

Let's discuss an example. Avoiding usual friends and acquaintances is a common example of a response to being depressed. This has positive and negative aspects. On the plus side, people often feel they are less overwhelmed by responsibilities and feel less inferior or guilty when they are not around other people who are feeling well. Often isolation is a means to cope with irritability or anxiety in social situations. On the down side, withdrawal from people leads to less positive feedback from others and fewer enjoyable experiences. This can lead to feelings of guilt and low self-worth. Sometimes other people gradually begin to expect less of the person who is depressed. They may express that he or she has hurt or angered them. Often there are also material bad effects, such as loss of work time and income. Although there may be times when isolation can be very helpful, for example, during bouts of severe irritability, it is usually wise not to select isolation as the one and only way to cope.

Let's select an example from your list on the board.

Therapist Directions
Next, the therapist will facilitate group participation in a cost-benefit analysis of at least one or two responses, selected from the group list by the group members. If participation is at a stalemate, then select examples from the generic list. Take care to be nonjudgmental when doing the cost-benefit analysis of "ineffective" coping responses to depression and stress. The therapist may use Exhibit 13 ("Responses to a Depressive Episode/Stress That May Trigger a Depressive

Episode—1: Costs and Benefits") to complete the cost-benefit analysis. Keep in mind that there are no perfect "responses," and most responses, if used in a limited manner, can help a person cope with depression and stress.

Group members may or may not list substance use or suicidal behavior among their examples. If they do, the therapist should integrate the content of Focus Point 3 into the discussion during Focus Point 2. If substance abuse and suicidal behavior are not mentioned by group members, the therapist must continue with Focus Point 3 as written.

FOCUS POINT 3: Recognize substance abuse and suicidal behavior as ineffective coping strategies for managing stress and depression and begin to understand their high rates of comorbidity with manic-depressive disorder.

Therapist Directions
Some group members may be recovering from alcohol or substance abuse disorders, whereas others may never have had problems. Some group members may be actively using, and others may be abstinent. Most important, each will have a different experience of the role substances play in their illness and their life (e.g., cause of episodes, self-medication of symptoms, no obvious relationship to mood state). Experiences with substance use should be listed on the board, and the costs and benefits of using drugs and alcohol should be acknowledged in a nonjudgmental manner by both other group members and the therapist.

Greater emphasis will be placed on substance use in Phase 2, wherein exploration of the costs and benefits for group members' personal Life Goals can provide more leverage for change in those for whom substance use is a current problem. At this point, the therapist elicits group discussion about, in a nonpersonal way, the negative roles substance use may play and the high rates of comorbidity.

Therapist Didactic.   How about the use of alcohol and/or drugs?

- What happens when a person drinks or uses drugs when he or she is depressed?
- Why do you think substance abuse rates are so high in persons with manic-depression?

Therapist Directions
Complete a cost-benefit analysis of suicide as a coping response using group member contributions for the lists.

Unfortunately, there are high rates of suicide in people with manic-depression and other mood disorders. Furthermore, when combined with substance use, suicide rates are even higher. Although it is difficult for many people to talk about, contemplating suicide is a coping response we need to include in today's discussion.

- How about considering suicide as the solution to depression or stress?
- At what point in depression might a person think about suicide?
- What do you think are the reasons that people with manic-depressive disorder are at high risk for suicide?
- What are the costs and benefits of suicidal behavior?

I want to conclude discussion on this very important topic by saying that contemplating suicide can be thought of as a serious *symptom* of depression or as an *attempt to cope* with stress or depression. It has been our experience that early and continuous treatment helps people to avoid the hopelessness that may accompany stress and depressive episodes, and that suicidal feelings tend to decrease when people have reasons to live. Thus, building relationships and working on Life Goals are important safeguards against suicide.

Therapist Directions
Next, display and refer group members to Exhibit 14 ("Responses to a Depressive Episode/Stress That May Trigger a Depressive Episode—2: Costs and Benefits"), and have each group member construct a cost and benefit response to at least two of his or her major responses to stress and early signs and symptoms of depression. Suggest that each member select one that is on balance beneficial and one that is detrimental. Additional worksheets may be provided for further examples that the group members can complete in the group or at home.

Turn to Exhibit 14 "Responses to a Depressive Episode/Stress That May Trigger a Depressive Episode—2: Costs and Benefits" in your notebooks. Please take the next few minutes to go through a cost-benefit analysis of at one of your major coping responses when you get depressed. In other words, choose a way you typically respond to being depressed, and make a list of the good effects and the bad effects of this response. Then, refer to your list of Personal Triggers of a Depressive Episode. Identify one or two coping strategies for specific stressors, and list the costs and benefits associated with each response.

EXHIBIT 14 Responses to a Depressive Episode/Stress That May Trigger a Depressive Episode—2: Costs and Benefits.

Response:	
Good Effects:	**Bad Effects:**

Response:	
Good Effects:	**Bad Effects:**

Response:	
Good Effects:	**Bad Effects:**

FOCUS POINT 4: Develop a Personal Action Plan for Depression.

Now that you have developed your Personal Depression Profile and identified your early warning signs and some of the coping responses that you used in the past to try to manage stress and depression, we are going to develop a Personal Action Plan to cope with depression. This is a plan that you will write on a worksheet and a card. You can keep the card in your purse or wallet to take along with you. The reason to have a card that you can keep with you is that when you're depressed, it may be hard to think clearly and recall the topics we discussed today.

- What do you think would be important to include on an action plan for depression?
- Think about responses that worked well for you in the past, and consider what you learned about today.
- What do you think would be important to include in an Action Plan to cope with stress that may lead to depression?

Let's briefly review Exhibit 15 Action Plan: Outline of Coping Strategies for Depression/Stress That May Trigger Depression.

Therapist Directions
- Write the group member contributions on the board, and follow up each with a brief group discussion regarding the rationale behind the suggestions.
- Once the group member contributions have been exhausted, display Exhibit 15 "Action Plan: Outline of Coping Strategies for Depression/Stress That May Trigger Depression." Review the list, explaining the meaning of the strategies, particularly points 7 to 10 and ask group members to complete their Exhibit 15 worksheets.

I'm now going to pass out a wallet-sized card for you to write your personal Action Plan for Depression (Exhibit 16, "Action Plan for Depression"). Fill in the card and keep it in your wallet or purse.

Therapist Directions
The group members may require assistance, depending on their cognitive functioning level. The therapist may choose to discuss specific items on the wallet-sized card to stimulate completion of the group member cards. Terminate the session with acknowledgment of the group member contributions to the group and a reminder of the next session.

EXHIBIT 15   Action Plan: Outline of Coping Strategies for Depression/Stress That May Trigger Depression

1. Alert health care provider of early depressive symptoms and stress that may lead to depression.

2. Discuss medication changes for medical illness with health care provider.

3. Get early assessment and treatment of physical illness.

4. Avoid alcohol and drugs. (Note: Even increasing tobacco can undo the effects of prescribed medication.)

5. Maintain daily routine.

6. Minimize changes in sleep routine.

7. Activate support persons: _____   _____

8. Know your personal coping skills. List specific things to do:
   -
   -

9. Know your personal coping skills. List specific things *not* to do:
   -
   -

10. Suicide prevention:
    -
    -

EXHIBIT 16   Action Plan for Depression

Action Plan for Depression

1. Check meds
2. Check: alcohol/drugs/
   nicotine
3. Recognize stress triggers:
   • Physical
   • Emotional
4. Maintain daily activities
5. Activate support persons:

6. Coping skills/to do:
   _____
   _____
7. Coping skills/not to do:
   _____
8. Contact provider
   Phone: _____
9. Support group
   Phone: _____

Action Plan for Depression

1. Check meds
2. Check: alcohol/drugs/
   nicotine
3. Recognize stress triggers:
   • Physical
   • Emotional
4. Maintain daily activities
5. Activate support persons:

6. Coping skills/to do:
   _____
   _____
7. Coping skills/not to do:
   _____
8. Contact provider
   Phone: _____
9. Support group
   Phone: _____

Action Plan for Depression

1. Check meds
2. Check: alcohol/drugs/
   nicotine
3. Recognize stress triggers:
   • Physical
   • Emotional
4. Maintain daily activities
5. Activate support persons:

6. Coping skills/to do:
   _____
   _____
7. Coping skills/not to do:
   _____
8. Contact provider
   Phone: _____
9. Support group
   Phone: _____

SESSION 6: TREATMENTS FOR MANIC-DEPRESSIVE DISORDER

SESSION RATIONALE

This session is designed to conclude Phase 1 with a completed Personal Care Plan. It provides group members with the basis for a collaborative practice model with their provider to complement the individual's self-management skills developed in Sessions 1–5. The role of pharmacological, electroconvulsive (ECT), and biological rhythm therapies is described. Emphasis is also placed on the essential role of adjunctive psychosocial treatments, including self-help programs, individual, group, and family psychotherapy, and psychoeducation to stabilize manic-depressive disorder.

Therapist Directions
Session 6 is intended for the group cohort. This session may be repeated with group members accompanied by family members, friends, or significant others that are involved in their treatment. This may take place in a group or individual format.

SESSION GOALS

1. Group members will learn that the goals of treatment for manic-depressive disorder are to improve clinical and functional outcome and to reduce personal costs, including impaired relationships, wages, and productivity.
2. Group members will understand the collaborative practice model and essential role of clear and jointly defined treatment goals, effective communication, mutual respect, and division of responsibility between the individual and his/her provider.
3. Group members will learn the importance of healthy living habits such as a structured daily routine and sleep–wake cycle regulation to improve stability in manic-depressive disorder.
4. Group members will learn the major pharmacologic interventions used as the cornerstone of treatment for manic-depressive disorder. A brief summary of the clinical and scientific legitimacy for the use of electroconvulsive therapy is presented.
5. Group members will recognize the role of self-help programs; individual, group, and family psychotherapy; and psychoeducation as essential adjuncts to the biologic treatments for manic-depressive disorder.

Focus Points

Focus Point 1: Describe the session rationale.

Orient the group members to the session rationale: to understand the goals of treatment for manic-depressive disorder, to develop skills to participate in a collaborative relationship with their provider, and to learn about the multiple complementary treatment modalities to improve mood stability. These include circadian rhythm regulation, pharmacologic treatments, and psychosocial treatments. Throughout the session, group members will be developing their Personal Care Plans for manic-depressive disorder.

Focus Point 2: Present the Collaborative Practice Model.

A Collaborative Practice Model combining the mutual skills and experience of individual and provider may improve the outcome in manic-depressive disorder. Essential to an common jointly defined goals, effective collaborative relationship are effective communication, clearly defined division of responsibility between individual and provider, mutual respect, and contingency plans for ready access to the provider with whom the patient has a collaborative treatment alliance.

Focus Point 3: Describe the regulation of circadian rhythms.

Social routines entrain, or synchronize, circadian rhythms. Social contacts, activities of daily living, and other environmental factors cue the body's clock and synchronize biological rhythms, particularly sleep. There is evidence that points to a relationship between the disruption of circadian rhythms and the onset of acute mania and depression. Minimally, the maintenance of circadian rhythms may complement medical and psychosocial treatments. Restoration of normal sleep–wake cycles is a primary step to manage mania and may commence a positive treatment response in depression.

Focus Point 4: Discuss medication management, the cornerstone of treatment for manic-depressive disorder.

Psychopharmacology is the foundation for treatment of manic-depressive disorder. A brief overview of the mainstay pharmacologic agents used to treat manic-depression is provided. Specific medications are not suggested. Rather, emphasis is placed on the collaborative relationship between provider and group member to share decisions regarding medication management and to discern the costs and benefits of each member's Personal Medication Plan. The group members' role to knowledgeably report medication side effects and describe their treatment response is accentuated. Electroconvulsive therapy is recognized as an effective treatment with clinical and scientific legitimacy.

Focus Point 5: Discuss self-help programs; individual, group, and family psychotherapy, and psychoeducation for manic-depressive disorder.

Self-help, psychotherapy, and psychoeducation are essential adjuncts to the medical treatment of manic-depressive disorder. Despite improvements in psychopharmacology, manic-depressive disorder is characterized by chronic symptoms, functional disturbances, and high rates of disability. Psychosocial treatments aimed at providing support, ameliorating the impact of stressful life events, and improving relationships may improve outcome and affect social and occupational functionality.

Focus Point 6: Complete a Personal Care Plan for manic-depressive disorder.

There are multiple personal characteristics to consider for an optimal personal plan of care. The Personal Care Plan elaborates on information gleaned throughout the session and includes information from the group members' personal mania and depression profiles, personal triggers of a manic and depressive episode, and each group member's medication plan.

SCRIPT

FOCUS POINT 1: Describe the session rationale.

Therapist Directions
Welcome the group, and distribute notebooks and worksheets as appropriate. We recommend the therapist provide multiple copies of the exhibits used in session 6 because the Personal Care Plan can be expected to change over time.

Therapist Didactic.   For the past 5 sessions we have discussed what manic-depressive disorder is, its causes, and the impact of psychiatric stigma. Each of you has been working on assembling your Personal Manic and Depressive Profiles, your personal list of stressors that may trigger a mood episode, and specific strategies to cope with both the stressors and early occurring mood symptoms. Today we are going to talk about treatments for manic-depressive disorder and each of you will complete a Personal Care Plan.

We will begin by discussing the overall goals of treatment and how to have an effective relationship with your health care provider. We believe that this is essential to good treatment. We will clarify the role of healthy living habits such as structuring your daily routine and sleep patterns and how these strategies help regulate mood. Then we will discuss specific issues about medications and other treatments. To complete the session, we will present a menu of therapies that are available to group members and their families that can have a positive influence on the outcome of your treatment. By the end of today's session, each group member will have a well thought out Personal Care Plan. This Personal Care Plan is the last task of Phase 1 of the Life Goals Program, however, this plan will likely need many revisions throughout the months and years ahead, so we are providing multiple copies to each of you. Additionally, the Personal Care Plan is a tool for you to use in working with your providers.

- Does anyone have any questions?

Let's begin by talking about treatment goals. By "goal," we mean what you want to get out of your treatment.

- What are your overall goals or expected outcomes of treatment for manic-depressive disorder?

Therapist Directions
As members contribute their ideas and beliefs about the goals of treatment, write them on the board. Do not make corrections or comment on the list, although some contributions may not be realistic. Once group contributions have been exhausted, display Exhibit 17 ("Goals of Treatment for Manic-Depressive Disorder"). Discuss them, and welcome feedback from the group members. Integrate the group member board list into the discussion.

Let's look over Exhibit 17, Goals of Treatment for Manic-Depressive Disorder.

- Are there any questions?

Now that we've reviewed the goals of treatment for manic-depressive disorder, turn to your Personal Care Plan (Exhibit 18A–E) in your notebooks. Take a moment to write one or more of your treatment goals in the spaces provided.

In Phase 2 of this program, we focus further on personal goal attainment. We will work together as a group to troubleshoot problems that interfere with reaching personal and other treatment goals.

FOCUS POINT 2: Present the Collaborative Practice Model.

There are many models of care in mental health treatment. Many of you have had experiences with different models. Some of these may have been

EXHIBIT 17   Goals of Treatment for Manic-Depressive Disorder

1. To improve symptoms:

   - Recognize, prevent, limit, and/or manage depressive mood symptoms.

   - Recognize, prevent, limit, and/or manage manic mood symptoms.

2. To improve functioning:

   - Improve or maintain social relationships.

   - Improve or maintain family relationships.

   - Achieve personal life goals in work, leisure, and social activities.

3. To improve life stress management skills:

   - Develop skills to prevent and/or manage life stress to prevent or limit stress-triggered mood episodes.

EXHIBIT 18   Personal Care Plan

18A: Treatment Team

**Person to Contact in
Case of Emergency**

Name: _____   Name: _____

Address: _____   Address: _____

Day/work phone: _____   Relationship: _____

Evening phone: _____   Day/work phone: _____

                             Evening phone: _____

Personal treatment goals:

1. _____
2. _____
3. _____
4. _____

Treatment Team   **Phone Numbers**

Name: _____   _____

Medication prescribers: _____   _____

Group therapist: _____   _____

Individual therapist: _____   _____

Prescriber alternate coverage: _____   _____

Things I will expect from my provider:

1. _____
2. _____
3. _____
4. _____

Things I will do to effectively collaborate with my treatment team:

1. _____
2. _____
3. _____
4. _____

EXHIBIT 18B   Personal Daily Activity and Sleep Routine

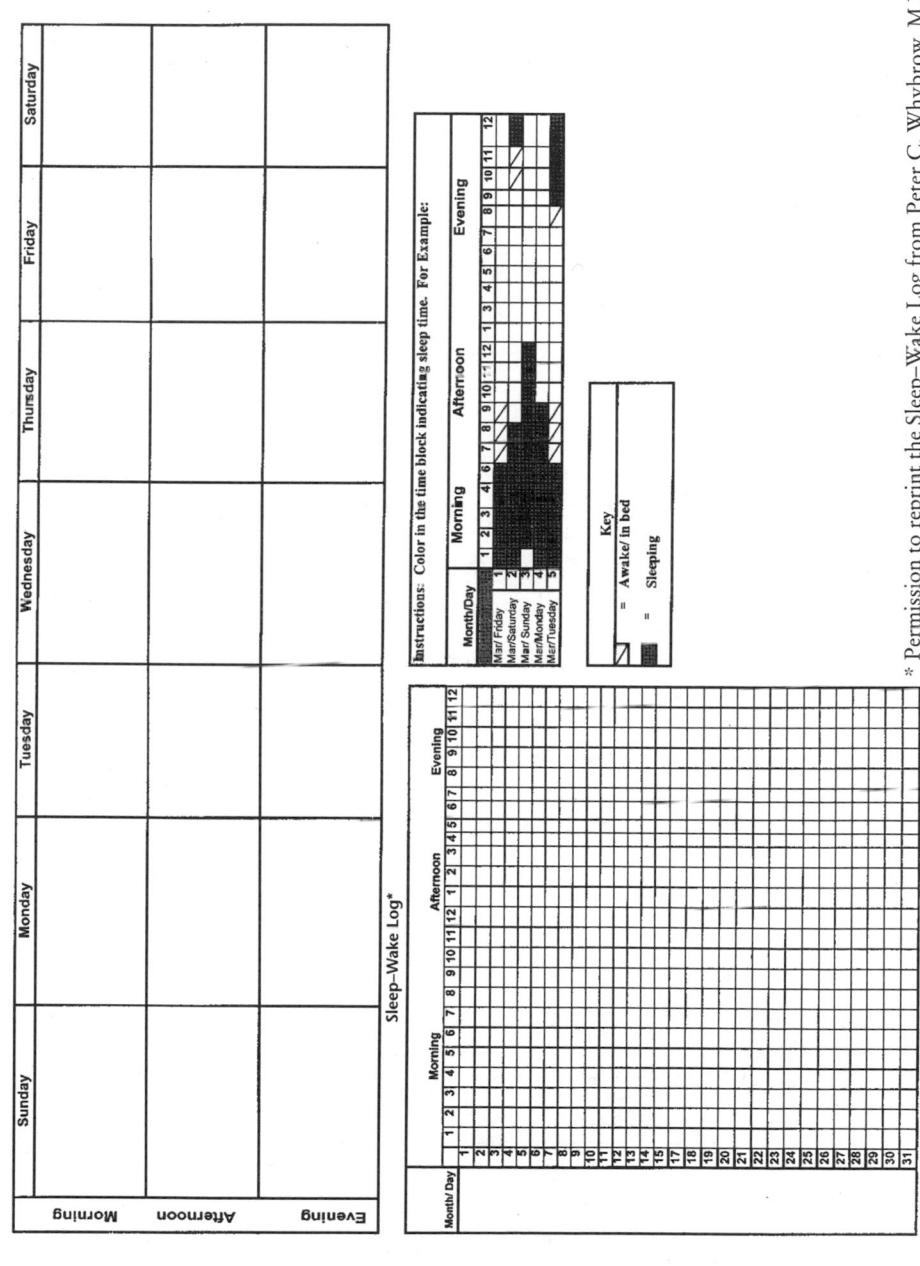

* Permission to reprint the Sleep–Wake Log from Peter C. Whybrow, M.D.

EXHIBIT 18C   Current Medications*

Date   Mood Stabilizers   Dose   Instructions

_____ _____ _____   _____
_____ _____ _____   _____
_____ _____ _____   _____
_____ _____

Date   Antidepressants   Dose   Instructions

_____ _____ _____   _____
_____ _____ _____   _____
_____ _____ _____   _____

Date   Antipsychotics   Dose   Instructions

_____ _____ _____   _____
_____ _____ _____   _____
_____ _____ _____   _____

Date   Other Psychiatric Medications Dose   Instructions

_____ _____ _____   _____
_____ _____ _____   _____
_____ _____ _____   _____

Date   Medical Medications   Dose   Instructions

_____ _____ _____   _____
_____ _____ _____   _____
_____ _____ _____   _____

* Update and add additional sheets as necessary to keep current and to provide a handy "look-back" at your treatment history.

EXHIBIT 18D   Costs and Benefits of Treatment

Medication or Other Treatment:	
Good Effects:	**Bad Effects:**

Medication or Other Treatment:	
Good Effects:	**Bad Effects:**

Medication or Other Treatment:	
Good Effects:	**Bad Effects:**

EXHIBIT 18E   Personal Care Plan—Self-Help and Psychotherapy

These are the therapies I am selecting and the reasons why:

_____ Individual therapy

_____

_____

_____

_____

_____ Family therapy

_____

_____

_____

_____

_____ Group therapy

_____

_____

_____

_____

_____ National Depressive and Manic Depressive Association

_____

_____

_____

_____

_____ National Alliance of the Mentally Ill

_____

_____

_____

_____

helpful and others not as helpful. It has been our experience that the most effective and satisfying treatment relationship occurs when individuals and their providers work *collaboratively* to manage manic-depressive disorder. To collaborate means that both the individual and provider actively participate in manic-depressive symptom recognition and in making decisions about the individual's mental health treatment. Each person brings his/her special skills to the relationship. For instance, your provider has special training and skills in treating manic-depressive disorder, as well as experience with what has helped other people. However, you also have special skills and experience in what *your* pattern has been—this is much of what we have been working on in Phase 1. In addition, family members or other important people in your life may be able to contribute constructively. Keep in mind that relationship building is a process that takes the effort of people, time, and patience.

- What do you think the ingredients are for an effective individual–provider relationship?
- What are the characteristics you want in your provider?
- What is your responsibility in the treatment relationship?
- What makes treatment relationships that you have had go well?
- What makes the relationship go poorly?
- Who do you call when your provider is off duty or on vacation?

Therapist Directions
Write group member contributions on the board. Briefly discuss each contribution as it is listed. Once group member contributions are exhausted, display Exhibit 19 ("Essentials of a Collaborative Treatment Relationship"). Discuss items on the list. Emphasize the importance of communication, especially early symptoms of mania, depression, and any problems with treatment.

Take a moment to turn to your Personal Care Plan (Exhibit 18), and complete 18A, "Treatment Team." Then, list the things about a provider that are important to *you* and the things *you* will do to collaborate in your treatment. Also, indicate the name and telephone number of the person to contact when your provider is off or on vacation. Some of you may need to discuss this during your next appointment with your provider. You are strongly encouraged to bring your Personal Care Plan to your appointments. Discuss and review it frequently with your provider(s). Remember working effectively with your provider is a process that takes time, effort, and a lot of reinforcement.

EXHIBIT 19   Essentials of a Collaborative Treatment Relationship

1. Clearly defined treatment goals
   - The individual and provider are working together to achieve a common purpose and jointly set realistic goals.

2. Effective communication
   - The individual understands the meaning of what the provider is communicating.
   - The provider understands the meaning of what the individual is communicating.
   - The individual communicates his/her symptoms of mania and/or depression
   - The individual communicates problems with treatment side effects

3. Complementary skills and division of responsibility
   - The individual and provider recognize each other's knowledge, skill, and ability.

4. Mutual respect
   - There is a mutual absence of stigmatizing behavior.

FOCUS POINT 3: Describe the regulation of circadian rhythms.

During Session 1, we discussed the biological basis underlying manic-depressive disorder. We learned that all thoughts, feelings, and behaviors are regulated by brain cells. We learned that brain cells contain substances called neurotransmitters and that it is an imbalance in this system that leads to manic and depressive mood episodes. The system in the brain that regulates mood is related to another system that regulates biological rhythms, or our body's "clock." Our body's clock regulates our sleep and wakeful activity cycles. We also learned that factors in the environment like stress, can affect these systems and cause symptoms. We discussed various ways to handle these stresses in Sessions 2–5. Stresses to your "clock" can also affect your neurotransmitters and cause symptoms.

Therapist Directions
During the discussion above, refer to Exhibits 3 and 4 in Session 2 to facilitate understanding of the biology being discussed. Draw the following diagram of the feedback loop to facilitate group member understanding of the relationship between mood and biological rhythms.

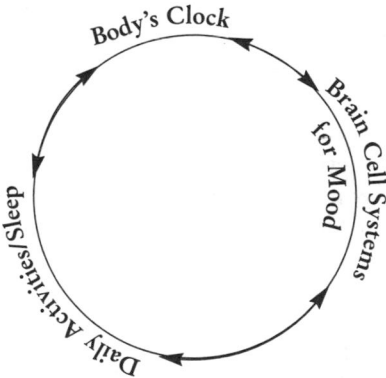

- Are there any questions so far?

Our daily activities and sleep patterns help to regulate or "set" our body's clock. Structuring a routine of daily activities and sleep may be protective and help to regulate moods in manic-depressive disorder. People with manic-depressive disorder are often very vulnerable to changes in routine because these changes may lead to mood episodes. Forces that help to set the body's clock include social contacts and activities of daily life. They act as "cues" and signal the brain to set our biological rhythms (body's clock). Among the most powerful "cues" for our body's clock are light and daily activities. We think maintaining a structured routine is a very important part of managing manic-depression.

- What would you include on a list of structured daily activities?
- What are some of the activities you do each day as part of your personal care?
- How about routine contacts with family, friends, or coworkers? Meal and medication times?
- What do you do each day for relaxation or exercise?
- What is your sleep routine?

Therapist Directions
Write group member contributions on the board. Once the board list is complete, refer group members to Exhibit 18B ("Personal Daily Activity and Sleep Routine Schedule"). Provide examples of how to complete the Daily Activity Schedule using examples from the group list.

Now that we have a list of things that may be included in a structured daily activity and sleep routine, you may begin to work on Exhibit 18B ("Personal Daily Activity and Sleep Routine Schedule"). You may need more time following the group to complete it at home. As you become more familiar with your daily activity and sleep schedule, you may come to notice that stress can disrupt your schedule and lead to early symptoms of mania and depression. Keeping your daily activity and sleep schedule is one strategy you can maintain to help limit major mood disturbances.

Notice the section on the Personal Daily Activity and Sleep Routine in the lower left corner called "Sleep–Wake Log." Directions for using this log are provided on the right lower section of your exhibit. The Sleep–Wake Log is simple to use and can be a valuable resource to the overall management of manic-depressive disorder. For example, it may be useful as a tool for you and your provider to monitor progress while treating a sleep disturbance. Sleep loss is often a symptom of mania. The "log" may help to signal early manic symptoms.

- Can you think of other examples of how the Sleep–Wake Log may help with your treatment?

Because a stable sleep routine is an essential tool for managing manic-depressive disorder, let's review some of the "rules" of good sleep hygiene together.

> **Therapist Directions**
> Refer to Exhibit 20 ("Good Sleep Habits"). Briefly review each of the items listed.

FOCUS POINT 4: Discuss medication management, the cornerstone of treatment for manic-depressive disorder.

Therapist Didactic.   Now we are going to discuss several important topics about the medications used to treat manic-depressive disorder. We will *not* review each group member's personal medication plan. Rather, our goal today is to discuss strategies to help you to be confident and knowledgeable when you make treatment decisions with your prescriber about medications and other medical treatments. Specifically, we would like you to use your personal cost-benefit analysis skills to evaluate at least one medication you are using. This approach will help you later when making treatment decisions with your prescriber.

But first, a little bit of background. We will start with a brief review of the four major medication groups used to treat manic-depressive disorder.

- Are there any questions?

There are basically four groups of medications used to treat manic-depression. They are the mood stabilizers, antidepressants, antipsychotics (also known as neuroleptics or major tranquilizers), and benzodiazepines (also known as minor tranquilizers).

> **Therapist Directions**
> Refer to Exhibit 21 ("Medications Used in the Treatment of Manic-Depressive Disorder") throughout this discussion. You may briefly review specific medications. Encourage group members to bring specific problems to their providers. Base your rationale on the importance of the collaborative treatment relationship between individuals and their providers.

EXHIBIT 20   Good Sleep Habits

1. Use your bedroom only for sleeping. Read, watch television, and talk elsewhere.

2. Do not go to bed until you are drowsy.

3. Get up at about the same time every day, even on weekends—it's hard to shift your sleep and wake times back and forth.

4. No naps!

5. No alcohol within 2 hours of bedtime.

6. No tobacco within 2 hours of bedtime.

7. No caffeine within 6 hours or more of bedtime (caffeine is in coffee, tea, chocolate, cola, and many other types of soda).

8. Avoid lots of fluids before bed, and empty bladder before retiring. Adjust the time to your personal response.

9. Take any bedtime or "qhs" medications 1 hour before retiring.

10. Maintain regular exercise (best in the morning or afternoon).

Notes:

- Follow the guidelines religiously.
- Don't expect quick changes; 2 or 3 weeks may pass before you notice any improvement.
- If you want to wake up earlier because you're oversleeping, move your wake-up time back by ½ hour each day until you're getting up at the time you want. This also works if you want to get to sleep earlier at night.

EXHIBIT 21 Medications Used in the Treatment of Manic-Depressive Disorder (Generic [chemical] name is followed by common brand name(s))

Putative Mood Stabilizers

Carbamazepine	Tegretol
Lamotrigine	Lamictal
Lithium	Eskalith
	Lithobid
Valproate	Depakote

Antidepressants

- **Tricyclics**

Amitriptyline	Elavil
Amoxapine	Asendin
Clomipramine	Anafranil
Desipramine	Norpramine
Doxepin	Sinequan
Imipramine	Tofranil
Nortriptyline	Aventyl
Protriptyline	Vivactil
Trimipramine	Surmontil

- **Selective Serotonin Reuptake Inhibitors**

Citalopram	Cylexa
Fluoxetine	Prozac
Paroxetine	Paxil
Sertraline	Zoloft

- **Serotonin-Norepinephrine Reuptake Inhibitors (SNRIs)**

Mirtazepine	Remeron
Venlafaxine	Effexor

- **Heterocyclic Agents**

Bupropion	Wellbutrin
Nefazodone	Serzone
Trazodone	Deseryl

- **Monoamine Oxidase Inhibitors (MAOIs)**

Phenelzine	Nardil
Tranylcypromine	Parnate

Antipsychotics—Typical

Chlorpromazine	Thorazine
Fluphenazine	Prolixin/Permitil
Haloperidol	Haldol
Loxapine	Loxitane/Daxolin
Mesoridazine	Serentil
Molindone	Moban
Perphenazine	Trilafon
Pimozide	Orap
Thioridazine	Mellaril
Thiothixene	Navane
Trifluoperazine	Stelazine

Antipsychotics—Atypical

Clozapine	Clozaril
Olanzapine	Zyprexa
Quetiapine	Seroquel
Risperidone	Risperdal
Ziprazodone	Geodon

Benzodiazepines

Alprazolam	Xanax
Chlordiazepoxide	Librium
Clonazepam	Klonopin
Clorazepate	Tranxene
Diazepam	Valium
Flurazepam	Dalmane
Halazepam	Paxipam
Lorazepam	Ativan
Oxazepam	Serax
Prazepam	Centrax
Temazepam	Restoril
Triazolam	Halcion

Other Agents

Buspirone	BuSpar
Gabapentin	Neurontin
Methylphenidate	Ritalin
Pemoline	Cylert
Tiagabine	Gabitril
Topiramate	Topamax
Zolpidem	Ambien

The mood stabilizers include lithium and a group of medicines known as the anticonvulsants. The mood stabilizers are the cornerstone of treatment for manic-depressive disorder. They are mainly good for treatding mania, but are often give long term to prevent future mania. This means they are the foundation for treatment. Many of the mood stabilizers have a range of values for a therapeutic level. Also, medications generally have two names, the generic name and the trade name. We have them listed for you.

The next group of medications are the antidepressants. They may be used to treat the depressive phase of manic-depressive disorder. Antidepressants are prescribed only if the individual is protected (from mania) with a therapeutic blood level of one or more mood-stabilizing medications. Some of the antidepressants are sedating and are used to induce sleep. Others are more energizing, for people who are slowed down by their depression.

The antipsychotics are often prescribed to treat psychosis, the hallucinations and disturbances in thinking that can accompany manic and depressive episodes. They are also used to treat mania. This group has several names. In addition to being called antipsychotics, they may be referred to as neuroleptics or by their older name, the major tranquilizers.

Please refer now to Exhibit 18C, Personal Care Plan—Current Medications. Fill in your medications using the spaces provided.

Therapist Directions
Time must be provided for group members to fill in their medications. Then, facilitate an example of a cost–benefit analysis of a specific medication chosen by the group using Exhibit 18D. The therapist may wish to refer to the tables of efficacy and side effects for classes of medications in chapter 4, or to individual drug profiles in the *Field Guide for Psychiatric Assessment and Treatment* (Bauer, 2003).

We are all aware that there are advantages and disadvantages associated with the personal use of specific medications. Take a moment to complete a cost–benefit analysis of one or two of the medications you are taking. Let's discuss an example.

Therapist Didactic. The media provides lots of information about new treatments, medications, nutritional supplements, and alternative therapies for a variety of disorders. Media information can be very influential to consumers. Whether you are listening to an advertisement or discussing traditional medications with your prescriber, it is important to make informed decisions, be able to evaluate what you hear, and weigh the personal costs and benefits.

For example, lithium is the primary agent used to stabilize mood in manic-depressive disorder. Its effectiveness has been demonstrated repeatedly in good scientific research studies. Some people who take lithium have few, if any, side effects. Others may have problems with hand tremor, thirst, and frequent urination. Tremor may not be a problem for some, but it may be a big problem for a toolmaker, seamstress, or violinist. In this case, to make an informed decision, you would weigh your decision based on the way your own illness responds to lithium and the side effects you might experience.

Let's consider another example. Electroconvulsive therapy (ECT), because of its controversial history, was almost eliminated as a medical treatment two decades ago. Also, many people have strong feelings about ECT because of how it has been portrayed by the media. However, there have been many reputable clinical trials demonstrating it as a significant treatment for depression and mania. These trials have been published in reputable journals. ECT is usually considered when other treatments fail, when there are complicating medical illnesses prohibiting the use of other treatments, or when the situation calls for fast treatment results. There are treatment procedures that now guide ECT practice. As with other treatments for mania and depression, a person should weigh the costs and benefits.

Therapist Direction
You may provide time for a brief discussion of ECT. Emphasize that selection of ECT is commonly done as a result of an individual weighing the costs and benefits with his/her provider.

It can be easy to believe advertisements, especially when they promise breakthrough results. Herbal and "natural" treatments are well publicized. In fact, it has been estimated that 20% to 30% of the U.S. population uses one or more herbal remedies. It seems that most of the people using these agents have chronic illnesses. Because something is called "natural" or "herbal" does not mean it is safe or better than traditional medicine. In fact, there are no FDA (Food and Drug Administration) restrictions that ensure quality control with regard to these products. That means we cannot rely on the label to tell us that what is advertised is actually in the product or present in the amount described. It's left up to the manufacturer to decide. Many of these over-the-counter products have side effects, can have interactions with other medicines, and may cause medical problems that can be dangerous. Always talk with your provider before starting one of these remedies. The decision to use them is, of course, up to you. But your provider may have helpful information or experience to share. At the very least, he or she should know what you are taking because of drug interactions and side effects.

- Any questions?
- What are some questions you would ask yourself or your provider selecting medication, over-the-counter products, or other therapies to treat manic-depressive disorder?

Therapist Directions
As group members contribute their ideas about questions that should be asked to make informed decisions, make a list on the board. Keep the group focused. Be sure not to correct contributions or be judgmental. Once the board list is complete, refer to Exhibit 22 ("Making Informed Decisions and Evaluating Treatment"). Review the items in the exhibit, emphasizing the contributions made by the group members.

Now let's review Exhibit 22, Making Informed Treatment Decisions and Evaluating Treatment.

We encourage you to ask yourself these questions, discuss them with your provider, then decide whether to take a specific medication or try a new treatment. Be sure to discuss your response to the treatment and any side effects with your provider during your next appointment or sooner if you're having problems.

FOCUS POINT 5: Discuss self-help programs, individual, group, and family psychotherapy, and psychoeducation for manic-depressive disorder.

Thus far in this session we've discussed several topics of importance as you develop your Personal Care Plan: the goals of treatments, forming a collaborative decision-making alliance with your health care providers, the value of having a structured daily activity and sleep schedule, and important things to consider with your provider when you make decisions about your choice of medication and other treatments. Next, we are going to discuss the therapies, educational sources, and self-help programs available to help people with manic-depressive disorder.

We talked in Sessions 2 and 4 about personal stressors that may trigger a manic or depressive episode. Although manic-depressive disorder is a medical condition with a biological basis and is effectively treated with medications, stress and social support also play a crucial role in how a person's condition behaves. Stress can trigger an episode of depression or mania and can affect recovery time. The support of helpful people can reduce the impact of stress.

EXHIBIT 22   Making Informed Decisions and Evaluating Treatment

1. Where did you hear about this treatment? Was it from a reliable source?

2. Was proof of the benefit determined in scientific studies?

3. Were the results published in a reputable journal?

4. Were the people in the study similar to you (age, gender, lifestyle)?

5. Could other factors lead to the same results (seasonal changes, other treatments or medications)?

6. Does the treatment require that you stop another medication or treatment or change your diet?

7. Is information about the potential dangers or "costs" associated with the treatment listed?

8. How much does it cost financially?

9. How does the new treatment balance out in a cost-benefit analysis?

10. Is the new treatment worth it (benefits)?

11. What is your provider's recommendation about this treatment?

Psychotherapies are designed, in part, to buffer stress. Stress is a problem for everyone, not just people with mood disorders. For this reason, these therapies are helpful to many people, not only people with manic-depressive disorder.

Therapist Directions

List group member contributions on the board under the headings "Individual Therapy," "Family Therapy," "Group Therapy," and "Self-Help." Provide a separate list of local chapters of the Depressive and Bipolar Support Alliance (DBSA; formerly called the National Depressive and Manic-Depressive Association; NDMDA) and the National Alliance for the Mentally Ill (NAMI). Once the group list is exhausted, refer to Exhibit 23 ("Psychotherapies for Manic-Depressive Disorder"). Briefly review the list. Next, refer group members to Exhibit 18E ("Personal Care Plan—Self-Help and Psychotherapy"). Ask group members to place a check mark in the spaces provided next to therapies that may be beneficial to them.

They include individual, family, and group psychotherapies and educational programs. Additionally, there are self-help support groups in the community. Let's take a moment to look back to Exhibits 6 ("Personal Triggers of a Manic Episode") and 12 ("Personal Triggers of a Depressive Episode").

As you review your worksheets:

- What are some problems or stressors that may benefit from individual therapy?
- What are some problems or stressors that may benefit from family therapy?
- What are some problems or stressors people with manic-depressive disorder might have that may benefit from attending group therapy?
- How might a person benefit from attending a self-help support group?

Let's review Exhibit 23, Psychotherapies for Manic-Depressive Disorder.

Next, look at Exhibit 18E, Personal Care Plan—Self-Help and Psychotherapy. Write in the spaces provided the reasons you may be involved with a specific therapy or self-help group.

- How will you access therapy if you've selected one?

EXHIBIT 23   Psychotherapies for Manic-Depressive Disorder

Goals of All Psychotherapies

- Support in meeting the challenges of manic-depressive disorder
- Education about manic-depressive disorder
- Improving daily life function despite manic-depressive disorder
- Learning illness management skills
- Management of beneficial and harmful feelings, thoughts, and behaviors

Individual Therapy

- Dealing with past life events (especially psychodynamic, supportive therapy)
- Dealing with social relationships (especially interpersonal therapy)
- Improving patterns of thought and behavior (especially cognitive-behavioral therapy)
- Stabilizing social rhythms (especially social rhythm therapy)

Group Therapy

- Mutual support
- Mutual education through shared experiences
- Improve social skills
- Stigma reduction

Family Therapy

- Assist in conflict resolution and conflict prevention between family members
- Educate family members about manic-depressive disorder
- Increase supportive family relationships

Self-Help Groups

- Wide-ranging information about manic-depressive disorder
- Mutual support
- Advocacy
- Stigma reduction
- Examples of stable and collaborative support groups

    - Depression and Bipolar Support Alliance (DBSA; formerly National Depressive and Manic-Depressive Association; NDMDA; www.NDMDA.org; www.NDMDA.org; National office phone: 800-826-3632; Local chapter phone: _____)
    - National Alliance for the Mentally Ill (NAMI); www.NAMI.org; National office phone: 800-749-3197; Local chapter phone _____)

FOCUS POINT 6: Complete a Personal Care Plan for manic-depressive disorder.

Therapist Didactic.   Each of you has developed a Personal Care Plan. This plan is intended to be an ongoing process, and it's likely it will change and evolve through the months ahead. Look it over carefully. We encourage you to take this plan to review with your provider, therapist, and someone in your life who is helpful or could learn to be helpful to you. Remember, it is not expected that you learn everything about manic-depressive disorder in just 6 weeks. It takes a lot of practice to use these skills and develop your resources. Many times group members select topics from their Personal Care Plan or Sessions 1–5 to focus on during Phase 2.

Phase 2 begins (date, time, and location). Phase 2 of the Life Goals Program is different from Phase 1. During Phase 2, there are no formal presentations by the group leader; however, we will go over any of the material from Phase 1 you would like to review. Phase 2 is an open-ended group where members work on goals that are meaningful to them and review the skills learned in Phase 1. Doing this in a group allows us to brainstorm solutions together to problems common to many people and get support to manage stress.

- Any questions?

Therapist Directions
Close the group. Thank members for their participation. Provide information about the date, time, and location of Session 6 for families of those interested group members. Provide the date, time, and location of Phase 2.

Chapter 8

The Life Goals Program Phase 2

And see the great Achilles, whom we knew,
Though much is taken, much abides; and though
We are not now that strength which in old days
Moved earth and heaven; that which we are, we are;
One equal temper of heroic hearts,
Made weak by time and fate, but strong in will
To strive, to seek, to find, and not to yield.

Alfred Tennyson, *Ulysses*

OVERVIEW

The Goals of Phase 2 of the Life Goals Program are (1) to improve clinical outcome by helping group members to collaborate effectively with their treatment team and to reiterate and strengthen the illness management skills developed in Phase 1 and (2) to improve functional outcome by helping group members to achieve functional goals that they have not been able to attain because of illness. Phase 2 is organized not by weeks but by specific goals. It uses primarily behavioral and cognitive techniques, but also integrates low-intensity interpersonal and psychodynamic therapeutic interventions aimed at supporting, motivating, and facilitating group members' working through their personal goal agenda. The group member agenda shifts week to week depending on members' progress with their personal goals, illness manifestations, treatment side effects, experiences with psychiatric stigma, and interpersonal relationships within and outside the group. Phase 1 material is revisited in the course of conducting Phase 2 sessions over and over again. Group members may assimilate illness management skills differently throughout the program as they grow and learn.

233

The backbone of Phase 2 treatment is behaviorally structured to facilitate group member identification of their overall goals, break them down into meaningful and realistically attainable subgoals, construct and carry out the behavioral steps toward reaching each goal, and troubleshooting roadblocks to goal attainment. These stages are summarized in Table 8.1. An orientation session is included as a guideline for the therapist to facilitate the first few meetings of Phase 2.

The goal-attainment plan is structured into a working format according to the four principles, summarized in Table 8.2. First, the goal must be chosen by the individual and be important to his or her quality of life. Second, the goal must be specifically measurable. Third, the goal must be formulated to depend primarily on the actions of the individual himself or herself and not depend on the cooperation of another person. Fourth, the goal must be broken down into a series of small, realistically attainable steps.

Recall from chapter 6 that individuals are assumed to act in their own self-interest in managing manic-depressive disorder and its attendant morbidity. However, their strategies to cope may be ineffective and lead to less than optimal results and concordant patterns of thought, feeling, and behavior.

It is important to emphasize, as with illness coping skills discussed in Phase 1, that functional coping strategies are also not random or haphazard. Rather, they are a product of the individual's personal cost–benefit analysis. In the course of Phase 2, as in Phase 1, the group member will become more conscious of the impact of his/her coping choices, and revise as necessary for better outcome. Thus, various roadblocks to goal attainment are expected. There are several types of roadblocks common to group members. For example, motivation may wax and wane as part of the change process (Prochaska & DiClemente, 1984); a simple lack of experience in thinking in terms of goals and realistically attainable steps frequently needs to be overcome. Symptoms of mania and depression will disrupt progress from time to time, and for some persons, chronic low-grade symptoms and medication side effects may inhibit progress over a long period of time. Other roadblocks are caused by treatment nonadherence, problems accessing resources, competing challenges related to family or other personal relationships, and academic or employment circumstances. Additionally, group member Roadblocks may manifest as negative thinking styles and dysfunctional attitudes consequent to losses incurred by the illness. Multiple losses may lead to hopelessness, isolation, and lack of peer modeling, as well as the sequelae of psychiatric stigma. Roadblocks are addressed through the judicious use of cognitive and interpersonal group techniques.

Progress, or outcome, in Phase 2 is tracked by assessing status with respect to clinical outcome and progress toward personal goals. Progress is here defined as achievement of behavioral steps or coping with roadblocks originating from the illness, the environment, or other personal factors.

TABLE 8.1   Five Stages in Goal Attainment

1. Description of the Challenge
2. Overall Goal Identification
3. Subgoal Development
4. Construction of Behavioral Steps and Monitoring Progress
5. Troubleshooting Roadblocks

TABLE 8.2   Four Principles for Goal Development

1. Goals must be chosen by the individual and be important to his or her quality of life.
2. Goals must be formatted so that progress is objectively measurable.
3. Goals must be formatted to depend primarily on the actions of the individual himself or herself and not depend on the cooperation of another person.
4. Goals must be broken down into a series of small, realistically attainable steps.

Progress may be further defined as recognizing the unrealistic quality of a specific goal and rethinking a more realistic overall goal. Progress with behavioral steps is facilitated by simple progress tracking sheets, used by the group member and reviewed by the therapist. Once an overall goal is reached, the process can begin again with a new overall goal, or treatment may be terminated. Participation is thus open ended. Often, the group will become more cohesive over time, and group members with chronic symptoms will seek to continue and benefit from its interpersonal, supportive, and goal-focused profit.

This section of the manual has a hybrid organization. As in Phase 1, the core of this section consists of a highly structured outline of components of the therapy and specific therapist guidelines to achieve the therapeutic objectives. This edition of the manual also provides the therapist with an optional Phase 2 session outline. In this example, the guidelines provide language that may help facilitate group member understanding of the theoretical underpinnings, purpose, and methods used in Phase 2. The example includes the *Five Stages of Goal Attainment: Description of the Challenge, Goal Identification, Subgoal Development, Construction of Behavioral Steps and Monitoring Progress, and Troubleshooting Roadblocks* (see Table 8.1). Each of the stages is organized into components that include the objective to be reached by the member and the therapist directions that delineate in succinct terms the therapist's input and response to help the group member achieve the objective.

During each step of working toward goals, group members will typically need a highly active therapist offering a road map for goal development (see Table 8.2) and support for group members in their efforts. Additionally, the therapist will have proficient assessment skills and use therapeutic interventions to address the multitude of roadblocks that may interrupt group member progress. Group members are likely to encounter roadblocks at each stage of goal attainment. For the purpose of clarity, group member barriers or obstacles are referred to as roadblocks, which are discussed in detail, as are therapist strategies for addressing them. Types of roadblocks and strategies used to address them are summarized in Table 8.3. For simplicity, roadblocks are grouped together and covered separately in the section that follows the individual stages of treatment, rather than being repeated under each stage. This is because similar roadblocks may appear at any juncture of the stages in the goal attainment process. If the therapist strategies to respond to these roadblocks differ substantively in different stages, notations are made where appropriate. Additionally, case examples, or *Vignettes,* are provided to illustrate the more complex roadblocks and interventions that may be helpful. Table 8.4 offers a quick reference with examples of therapist strategies for roadblocks to goal attainment.

To complement the basic structure of this section of the manual, individual components are amplified by narrative text. These comments have been added to emphasize the points made and relate specific aspects of the therapy to its theoretical underpinnings. The comments provide background, amplify strategies, and offer rationale.

ESTABLISHING THE GROUP CULTURE AND BOUNDARY CONDITIONS

Using the first session, and oftentimes part of subsequent sessions of Phase 2 to establish the group culture and reviewing the rules and objectives will allow the further development of group cohesion and empathy and is time well spent. It is recommended that the first few Phase 2 sessions focus on orientation of the members to the methods that will be used during the upcoming sessions to facilitate goal attainment, and also to review illness management skills (e.g., Action Plans, Personal Care Plans). It is important to reiterate guidelines specific to the development and maintenance of a supportive group culture, as was done in the first session of Phase 1. It is also recommended that the therapist review these topics whenever the group needs reinforcement or if new members enter an ongoing group cohort.

The therapist should explain the rationale for having goal attainment as the focus of Phase 2 of the program. This discussion should focus on the issue that persons affected by manic-depressive disorder may have a severe

TABLE 8.3   Roadblocks to Goal Attainment

Source of Roadblock	Addressed by
Lack of experience in thinking in terms of Goals and Behavioral Steps	Behavioral strategies Personal cost-benefit analyses Interpersonal group techniques (e.g., imitative behavior, interpersonal learning)
Disease symptoms	Illness management skills Pharmacotherapy Cognitive techniques
Dysfunctional attitudes	Cognitive techniques
Demoralization, isolation, stigmatization	Interpersonal group techniques (e.g., instillation of hope, emphasis on universality, strengthening of group cohesiveness, catharsis)

illness that may have disrupted progress to reach their Life's Goals, and may also have hampered mastery of the tasks associated with working toward goals. The skills associated with organizing effective plans to reach their goals and concurrently cope with the challenges of daily life and living with manic-depressive illness may need to be learned, old learning may need to be reinforced, or a backbone of solid support, such as the group, may be needed to overcome roadblocks and gain success. As in Phase 1, it is important to facilitate member sharing from a general to a more personal level about how the illness may have generated multiple problems including devastating personal, social, economic, and occupational losses. Additionally, the demoralization associated with psychiatric stigma may have added to the person's trauma, and acknowledging this supports the building of empathy both between the therapist and individual members and among the members themselves.

Helping members to cope with the effects of psychiatric stigma is an ongoing process in Phase 2 groups. Psychiatric stigma can be regarded as an unavoidable reality in the members' lives, and its impact will be manifest in several ways. Low self-confidence, hopelessness, anger, avoidance, and nonadherence to treatment and are frequent effects of stigma. Specific social and occupational behavioral plans such as job applications and sharing information with new acquaintances will require active group support to identify coping strategies that have fewer costs for the member.

The therapist is encouraged to discuss how group members may help each other identify ways to manage their illness and its sequelae and the value of doing this work in a group. Members can share their ideas with others who

TABLE 8.4 Examples of Therapist Strategies for Roadblocks to Goal Attainment

Roadblocks to be prepared for	Examples of therapist strategies for Goal Attainment
1. No Goals identified due to lack of experience in thinking in terms of Goals and behaviors	• Ask members to provide examples of goals they have had in their lives and how they have gone about approaching them. • As group members vent their personal challenges and problems with their illness, extract goals from the discussion. • Brainstorm. • Seed examples if the group does not generate their own. Example statement: "As I listen to you talk about _____ I'm aware of multiple opportunities for you to identify specific goals."
2. Overly ambitious Goals and steps identified due to inexperience	• Reconstruct an overly ambitious goal into several realistic subgoals. • Reinforce the rationale for more realistic goals and subgoals is to be able to know when and how the goal was attained.
3. Imprecise Goals and steps are identified due to lack of experience	• Help participant formulate goals into measurable and behavioral terms. • Brainstorm with the group. Example statement: "Let's state your goal in a way that we will know when and how you attained it." .
4. Goals and steps are formulated to depend primarily on others	• Focus goal formulation on the individual's role in attainment. Example statement: " Although we will often work with and around other people, goals are attainable only when we rely on ourselves to reach them." .
5. Writer's block	• Explicitly point out the uncomfortable dynamic (feeling like the student). • Point out that if a person does not set out a concrete and specific goal, he or she can never recognize success. • Set members up for success by helping them set realistic, achievable goals. • Identify the faulty assumptions underlying the thought that "If I adopt a small goal I am a less capable or worthwhile person."

TABLE 8.4 (*Continued*)

6. No Goals or steps are identified due to depressive symptoms	• Structure modest, symptom-related goals and steps, (e.g., depression management). • Begin each session with a query about how group members' illness has behaved over the past week. • Accept and support the depressed member at his or her level of participation. Example statement: "Coming to group when depressed is a goal accomplished."
7. Overly ambitious Goals and steps are identified due to hypomanic symptoms	• Refer to action plans for mood episodes. • Refer to each member's personal mania profile. • Elicit a cost-benefit analysis of hypomania. Example statements: "I am noting a change in your mood. Is this something you've noticed? What has been the advantage of having a mood such as this? What is the disadvantage?"
8. No Goals or steps are identified due to demoralization and hopelessness derived from chronic illness	• Counter hopelessness with personal cost-benefit analysis (e.g., point out that having no Goals means avoiding exposure to the humiliation of failure of some type). • Counter hopelessness with group supportive feedback. • Refer to the change principles outlined in chapter 7. • Explore sources of expectations for failure using cognitive techniques. • Watch for irrational thinking, such as minimizing success, magnifying adverse experience, or appraising other individuals erroneously. Example statement: "What would you like to have in your life next year at this time, different from today?"
9. Overly ambitious Goals and steps are identified due to self-esteem deficits or to denial	• Point out the need to set oneself up for success. • Ask if this has been a trend in the past and how it worked out. • Help group members focus on taking information from their overly ambitious goal, and formulate several subgoals that are realistically more attainable. Example statement: "In order to relearn belief in oneself, one needs to succeed. Let's start with small steps, and they will grow into larger successes."

have had personal experience something like their own. Members can share their experiences and help one another to think about strategies to reach their Goals, solve problems, and overcome the effects of these and other trauma. Through techniques like listening, speaking one at a time, offering general and personal information, and offering feedback and encouragement, members will benefit from interpersonal learning. This will translate into progress managing personal challenges and the tasks associated with work on personal Goals.

The therapist will model and reinforce the technique of brainstorming, which is a way for group members to share their views and generate a list from which ideas may be selected that the person thinks would be helpful to solve a problem, reach a Goal, or make a decision. A personal cost-benefit analysis, as was introduced in Phase 1, is useful here. In Phase 2, members can be reminded that this process also provides a way to look at particular coping strategies in terms of negative or positive outcomes.

Components of the group "culture" or management of the group milieu is reviewed during the initial sessions, whenever a new member joins the cohort, or whenever a group milieu requires redirection. Although there are benefits to having Phase 1 cohorts stay together for Phase 2, there may be times specific group members would benefit from transfer to a different Phase 2 cohort. Although the manual provides a basic model, each group will develop a unique style of relating and rules of participation. The therapist's role is to facilitate member contributions regarding how they would like their group culture structured and provide boundaries as needed.

During these introductory sessions, include a discussion about attendance. Recall that membership requires only that a person has a goal and wants to work on it. Premature dropout often indicates that a member is having trouble. Missing appointments and premature termination may be a sign of mood worsening or frustration with goal attainment, having difficulty dealing with strong feelings about the group or a person in the group, or other reason. In fact, it is likely that moods associated with manic-depressive disorder may further intensify uncomfortable perceptions, thoughts, and feelings. It is important that the therapist proactively relate that this is expected to occur at times and encourage group members not to give in. The therapist should remind members that the goal as a group is to overcome roadblocks that get in the way of reaching personal goals.

There may be times that the therapist will elect to meet with a group member individually to further troubleshoot problems. The intervention is low intensity, always protective, and supportive. There may be times when the therapist and the group member will conclude, after a careful cost-benefit analysis, that time out from the group or group termination may be the most beneficial solution. Sometimes group members may benefit from a transfer into another Phase 2 cohort because the culture may be more suitable for the member's issues. For example, one Phase 2 cohort may have a chronically functionally disabled membership, and another is more socially or occupationally stable. Regardless, we find that having a mix of group members with diverse experience attaining personal goals and managing their illness will optimally provide the foundation for active group participation and growth of its members.

Issues regarding membership and attendance are especially pertinent to the person with a comorbid substance abuse disorder. We hope that members with an active substance use disorder work on Goals related to management of that disorder. We have not allowed members to participate in a group if they arrive under the influence of alcohol or drugs. Rather, they are referred for emergency or other appropriate clinical services. This should be clearly stated during Phase 2 orientation and whenever the situation deems it necessary. It is expected that members will occasionally report drug or alcohol use between sessions, and this is not grounds for termination. We do scrutinize, by way of cost-benefit analysis, any drug or alcohol use between sessions— always in the spirit of care and concern. A motivational enhancement approach (Miller & Rollnick, 2002) may be used to encourage group members with active substance use disorders to choose abstinence as a goal to work toward.

Several other group process issues are worthy of note during the first few Phase 2 meetings and whenever the situation deems it prudent. The management of giving and receiving feedback should be renegotiated during Phase 2 because it is likely that since the group has been together for 6 weeks, members may be comfortable with a more relaxed style. Recall that in the beginning of Phase 1, it was established by the therapist that feedback was only to be given with the verbal permission of the member. Alternately, a change from the Phase 1 ground rules for feedback may be postponed at the discretion of the therapist depending on group readiness.

Illness management skills for specific mood symptoms were developed during Phase 1. We recommend that the therapist refer to specific Personal Care Plans and other Phase 1 Worksheets such as the Personal Mania and Personal Depression Profiles to help a group member deal with emerging symptoms of hypomania and manic, mixed, or depressive symptoms. Practice is essential to mastery! Review with members that during mood episodes changes in thoughts and feelings often affect insight, judgment, and behavior. Having members of the group support each other during episodes may help reduce the painful sequelae in a mood episode, and may also prevent dropout from group if members prearrange how they will handle depressive and hypomanic episodes.

Group contingency planning for major mood episodes is best accomplished at this juncture in the life of the group, because members are becoming more at ease with each other and it will increase the member's alliance with the group during a difficult time. Left undone, group members may bear unnecessary costs and losses associated with the negative sequelae of the episode. Suicidal and aggressive behavior during group can also be better managed with contingency plans. Contingency plans for mood symptoms, aggression, and suicidality may be added to the group member Personal Care Plan and optimally will include details for provider access and social support. Formally writing contingency plans contribute to the commitment group members have to the plan. It also offers a point of reference if an episode negotiation is needed. This group activity also provides an opportunity for the therapist to further assess group member's collaborative capacity with the group, providers, family, and other social support and their illness management skills.

In traditional interpersonal therapy groups (e.g., Yalom, 1975), a spectrum of inappropriate behavior during group sessions is sometimes processed for its psychodynamic source. Such behavior is frequently illness-driven in individuals with manic-depressive disorder. Alternatively, inappropriate behavior may also mean that the member is acting to avoid strong emotion associated with sequelae from the illness or other underlying psychopathology. Sometimes the longitudinal perspective can help differentiate: for members exhibiting more effective coping with feelings, thoughts, and behaviors during periods of remission, psychopathological behaviors are likely driven by mood.

Regardless, the strategy within the structured setting of the Life Goals Program is very different from the "uncovering" approach typical of interpersonal therapy groups. Strategies to interpret these behaviors into mood symptoms and, when applicable, effects of personal stress are encouraged. Typically, the therapist will help the member to restore equilibrium by bringing the group, and the member, back to a more concrete, here-and-now focus on illness management and goal-driven agenda. The therapist can support the member by refocusing him or her to the steps outlined for goal development or for translation of the behavior by referring to appropriate worksheets used for symptom tracking and stress triggers. These therapeutic interventions are protective and serve members well in their overall attempts to cope. They also provide group members, by way of modeling, an effective strategy to cope with negative thoughts and feelings.

Interpersonal therapy groups usually prohibit members from having contact outside the group forum, and require that when such contacts do occur, they be processed during the groups for their psychodynamic content. The Life Goals Program in contrast does not restrict members from outside contact or process contacts for their psychodynamic relevance. Outside contact may allow members to be supportive to each other and for some, may actually represent their first successful postillness attempt at building social relationships. Outside contacts can also deter members from more appropriate coping plans and put other group members in awkward situations (e.g., if one member repeatedly calls another when suicidal, or when one member seeks more intimacy with another than the latter is comfortable with). Each group should establish their own guidelines for managing member contacts outside of the group. The cost-benefit rubric provides a useful format for thinking through this issue. Guidelines will minimally include contingency plans for potential problem areas such as a call for help. Most important is that outside contacts between members, problematic or not, are not a secret from the group. These contacts should be openly discussed. This will facilitate trouble-shooting problems should they arise.

Group members may also choose to build social relationships and exercise collaborative skills by planning specific group goals or special activities that take place in the group. For example, group cohorts may plan healthy living routines, holiday celebrations, recreational events, and other activities. Planning group goals offers group members an opportunity to practice using the five stages of goal attainment. Planning an activity and working on a goal as a group can also be less threatening than the process of goal attainment faced by individual members.

PHASE 2 ORIENTATION SESSION

The following outline offers the therapist a guide for presenting group orientation of Phase 2 to the group members.

INTRODUCTION

Therapist Directions
Welcome group members, introduce participants. The therapist may have group members from various cohorts coming together for Phase 2. Encourage group members to have their notebooks from Phase 1 with them during Phase 2 meetings for reference, because a goal of Phase 2 is to "fine-tune" their illness management skills.

Therapist Didactic.   Welcome to Phase 2 of the Life Goals Program. Some of you may have been together during Phase 1, and others may be new to you. Let's begin with going around the table and (re)introducing ourselves to one another.

Today we will discuss the purpose of Phase 2 and review the ground rules for being a member of a group such as this. It will be helpful for you to have your Phase 1 notebooks on hand during these groups. They will be handy resources as you become more acquainted with the personal aspects of your manic-depressive disorder and work on managing it.

Recall that symptoms of mania and depression affect the way a person thinks, feels, and behaves. This can affect a person's ability to work on relationships, manage anger, start or complete projects, and make plans for school, work, and leisure time. For this reason, Phase 2 has been developed to provide an opportunity for you to work on personal Goals that *you* will choose. Also, we are all aware that manic and depressive episodes can recur. With this in mind, we will continue to work on coping strategies to manage this condition. In fact, during these groups members learn to work on personal Life Goals while they continue to focus on issues related to coping with manic and depressive episodes.

- Are there any questions thus far?

Another thing about this group: There will be less teaching than there was in Phase 1. We'll talk about the events and topics that are important to you, your goals and symptom management.

BRAINSTORMING

Therapist Didactic. So, during Phase 2, we will be working on Goals that are individually selected and meaningful to you. Group is an ideal place to do this because we can all benefit from the ideas we share with one another. We don't tell each other what to do, but a lot of brainstorming takes place here to explore ways to work on goals. Brainstorming is when the group shares their ideas about ways to format challenges into goals or manage a roadblock that is in the way of reaching a goal. It is one of the major reasons this program is formatted for groups and not one-on-one therapy.

MANAGING SYMPTOMS

Therapist Didactic. Let's review some of the ground rules for being a member of this group. First of all, even if you are having problems with symptoms, we encourage you to come to the group. The group can be a strong source of support. In fact, as a group, we can plan ways to help one another during mood episodes. Here, you will be working with people who understand something about what it means to have manic and depressive symptoms. In fact, I've had group members tell me they've missed group because they were depressed and didn't want to "bring other people down." This is a "come as you are" program. We expect that there may be times when you'll feel like giving up, and we're here to help you get through that. On "down" days you needn't talk—it's important just to be here!

> **Therapist Directions**
> It is prudent to discuss contingency plans for an acute mood episode and suicidality during one of the initial group sessions. The following guidelines are offered. List group member contributions on the board. Each group member should write explicit directions in his or her personal care plan for the group to follow regarding group feedback for symptoms of depression and mania.

In fact, let's spend time now talking about how the group might be helpful should you have a mood episode or become severely suicidal. Mood episodes can recur, or continue longer than you'd like. Practicing your Phase 1 skills can be very important at these times. One of the benefits of this group is to support one another should that happen. Open your notebooks to your Personal Mania and Depression Profiles and your Action Plans for coping with these mood episodes. It can help to review these now. Recall that mania and depression may come on quickly or slowly over a period of time.

- How would you like to receive feedback if the group notices you are having symptoms of mania? Depression? Are suicidal?
- What would help if you seem to have trouble hearing our feedback?
- What are your personal Action Plans for a manic episode? Depressive episode?
- Does anyone have a specific plan for coping with being suicidal?
- What is it?

Take a few minutes to write this into your Personal Care Plans.

> **Therapist Directions**
> You may provide group members with an additional sheet of paper to add to their Personal Care Plans, for example, "Group Contingency Plan."

These are the "directions" for the group to follow to help if you become suicidal or if symptoms of mania or depression are recognized by the group. This can be thought of as your Group Contingency Plan. We will refer to it and use it as a guide so the group may be helpful during those times.

CONFIDENTIALITY

Therapist Didactic.   Confidentiality continues to be an important topic for this group. Keeping what people say here confidential and never talking about group members and what they say to people other than treatment staff continue to be important rules for membership.

MEMBERS MEETING OUTSIDE THE GROUP

Therapist Didactic.   Some of you may decide to get together at times other than in group. Some group programs don't allow outside contact. Outside contact with other group members can be helpful, and sometimes it can lead to problems. We do feel it is important that if you meet outside the group, we will discuss it during group, so everyone is comfortable being open with one another.

- What do you think would be some of the potential costs and benefits of meeting each other outside the group?
- What would you do if another group member calls you in crisis? If you feel burdened or overwhelmed by these contacts?
- What would you do if another group member called you with a suicide plan?

Therapist Directions
Facilitate a cost-benefit analysis of outside contacts between group members. We suggest contacts only when it is wanted by the individual, never when it is unwanted. Typically, costs will include having another member call in crisis or to discuss another member. Benefits may be having someone to ride with, share a difficult task, or attend a support group meeting. Facilitate discussion and list contributions for member boundaries outside group. For example, boundaries should include clear restrictions about calling another group member if an individual is suicidal, or if the call is unwanted.

ATTENDANCE

Therapist Didactic.   We ask that you continue to tell us if you are having a problem. We are here to help you to plan a way to cope with problems, should they come up. Sometimes a group member may feel a need to leave the group before it's over. That's okay. Sometimes thinking through ways to cope with a feeling or a problem by taking a moment or two outside the group can help. Most important is that you return to the group or minimally touch base with us before you leave for the day.

- Can we all agree to do that?

If you are going to miss a group session, let us know. Missing sessions and leaving the group without notice may be a sign of feeling worse or having difficulty dealing with strong feelings about the group or a person in the group. Sometimes the moods associated with manic-depressive disorder may further intensify these uncomfortable thoughts and feelings. It is important that we recognize that this can be expected to occur at times and not give in, keeping in mind that our goal as a group is to overcome roadblocks that get in the way of reaching personal goals. For some people, coming to group can be more difficult than they would have expected. This is completely understandable. Many people with manic-depressive disorder have been isolated, may have difficulties sharing their thoughts and feelings with other people, or feel other members of the group are insensitive. This can occur because of problems with others in the past or because other members are not being very helpful.

• Can we agree that if you have a problem and it makes coming to group difficult, we will discuss it here or spend a few minutes discussing it in an individual appointment?

Therapist Directions
It sometimes happens that a group member will leave during a group or drop out of the Life Goals Program without notice. This may occur for several reasons. The member may have mood disturbances with co-occurring disturbances in perceptions, thoughts, and feelings. Additionally, Axis II psychopathology may make it difficult for a member to tolerate the group milieu. Specific interpersonal factors between the member and the therapist or the member and other members may interfere. For these reasons, having contingency plans regarding attendance is addressed here, as it was in Phase 1. A suitable intervention will lead the therapist to help the member to identify the trigger leading to his or her leaving the group or not attending at all, and identification of the costs and benefits associated with their decision and alternate strategies. Keep in mind the member is making attempts to cope as effectively as possible within the limits of their personal resources. The therapist leading groups such as these should have an active outreach protocol that includes telephone calls to members who have cancelled or did not keep their group appointment, and arranging individual sessions for members who are having difficulty in group or with attendance.

It is a goal of these groups that you feel free to participate as much or as little as you feel comfortable. You may have days when you prefer to sit quietly observing and others when you have more to say. We will support that.

ALCOHOL AND DRUG USE

Therapist Didactic. Some members of these groups have active problems with alcohol or drugs; others may not. We continue to ask that you not show up to group under the influence of alcohol or drugs. However, if you use alcohol or drugs during your membership in Phase 2, we will ask that you describe its costs and benefits. We will work with anyone who has a drug or alcohol problem to stabilize the problem. Alcohol and drug problems are common to people with manic-depressive disorder, and their use often leads to problems stabilizing the disorder and achieving personal goals.

- Is this agreeable to everyone?

Therapist Directions
Specific agency and facility policy for management of persons under the influence of alcohol and/or drugs should be clearly described to the group. For example, not allowing intoxicated group members to leave the facility unless their alcohol level is at or below the legal limit.

- We have a policy in our facility that we as staff, are obligated to follow. It states that _____.

GIVING AND RECEIVING FEEDBACK

Therapist Didactic. During these groups, you'll be working on issues and problems common to many of you. At times, you may be of help to others in the group, and at times others may be helpful to you. Part of group building is giving and getting feedback or advice from your associates here. It is our experience that feedback and advice can be helpful if it's wanted by the other person, and not so helpful if it's not wanted. In Phase 1, we asked that you find out first if your advice was wanted before giving it. That way, people were able to decide for themselves if they were able to hear advice and feedback at that time. Something else we learned is that feedback is most helpful if it is offered as a suggestion, and not as a criticism.

- Are these the rules that we want for Phase 2?

Therapist Directions
The group may renegotiate the rules for giving and receiving feedback at this time and in subsequent sessions. It is recommended that the therapist use his or her judgment as a guide. Individual members may not feel ready or able to relax their posture on this subject at this time, especially if there are new members in the cohort.

INTRODUCTION TO GOAL SETTING

Therapist Didactic. Having manic-depressive disorder usually disrupts progress toward personal Life Goals. Having manic-depressive disorder may interfere with, or lead to, occupational, financial, relationship, or other types of losses.

Vignette

(The therapist may feel free to use a vignette of their own). I'll tell the story about a group member who first had a manic episode in his 30s as an example. He was a teacher in a public high school. After his hospital stay, his wife moved to another state with the kids, and he lost his job. He came into a Life Goals group when he was on the inpatient unit. At that time, he was homeless. Once discharged, he moved into a shelter and began trying to find a job. He was angry he had this illness and had a lot of feelings about his losses. He didn't trust. He felt hopeless. During group, he worked on Goals to get a job but didn't get hired. He moved from the shelter to a group home. The group home offered support in areas of his life that he needed. As a pastime, he started to draw, and eventually painted beautiful murals on the walls of the group home. Soon he applied to a local college and began classes. His goal was to become an art therapist. There were many times he felt like giving up along the way. Mania interfered with his education, and at times he had to take incompletes in courses. There was a lot of family stress. In fact, he had problems accepting his diagnosis and that interfered with his taking medications independently for several years. Several times he refused them. This led to more manic episodes and several hospitalizations. Today, though, this group member has successfully completed 75% of the course work required for a bachelor's degree in art. He is now an employee at a shelter and is living independently. He's also had several successful art shows. The group helped this member in many ways: through encouragement to continue despite many recurrent disappointments and setbacks. It helped him to overcome his personal battle with psychiatric stigma that led to his resistance to taking prescribed medications. It helped him to develop, and practice, good illness management skills. And it helped him problem-solve around trying to reach his goal of going to art school.

- What are some of the problems that you have encountered when trying to pursue your goals?

It is important to remember that frustrations and roadblocks to achieving Life Goals are the rule and not the exception. This is not unique to people with manic-depressive disorder! In fact, there are many groups like this for people in all walks of life. Something all people have in common are barriers or roadblocks to reaching their goals. When people get stuck, they may feel like quitting. A purpose of the group is to help people deal with setbacks and delays as they work toward their goals. A lot of the time spent working on goals is involved in identifying strategies to overcome roadblocks and working on coping with the feelings that roadblocks may lead to. This is especially important if mood symptoms erupt.

- Can anyone recall a difficult time reaching a personal goal?

Let's discuss some basic facts about goals. First of all, a goal isn't necessarily something complicated. It can be "staying out of hospital this year," "returning to school," or learning to cope with a stress that has led to a manic-depressive episode in the past. Sometimes goals are about changes in the way you handle your feelings or structure your daily routine. Most important in this program is that your goal is chosen by you and be important to your quality of life. No one can decide for you what goal you should work on.

> **Therapist Directions**
> Write the Stages of Change on the board as you describe the process in the following discussion. They are (1) not thinking about change, (2) thinking about making a change, (3) taking action to change a behavior, and (4) continuing change.

Something else to keep in mind is that whenever we work on change or want to make something about our lives different through a new goal, we need to expect it to take time. Clearly, change is a process that takes place over time and is not an event. People go through different Stages of Change. They are

1. Not thinking about change (precontemplation).
2. Thinking about making a change (contemplation).
3. Taking action to change a behavior (action).
4. Continuing change (maintenance).

The time each person spends in each stage of change is very personal. For example, a person may spend several weeks or even months thinking about making a change. Something else to keep in mind is to avoid giving up if you choose to work on changing something about yourself and find things are back to the way they were when you started. It can take quite a few times journeying through the stages of change before a new behavior becomes stable. This is true for the way we might think about things as well as the way we do things. For example, a person may habitually put himself or herself down. Changing the way we think about ourselves usually takes practice!

- Have you ever made a change and later found yourself doing things the same way you did before? Even after successfully changing?

There are other important guidelines to keep in mind when we work on *goals*. Goals must depend primarily on *your* actions. We cannot depend on the cooperation of another person for us to reach our goals. And goals are easier to accomplish when they are broken down into a series of small, realistically attainable steps. For that reason, we have a format available to help with that. It's the Life Goals Worksheet (Exhibit 24).

Therapist Directions
During this discussion, write the Five Stages of Goal Attainment on the board: 1. Describe the Challenge. 2. Identify the overall Goal associated with the Challenge. 3. Identify the Subgoals related to each overall Goal. 4. Identify the Behavioral Steps to take to reach the Subgoals and monitor progress. 5. Troubleshoot Roadblocks. (Refer to Table 8.1, p. 235.)

The first step is to identify your goal. This often begins with a description of the challenge you are facing, especially if it seems as if what you are attempting to do seems complicated or entangled with other areas of your life. Typically, the overall goal is selected from a part of the description of the challenge. Once the goal is clear, you can begin the process of breaking down the overall goal into smaller goals we call subgoals. Finally, the actions you take to reach your goals are identified as multiple steps. Once an individual has completed this part of goal attainment we work together to monitor progress accomplishing the *steps*. Often, an individual will face roadblocks that get in the way. Roadblocks are barriers or obstacles that interfere with completing a step toward attaining a goal. Usually, we spend a lot of time in these groups talking about roadblocks. This is true for everyone working on goals, whether it is people with manic-depressive disorder or a group of business leaders.

Vignette

I'm going to share an example of how this works. A group member explained that he wanted to get a job. He'd been battling depression with psychosis for a period of time. He felt sedated in the morning and had a hard time "getting going." The psychosis had been improving

EXHIBIT 24   Life Goals Worksheet

Name: _____   Date: _____

Description of the Challenge: _____

_____

_____

Overall Goal: _____

                                    Date completed: _____

Subgoal:	Subgoal:
Date written: _____	Date written: _____
Step 1: Date completed: _____	Step 1: Date completed: _____
Step 2: Date completed: _____	Step 2: Date completed: _____
Step 3: Date completed: _____	Step 3: Date completed: _____
Step 4: Date completed: _____	Step 4: Date completed: _____

but was continuing to be a problem. He spent a lot of time alone at home because he had no car and felt self-conscious walking through town. He'd tried to work several times but got fired because his employer said he was too slow. This group member's Description of the Challenge demonstrated several Subgoals to work on as he approached his overall goal to get a job. They were (1) to reduce his daytime sedation, (2) to reduce the symptoms of psychosis, and (3) to begin a work readiness plan that meant spending more time with others.

Here's how he worked this worked out:

Therapist Directions
You may write the example provided below on the board or select an alternate example provided by the group that will demonstrate the processes used on the Life Goals Worksheet.

Description of the Challenge

- Wants to get a job
- Depression with psychosis for a period of time
- Sedation in the morning and a hard time "getting going"
- Psychosis improving, but a continuing problem interfering with concentration
- A lot of time alone at home because no car and feels self-conscious walking through town
- Tried several jobs but fired because of being "too slow"

Overall Goal: Get a Job

Subgoal 1	Subgoal 2	Subgoal 3
• Reduce daytime sedation	• Reduce the symptoms of psychosis	• Begin a work readiness plan • Spend more time with others

This group member then identified the steps to take to reach his Subgoals. They were:

Steps:	Steps:	Steps:
• Contact provider about medication • Take hs meds earlier in the evening	• Monitor symptoms using a daily journal • Report symptoms to his provider	• Attend weekly group and NDMDA meetings
Roadblocks:	Roadblocks:	Roadblocks:
• Appointment in 1 week	• Forgot to write in journal several days	• Early A.M. meetings

- Can you think of any other potential roadblocks this group member may have to manage?
- Any questions?

Now, I want each of you to begin to think about goals that are meaningful to you so you can get started. It may make sense to begin working on goals by selecting something that has to do with improving the management of your manic-depressive disorder. It may be to complete the daily activity and sleep schedule that is part of your Personal Care Plan or to get ready to discuss things of importance to you with your treatment team or find ways to manage a stressor that keeps interfering with your mood stability. Remember, selecting a goal, working through the steps, and overcoming roadblocks takes time.

- Does anyone have a question?

During our upcoming group sessions, we will be reviewing the topics we discussed today, and take more time to think about them. It usually takes a few sessions to understand the steps to goal attainment and the process of change.

Therapist Directions
Close the session, reminding group members of the time, date, and location of the next session. Thank all members for their participation.

THE FIVE STAGES OF GOAL DEVELOPMENT: CONTINUING PHASE 2

Subsequent Phase 2 sessions are based on a review of the topics discussed in the Phase 2 orientation session and guidelines provided in the remainder of this chapter. Although we've provided an orientation session for Phase 2, subsequent sessions are not outlined but may be used as the basic mechanics to facilitate subsequent Phase 2 sessions. The focus of Phase 2 sessions is the goal-attainment process. Recall that the purpose of the Life Goals Program is to improve outcome in manic-depressive disorder across three domains: disease-specific domain, functional domain, and illness costs.

The framework of each Phase 2 session is based on member progress as he/she works toward personal Life Goals. Practically speaking, this requires the therapist to take a very active role to direct and redirect group member attention to the goal-attainment process. More likely than not, a substantial amount of time is spent trouble-shooting roadblocks, often mood symptoms, that inevitably interfere with personal functional goals. A considerable amount of time is spent working with individual members using dynamics that foster the group's participation reviewing and refining illness management skills introduced in Phase 2, referencing the Personal Care Plan and other Phase 1 worksheets.

Recall the therapeutic orientation of Phase 2, summarized in chapter 6, derived from a blend of low-intensity interpersonal, cognitive, behavioral, and psychoeducational theoretical paradigms. During Phase 2 sessions, the therapist selects specific therapeutic interventions based on "here and now" dynamics taking place with individual members and the group as a whole. Thus, the therapist is constantly assessing the group and individual members and selecting the therapeutic intervention that will most likely support the group process at any given moment in time. Overall, the therapist's goal is to actively mentor, inspire, and facilitate member progress to refine the group member's illness management skills and reach personal life goals (functional domain).

STAGE 1: DESCRIPTION OF THE CHALLENGE

Objective

Although some group members may come to the group with a specific and focused goal, many will describe a complex problem with multiple issues in need of translation into specific goals. The first step to goal identification will be to describe an overarching Challenge or problem. This description offers the specific member and the group the contextual information from which goals may be identified. Hence, the therapist facilitates member communication of the Challenge as a natural first step in the series of stages of goal attainment. Facilitating the Description of the Challenge reinforces this stage as an expected and formidable step in the process of goal attainment and through this process may build confidence in those having difficulty identifying a goal. Once the Challenge is articulated, the therapist may then facilitate active group member participation to begin sorting through the Challenge to identify one or more goals. Complex problems require step-wise solutions. The key here is to simplify the process as much as possible and to formulate the solution into behaviorally operationalized and manageable goals. Once goals are cast in specific, behavioral terms based on the Description of the Challenge, they are given a priority status.

The therapist facilitates the discussion and has group members simply share what their Life Goals and frustrations have been in the wake of their illness. Alternatively, for a less cohesive group, the therapist may begin with a more general discussion on how Life Goals may be affected by manic-depressive illness and the types of life problems that may be generated by the illness. This technique, first implemented in Phase 1, allows group members to elect the degree of personal disclosure they are ready for by sharing information from a general to a more specific and personal level.

The therapist should reinforce that frustrations and roadblocks to achieving Life Goals are more the rule than the exception, and that this is not unique to persons with manic-depressive disorder. The process of opening and sharing is gradual, even though the individuals have been in group together for at least 6 weeks and have come together with explicit and similar therapeutic purposes in mind.

> **Comment:** For the benefit of the specified group member and other members of the cohort, reinforce that managing *Challenges* and making progress-reaching goals are part of a process. Success is met with time, patience, support, and perseverance in overcoming roadblocks. For many group members, especially those with chronic symptoms, the journey from *Description of the Challenge* to realization of *goal attainment* may take weeks, months, or even years.

It is suggested the therapist use Exhibit 24 ("Life Goals Worksheet") as the basis for Phase 2 goal attainment. There is a space at the top of Exhibit 24 where members may write about a Challenge (problem) that they are experiencing, but that they are not yet able to articulate in terms of a specific goal. Instruct group members to describe their Challenge or an area of their life that they would like to change. Questions such as "What would you like to have in your life next year that is/are different from today?" may be a good starting point. Depending on the level of sophistication of the group members, they may benefit from having the therapist write an example of a Description of the Challenge on the board.

Optimally, this will be derived from a group volunteer sharing a personal story. This accomplishes two things. First, it provides the group with a visual example of the task that may be confounding everyone. Second, it provides an opportunity for the therapist to model the process of Describing the Challenge with its contextual underpinnings.

> **Comment:** The Description of the Challenge will not explain the problem in behavioral terms, but it will offer a rich source of information about an area in the group member's life that is of importance. Though nonspecific, this is the material that will later become formulated into objective and measurable goals, subgoals, and behavioral steps. Additionally, sources of potential roadblocks to goal achievement may be gleaned from the original story presented.

STAGE 2: IDENTIFICATION OF AN OVERALL GOAL

Objective

The second step in developing a successful goal-attainment strategy is to identify an overarching Goal on which the group member wants to work. The overall Goal should have several characteristics, also applicable to the subgoals and behavioral steps of the following stages (see Table 8.2). First, the Goal defines an area that is important to the individual's quality of life. Second, the Goal must be articulated such that the member and therapist, as well as other group members, will know whether it has been attained. This means that the Goal must be articulated in explicit, behavioral terms. Third, the Goal must depend primarily on the group member's behavior, not on the behavior of others. Finally, the Goal must be able to be broken down into measurable subgoals and behavioral steps.

Examples of initial formulation of Goals may include "Reporting my symptoms of mania to my provider more promptly," "Reporting side effects to my provider before discontinuing my medication," "Staying out of the hospital this year," "Getting a job," "Making two more friends this year," and "Taking charge of my own medication dispensing." The acid test for an overall Goal is whether it can be broken down into subgoals and behavioral steps that can be formulated primarily in terms of the individual member's own efforts.

We strongly urge that the first Goal identified for each member in Phase 2 be related to managing his or her own illness and strengthening the collaborative treatment alliance with his or her provider. Illness management Goals are a useful place to begin for several reasons. First, working initially on an illness management goal will lead to reinforcement and application of the concepts and skills that were recently introduced in Phase 1. Most group members need to practice their newly identified skills. Second, this is frequently an area in which the group member will need help, unless the illness is completely in remission. Many of the illness management strategies introduced during Phase 1 will be novel to the group members. Third, illness management Goals and issues regarding the collaborative member–provider treatment alliance may be easier for the member to discuss with fellow group members, who are relative strangers than, say, their social or occupational dysfunction. Discussing perceived shortcomings of the latter type often can be threatening to one's self-esteem, whereas illness management provides an area for sharing and group identification.

It is wise to spend time during the initial Phase 2 sessions reviewing the Personal Care Plan and exploring any roadblocks to their implementation. Notably, group members may have difficulty implementing the elements of the Personal Care Plan or in other ways establishing a stable treatment alliance. They may have difficulty mastering basic illness management skills such as implementing a structured daily activity and sleep routine. Strategies to improve the relationship between a group member and his or her primary mental health provider and implement illness management skills will lead to improved stabilization of mood and greater likelihood of success in the Life Goals Program.

Comment: Depending on the member's level of sophistication, the concepts of Goal and goal attainment may not be clearly understood. It has been our experience that some individuals may perceive that a Goal is something big and extraordinary. It helps members to learn that Goals may also have to do with managing everyday life issues, such as establishing a daily routine that fosters mood management, learning to use their support systems effectively, and improving communication with family and friends. The choice of illness management and the collaborative treatment relationship as the initial Goals on which to focus gives the individual an opportunity to employ the process of describing the challenge, overall goal identification, development of subgoals, construction of behavioral steps, monitoring progress, and troubleshooting roadblocks in a fairly straightforward area of their lives.

The Goals initially articulated by the individual, as in the examples listed, may vary greatly in terms of topic, complexity, and specificity. Even more general Goals, such as "Being less depressed" and "Feeling less empty," are also typical starting points originating from a description of the challenge. Sometimes quite ambitious Goals are articulated, such as "Being president of my own corporation." Selection of such lofty Goals, if they are not realistic, may be due to hypomanic symptoms, to personality factors, or simply to naivete. The key qualities of the Goal are that it must be important to the person's quality of life and must be a realistic starting point from which to develop subgoals and behavioral steps at which the group member is likely to succeed.

This second step of goal identification alone may take several weeks. At first, members may not be able to articulate Goals beyond illness management. Reasons include chronic mood symptoms, demoralization due to past failures, stigma, and inexperience in thinking in terms of Goals and problem solving. Nonmanic-depressive illness-based psychopathology may also interfere with relating with others.

The members' Personal Depression and Mania Profiles and the other exhibits from Phase 1 should serve as references from which members can reinforce their knowledge about manic-depressive disorder and their personal illness characteristics and learn to apply this knowledge to their everyday life.

As the therapist guides sharing of Goals, particularly illness management Goals, and strategies for an effective collaborative treatment alliance, he or she works with individual members to make the Goal identification processes explicit to other members. This moving back and forth between group level and individual level accomplishes two things. First, the focus on issues with an individual group member can serve as a model for the other group members, allowing imitative learning to take place. It also breaks down the isolation the other members experience as they realize that a peer has the same issues, problems, and deficiencies that they perceive themselves to have. Second, the individual receives peer support as the therapist facilitates other group members to comment and assist in work with him or her.

Comment: It is worth noting Eidelson's comments about the adaptation of cognitive techniques from individual to group modalities (Eidelson, 1985). She emphasizes the importance of "translating the members' individual concerns into universal problems." That is, the therapist must find common themes among individual members' specific problems such that the learning of one becomes applicable to others with the same themes. For example, on the surface, difficulty completing behavioral steps may seem similar to poor work performance, but common themes may produce both, such as depressive symptoms, medication side effects, hopelessness, and lack of self-esteem. In addition, finding commonalities in individual themes allows the group members to provide feedback and support to each other from a position of empathy and experience.

STAGE 3: DEVELOPMENT OF SUBGOALS

Objective

In Stage 1, the Description of the Challenge is articulated. In Stage 2, the overall Goal is identified. Typically, if the challenge is complex, there are multiple issues to address. This defines the areas in which the member will begin to work, and the ultimate goal he or she wishes to achieve. In Stage 3, the overall goal is broken down into a series of component Subgoals. These Subgoals serve to break down what is often an overwhelming task into more manageable component subtasks. For example, if a member identifies as an overall goal "Getting a job," then there are several component steps necessary to achieve this. These may include further stabilizing his or her depression, reducing daytime sedation due to medication, creating a resume, working on interviewing skills, talking to potential contacts, and making formal application for a position. If a member identifies as a Goal "Dating at least once a month," this may break down into such Subgoals as (in reverse sequential order) asking someone out on a date, putting oneself in a position to meet potential persons to date, and even such basic requirements as improving personal hygiene or learning to leave the house without panic.

As in the examples above, Subgoals may or may not be sequential, in that completion of one is necessary for beginning to address the next. Typically, they are at least interdependent.

As noted for overall goals Stage 2, Subgoals must also be behaviorally measurable and realistic. At this stage, they must also rely on the individual's own efforts.

During this stage, the therapist continues to use Exhibit 24 ("Life Goals Worksheet"). Each member is instructed to identify and write down a series of Subgoals that are necessary for achieving the overall goal. Because of space constraints on the Worksheet, there is space for only two Subgoals on each sheet. However, it is likely that many overall goals will require three or more Subgoals. Separate Worksheets should be used in such cases. The therapist, as during Stage 1, works at both the individual and group level, emphasizing the commonalities among members' endeavors and encouraging group interaction and feedback specific to the Subgoal.

Several examples of completed Life Goals Worksheets are found in Figures 8.1A–C. These examples are described in the Vignettes that accompany many of the roadblocks.

Comment: Recall that it is advisable that the first overall goal pertains to some aspect of illness management, so that members should be working on similar problems. Discussion of one member's Subgoals will likely enhance the efforts of the others if they are working on similar topics.

The principles of goal development (Table 8.2) should be kept in mind when formulating specific Subgoals. The principles of behavioral measurement and self-dependence are particularly applicable to this stage. First, the Subgoals, as the overall goal, must be articulated in behaviorally measurable terms so that the individual, therapist, and other group members can know

Name: _Ms J._____ Date: _12/7/02_

Description of the Challenge: _Since leaving school, I've felt empty and alone. I've lost contact with my college friends. It's difficult to join in with other people; feeling depressed, lost my confidence._

Overall Goal: _Increase social activity and make friends._

Date completed: _____

Subgoal: Improve mood Date: _____	Subgoal: Develop my friendship with Sarah and other people Date: _____
Step 1: Monitor symptoms of depression and report them to my MD Date completed: _____	Step 1: Invite Sarah to lunch Date completed: _____
Step 2: Set up my meds in a weekly dispenser and take them as prescribed Date completed: _____	Step 2: Return Sarah's phone calls the same day Date completed: _____
Step 3: Exercise three times a week by walking 2 miles Date completed: _____	Step 3: Say thank you when Sarah compliments me Date completed: _____
Step 4: Stabilize my sleep cycle – go to bed at 11pm and get up at 7am Date completed: _____	Step 4: Accept invitations to go out when asked Date completed: _____

FIGURE 8.1A   Sample of a completed Life Goals Worksheet.

Name: _Mr. T._   Date: _2/2/02_

Description of the Challenge: _When depressed I go to my room and think alot about suicide for days. I'm irritable and think I should avoid others so I won't hurt them. Everyone would be better off without me_

Overall Goal: _____ Don't hurt anyone or myself_

Date completed: _____

Subgoal: Get help for anger and depression with suicidal thoughts Date: _____	Subgoal: Don't hurt myself or other people Date: _____
Step 1: Make an appt. with my doctor as soon as I notice depression Date completed: _____	Step 1: Tell my family when I get depressed and I don't blame them Date completed: _____
Step 2: Maintain my Daily Activity schedule if I do get depressed Date completed: _____	Step 2: Take a walk if I get angry at home Date completed: _____
Step 3: Learn more effective ways to handle my anger— join the anger group Date completed: _____	Step 3: Stop drinking coffee and soda containing caffeine Date completed: _____
Step 4: Make a plan with my doctor for safety if I get alot of suicidal thoughts Date completed: _____	Step 4: Get more exercise— go to the gym 3Xs a week Date completed: _____

FIGURE 8.1B Sample of a completed Life Goals Worksheet.

Name: _P. L._

Date: _9/10/01_

Description of the Challenge: _Trouble getting up in the a.m. I lie in bed and think about my past when I beat people up, set a fire in the house. I feel too ashamed to face the day. I lost my job for coming in late._

Overall Goal: _Have a schedule that allows me to function_

Date completed: _____

Subgoal: _Quickly manage episodes of depression and hypomania_	Subgoal: _Develop a Daily Activity and Sleep Schedule_
Date: _____	Date: _____
Step 1: _Monitor my signs and symptoms closely_	Step 1: _Walk the dog by 8 am_
Date completed: _____	Date completed: _____
Step 2: _Discuss a plan with my MD to report my symptoms promptly (next appt.)_	Step 2: _Volunteer at the Sr. Center 2 days a week and help others_
Date completed: _____	Date completed: _____
Step 3: _Accept group feedback if they notice my symptoms_	Step 3: _Go to bed at 11 pm stop all naps_
Date completed: _____	Date completed: _____
Step 4: _Take my prescribed medications every day_	Step 4: _Schedule my day and change my activity whenever I think about the past_
Date completed: _____	Date completed: _____

FIGURE 8.1C   Sample of a completed Life Goals Worksheet.

when it has been achieved. Second, the Subgoal must be articulated in terms that depend on success only on the action of the individual himself or herself, and not on the response of others. Thus, for instance, doing something with another is recast as asking someone to do something. The idea is that the member will keep trying (asking others, or being persistent with the same other person) until he or she succeeds, rather than call the effort a failure if that other person does not respond as desired.

Note at this juncture that at this stage the therapeutic interventions begin to focus solely on individual members' behavior and reactions to success or failure in their efforts. Subgoals and subsequent behavioral steps are constructed in terms of an individual member's actions. This serves two purposes.

First, in the event of success, the individual can recognize that it was in large part his or her efforts that have achieved the stated objective. Second, if the Subgoal is unattainable, the member has the opportunity to rethink and revise strategies, to try again, and to deal with the emotional impact with group support. Analysis of this experience—focusing on one's own role in its success or failure—allows the member to make accurate (cognitive) attributions to himself or herself or to outside forces. This is an important realization to strive to have members make in order to combat the negative cognitive set so endemic in persons with manic-depressive disorder. At the same time, it allows members to realize, when applicable, that the world is not always the kind, loving, supportive place that we often wish it to be.

The importance of this approach can be seen in following the "Getting a Job" scenario. If the person works through the Subgoals and behavioral steps yet cannot stabilize his or her depression or find a job, then he or she is less likely to attribute that failure to internal, global, or stable causes. At least he or she has fought the good fight and picked up pertinent skills along the way. Perhaps the group member is a better collaborator with his or her treatment team or has learned more about how to gain access to the system of care where he or she is treated. The member will be better prepared for the next attempt, and with the help of the group work through the emotional, cognitive, and behavioral impact of failure or postponement of an endeavor.

Comment: The space in Exhibit 24 labeled "Description of the Challenge" allows the member to expand on the contextual areas of the overall Goal and offer personal detail about the issues relevant to the individual and his or her Goal. Subgoals are derived from this description. For example, if the overall Goal is "Getting a full-time job," the member's Description of the Challenge will provide a source of the problems that the Subgoal will address. These descriptions need not necessarily be behaviorally specified; "Depressive symptoms," "Problems with energy," Lack of confidence," "Lack of experience," and the like may be used as starting places from which to develop specific, behaviorally specified Subgoals. Corresponding Subgoals might be, for example, "Improving mood," "Change medication times," "Practicing job interview skills to reduce anxiety," and "Asking my brother for part-time work in his business."

STAGE 4: CONSTRUCTION OF BEHAVIORAL STEPS AND MONITORING PROGRESS

Objective

The objective of Stage 4 is to have each member formulate specific Behavioral Steps toward achieving each subgoal and carry them out successfully. The Behavioral Steps may in some cases be sequential, in that completion of one depends upon completion of a prior Step; alternatively, Steps may be constructed to be carried out in parallel. It is critical that the therapist guide the member to Steps that are sufficiently modest so as to have a high likelihood of success. This strategy of setting a person up for success supports confidence building and reduces the opportunity for strengthening of a sense of hopelessness.

The therapist continues to work from Exhibit 24, helping each member to construct and write down individual Steps for each subgoal. Because multiple subgoals may have been articulated, the therapist may wish to work on constructing Steps only for one subgoal at a time, or may wish to have the member work on several subgoals simultaneously. This will depend on the judgment of the therapist based on assessing the group member's ability.

The therapist should keep in mind that it is of paramount importance not to overload members with multiple concurrent tasks, since this will increase the likelihood of failure at tasks. It is possible for some individuals to work on multiple subgoals simultaneously, and in some instances the therapist may wish to have the member outline all Behavioral Steps for all subgoals at the outset. This sort of "road map" can be helpful to some members, but both the therapist and the individual member should be wary of being over-ambitious. Alternatively, the therapist may advise the member to work only on Steps for one subgoal at a time, delaying work on others until there is significant progress in working on the Steps for the first subgoal. Sometimes a member may have steps listed and cannot see that they are making progress. Through discussion, it may be possible to identify the individual's progress on his or her goal that was overlooked and not listed. Then the therapist may reinforce the individual's effort and add these steps to the list for recognition.

As in the earlier stages, the therapist moves between the individual and the group level. This emphasizes the commonalities among members' endeavors and allows the therapist to employ interpersonal group techniques to address roadblocks, as outlined in the next part of this chapter.

In constructing the Behavioral Steps, the therapist must ensure that the goals are formatted according to the guidelines from Table 8.2. These elements are even more important in constructing Behavioral Steps than in formulating goals, because the Steps will serve as the guides for specific behaviors on the part of the individual. It is worthwhile to review the key principles as they apply to constructing Behavioral Steps.

First, goals must be formatted so that progress is measurable objectively. This does not mean that the behaviors need to be numerically quantifiable; rather, they must be sufficiently objective so that the individual, the therapist, and, if applicable, the other group members know when they have been achieved. Otherwise, there can be no success. Simply "being more active" or "having more confidence in social situations" or "appreciating my wife" is not measurable. On the other hand, the following are measurable: "Getting out of the house every day for at least an hour" or "socializing at the club at least once a week" or "telling my wife I appreciate something about her at least five times a week." Simple yes/no behaviors are also considered measurable.

> **Comment:** This measurable behavioral orientation is not unlike that which clinicians use for treatment planning. It is also similar to more formal treatment study paradigms in which researchers investigate quantifiable outcomes.

Second, Behavioral Steps must be formatted to depend primarily on the actions of the individual himself or herself and not depend on the cooperation of another person. This was noted to be important in formulating subgoals, for reasons discussed in Stage 3. It is even more important in constructing Behavioral Steps, for the same reasons. Steps must focus on what the individual himself or herself can do to bring about success, in order to avoid the passive hopelessness that often exists in persons with manic-depressive disorder. Strategies that do not work can be revised, gradually giving the individual more control over his or her component of work toward goals. If Steps are properly constructed, the risks of failure are minimized; and if failure does occur, it can be explored on the basis of likely roadblocks, using behavioral, cognitive, and interpersonal techniques to minimize their impact.

Finally, Behavioral Steps must be realistically attainable. Setting the member up for success can be important in motivating individuals who feel that they have experienced little but failure for most of their adult lives. Confidence building and dealing with anxiety are key components of a successful goal-attainment strategy, and anxiety can depend to a large degree on the complexity of the Step to be completed.

Comment: It is important to look carefully at Behavioral Steps to make certain that they do not contain multiple Steps bundled into one.

Up until this point, the work of the group has focused on matters that take place within the group setting. Initially, in Phase 1, members were learning about manic-depressive disorder together, sharing their experience with the illness, and eventually constructing Personal Care Plans for themselves. Subsequently, in the first three Stages of Phase 2, the members focused on developing plans for working on meaningful goals. This is the first stage of treatment that the member may have formal expectations for his or her behavior outside the group setting.

While we are hesitant to label the tasks at hand "homework" because of the schoolwork connotation, the therapist and individual members need to begin to expect work at home or elsewhere in the lives of the members. This follows naturally from the fact that the goals that individuals have will have to do with important areas of their personal lives.

Comment: Some Behavioral Steps may focus on behaviors within the group setting (e.g., "Speaking up when I do not understand what is being said"), and in fact intragroup behaviors can be a good place to start gaining confidence in social skills and decreasing anxiety about social situations. Ultimately, however, these are in the service of reaching goals outside the group proper because the member lives the vast majority of his or her life outside the group, succeeding or failing to adjust in the world at large.

We recommend that the therapist begin each session asking members how their illness has been behaving and how things have gone since the last session in terms of working on their behavioral plan. This reliably brings up discussion about mood symptoms as thoughts and feelings and reports of behavior that can be addressed using psychoeducation about illness management and interpersonal and cognitive techniques. It also provides validation that, regardless of the plan, symptoms of manic-depressive disorder may resurface and interfere with their goals.

Sometimes there is a reticence to share experience and feelings. It is important to be aware of how personal some of these issues can be to members (i.e., how sensitive their self-esteem is to talking about their hopes, aspirations, failures, and even successes). Just as in Phase 1, as the therapist works from the general to the personal in describing manic-depressive disorder, so must he or she begin gradually and slowly to move the focus to the most sensitive areas of an individual's thoughts, feelings, and behaviors.

The issue then becomes how to motivate and how to monitor work on these Behavioral Steps that depend largely on behaviors outside the group. Motivation, as we have proposed in chapter 6 and elsewhere this chapter, derives from the individual's tendency toward adaptive coping to the world around him or her. If individuals feel that they can succeed in areas that are important to them, they will make efforts in those areas. However, in each individual's life multiple roadblocks exist. Much of the work of this stage of treatment is to help the member to overcome those roadblocks discussed in Step 5.

Comment: It is important to note that groups may become "centrifugal" by focusing primarily on process issues within the group, or on various issues in the lives of individual members that are not related to goal attainment. There is usually sufficient material in each member's life to fill a lifetime of group work. The therapist must balance this centrifugal tendency of the group with too tight a focus on the behavioral plans that can lead to the appearance of insensitivity to current concerns of the members and feelings on the part of the members that the group is irrelevant to their lives. The essence of the group discussion may be translated by the therapist into their goal agenda. It is useful to use the rule of thumb that if group process issues are in the service of the behavioral plan, then they should be pursued. If not, they should be deemphasized. As with the situation the therapist finds himself or herself in when trying to work with individuals and generalize to group experience, he or she should try to find and focus on themes in the group process that relate to individual members' behavioral plans.

It should be noted that there is also a tendency for members to avoid dealing with progress on reaching goals and to talking about other areas or periods in their lives. Gentle but persistent refocusing on the tasks at hand is usually indicated at these times.

At other times, the members of the group may not be able to focus on the tasks at hand because there are dynamics within the group that are interfering with the process. It is especially important for the therapist to assess resistance, including its source, to select an intervention, and to evaluate its effectiveness before pursuing the group goal-attainment task. Otherwise, it is likely that the themes of discontent will resurface over and over again and impede the process of goal work.

Recall that progress in Phase 2 is conceptualized in terms of progress toward goals and not in terms of specific number of weeks or sessions. Accordingly, the "end" of Phase 2 occurs when the member has reached the overall goal he or she has set. This typically takes place over months or longer. In our initial studies, time to attainment of the first goal was 8 months on average, with a range of 2 to 17 months.

At the end of this first goal-attainment cycle, the member may opt to continue group to delineate and address another goal. Thus, the process may be continued through multiple iterations or cycles of goal identification, subgoal development, behavioral steps, and troubleshooting roadblocks.

Comment: It is likely that the members will be working on multiple goals simultaneously in their lives during group attendance. However, formal group work may focus on a single goal at a time, putting this goal "under the microscope" for particularly close work and support. Additional areas of an individual's life can be examined sequentially.

As the therapist encourages members to report back their experiences in pursuit of their Behavioral Steps, he or she watches for problem areas and identifies the roadblocks that cause the problems. Positive reinforcement is given liberally for completion of tasks as well as for the exploration of the roadblocks that members discuss in group that have impeded their progress. In fact, it has been our experience that the roadblocks to reaching goals are more the rule than the exception, and more time is spent brainstorming to understand and find solutions to the roadblocks than time is spent discussing achievement.

Members will need to deal with and learn from misstarts, failures, and adjusting to successes throughout the process of attempting these specific Steps. The therapist employs cognitive and interpersonal group techniques, as outlined under the specific roadblocks listed below. It is important to move back and forth from the group to the individual level, remembering to relate individual interventions to common themes of the group so that the group does not feel left out during times of extended work with one individual.

Instruct members to date their worksheet in the space provided when an individual Step is completed, and again when a Subgoal or overall goal is achieved.

STAGE 5: TROUBLESHOOTING ROADBLOCKS

In the Life Goals Program, Troubleshooting Roadblocks is a critical step in the process of achieving goals for group members. Formally demarcating this as the fifth step in the goal-attainment process has several advantages. First, it gains group member recognition as a formal step in the goal-attainment process. Otherwise, the expectation may be that work on goals is a process culminating in achievement without the struggles encountered in managing roadblocks. The roadblocks commonly encountered by group members and some suggested therapist strategies are delineated in detail in the next section, "Roadblocks and Therapist Strategies."

> **Comment:** It is critically important that group members recognize that this step is a part of the goal-attainment process for everyone, not just people with manic-depressive disorder. In fact, the bulk of work in the Life Goals Program and life in general is identifying and working through Roadblocks, brainstorming solutions, and activating steps to resolve them. Group members will be more aware and prepared.

Second, as a step in the goal-attainment process, overcoming roadblocks provides opportunities for group members to gain experience with working through difficulties with the support of the group. Though common to all group members is the manic-depressive diagnosis, the process of exposing their personality to a group of other people, simultaneously developing self-awareness, and having others work along with them despite their shortcomings may be extraordinary. Many people with mental illness are socially derailed and have limited social support. Additionally, making contributions that aide the success of another group member is especially meaningful to persons who, through the multiple losses associated with their illness, have come to view themselves as useless or discredited.

> **Comment:** This is when the group-building process truly makes gains in the areas of interpersonal learning, group cohesiveness, universality, altruism, hope and catharsis. It is the group process and the relationships between group members that ultimately heal the impact of loss due to illness. For this reason, the Life Goals Program is formatted specifically for group application.

There may be times when it is necessary for a member to shift his or her focus from one goal to another because it must take precedence. For example, managing an acute depressive episode may require temporary cessation of work on job seeking. Also, as is true in life outside the group, an unforeseen event may occur in the life of a member that must take priority over his or her original goal (e.g., job loss). In that case, the original goal may be placed on the back burner as the member works on the more pertinent goal.

Losses incurred by the illness may lead to negative thinking styles, dysfunctional attitudes, feelings of hopelessness, isolation, lack of peer modeling, and the sequelae of psychiatric stigma.

> **Comments:** As noted above, there will be times when the focus will need to shift from one Goal to another, more pertinent goal. For example, if a member should become hypomanic or depressed, as frequently occurs during the course of the group program, the goal may need to shift to managing the illness episode. During this time the concept that illness management must precede attainment of Life Goals is reinforced. It may not be necessary to stop all effort on the first goal. In fact, the group experience may provide the initial guidelines for the development of specific coping strategies to manage an illness episode in lieu of Life Goal work.

Let us now turn to specific roadblocks and some strategies the therapist may use to help the members in combating them. These will be discussed in some detail so that they can be applied by the therapist in diverse but similar situations when they may arise.

ROADBLOCKS AND THERAPIST STRATEGIES

OVERVIEW OF ROADBLOCKS

The conceptual framework for understanding progress in therapy is derived from viewing a member's behavior as driven by efforts to cope adaptively, as summarized in Chapter 6. Accordingly, the individual will act in his or her best interest as he or she perceives it, even if it appears to an outsider to lead to unproductive, odd, or self-defeating behavior. It is often the only avenue the person sees available, or the one that entails the least risk to self-esteem or risk of outright failure. These mechanisms apply not to the signs and symptoms of manic-depressive disorder itself, which we assume to have a strong biological component. Rather, these mechanisms apply to how the person carries his or her illness and how he or she attempts to live around it.

The corollary of this understanding of how an individual behaves is that the person will act in healthy ways if certain impediments are removed. Such impediments, or Roadblocks, include lack of knowledge; signs and symptoms of manic-depressive disorder; and, most important and most difficult to address, certain types of psychopathology, broadly defined.

We consider these last processes to be psychopathological only in the broadest sense because they interfere with optimal functioning. It is not terribly important for treatment in the Life Goals Program to divine whether such maladaptive coping behaviors derive from diagnosable DSM-IV-R axis II disorders, from personality characteristics that track along axis II dimensions, or simply from variants of normal due to individual experience. Rather, it is important to recognize that these roadblocks to adaptive function exist, and that, if removed, the individual has a much greater chance of attaining the goals that are important in his or her life.

Recall that individual roadblocks for a member may reoccur at several, or all, stages of the goal-attainment process. The therapist strategies are usually similar, though the specific content of the intervention may differ depending on whether, for example, the therapist is addressing hopelessness during overall goal identification or during implementation of behavioral steps.

It should be noted that, as the therapy progresses toward more specific expectations, more of the psychological burden of having manic-depressive disorder will surface. Dealing with stigma, loss, hopelessness, poor self-esteem, negative cognitive set, and simple lack of experience (e.g., in holding a job, maintaining personal relationships, or managing personal affairs) will all make constructing and carrying out realistic goals difficult.

Thus, the going will get tougher as the therapist moves members from articulating the *Description of the Challenge* and *overall Goal,* to identifying component *Subgoals,* then to constructing and monitoring *Behavioral Steps.* The therapist will need to maintain the focus on the behavioral program that serves as the backbone of treatment. At the same time, he or she will need to use interpersonal and cognitive interventions to address the Roadblocks that will inevitably develop. Interpersonal or process group interventions are often time-consuming and take place over weeks, with behavioral goal tracking needing to be interspersed to keep the group members focused on their purpose in group.

Roadblocks below are grouped roughly into three categories and presented in order of increasing complexity. At a most basic level, simple inexperience in working in the goal attainment format may be responsible for an individual not progressing toward goals that he or she feels are meaningful. This is dealt with in Roadblocks 1 through 5 (see Table 8.3, p. 237). In addition, disease symptoms may complicate goal-attainment, as outlined in Roadblocks 6 and 7. On a more complex level, goal attainment may be thwarted by ineffective coping patterns driven by certain psychopathological (broadly defined) characteristics; these include particularly dysfunctional attitudes and several factors addressed by interpersonal group techniques. These are addressed in Roadblocks 8 and 9. The reader is referred to Table 8.4 (p. 238) for a condensed reference to Therapist Strategies for Overcoming Roadblocks. On a more practical level, Roadblocks may be due to securing and applying the appropriate resources.

ROADBLOCK 1: NO GOALS OR STEPS IDENTIFIED DUE TO LACK OF EXPERIENCE IN THINKING IN TERMS OF GOALS AND BEHAVIORS

It is unusual that a member will immediately identify and write down a Goal on which to work. Thus, the process in the first Stage, "Description of the Challenge," may help group members to recognize goals within the context of meaningful experiences and and events actually taking place in their personal lives. The value of listening to group members' personal "stories" is that they offer a pool of data about the context from which they will work on their goals and the enfolding background that may affect their success.

This long period of time may be due to several factors. Group members may hesitate sharing details about their personal aspirations and challenges (problems) in the group setting. In addition, on a most basic level, many people do not tend to think in terms of specific goals in their lives. Consequently, specific mental tools and strategies for identifying specific goals are often not well developed. These types of host factors, though not well defined, clearly affect how an individual will respond to the challenges of functional deficits due to manic-depressive disorder.

Lack of experience in thinking in terms of goals in a formal way and specific plans to reach them is the rule rather than the exception. Most individuals, though they certainly have goals for their lives, do not necessarily think of them as tied to explicit behaviors on their part. Some group members who present as thwarted by the prospect of developing a goal for the group will discover during less formal group discussion one or more goals they are actually accomplishing. For others, goals and subgoals may be thought of as something that just "happen," or may be seen as dependent primarily upon other people, or luck, or some other external factor.

Therapist Strategy: Countering Lack of Experience in Thinking in Terms of Goals and Explicit Behavioral Steps

To address this issue, the therapist may use techniques such as brainstorming to allow each of the members to speak about his or her own experience in setting goals. In Stage 1, the therapist simply asks the group to talk about an area in their lives they would like to change. This strategy often will lead to group member statements, such as they would like to have improved symptom management, resolve sleep problems, or increase their effectiveness coping with a specific stressor. Another strategy is to ask group members for examples of goals they have had in their lives and how they have gone about approaching them. The therapist may go around the room if no one volunteers. In this exercise, it is useful for each member to produce at least one example of a goal that he or she has worked on at some time. Throughout the group process, the therapist may also tune into the content of group member discussions and translate their contributions into goals. In Stages 3 and 4, the therapist queries group members about their experiences in working on projects (goals) that they had to divide into individual steps in order to complete. The dependence of success on formulating a specific plan is the point of emphasis.

Occasionally, the group will not elicit personal information or examples of goals spontaneously. The therapist may "seed" the group with examples. He or she may also return to examples of illness management goals and steps that were discussed by members in Phase 1. Note that certain aspects of Phase 1 actually represented goal attainment as well, such as the successful identification or truncation of an episode. This also provides the therapist with an opportunity to work on a group goal. For example, developing contingency plans for a group response to members presenting with mania or depression is an appropriate starting point for group members to get experience using the stages of goal attainment. Additionally, group members may spend time discussing and integrating the information learned during Phase 1 and refine their Personal Care Plans. Certainly, the fact that members are present in Phase 2 of the program offers a rich segue for the therapist to demonstrate the process of goal attainment.

Comment: Once again, the difficulty is not that individuals do not have goals for their lives; rather, they simply do not recognize the goals they have and think in terms of explicit behaviors of their own to meet them.

Vignette

Mr. C. joined a Phase 2 cohort after completing Phase 1 with a different cohort. It was thought he would benefit from this group because the group members had similar backgrounds. He was a quiet man who had predominantly mixed episodes. In the past, when Mr. C. had mixed episodes, he was aggressive. He learned that these behaviors were not acceptable and initially did not discuss them, thinking that was not acceptable either. Typically, when Mr. C. had a severe episode, he spent most of his time alone on his fishing boat. During Phase 1, Mr. C. became quietly aware that psychosis was part of his mental illness.

Though often queried by his treatment team, he did not disclose having auditory hallucinations associated with paranoia. The concepts associated with integrating illness management, manic-depressive disorder, and goals were also very difficult for Mr. C. to understand. During group meetings, Mr. C. verbally participated, though he did not disclose his secrets. Mr. C. listened as other group members shared their symptoms of psychosis and strategies to manage them. Mr. C. then shared his experience with psychosis and aggression and developed a goal to improve management of his auditory hallucinations and paranoia, having recognized the relationship between these symptoms.

This goal was further processed to include subgoals to collaborate more effectively with his treatment team and to discuss his symptoms quickly after they emerged. Mr. C. further disclosed his fears of being hospitalized should he share his symptoms with his provider, and this interfered with his being an effective collaborator in managing his illness. The therapist educated Mr. C. that psychosis alone was not grounds for commitment to a psychiatric facility. Because he had a stable support network in the community and control of his behavior, he could think of the hospital as a resource if he felt he needed it. He was given positive feedback about the effective coping strategies he was already using, such as sharing these concerns with the group and taking time out away from people in his fishing boat. He included these in his illness management plan.

ROADBLOCK 2: OVERAMBITIOUS GOALS AND STEPS IDENTIFIED DUE TO INEXPERIENCE

It is not unusual for a member to identify a goal that is unrealistic in terms of his or her abilities, experience, or disease prognosis. This may be due to several factors, including simple lack of experience, self-esteem deficits that make only the loftiest goals acceptable, and clinical hypomanic symptoms.

Therapist Strategy: Developing Experience in Realistic Goal Choice and Step Construction

In the case of simple inexperience, it is important that the therapist respond in a manner that frames the member's capabilities in a positive light, while not minimizing the realities of his or her situation. One way this can be done is to reconstruct an overly ambitious goal into several more realistic subgoals. The member is urged to "work up to that one." Recall that the first goal optimally will deal with improved illness management, so this provides further grounds for deferring particularly overambitious goals.

For the more impaired members, an apparently simple step to improve self-determined illness management skills may be "Dispensing my own medications." This goal may actually break down into many steps. These may include locating a store where a 7-day pill dispenser may be purchased, putting the money aside and buying one, scheduling time with a family member or case manager to review the medication list, filling the dispenser, developing and maintaining a checklist of medications dispensed, and discussing any problems with the group as the process unfolds. Each of the steps represented provides ample opportunity for anxiety and failure. Success means making sure that each of these steps is carefully thought out and addressed separately. In the example above, each step taken toward "dispensing my own medication" was accomplished in sequence.

It is also advisable that the therapist be quite upfront and explicit with the members regarding the strategy of "setting them up for success." This should be no therapeutic secret. In essence, what the therapist communicates to the group in a general way is that they may be disappointed in themselves due to multiple losses as well as failure achieving certain goals in their lives. This is not their fault, at least, not nearly so much as they believe it to be. To be sure, everyone has failures to which he or she has contributed, but that is not the main focus here. The illness of manic-depression makes it difficult to work at achieving Life Goals. These frustrations breed lack of self-confidence, and this self-confidence needs to be rebuilt. To relearn this belief in oneself—or to learn it for the first time—one needs to succeed. "We will start with accomplishing small steps that will grow into larger successes."

Vignette

Mr. P. was a bright, educated person with a severely disabling manic-depressive illness. He had a PhD and could read and write several languages. Mr. P. lost his inheritance on manic spending sprees and his job due to alcoholism and cocaine dependence. Through aggressive outpatient psychopharmacology and group program support, Mr. P. had no hospitalizations for 2 years. Mr. P. described his goal to cope more effectively with his depressive symptoms so he could write a novel. It was gleaned from his "Description of the Challenge" that Mr. P. had been nonadherent to his medication plan whenever he felt depressed and decided to give up. When depressed, Mr. P. would not maintain any semblance of a schedule, and his sleep–wake cycles were haphazard. His subgoals were identified as "Adherence to a Structured Daily Activity/Sleep Schedule" and "Medication Plan." While constructing the daily activity schedule, Mr. P. completed a cost-benefit analysis of each item considered for his list. Regardless of the severity of his depressive symptoms, he adhered to the schedule. He worked closely with his provider and adhered to his appointments and medications, both dedicated to minimizing the intensity of his depressive episodes. Eventually, over the course of several months, Mr. P. had fewer depressive symptoms and more days well. With many misstarts and delays to write a novel, he eventually completed it.

ROADBLOCK 3: IMPRECISE GOALS AND STEPS IDENTIFIED DUE TO LACK OF EXPERIENCE

The cornerstone of treatment in Phase 2 is to identify and achieve realistic goals that are important to the individual member's quality of life via specific behavioral plans. This cannot be achieved if the member cannot articulate goals or steps in sufficiently precise behavioral terms so that the individual and the therapist know when they have been reached.

Therapist Strategy: Goal and Step Formulation in Measurable and Behavioral Terms

With regard to behavioral precision, the goal must be stated in behavioral terms such that all would agree when the goal has been reached. Goals such as "Being a business success" or "Not being lonely" clearly take more work. However, they also are very valid and useful starting points for therapeutic work. Not being lonely can clue the therapist into the fact that this member wants to work on social relationships. This may be reformatted into more specific terms, such as "Dating at least once a month" or "Making at least two new friends this year." In this latter example, what exactly a friend is to the individual needs to be defined, but once done, it will be clear when he or she has achieved the objective. Being a business success may be reformulated as "Getting a full-time job," "Becoming financially independent of my parents," or some other ambitious desire for increased income or peer recognition.

> **Comment:** Note that the first articulations of the Description of the Challenge and overall goals do not allow anyone, even the member, to know when they have reached his or her Goal. Formulating Subgoals and Behavioral Steps that clearly define outcome in concrete terms makes it possible for the member and the group to understand exactly what he or she strives to accomplish and incremental progress made in each Behavioral Step.

The principle of behavioral measurability for formulating goals, subgoals, and behavioral steps is similar. It is critically important that as the planning becomes more concrete—as the process moves from description of the challenge, overall goals to subgoals to behavioral steps—the therapist emphasizes behavioral measurability. For example, the therapist will not be able to give meaningful positive feedback for achieving specific behavioral steps if he or she cannot recognize that a step has been completed. Similarly, the individual members and their peers cannot provide recognition on a job well done. Neither can the therapist work with members on specific problems that develop unless the steps are sufficiently behaviorally articulated.

Vignette

Ms. J. (see Figure 8.1A, p. 261) was a college student who had experienced a devastating manic episode during her sophomore year. She was subsequently bothered by chronic depressive symptoms that had not responded to trials of several antidepressants and adjustment of mood stabilizers. Her initial Description of the Challenge on the Life Goals Worksheet focused on her feelings of emptiness and isolation. During group discussion it was clear that she craved a more active social life and more intimate friendships with several of her classmates.

The therapist worked with Ms. J. to develop Goals that were explicit and realistic. They focused on developing a single friendship, and the formulation of explicit Subgoals and Behavioral Steps allowed them to track progress. Over several months Ms. J. made modest progress on her plan, but the progress that she did make was explicitly apparent to both the therapist and to her. This in turn led to a more realistic appraisal of her own limitations and her own progress, and her chronic dysphoria diminished somewhat, suggesting that guilt about not living up to her self-perceived potential was a contributing factor.

ROADBLOCK 4: FORMULATION OF GOALS AND STEPS THAT DEPEND PRIMARILY ON OTHERS

Sometimes an overall goal is initially formulated in terms that depend primarily on others. Clearly, virtually all goals that are meaningful in the realm of functional outcome—that is, social and occupational function and subjective health-related quality of life—will depend to some extent on others. We are, after all is said and done, social human beings. On the other hand, it is important to specify the overall goal in such a manner as to construct subsequent building blocks of subgoals and behavioral steps that will be under the individual's control.

A balance must be struck between a goal that reflects a person's life in a social world of intricate interdependencies and the need to focus on what the individual himself or herself can bring to those social situations to maximize the probability of success. The goal "Getting a job" clearly depends on an appropriate job being available—and so similarly for dating, making friends, and getting married.

The "acid test" for goal identification is whether the goal can be broken down into discrete subgoals and behavioral steps that depend on the individual's own efforts and whether there will be ambiguity for either the member or the therapist in terms of knowing whether or not the member has reached his or her goal.

Comment: This approach sets the member up to work on his or her goal-attainment plans in a meaningful sphere of his or her life, which will likely involve interactions with others in a social manner. However, focusing subsequent work in Stage 3 and particularly Stage 4 on the components of these interactions that are under the individual's control will help the person to develop a reasonable view of his or her own successes and limitations along the way. It also will put the therapist in a position to help the member to develop better goal-attainment strategies and to overcome the Roadblocks that the individual may bring to these situations.

Therapist Strategy: Goal Formulation, with a Focus on the Individual's Role in Attainment

What is important at the stage of goal identification is that the goal not depend exclusively on the vagaries of fortune or the good will or interest of someone else. Goals such as "Winning the lottery" and, more commonly, "Being able to live without medications" depend primarily on matters outside of the individual's control. In the first example, it is chance. In the second, it is the individual's biology, which in most cases, is minimally under the control of an individual's will, habits, behaviors, and wishes.

However, even behaviorally specified goals such as "Making new friends" and "Getting a job" will depend to some extent on others. This is appropriate for the reasons outlined above. It is in the subsequent two steps of subgoal development and construction of behavioral steps that the therapist will focus the individual's efforts on what he or she can do to achieve the overall goal.

Formulation of subgoals should focus more on the member's own role in the completion of tasks, and behavioral steps should be formulated exclusively in terms of the individual's own efforts. To continue the example of seeking employment, one subgoal might be "Practicing job interviewing skills with mock interviews." Although successful attainment of this sub-goal clearly depends on having someone with whom to practice, the focus is clearly on the member's own actions.

In developing the specific behavioral steps to achieve this subgoal, the focus must be exclusively on the individual's efforts. For example, "Asking my brother to practice job interviewing skills with me" is preferable to "Practicing job interviewing skills with my brother at least five times."

Under the latter formulation, the step may not be completed because of factors not under his or her control: The brother may or may not want to do this, may or may not have time to do this, and may or may not be in town for the next 2 months. This leads to failure to complete a step that is not the result of the member's own efforts. This in turn leaves the member with a sense of failure due to external factors, emphasizing his or her passivity and victimization in a hostile world. It also leaves the therapist without an opening with which to address Roadblocks that may have kept the member from being able to attain the Goal.

Under the formulation "Asking my brother . . ." the member and therapist should focus on the member's own actions. If he or she has asked the brother, then the step is successfully completed. If the brother, for whatever reason, does not wish to comply, it is accurately seen as a function of the brother's choosing and not the member's. The member can then formulate alternate plans (e.g., ask a friend or another family member to practice interviewing).

Comment: There is clearly the potential to investigate the brother's decline of the request to practice job interviewing in terms of the member's own difficulties or inadequacies. For example, the member may bring up the thought that the brother doesn't like him or her because he or she is "sick," "irresponsible," "inconsiderate," or any one of a thousand qualities that may be associated with persons with manic-depressive disorder whose behavior is not considered a function of an illness.

There is certainly an opportunity to focus on issues of stigma and hopelessness using interpersonal group techniques. However, two points should be made. First, these issues will not emerge with clarity unless the member's action (asking) and the brother's response (declining the request) are separated.

Second, the decision to delve into these intrapsychic or interpersonal issues should be determined by whether they will ultimately serve the individual's behavioral plan. If they will address specific Roadblocks, then the therapist should pursue them. If not, and they typically do not, they should be deferred. Recall that there is no limit to the amount of process-oriented work that can be done with each individual member in group. The strategic question for the therapist is which of these many avenues to follow. The guideline is to follow those that will result in improved ability to attain the specified goals on which the member is working.

Vignette

Mrs. H. wanted very much to "meet someone special and get married." She had been living alone for many years since she'd had a manic episode. The manic episode led to her dropping out of law school, which left her devastated. She also believed it had greatly disappointed her father before he passed away. She described how she had lost contact with many of her old friends over the years and hadn't been out socially for quite a while. The group recognized and discussed the pitfalls that were associated with depending on the cooperation of another person to attain a goal and helped Mrs. H. reframe her goal to her going out and participating in activities where she may socialize and meet others. Mrs. H. elected to schedule part of her day exploring the town in which she lived and making conversation with shopkeepers along the way. She also joined a dancing class. Over several months, these activities led to her meeting someone and dating. She eventually got married and began a family.

ROADBLOCK 5: "WRITER'S BLOCK"

It is not uncommon to hear a member say, "I know what goal/plan I want to work on, I just don't like to write it down." Sometimes the person may even have articulated a goal or behavioral steps in fairly specific terms, yet not want to write it down. This resistance can be due to one or more factors.

Individuals may simply not have come from writing-oriented backgrounds, and the most day-to-day writing they have done is filling out bank checks or writing shopping lists. They may not have had extensive education, or they may even be dyslexic. Sometimes they are simply not comfortable expressing intimate details of their hopes, goals, and often failures in writing. More frequently, however, resistance to writing comes from two Roadblocks that need to be a focus of treatment.

Therapist Strategy: Countering the "Schoolhouse Dynamic"

First, members may feel that writing recapitulates the school environment in which many of them have failed or at best found irrelevant to their lives. Many feel that this puts them in a student role and the therapist in a teacher role. Although there is some truth to this, the fear is that they will find themselves in the position of being checked and graded or otherwise evaluated punitively. They know that if they write down a goal on paper, that sooner or later the "teacher" will ask them to take out their "homework" to be "checked." They anticipate evaluation and eventual failure, and sometimes even feel infantilized and resentful.

> **Comment:** As noted above, as the expectations become more concrete, there will naturally develop more resistance. Even the name "Homework" for Stage 4 may conjure vivid memories and strong feelings that derive from a member's childhood experience in school.

The therapist is best advised to approach this Roadblock head on, using two interventions. First, outlining explicitly to the group the specific dynamic that leads to this type of resentment can help to dissipate the ill feelings and resistance. Second, pointing out the benefits of writing is important (here as elsewhere, the cost-benefit paradigm can be helpful). It is particularly important to point out that if the person has not set out a concrete goal, he or she can never know when success has been achieved. This typically relieves some tension and resistance, but it also brings up the specter of failure. In addition, in the construction of a multistep behavioral plan, it is just plain difficult to remember everything—for the therapist as well as for the individual member.

Vignette

Mr. Z. refused to write anything at all during both Phase 1 and Phase 2 of the group program. During his initial assessment, his clinicians recognized that he had had learning difficulties in school and had dropped out at an early age. During Phase 1, the therapist recognized that it was possible that Mr. Z. had writing and reading deficits. Though not ready to disclose this to the group or the therapist, Mr. Z. agreed to allow the therapist to write for him on the Life Goals Worksheet.

Therapist Strategy: Minimizing Fear of Failure by Setting the Members up for Success

This second source of resistance, fear of failure, is omnipresent in individuals with manic-depressive disorder. Writing a goal down on paper represents a greater level of commitment than a verbal articulation of the goal. To make such an explicit commitment means to open oneself to the possibility of failure.

Recall that the therapist must provide guidance to "set members up for success." This means helping them to set realistic, achievable goals that they are likely to be able to reach. It is important to emphasize this strategy, making it explicit if necessary.

> **Comment:** A second process often sets in at this point. The individual will think that to set achievable goals is beneath him or her. This is the same dynamic that drives the Roadblock of setting ambitious goals and needs to be addressed with the same types of strategies. Substantial time in interpersonal interventions is often necessary to progress through this Roadblock, as it is supported by stigmatization, isolation, and hopelessness. Cognitive interventions may also be useful to identify the faulty assumptions underlying the thought that "If I adopt a small goal, I am a less capable or worthwhile person."

ROADBLOCK 6: NO GOALS OR STEPS IDENTIFIED DUE TO DEPRESSIVE SYMPTOMS

It is clear from psychopharmacologic and psychotherapeutic research that there are aspects of the depressive syndrome that are amenable to biological interventions. For example, those with more severe depressive symptoms tend not to respond to psychotherapy alone but do respond to pharmacotherapy with psychotherapy. The most that psychosocial interventions can do in that situation is to provide support. Thus, it is likely in dealing with persons with manic-depressive disorder in the group setting that there will be times when the therapist and group are confronted with a member who is so depressed that he or she cannot participate actively in goal identification and the subsequent steps. In this instance, there are several responses the therapist can make.

Therapist Strategy: Working with and Around Depressive Symptoms

Typically, the therapist will suggest that the group member select depression management as the goal. As the description of the challenge unfolds, it will become evident what subgoals will most effectively contribute to meeting successfully the goal of depression management. In the most severe cases, it may be necessary to directly ask the member to construct a subgoal to contact his or her primary clinician or psychiatrist regarding a their current treatment plan. Addressing potential suicidality, individually or in the group setting, as a contingency plan is also appropriate and necessary in certain cases. This has the additional benefit of facilitating group support when it is most needed. (See Phase 2 session orientation for guidelines.)

It is often possible also to maintain work in the goal-attainment process, with certain key adaptations. As noted previously, we strongly urge that the first set of goals that group members work on focus on improved illness management skills. The depressive episode provides the perfect opportunity to identify and work on subgoals related to this. Reasonable subgoals, for example, include "Discussing with my doctor that I need more help with my depression" and "Work with my doctor to get a new antidepressant." These subgoals can be broken down into simple steps, such as "Calling the clinic to arrange an appointment for my doctor," "Arranging transportation to the clinic on the appointment day," "Arranging child care so that I can attend the appointment," "Telling my doctor my symptoms," "Telling my husband/wife I am feeling depressed again and asking them for help in . . . ," and the like.

It is important to structure modest goals for individuals during periods of depression, because they are less able to perform to their full potential cognitively or emotionally. The key here is not to let the member set himself or herself up for failure, which will doubtless be magnified in his or her own mind. The therapist may also take the opportunity to reinforce and reemphasize the logic associated with having the goal to improve depression management take priority over other personal goals as needed.

In addition, it is important for the therapist to be alert for internal, global, or stable attributions from depressed group members. Questioning the assumptions of these attributions can be important in redressing their negative cognitive set.

Finally, it is important to accept the depressed member at his or her current level of comfort for group participation. Sometimes the person will only be able to listen for several sessions, and sometimes the person may be so uncomfortable that he or she asks for a "vacation." The therapist should help the member in assessing whether this is in his or her own best interest, using a personal cost-benefit analysis. If so, he or she works to support the member in the individual's temporary nonparticipation with the other group members.

Comment: One can see the differences between the Life Goals approach and the primarily interpersonal group approach to nonparticipation of members. In the Life Goals approach, depression is accepted as a common occurrence, the expression of which is only partially under the individual's control. The individual and the group respond based on the individual's current capabilities rather than according to the primacy of group process. Confrontation and stimulation are minimized, expectations are temporarily lowered, and the focus of intervention is shifted toward the main problem at hand: managing what is undoubtedly a painful, frustrating, even humiliating depression. Most important is that the group member clearly understands that the group values the member's presence, regardless of his or her level of active participation.

Vignette

Ms. L. had a history of seasonal depressive episodes that recurred every autumn and lasted into early spring. During these episodes, she had extreme social withdrawal, and at times she locked herself into the basement to avoid all social contact. She also attempted to self-regulate her medications and tried several times to end the depression and induce hypomania by discontinuing lithium. Subsequently, on a least one occasion, this led to active suicidal behavior and hospitalization. As the end of the summer drew near, Ms. L.'s goal-attainment work was replaced by obsessive concern about her well-being during the coming months. Ms. L. shared her feelings of resignation about winter approaching and her anticipated misery. The group worked with Ms. L. to help her to think more about the outcome of her behavior when depressed and regarded these behaviors as efforts to cope. With the group support, Ms. L. did a cost-benefit analysis of her strategies to cope with depression: stopping lithium and isolating in the basement. Then the group helped Ms. L. to identify more effective coping strategies to deal with her impending depressive episode.

What is notable in this example is that, although the group members had "intellectually" talked about illness management and the processes instrumental to undertake it, Ms. L. had not integrated these principles in a way that she could apply them to her personal dilemma. Ms. L. formulated her overall goal into coping more effectively with the potential for a seasonal depressive episode. Her subgoals further defined her strategies to cope. They were (1) maintain strict adherence to her daily activity plan and (2) develop a treatment plan with her provider for more aggressive depression management. Ms. L. identified specific behavioral steps that translated into strategies to replace the ineffective coping strategies used in the past: She made an appointment with her physician to discuss antidepressant therapy, volunteered to take responsibility for a fall fund-raising project, and made a commitment to attend the group where she could troubleshoot difficulties and get other moral support.

The depressive episode began as anticipated; however, it was not as intense as it had been in other years, an effect of her taking antidepressant medication and planning social interaction through group and volunteer activity. There were times that Ms. L. did not keep her appointments, but they were rare. When her level of participation fell off, Ms. L. received group support for her occasional "vacations" from group and positive reinforcement for attendance. One aspect of the positive reinforcement was to confirm that the group accepted her coming and sitting quietly without participating verbally when she was feeling particularly overwhelmed.

ROADBLOCK 7: OVERAMBITIOUS GOALS AND STEPS IDENTIFIED DUE TO HYPOMANIC SYMPTOMS

Yalom (1975) was not incorrect in his assertion that hypomanic individuals could be disruptive to groups, although it is unfortunate that he overstated the case so dramatically (see chapters 5 and 6). However, in a homogeneous group of persons with manic-depressive disorder who have similar Goals for group participation, the verbalizations and behavior are relatively less foreign and disruptive, and they can be dealt with in a more straightforward manner. Furthermore, contingency plans for mood episodes, gentle but firm redirection, and even one-on-one reinforcement of illness management skills learned in Phase 1 may be required. Infrequently, there may be times the therapist and the group member elect for the member to take a brief "time-out" from one or more sessions to reduce the stimulation of the group setting that may fuel the hypomania. However, hypomania may also present the more subtle fueling of unrealistic goals and expectations.

Occasionally, persons with manic-depressive disorder type II build their coping skills around hypomania. This can be seen, for instance, in salespeople, artists, writers, consultants, and others in whom productivity does not depend on consistency. Even in those for whom hypomania has fueled success, it is important to point out that inconsistency is usually the source of substantial interpersonal and occupational morbidity in manic-depressive disorder. For example, it is not necessarily being the life of the party that is detrimental to a person's social life when he or she has manic-depressive disorder; rather, it is setting up the expectation in others that the person will always be optimistic, self-confident, loquacious, humorous, and energetic. This is a tall bill to fill for anyone, even for those with chronic hypomania. Other people, whether in business or in social relations, are simply confused and often offended when the individual seems to withdraw from them when not hypomanic. The question they frequently ask is, "What have I done to make him or her respond differently to me?" The answer, of course, is nothing; it is an internal change driven by the illness. Nonetheless, this inconsistency frequently leads to alienation from friends and family, and not infrequently to failure in business, when the hypomanic episode has run its course. Furthermore, the individual's self-esteem often comes to depend on hypomania. This leaves the person very little room to accept his or her shortcomings, depressive periods, even normal periods of quiescence, self-doubt, and inward focus.

Therapist Strategy: Working with and Around Hypomanic Symptoms

It is important that the therapist recognize hypomanic expectations, even in those who appear to build success on their hypomanic episodes. The strategy here is, as in dealing with depression, supportive and positive rather than confrontative.

Note that focused support, referencing group contingency plans, and Phase 1 Worksheets: Personal Care Plans and Action Plans for Mania and even "time-out" may be necessary to maintain group decorum, as noted above. Dealing with hypomanic expectations in goal and step development, conceptually a different matter altogether, is the focus here. The focus must be shifted from the short-term benefits of hypomania to the longer-term, and more grounded, benefits of improved mood stability, constancy in behavior, and successful goal attainment. This, of course, includes not only hypomanic periods but also depressive periods and periods without symptoms. What are the goals that will be important through all these times? What are the goals that will be realistic throughout all moods? Personal cost-benefit analysis using the "worst case scenario" (i.e., persistent cycling, always starting over, and incurring further loss) often helps to bring the hypomanic person's perspective back to a more realistic grounding.

It is important to note that as the therapist and member focus on longer term management and away from episode-driven perspectives, they are reframing the person as being an *individual with an illness as a burden* that he or she carries, instead of considering the illness to be something that is part of him or her as a person. This therapeutic maneuver may, when repeated over time, unload some of the guilt that a person with manic-depressive disorder carries for his or her failings. These failings can then realistically be attributed by the individual to having a serious, though unrecognized, illness rather than be attributed to a character flaw or moral weakness. By the same token, looking past the hypomanic behavior to longer term goals and values allows the therapist and group member to focus the member as a person with values, goals, and abilities beyond those driven by hypomania.

Vignette

Mr. F. had been a captain on his city's police force prior to the onset of his manic-depressive disorder. During the illness, he often discontinued his lithium in order to generate hypomania and complete projects by working through the night. He was still involved in many community activities, and he valued the prestige that came with participating as a leader. As well as being more productive during hypomanic episodes, Mr. F. became irritable and verbally aggressive with members of the community groups and his family. He also had a tendency to take on too many projects, become overburdened, and project blame onto others for "not doing their share of the work." Many times his dialogue during group meetings focused on his anger toward members of the community groups he served. Mr. F. did not share other personal information, and he was resistant to the group guidelines regarding goal work.

The therapist's intervention was to interpret that Mr. F.'s overambition, anger, and irritability with regard to his community service and overall behavior appeared to be fueled by hypomania, because it was episodic and inconsistent. Eventually, the therapist suggested that this feverish activity was due to hypomania that was in turn generated by nonadherence to the treatment plan. The therapist eventually proposed that Mr. F. might not like himself much because of the problems associated with his hypomanic behavior. The therapist reframed Mr. F.'s dilemma into a goal that he had a central role in facilitating: become a more active comanager of his illness and treatment plan. This strategy protected Mr. F.'s fragile self-esteem while providing an opportunity for his personal investment to change his illness management strategies and unwanted behaviors.

Gradually and persistently, the group gave feedback about how they felt when Mr. F. was hypomanic: pressured, impulsive, and angry during the groups. The hypomanic episodes became fewer, and he began to experience the benefits of mood stability through his improved relationships with the group and his family. Mr. F. reduced the number of commitments he had in the community and began to discuss more meaningful goals for improving relationships in his family.

ROADBLOCK 8: NO GOALS OR STEPS IDENTIFIED DUE TO DEMORALIZATION AND HOPELESSNESS DERIVED FROM CHRONIC ILLNESS

In addition to lack of experience or disease symptoms, there are more complex reasons related to psychopathology, broadly defined, that may inhibit goal identification and step construction. Recall from chapter 6 that the basic choices made by an individual are driven by efforts to cope. Although certain behaviors may seem dysfunctional, they are adopted by the individual if not to maximize their chances of success in life, at least to minimize the chances of further loss and subjective discomfort. Of particular relevance to Phase 2 is the recognition by the therapist that not having certain goals in life or difficulty in developing plans to meet them is likely due to an adaptive coping strategy as well. This needs to be identified by the therapist and made explicit to the group members.

It is common that members will voice hopelessness about achieving meaningful goals in their lives. This can be a product of depressive symptoms, but frequently it is a reflection of their own life experience, which may be peppered with failures due to illness and other factors. A college career disrupted, a marital breakup, a business failure, the loss of friends—all these are common sequelae of manic-depressive illness. Understandably, they may lead to demoralization and hopelessness.

Various therapeutic strategies are available. These include the personal cost-benefit analysis, to which group members were introduced in Phase 1; cognitive techniques; and interpersonal group techniques.

Comment: Which of the various strategies the therapist chooses depend on the mechanism producing the Roadblock. This is frequently obvious to the therapist from the context. Sometimes additional probing by the therapist will clarify the source. Observation of an individual's interaction with other group members can also help to identify the source. This is one of the benefits of group psychotherapy: The here-and-now interactions of individuals are directly observable by the therapist rather than being reported secondhand by the individual in treatment. Not infrequently, multiple mechanisms contribute to producing a Roadblock. In some cases, the therapist chooses a strategy intuitively, working by trial and error until progress is made.

Therapist Strategy: Countering Demoralization with Personal Cost-Benefit Analysis

One strategy to use with this type of Roadblock is the personal cost-benefit analysis, which was introduced in Phase 1. The therapist responds to a member who verbalizes hopelessness as a reason for lack of goal identification or planning. Remembering that this also represents a type of adaptive coping, the therapist explores the ways in which the member may have benefited from having no explicit Life Goals. Typically, having no goals means not having to expose oneself to the humiliation of failure of some type. The therapist works to make these benefits explicit, perhaps writing them on the flip chart or blackboard.

The therapist then leads the member to list the benefits of identifying a specific goal in the area of life function that he or she would like to change. Not surprisingly, the metric usually tips the balance in favor of having a goal, though perhaps not the goal initially discussed by the therapist and group member. If the balancing of costs and benefits reveals that working on a particular goal will lead to too much cost or too much threat of loss, then the goal should be revised or discarded. This may be because the initial goal is overly ambitious.

Comment: Goals and subgoals at this stage may be too lofty or complex and will be prone to failure. The member should be guided toward the choice of a meaningful yet modest and attainable goal, such that he or she may have a successful experience in goal attainment; be recognized by the group and the therapist for such; and experience for himself or herself the positive reinforcing value of success, however modest. Overly ambitious goals or subgoals may themselves represent Roadblocks.

Vignette

Mr. T. (see Figure 8.1B, p. 262) had severe manic-depressive illness with rapid cycling. Major depressive episodes led to mixed episodes and later a state of chronic subsyndromal depression. Mr. T. had difficulty identifying a goal. He had many acute suicidal and assaultive episodes both at home and in the workplace. Much of his time was spent in isolation. It was a standard coping response for Mr. T. to refuse food, fluids, and medications when he was depressed and feeling hopeless. Mr. T.'s behaviors—suicide attempts, social isolation, violence, and refusal of basic self-care needs—were reframed as the "coping strategies" he had developed in order to manage his thoughts, feelings, and behaviors associated with depression. The group, by way of therapist interventions, was able to identify with Mr. T.'s hopelessness and suicidality as feelings they too had experienced. The group offered both statements of concern and confidence in Mr. T.'s ability to work on alternative and more effective strategies to cope with his depressions.

Once Mr. T. began to view his suicidal, violent, and other self-defeating behaviors as efforts to cope, it became possible to examine them together more objectively through a cost-benefit analysis. For example, Mr. T. often sat in a dark room when he felt depressed. The first step in the cost-benefit analysis was to list how this behavior was helpful to Mr. T. The benefit to this strategy was that social isolation provided a sense of safety and security. It was his objective to stay away from other people so he would not become more irritable and hurt someone. Once the benefits of the coping behavior were reinforced and acknowledged for their value, the group went on to look at the costs of sitting in a dark room alone. Mr. T. identified the costs of this behavior as increased feelings of loneliness, focused thinking on his mistakes, and feeling more depressed, angry, and hopeless. The next step was to help Mr. T. to identify coping strategies that had fewer costs but still provided the safety and security the dark room and isolation offered.

Mr. T. was able to identify an overall goal to improve management of his mood. Subgoals were (1) avoid hurting others and (2) activate more intense support from his treatment team during these episodes (get help for anger and depression with suicidal thoughts).

Comment: It is important that the therapist emphasize that all behavior has costs and benefits. It is through thoughtful consideration and trial and error that a person may recognize which behaviors are more helpful and which are more harmful. The therapist should also stress that a cost-benefit analysis may only be fashioned by the individual for whom it is intended. Henceforth, the member's response to group brainstorming sessions may be met with less resistance. In this way, every contribution may be regarded as valuable even though it may not become part of the final plan.

Note that as the treatment moves through the stages of goal and subgoal identification to the development of behavioral steps, the therapist and members will focus more on concrete plans. This entails a greater risk of failure as expectations become more specific. It is likely that resistance will become greater. The need for support will increase as the therapist intervenes to help the members address their Roadblocks.

Personal cost-benefit analysis in the construction of behavioral steps should be somewhat familiar to the members and the therapist from their work in Phase 1. Much of this work was in actuality the construction of a behavioral plan for improved management of the member's illness. This can be referred both to increase the member's sense of mastery and for examples of behavioral plans on which to build. In this example, Mr. T. developed Action Plans with his treatment team to ensure easy access to appointments once he and his spouse recognized his early symptoms. The behavioral steps included arranging an appointment with his provider to discuss these plans and activating the participation of his spouse who was, fortunately, supportive.

During the construction of behavioral steps, there may be many cost-benefit analyses that can be done to help choose which of several types of steps are most appropriate. The therapist is advised to emphasize simplicity and to make sure that multiple steps are not bundled into one (see Roadblock 3). Recall that each of the component behavioral steps may have a personal cost-benefit analysis that makes adopting that step difficult. As another example, a trip to a local store may be difficult to complete due to social anxiety or due to anxiety simply about getting lost. The member may not be conscious of the personal cost-benefit analysis that makes it preferable to stay at home rather than to risk that anxiety and potential failure. It is important to identify such hidden costs when individuals do not easily formulate or carry out what seem to the therapist to be relatively simple steps.

Vignette

Ms. D. had recently separated from her husband and moved into an apartment in an unfamiliar area of the city. Through-out her marriage, she had become increasingly dependent on her partner, who carried out most of the activities and decisions that were part of everyday living. The family system was closed to outsiders, and she had few social contacts or support. One goal that Ms. D. identified was to enhance her independence. The subgoal identified was to begin to have social contacts outside her family. One behavioral step she wanted to accomplish was to meet her new acquaintance at a coffee shop near her home.

Several weeks passed, and Ms. D. hadn't completed that step. The group queried her about possible Roadblocks to accomplishing her Steps and made genuine attempts to offer support and encouragement. As Ms. D. became more comfortable, she disclosed that she never before took a walk like that on her own. She feared having a panic attack if she ventured out and lost her way and was embarrassed to tell the group about the degree of her limitations. Clearly, Ms. D. had identified a behavioral step that was unattainable. Her problem was reframed by the therapist as progress and not a failure. Included in that discussion was reinforcement that it is more the rule than the exception for people to meet up with Roadblocks when trying to reach their goals. Often, a person will get stuck at that point and exit from proceeding to achieve his or her goal. One of the goals of the group is to help people to realize this and to take the next step, that is, to try to identify strategies to overcome Roadblocks.

Ms. D. reconsidered her problem and decided that several additional steps were needed. She decided to discuss the occurrence of these panic attacks with her provider, as it was realized through the group discussion she had a panic disorder. Treatment of this comorbid disorder followed by the purchase of a street map of the city, becoming familiar with the route to and from the coffee shop, and practicing the walk before the "coffee shop meeting" took place all contributed to her success.

Therapist Strategy: Countering Hopelessness with Interpersonal Techniques

Hopelessness can also be a function of those factors, only partially defined, that are responsive to interpersonal group psychotherapy techniques. Recall that, as outlined in Table 6.4 putative therapeutic interpersonal group factors were proposed by Hogue and McLoughlin (1991) and by Yalom (1975).

It is important that the therapist balance the structured behaviorally driven, goal-directed aspects of Phase 2 with a less structured interpersonal approach, allowing the development of group cohesion. This may appear to "delay" the group agenda, but the time spent in developing and supporting these aspects of treatment will provide further tools for goal attainment for the members.

Comment: Eidelson (1985) notes that "[h]ighly qualified cognitive therapists often have difficulty applying their skills in a group setting because they fail to take 'process' factors into account." She rightly proposes that a balance must be struck between the "classroom" aspects of cognitive and behavioral therapies and the concerns of process groups on individual conflicts. She further proposes that selection of group members, individual conferences outside of group with problem members, and a problem-solving approach on the part of the therapist all help to reduce this problem. Our approach differs somewhat in proposing that process aspects of the group experience are seen as active therapeutic ingredients of the treatment, and that the group will benefit from their judicious emphasis and focal application.

The group members become more cohesive as they share their experiences in an environment that they gradually discover to be safe and supportive. As this cohesion develops, members become more comfortable giving and receiving feedback. Supportive feedback from peers in similar circumstances frequently carries more weight than feedback from a therapist who has not lived with the same illness, the same doubts, the same experiences as a member's peers. This is one of the benefits of using group rather than individual techniques to address the functional needs of persons with manic-depressive disorder.

Simply having one member advise another on how to deal with a similar situation can be helpful both to the giver and to the receiver, as long as the advice is given and received in a positive spirit. A more subtle form of advice giving is simply asking another member whether he or she has been confronted with a similar situation, and what worked and did not work successfully for him or her.

Comment: Recall that the process of feedback must be carefully controlled by the therapist so as not to lead to overly stimulating or confrontational interactions.

Vignette

Mr. C. had a recurrent substance abuse problem that involved the use of cocaine. His group attendance was sporadic, and he had a tendency while in the group to deflect the focus from his personal issues to a more superficial agenda. The goal he had identified was to recover from his cocaine dependence. Several of the other members of the group were themselves recovering from a substance abuse disorder. One member of the group, Ms. A., had expressed anger toward Mr. C. for not adhering to his goal and continuing to relapse. She thought Mr. C. should be discharged from the group.

The therapist realized that Ms. A. was also having difficulty maintaining the behaviors associated with her goals. The therapist's interpretation of the dynamics that fueled Ms. A.'s behavior were that she was projecting her rejection of herself onto Mr. C. and feared she herself would be discharged from the group for lack of progress.

The therapist, mindful of the Transtheoretical Model of Change (see Phase 2 Orientation Session), spoke in general terms to the group that it is common to need to reestablish and reinforce new behaviors several times before the individual begins to "own" them. Frequently, the therapist pointed out, work on particular steps must be repeated despite achieving the Step previously; the process of change, the therapist noted, is often cyclic rather than strictly linear.

Therapist Strategy: Countering Hopelessness with Cognitive Techniques

As discussed in Section 2, it is likely that a negative cognitive set in persons with manic-depressive disorder may be due to several factors. According to classical cognitive theory, a negative cognitive set is concomitant of the depressive syndrome, both producing and probably produced by the syndrome. In addition, data from Seligman's group indicates that negative attributions may be due to longstanding personal factors not directly related to clinical depressive symptoms (Peterson & Seligman, 1984; Seligman et al., 1990). Furthermore, there is evidence that persons with depression may actually experience more negative events, and perhaps have a more justifiably negative slant to their cognitive set, than do nondepressed persons. In dealing with persons with chronic mental illness, the therapist must recognize that there may be more "logic" and empirical data in the negative attributions of the former than would be expected from working with the latter.

Regardless of the source of the negative cognitive set, the goal of treatment is to structure the goal-attainment strategy for success. The key cognitive intervention in Phase 2 is to focus on the expectations for failure verbalized by the members and to explore their sources. It is likely that the source of expectation for failure is multifactorial. Sometimes members may have overly ambitious goals that lead to failure (see Roadblocks 2 and 9). Frequently, though, members will have a negative cognitive set that leads the individual to conclude that their failure to have reached reasonable goals, or even to be able to identify goals, is so because of their personal shortcomings (internal), is true of all areas of their lives (global), and was always true and will always be true throughout their lives (stable).

The therapist explores these cognitions with an individual member in terms of a "response chain": Stimulus or event leads to thought, then to feeling, then to behavior (Beck et al., 1979). Through the exploration of overly negative attributions (self-defeating beliefs), members may be helped to conclude objectively whether or not their appraisal is justified and behavior response is effective.

A typical therapist intervention would be to introduce explicitly to the group the concept of the response chain:

EVENT → THOUGHT → FEELING → ACTION

and the potential variations in this model that may be induced by depression:

FEELING (DEPRESSION) → ALTERED PERCEPTION
OF EVENT (THOUGHT) → FEELING → ACTION

Making explicit the response chain can help the resistant individual who may be demoralized by defeat and adverse to group discussion about his or her "negative" personal thinking style. Once the members have participated in interactive learning experiences about these topics using generic examples as a group, the therapist may lead the target member into electing to participate on a more personal level.

Likewise, it is important that the therapist query the group in a general and nonintrusive way whenever statements are heard during group discussion that minimize success, magnify adverse experience, or appraise individuals in an erroneous way. The statement may be explored and the response chain evaluated formally or informally. Likewise, realistic ways of thinking and responding may be reinforced. This is most effective and more acceptable to group members when the therapist facilitates member identification of "neutral" versus "positive" thoughts to replace the negative (Greenberger & Padesky, 1995). Neutral versus positive may be considered a halfway mark to reframing self-appraisal. A key element in the therapeutic process is to identify whether the response chain elicits adaptive and effective or maladaptive responses.

Vignette

Mr. A. had a problem with anger management both during and outside major mood episodes for as long as he could remember. As he described it, he would encounter a situation and become angry immediately. He believed that his anger controlled him, and he felt hopeless. The group had gone over the cognitive strategies using the response chain during several of the preceding groups. During that time, other members discussed specific situations when they felt bad and recognized the association between their thoughts about an event and the feelings and behaviors that soon followed. Mr. A., however, was convinced that, in his case, his thoughts were not associated with his problem with anger.

It required endurance on the part of both the therapist and Mr. A. to pursue the strategy of using the response chain to help him with his problem. His Roadblocks were not at once apparent, and the process showed little week-to-week progress. One day, Mr. A. talked about a situation that resulted in his feeling angry. It happened immediately after being dropped off by his sister for a dental appointment. The thoughts that followed the event were that his sister would not return for him and he'd be left without a way home. Furthermore, he would not be able to find a way home for himself (his illness had led him to live quite a sequestered life). These thoughts led Mr. A. to feel shame that was quickly supplanted by anger. Once he was able to recognize the thoughts (regarding his own incapability) that were associated with his feelings (anger and shame) and how this potentiated negative behavior (withdrawal, verbal aggression, and indirect communication), it was possible to better facilitate his insight about the relationship between his thoughts, feelings, and behavior. Mr. A. found it acceptable to reframe his negative self-statements into more neutral versus positive statements. For example, "She would not return for him" was reframed as "She likely would return for him, but there was always a possibility she wouldn't." "He would never find his way home" was reframed as "It would likely take a while, but he would find his way home."

Comment: The reader is referred to a very user-friendly cognitive therapy workbook for patients, *Mind Over Mood* (Greenberger & Padesky, 1995) and its companion therapist guide (Padesky & Greenberger, 1995). Some group members may benefit from complementary therapies to increase their awareness of their negative thinking styles.

ROADBLOCK 9: OVERAMBITIOUS GOALS AND STEPS IDENTIFIED DUE TO SELF-ESTEEM DEFICITS OR DENIAL

Occasionally, individuals will be resistant to adopting realistic goals or developing step-wise behavioral plans, which they view as "beneath them." This is usually due to deficits in self-esteem that are made up for by adopting Goals that may make up for the deficits they themselves feel. Alternatively, individuals may use denial about the severity of impairment due to their illness to defend against recognition of those real-world losses. Unfortunately, failure at attaining such lofty goals usually follows, with subsequent further damage to self-esteem and sometimes increased depression. Without specific behavioral steps to reach goals, frequently nothing happens, as has been the case in the past for many members.

Therapist Strategy: Using Interpersonal Techniques to Emphasize Acceptance and Universality

Unfortunately, the individual is usually not conscious of such mechanisms, and neither are other group members. Other group members may look at such an individual as higher functioning than they and even look to him or her as a leader. Sometimes these are individuals whose premorbid function would have supported highly ambitious goals, but for whom they are no longer realistic.

In these situations direct confrontation is always avoided. It is more likely to be successful to focus on the commonalities between that individual and the others and to focus on common tasks, such as illness management skills. It is usually not too confrontative to point out the need to "set up for success" and to query the individual for instances in which he or she has not succeeded, then work to format the chosen area into manageable subgoals in Stage 3.

Vignette

Mr. K., an architect, was renowned nationally in his field. He was well-spoken and considered a prominent member of the professional community. However, during a manic episode complicated by alcohol abuse several years earlier, Mr. K. had lost his job, friends, and home in another state and had "fled" in embarrassment. He now lived with his parents. During the first several months of Phase 2, Mr. K. had quickly mastered the concepts of the Life Goals Worksheet and had no problem describing his identified goal, the specific problem units, subgoals, and steps. The scope of Mr. K.'s goals included a series of rather high-level and impressive business-related strategies to further his financial success, recruit new accounts, and market his designs. He presented them to the group typewritten and bound in a folder. For weeks, Mr. K. elaborated on his plans and the way he achieved his steps one by one. His goals, subgoals, and steps were realistic and attainable; however, Mr. K. was not dealing with his well-defended agenda associated with his social hardships and social anxiety without the use of alcohol.

Whenever sensitive material was shared by other group members regarding their difficulties with relationships and other social hardships consequent to their illness episodes or their use of alcohol and drugs, Mr. K. spoke enthusiastically about his business ventures without comment on the sensitive personal information the others were sharing. The therapist observed that prompts to elicit personal information sharing from Mr. K. led quickly to escalating anxiety. As the group culture for tolerance and acceptance grew, Mr. K. responded to prompts to offer advice to other members having difficulty coping with the negative outcomes associated with their manic episodes. Eventually, he disclosed his personal experience dealing with his own losses and began to work on more modest and appropriate social Goals.

In conclusion, the Life Goals Program offers individuals with an opportunity to develop and refine illness management skills to improve mood stability, and ability to cope with the sequelae of manic-depressive disorder. Additionally, Phase 2 provides guidance that is intended to assist members to reach personal Life Goals and move beyond the negative impact manic-depressive disorder has had on their lives—including the devastating personal, social, economic, and occupational losses.

Chapter 9

Program Evaluation

Treatment planning, clinical research, and health care resource management have developed from separate traditions; these include, respectively, clinical care and hospital accreditation concerns, research, and administrative management. However, in its own way each is concerned with the same central question: *Is what I am doing for the person doing them any good?* Our orientation is that there is more commonality among these apparently diverse endeavors than has commonly been assumed.

The recent focus on outcomes and services research seems to bear this out. For example, more and more clinical trials of psychotropic medications include components evaluating service utilization, traditionally more a concern of administrators than of clinicians. In addition, treatment planning has moved toward selection of explicitly measurable goals and tracking of progress toward those goals in quantitative terms, bringing a research orientation to general clinical practice. Furthermore, administrative resource management has in most institutions come to include measurement of quality of care, which includes process and outcome variables with applicability to both treatment planning and research.

The measures described in this chapter can be categorized as either process or outcome measures. *Process measures* relate to aspects of the caregiving, asking how well particular aspects of care are being delivered. In contrast, *outcome measures* tell you about the actual impact of treatment on an individual. Outcome measures, as reviewed in chapter 2, can be considered across three interdependent domains. These include *clinical outcome,* or signs and symptoms of the disease; *functional outcome,* including social and occupational function and subjective health-related quality of life; and *illness costs,* including costs of treatment (direct costs) and the additional financial burden of illness to the individual and society (indirect costs). Comprehensive measurement of all these outcome variables would require staffing—and group member cooperation—beyond that which can be reliably expected in general clinical practice. We have therefore chosen to target what we consider the key aspects of outcome with a small number of instruments easily adapted to use in the clinical setting.

Outcome measures are of course the most important measure of a program's worth. However, process measures can be informative in two ways. For research purposes, process measurements elucidate mechanisms by which changes in outcome are effected. For program management purposes, these indices may help to identify specific problems in the rendering of care that lead to suboptimal effects, or opportunities that stimulate further program development.

Though it may sound paradoxical, we have modeled our approach to evaluating the process of delivering treatment in the Life Goals Program after that for delivering pharmacologic treatments. Typically, in understanding medication effects, one wishes to know the amount of medication delivered and the level that is actually achieved in a subject. The delivery of medication is usually measured in terms of the dose given (e.g., milligrams per day). This is what the clinician *gives* to the person. However, once the person *ingests* the medication, his or her *absorption* or *metabolism* may differ from others, leading to differences in medication level in the body. Typically, these individual factors are accounted for by measuring the medication level in the blood.

Problems with resolution of depression, for example, could be due to the prescriber not administering a sufficient dose of antidepressant. Alternately, an appropriate dose of medication could have been delivered, but could have resulted in a low level of medication in the body because of variability in absorption or metabolism. Furthermore, levels may be low because of noncompliance on the part of the individual with the illness. Each of these problems points toward different solutions.

Because the Life Goals Program is manual-driven, we have the capability to measure the amount of treatment the therapist delivers by monitoring how closely he or she follows the prescribed program. This information can be used both in supervising therapists and in monitoring the uniformity of treatment across sites and across therapists. Additionally, there are several procedures to measure the amount of therapy "absorbed" by individual group members. For example, the therapist may do a wonderful job in delivering each focus point in a Phase 1 session, but if a member sleeps through the session, or does not come, it is not likely that he or she "absorbed" much of the therapy that day.

To develop a parsimonious yet comprehensive battery of process and outcome measures, we have been guided by several concerns.

• First, we have taken care to ensure that the measures are succinct and simple enough to be used by busy clinicians, and have avoided the more labor-intensive methods used in more extensive clinical research that require separate program evaluators. Although extensive research-oriented evaluations are more comprehensive and in some cases more precise, they are usually simply not feasible in clinical practice.

• Second, when using group member self-reports, we have kept those instruments as simple as possible. They have been completed successfully in our program even by persons who are of limited educational background and by those who are quite symptomatic at the time. Nothing decreases compliance like an overload of paperwork—and in our experience, this holds both for individuals and clinicians!

• Third, wherever possible we have chosen instruments for which reliability and validity in similar populations have been established, either by the original developers or in our own program.

Thus, we have attempted to glean from available research techniques those instruments that are simplest and quickest without compromising quality.

PROCESS MEASURES

TREATMENT DELIVERED

Treatment delivered by a therapist can be measured by having a supervisor review of the individual sessions, either by sitting in on the sessions and debriefing afterwards with the therapist or by reviewing video- or audiotapes. For Phase 1, the basis of measurement is the determination of whether the therapist adhered to the content and process goals of the Life Goals Program, and whether he or she covered the specific focus points for each session. The Therapist Monitors for each individual session in Phase 1 comprise Exhibit 25 (pp. 302–310).

For Phase 2, therapist adherence to the program is tracked using Exhibit 26 (p. 306), which can be filled out by a supervisor for each session initially and periodically as desired for subsequent sessions. Recall that the specific content of each session is much more dependent on the members, and not driven by a specific a priori agenda. Nonetheless, the therapist must still retain the orientation that his or her interventions are driven by the behavioral goal-attainment strategy, with cognitive, cost-benefit, and interpersonal interventions in the service of this end. The orienting image to be kept in mind is that of a behavioral backbone to the treatment plan supported by interventions of several types to identify and remove specific roadblocks.

EXHIBIT 25   Life Goals Program Therapist Monitor: Phase 1

SESSION 1, ORIENTATION

Date: _____

Therapist: _____

Supervisor:_____

Key: 1 = complete, 2 = partially complete, 3 = did not meet criteria

Content Goals:

Therapist came prepared and organized.

__ Therapist elicited clarification of member understanding of didactic content.

__ Therapist delivered didactic material in a matter-of-fact and friendly way.

__ Therapist exhibited expertise answering questions about manic-depressive disorder.

__ Therapist made appropriate use of visual aids and exhibits.

Process Goals:

Therapist recognized member ability level to (not) participate.

__ Therapist worked member discussions from a generic to a personal orientation.

__ Therapist addressed process issues but did not allow them to disrupt content agenda.

__ Therapist facilitated member discussion and interaction.

__ Therapist avoided judgmental feedback on member contributions.

__ Therapist avoided addressing interpersonal dynamic issues.

__ Therapist responded empathically to group member behavior (verbal, nonverbal).

__ Therapist initiated appropriate interventions for member symptoms manifested in group.

__ Therapist modulated overly stimulating feedback between group members.

Specific Focus Points:

Focus Point 1

__ Therapist established the therapeutic relationship environment.

Focus Point 2

__ Therapist explained the mood disorder spectrum.

__ Therapist introduced the concept of mood variation occurring as a response to stress and spontaneously.

Focus Point 3

__ Therapist described the elements of psychosis.

Focus Point 4

__ Therapist discussed neural transmission and brain organization based on member potential for understanding.

Focus Point 5

__ Therapist established the universality of manic-depressive disorder.

__ Therapist facilitated discussion about myths and inaccurate information about manic-depressive disorder.

__ Therapist discussed the impact of psychiatric stigma.

__ Therapist discussed coping with psychiatric stigma.

SESSION 2, MANIA PART 1

Date: _____

Therapist: _____

Supervisor:_____

Key: 1 = complete, 2 = partially complete, 3 = did not meet criteria

Content Goals:

Therapist came prepared and organized.

__ Therapist elicited clarification of member understanding of didactic content.

__ Therapist delivered didactic material in a matter-of-fact and friendly way.

__ Therapist exhibited expertise answering questions about manic-depressive disorder.

__ Therapist made appropriate use of visual aids and exhibits.

Process Goals:

Therapist recognized member ability level to (not) participate.

__ Therapist worked member discussions from a generic to a personal orientation.

__ Therapist addressed process issues but did not allow them to disrupt content agenda.

__ Therapist facilitated member discussion and interaction.

__ Therapist avoided judgmental feedback on member contributions.

__ Therapist avoided addressing interpersonal dynamic issues.

__ Therapist responded empathically to group member behavior (verbal, nonverbal).

__ Therapist initiated appropriate interventions for member symptoms manifested in group.

__ Therapist modulated overly stimulating feedback between group members.

Specific Focus Points:

Focus Point 1

__ Therapist established the session goals.

Focus Point 2

__ Therapist facilitated discussion about the variability of manic episodes and patterns of occurrence.

__ Therapist facilitated a production of a generic list of manic signs and symptoms.

__ Therapist facilitated member construction of a personal mania profile.

Focus Point 3

__ Therapist explained that episodes can occur spontaneously or in response to either good or bad stress.

__ Therapist facilitated a general discussion of potential triggers for mania.

__ Therapist facilitated member construction of a list of personal triggers of a manic episode.

SESSION 3, MANIA PART 2

Date: _____

Therapist: _____

Supervisor: _____

Key: 1 = complete, 2 = partially complete, 3 = did not meet criteria

Content Goals:

Therapist came prepared and organized.

__ Therapist elicited clarification of member understanding of didactic content.

__ Therapist delivered didactic material in a matter-of-fact and friendly way.

__ Therapist exhibited expertise answering questions about manic-depressive disorder.

__ Therapist made appropriate use of visual aids and exhibits.

Process Goals:

Therapist recognized member ability level to (not) participate.

__ Therapist worked member discussions from a generic to a personal orientation.

__ Therapist addressed process issues but did not allow them to disrupt content agenda.

__ Therapist facilitated member discussion and interaction.

__ Therapist avoided judgmental feedback on member contributions.

__ Therapist avoided addressing interpersonal dynamic issues.

__ Therapist responded empathically to group member behavior (verbal, nonverbal).

__ Therapist initiated appropriate interventions for member symptoms manifested in group.

__ Therapist modulated overly stimulating feedback between group members.

Specific Focus Points:

Focus Point 1

__ Therapist established the session goals.

__ Therapist reinforced the concept of personal mania profile.

__ Therapist processed the concepts of early versus late occurring symptoms.

Focus Point 2

__ Therapist explained the concept of coping behavior.

__ Therapist reinforced the concept of Personal Triggers of a manic episode.

__ Therapist explained the concept of "costs and benefits" of specific coping behaviors.

__ Therapist facilitated construction by the group of a list of responses to mania and stress that may trigger mania.

__ Therapist led group through cost-benefit analysis of mania.

Focus Point 3

__ Therapist included medication noncompliance and substance abuse in the discussion about coping behavior and elicited their costs and benefits from group members' contributions.

__ Therapist ensured that each member identified one coping response for mania and listed the costs and benefits of each.

__ Therapist ensured that each member identified one coping response for stress that may trigger mania and listed their costs and benefits.

Focus Point 4

__ Therapist facilitated group member contributions to include in the Action Plan: outline of coping strategies for mania and stress that may trigger mania.

__ Therapist facilitated construction of an Action Plan for Mania wallet card.

SESSION 4, DEPRESSION PART 1

Date: _____

Therapist: _____

Supervisor: _____

Key: 1 = complete, 2 = partially complete, 3 = did not meet criteria

Content Goals:

Therapist came prepared and organized.

__ Therapist elicited clarification of member understanding of didactic content.

__ Therapist delivered didactic material in a matter-of-fact and friendly way.

__ Therapist exhibited expertise answering questions about manic-depressive disorder.

__ Therapist made appropriate use of visual aids and exhibits.

Process Goals:

Therapist recognized member ability level to (not) participate.

__ Therapist worked member discussions from a generic to a personal orientation.

__ Therapist addressed process issues but did not allow them to disrupt content agenda.

__ Therapist facilitated member discussion and interaction.

__ Therapist avoided judgmental feedback on member contributions.

__ Therapist avoided addressing interpersonal dynamic issues.

__ Therapist responded empathically to group member behavior (verbal, nonverbal).

__ Therapist initiated appropriate interventions for member symptoms manifested in group.

__ Therapist modulated overly stimulating feedback between group members.

Specific Focus Points:

Focus Point 1

__ Therapist established the session goals.

Focus Point 2

__ Therapist facilitated a discussion of depressive signs and symptoms.

__ Therapist facilitated member construction of a personal depression profile.

__ Therapist helped members identify early versus late occurring symptoms.

__ Therapist facilitated discussion about the variability of depressive symptoms and patterns of occurrence.

Focus Point 3

__ Therapist explained that depression may occur in response to stress or spontaneously.

__ Therapist facilitated a general discussion of potential triggers of depression.

__ Therapist facilitated member construction of a personal list of triggers of a depressive episode.

SESSION 5, DEPRESSION PART 2

Date: _____

Therapist: _____

Supervisor: _____

Key: 1 = complete, 2 = partially complete, 3 = did not meet criteria

Content Goals:

Therapist came prepared and organized.

__ Therapist elicited clarification of member understanding of didactic content.

__ Therapist delivered didactic material in a matter-of-fact and friendly way.

__ Therapist exhibited expertise answering questions about manic-depressive disorder.

__ Therapist made appropriate use of visual aids and exhibits.

Process Goals:

Therapist recognized member ability level to (not) participate.

__ Therapist worked member discussions from a generic to a personal orientation.

__ Therapist addressed process issues but did not allow them to disrupt content agenda.

__ Therapist facilitated member discussion and interaction.

__ Therapist avoided judgmental feedback on member contributions.

__ Therapist avoided addressing interpersonal dynamic issues.

__ Therapist responded empathically to group member behavior (verbal, nonverbal).

__ Therapist initiated appropriate interventions for member symptoms manifested in group.

__ Therapist modulated overly stimulating feedback between group members.

Specific Focus Points:

Focus Point 1

__ Therapist established the session goals.

Focus Point 2

__ Therapist facilitated group member review of the Personal Depression Profile.

__ Therapist helped members to identify early versus late occurring symptoms.

__ Therapist facilitated group member review of the Personal Triggers of a Depressive Episode.

__ Therapist reviewed the concept of "coping behavior."

__ Therapist reviewed the concept of costs and benefits.

SESSION 5, DEPRESSION PART 2 *(Continued)*

___ Therapist facilitated construction of the group list of coping behaviors for depression, and stress that may trigger depression.

___ Therapist led group through cost-benefit analysis of at least one generic and one response from the group list to depression.

Focus Point 3

___ Therapist facilitated a discussion of the costs and benefits of alcohol and drugs in managing depressive signs and symptoms.

___ Therapist identified suicidal behavior as a member response or symptom of depression and facilitated a discussion of the costs and benefits.

___ Therapist ensured that each member identified one personal coping response for depression and one for stress and listed the costs and benefits of each.

Focus Point 4

___ Therapist facilitated group member contributions to include in the Action Plan: outline of coping strategies for depression and stress that may trigger depression.

___ Therapist facilitated member construction of an Action Plan for Depression wallet card.

SESSION 6, TREATMENTS FOR MANIC-DEPRESSIVE DISORDER

Date: _____

Therapist: _____

Supervisor: _____

Key: 1 = complete, 2 = partially complete, 3 = did not meet criteria

Content Goals:

Therapist came prepared and organized.

__ Therapist elicited clarification of member understanding of didactic content.

__ Therapist delivered didactic material in a matter-of-fact and friendly way.

__ Therapist exhibited expertise answering questions about manic-depressive disorder.

__ Therapist made appropriate use of visual aids and exhibits.

Process Goals:

Therapist recognized member ability level to (not) participate.

__ Therapist worked member discussions from a generic to a personal orientation.

__ Therapist addressed process issues but did not allow them to disrupt content agenda.

__ Therapist facilitated member discussion and interaction.

__ Therapist avoided judgmental feedback on member contributions.

__ Therapist avoided addressing interpersonal dynamic issues.

__ Therapist responded empathically to group member behavior (verbal, nonverbal).

__ Therapist initiated appropriate interventions for member symptoms manifested in group.

__ Therapist modulated overly stimulating feedback between group members.

Specific Focus Points:

Focus Point 1

__ Therapist explained the session rationale to develop a personal care plan.

__ Therapist facilitated group member entry of personal treatment goals on their personal care plan.

Focus Point 2

__ Therapist facilitated a discussion about the elements of a collaborative treatment relationship.

__ Therapist facilitated member completion of "things I will expect from my provider" and "things I will do to effectively collaborate with my treatment team" on Exhibit 18a.

SESSION 6, TREATMENTS FOR MANIC-DEPRESSIVE DISORDER *(Continued)*

Focus Point 3
__ Therapist described the relationship between biological rhythm regulation and mood.
__ Therapist facilitated group member construction of their personal daily activity and sleep routine schedule.
__ Therapist explained the importance of good sleep habits and the usefulness of the sleep log.

Focus Point 4
__ Therapist described the four medication groups used to treat manic-depressive disorder.
__ Therapist facilitated group member entry of their personal medications on their personal care.
__ Therapist facilitated discussion about making informed treatment decisions.
__ Therapist facilitated group members completing a cost-benefit analysis of one of the medications listed on their personal care plan.
__ Therapist reviewed Exhibit 22, Making Informed Treatment Decisions.

Focus Point 5
__ Therapist described the psychotherapies, educational, and self help programs available to people with manic-depressive disorder.
__ Therapist facilitated members selection of therapy and self help groups to add to their treatment plan.

Focus Point 6
__ Therapist concludes group member completion of a Personal Care Plan.
__ Therapist described the purpose of Phase 2.

EXHIBIT 26   Life Goals Program Therapist Monitor: Phase 2

Session Date: _____
Therapist: _____
Supervisor: _____

Key: 1 = complete, 2 = partially complete, 3 = did not meet criteria

Content Goals:

__ Therapist came prepared and organized.
__ Therapist exhibited expertise answering questions about manic-depressive disorder.

__ Number of members with goals addressed this session
__ Total members present

__ Number of Roadblocks identified this session
__ Number of Interventions:
    __ Personal cost-benefit   __ Interpersonal
    __ Cognitive   __ Other

Process Goals:

__ Therapist recognized member ability level to (not) participate.
__ Therapist translated discussion with individual members into relevance for the group.
__ Therapist avoided judgmental feedback on member contributions.
__ Therapist responded empathically to group member behavior (verbal, nonverbal).
__ Therapist initiated appropriate interventions for member symptoms manifested in group.
__ Therapist modulated overly stimulating feedback between group members.

TREATMENT "ABSORBED"

Treatment absorbed is determined by member participation and cooperation. If a member was not able to complete assignments or participate actively in group, despite adequate delivery of treatment by the therapist, this would suggest that one or more factors may be the cause, such as member psychopathology or lack of skills or motivation. Two types of assessments can be employed for this type of measurement. First, completion of the specific worksheets in Phase 1 and Phase 2 can be monitored. Clearly, the member is not absorbing treatment if he or she is not participating in this way. Although the member may be benefiting in other subtle ways from interpersonal group process factors, this aspect of the process of treatment delivery is quite difficult to measure beyond looking at the overall outcome measures discussed below.

Second, the group Progress Note (Exhibit 27) can be employed for more standardized and quantitative information during either phase. The top section of the Progress Note is the crux of participation tracking. After each session, the therapist should check the predominant level of participation that each member showed during group. The choices are arrayed from most to least participation. For example, the contribution of personal information is rated more highly than contributing generic information, which in turn is rated more highly than participating in discussions in more general ways. The bottom section of the form is a quick-and-easy way to track overall evident mood state for the day, based only on information gleaned from the session. Although this monitor is far from a valid indicator of mood state according to the DSM system, it can provide a general indicator of predominant behavioral state that may be helpful in interpreting the participation information above. We have found this metric particularly useful in tracking the occurrence of psychosis in members who are so afflicted from time to time. Additional progress notes can be made on the reverse side.

TWO ADDITIONAL PROCESS MEASURES

There are two additional measures related to the process of care that assess effectiveness of specific aspects of the Life Goals Program. These include a measure of the member's *knowledge about manic-depressive disorder* and a measure of intensity of *medication treatment delivered and resultant side effects.*

Measurement of a member's knowledge about manic-depressive disorder would be expected to increase during Phase 1, with additional improvement for some persons during Phase 2, as points made earlier are reiterated and eventually retained. We designed the simple instrument in Exhibit 28 to accomplish this.

EXHIBIT 27 Life Goals Program Progress Note

Directions: Place a check mark in the boxes that best indicate the member's level of participation and evident mood state.

Member Name: _____ Phase: ____

Level of Participation   Date: ____ ____ ____ ____ ____

Level of Participation					
Contributed personal information					
Contributed to group list					
Verbal during discussion					
Attentive, limited verbal					
Distracted					
Attended only part of the session					
No show/canceled					

Evident Mood State   Date: ____ ____   ____ ____

Evident Mood State					
Mania					
Hypomania					
Mood elevated (mild)					
Mood within normal range					
Mildly depressed					
Moderately depressed					
Severely depressed					
Check if psychosis evident					

Provider_____

EXHIBIT 28   Self-Assessment for Manic-Depressive Disorders Group Psychotherapy

Name: _____   Date: _____

1. Manic-depressive disorder affects the following proportion of Americans (circle *one*):
   1 out of 10   1 out of 1,000
   1 out of 100   1 out of 1,000,000

2. The following can occur as part of manic-depressive disorder (circle *all* that apply):
   Depression   Irritability   Hallucinations
   Mania   Hypomania   Diabetes

3. Alcohol and drug abuse affects the following percentage of persons with manic-depressive disorder (circle *one*):
   10%   20%   60%   90%

4. Mood episodes can occur without any apparent stress:
   True   False

5. Manic-depressive illness is caused by a lithium deficiency in the brain:
   True   False

6. The following can cause mood episodes in manic-depressive disorder (circle *all* that apply):
   Stress   Change of seasons   Physical exercise
   Physical illness   High-fat diet   Alcohol use

7. The following can occur as part of a manic episode (circle *all* that apply):
   Irritability   Hallucinations   Too much sleep
   Too happy a mood   Lying and stealing

8. You may or may not be aware of how your depressions begin. If you can, please list two of the earliest symptoms that tell you your depression is beginning:
   _____   _____

9. List two coping skills you use to combat depression:
   _____   _____

Scoring Key for "Self-Assessment for Manic-Depressive Disorders Group Psychotherapy"

Total Score = 25.

Answers:

1. 1 out of 100

2. (One point for each correct answer; total = 6)
   Circled: Depression, Mania, Irritability, Hypomania, Hallucinations
   Not circled: Diabetes

3. 60%

4. True

5. False

6. (One point for each correct answer; total = 6)
   Circled: Stress, Physical illness, Change of seasons, Alcohol use
   Not circled: High-fat diet, Physical exercise

7. (One point for each correct answer; total = 6)
   Circled: Irritability, Too happy a mood, Hallucinations
   Not circled: Lying and stealing, Too much sleep

8. Give one point for each different symptom listed, whether or not they are plausible.

9. Give one point for each different coping skill listed, whether adaptive or maladaptive.

With regard to measures of medication treatment, recall that one of the sources of the efficacy–effectiveness gap in treating manic-depressive disorder (see chapters 4 and 6) is most likely the fact that suboptimal levels of medication are delivered in general clinical practice. This has been demonstrated for mood disorders in general (Keller et al., 1986). Data from our program indicate that similarly low levels are typically given for manic-depressive disorder as well, and that changes in care delivery system can increase those levels (Bauer, McBride, et al., 1997b; Shea, McBride, et al., 1995).

Recall that one of the primary goals of the Life Goals Program is to improve the individual's illness management skills so that he or she may participate more effectively in treatment. If the group is successful in helping group members to become more effective collaborators in their care, then the therapist would expect in many cases to see increases in medication intensity, optimally without substantial increases in side effects. When this occurs, it is likely due to one or more of several factors. For example, adherence with a prescribed medication regimen can improve when individuals develop a better understanding of the purposes of treatment and more solid motivation as a result of reviewing the costs and benefits of treatment. In addition, more effective negotiation around costs and benefits of a given medication regimen, particularly its side effects, with a collaboratively oriented prescriber clearly will help adherence. In addition, it is our experience that members may actually increase their requests for medication management when they identify and begin to work on getting their most nettlesome symptoms under control.

Clearly, however, increased intensity of medication treatment represents the outcome of a complex interaction of multiple factors. Such factors include the effects of the Life Goals Program, the characteristics of the group member, and the availability of his or her prescribing prescriber and the prescriber's attitude toward a collaborative approach to treatment. Despite this complexity, measurement of biological treatments delivered can be instructive in assessing this potential impact of the Life Goals Program.

In the first edition of this book (Bauer & McBride, 1996), we included the Somatotherapy Index, an instrument to measure intensity of somatotherapy (i.e., pharmacotherapy plus ECT and bright-light treatment). The instrument was adapted from that used in the NIMH Collaborative Study on the Psychobiology of Depression (Keller et al., 1986). We continue to use an adaptation of that instrument in our research studies. However, pharmacotherapy for manic-depressive disorder has broadened so dramatically since the mid-1990s that the instrument itself has become much more complex. There are clear benefits to condensing all somatotherapy into a single number, as the Somatotherapy Index does. However, the instrument has become sufficiently complex, reflecting the broadening of pharmacotherapeutic options for manic-depressive disorder, that it has become cumbersome for use in general clinical practice. At this point, we recommend tracking intensity of treatment using the straightforward approach of tracking serum levels and doses of individual medications. For example, one might track lithium or anticonvulsant levels, or antidepressant or neuroleptic dosages. One might also assess compliance by tracking the number of consecutive prescriptions refilled. For those interested, the index and accompanying instruction manual are available from the authors.

The instrument to assess side effects is a self-report (Exhibit 29), with overall scores given for both the occurrence and the impact of side effects. There are two aspects of this instrument that are worth noting. First, the instrument reflects the fact that most persons with manic-depressive disorder most of the time are treated with multiple medications. It does not attempt to ascribe certain side effects to particular medications. Rather, it seeks to determine the overall level of side effects, regardless of specific source (though, of course, the list has been constructed based on review of side effect profiles of the specific medications commonly used for manic-depressive disorder).

Second, the instrument measures not only the side effects perceived by the person, but also the functional impact on their life, which may differ. For example, a person may be affected with a minor degree of tremor, but if he or she is a machinist or surgeon, this may have an impact beyond what would be expected from the severity of the side effect. In contrast, even severe tremor may not be as troublesome to a person who does not do work requiring fine motor coordination. Among both women and men, sexual dysfunction may vary greatly in its impact, depending on whether they are sexually active or not and depending on their attitude toward their own sexuality and self-esteem.

OUTCOME MEASUREMENTS

OVERVIEW

Outcome is the most important indicator of the worth of the program to individual members and is distinct from the above process measures. Although the process measures ask how treatment is delivered and focuses on intermediate characteristics that are thought to be important to outcome, outcome measures focus predominantly on how the member is doing in his or her life outside the group. To expand on the query posed in the introduction to this chapter, outcome measures simply answer the question Is what I am doing for the person helping, and if so, in what ways?

To be useful in program evaluation, the answer to this question clearly must be measurable and quantitative, although the specific methods chosen will likely vary depending on the specific clinical needs and experience of those implementing the Life Goals Program. To provide a comprehensive assessment of outcome, we recommend that outcome evaluation include measurements in each of the three domains of outcome described in chapter 2: clinical outcome, functional outcome, and illness costs.

EXHIBIT 29   Medication Side Effects Summary

Name/SSN: _____   Date: _____

Baseline   6 Months   12 Months   18 Months   24 Months

Please indicate whether you are experiencing any of these effects from your medications
and how much of a problem it now causes in your life:

	Does this happen to you?					How much does it cause problems in your life?				
	not at all	a bit		very much so		not at all	a bit		very much so	
Skin problems	0	1	2	3	4	0	1	2	3	4
Problems with vision	0	1	2	3	4	0	1	2	3	4
Dry mouth	0	1	2	3	4	0	1	2	3	4
Change in appetite	0	1	2	3	4	0	1	2	3	4
Upset stomach	0	1	2	3	4	0	1	2	3	4
Change in moving bowels	0	1	2	3	4	0	1	2	3	4
Change in passing water	0	1	2	3	4	0	1	2	3	4
Sex problems	0	1	2	3	4	0	1	2	3	4
Sleepiness	0	1	2	3	4	0	1	2	3	4
Getting dizzy or clumsy	0	1	2	3	4	0	1	2	3	4
Shakes or tremors	0	1	2	3	4	0	1	2	3	4
Getting restless or jumpy	0	1	2	3	4	0	1	2	3	4
Stiff muscles	0	1	2	3	4	0	1	2	3	4
No energy	0	1	2	3	4	0	1	2	3	4
Slow or confused thinking	0	1	2	3	4	0	1	2	3	4
Totals	_____					_____				

We review below several instruments that we have found useful for assessing outcome across these three domains. Most of the instruments chosen are self-reports. Though depending to a greater degree than clinician interview instruments on the individual's insight, degree of psychopathology, and willingness to comply, they are all fairly brief and require no standardization across clinical raters. Self-reports are likely to be much more feasible in a busy clinical practice than expecting therapists or other clinicians to conduct a separate interview and fill out a series of forms at periodic intervals.

The entire battery that we have used requires about 20 minutes to complete. We have used the battery at baseline, after Phase 1 (6 weeks), and at 3-month intervals during Phase 2. Some measures may be expected to change more quickly than others. For example, it is likely that a person's knowledge base will improve before his or her work status or living situation improves.

Finally, are there benchmarks, or external standards, of outcome that a therapist or program director should expect in assessing members' progress? Although formal studies of the Life Goals Program are currently under way, even these will not provide an a priori standard against which to judge a person's progress. Rather, individuals are likely to begin at varying baselines, so it is difficult to set absolute benchmarks for progress; however, it is expected that treatment success will by definition include progress toward a member's goals and improvement on relevant outcome measures. Note that data from our studies indicate that goal attainment will not be a quick process, with members needing 2 to 17 months (average almost 9 months) to reach their first self-defined goal in Phase 2 (Bauer, McBride, et al., 1998; see also chapter 5). Among process measures, though, we can be more definitive: It is anticipated that the therapist will meet over 95% of treatment delivery goals (Bauer, McBride, et al., 1998).

CLINICAL OUTCOME

For clinical outcome, we have chosen to use the Internal State Scale (ISS; Bauer et al., 1991; Vojta et al., 2001). A copy can be found as Exhibit 30, with instructions for completion in Exhibit 31 (pp. 323–324). This is a brief 100-millimeter visual analogue self-report scale that has the advantage of being validated for both manic and depressive symptoms. It is a "snapshot" of current function, geared to the prior 24 hours. Thus, measurement at only 5 weeks will not likely reflect mood symptoms over the past 5 weeks, but only on the day of administration. For more frequent measurement, it is reasonable to measure mood state on a weekly or even daily basis with the ISS. The repeated measures at this frequent time interval can be charted over time to reveal trends in mood state. We have used the ISS as frequently as daily for assessment of mood state during rapid cycling.

EXHIBIT 30   Internal State Scale (Version 2)

Name/SSN: _____   Date: _____

For each of the following statements, please mark an *X* at the point on the line that best describes the way you have felt *over the past 24 hours.* Although there may have been some change during that time, try to give a single summary rating for each item.

Today my mood is changeable.

0   100

Not at all   Very much so
Rarely   Much of the time

Today I feel irritable.

0   100

Not at all   Very much so
Rarely   Much of the time

Today I feel like a capable person.

0   100

Not at all   Very much so
Rarely   Much of the time

Today I feel like people are out to get me.

0   100

Not at all   Very much so
Rarely   Much of the time

Today I actually feel great inside.

0   100

Not at all   Very much so
Rarely   Much of the time

Today I feel impulsive.

0   100

Not at all   Very much so
Rarely   Much of the time

Today I feel depressed.

0   100

Not at all   Very much so
Rarely   Much of the time

Today my thoughts are going fast.

0   100

Not at all   Very much so
Rarely   Much of the time

Today it seems like nothing will ever work out for me.

0   100

Not at all   Very much so
Rarely   Much of the time

Today I feel overactive.

0   100

Not at all   Very much so
Rarely   Much of the time

Today I feel as if the world is against me.

0   100

Not at all   Very much so
Rarely   Much of the time

EXHIBIT 30   Internal State Scale (Version 2) *(Continued)*

Today I feel "sped up" inside.

0   100
└───┘

Not at all   Very much so
Rarely   Much of the time

Today I feel restless.

0   100
└───┘

Not at all   Very much so
Rarely   Much of the time

Today I feel argumentative.

0   100
└───┘

Not at all   Very much so
Rarely   Much of the time

Today I feel energized.

0   100
└───┘

Not at all   Very much so
Rarely   Much of the time

Today I feel:

0   100
└───┘

Depressed   Normal   Manic
Down   High

EXHIBIT 31   Key for the Internal State Scale (ISS)

DESCRIPTION

The ISS consists of four subscales: Activation, Well-Being, Perceived Conflict, and the Depression Index. A single-item Global Bipolar Scale has been added for reference to earlier single analog line mood scales for manic-depressive disorder.

SCORING GUIDELINES

Each item consists of statement followed by a 100-mm line, or an 11-bin Likert scale, with anchor points at 0 and 100. During duplication the 100-mm line may shrink or expand to a minor degree (e.g., 97–103 mm). This magnitude of error is negligible in overall scoring (± 3%). Such error can be minimized further by consistently measuring from the left-hand end of the line.

Note that several investigators are reporting similar performance with an ordinal scale (i.e., 0, 5, 10 . . . 95, 100) instead of a line, but we personally have not yet tested the discriminating ability of this format compared to the original.

The 0 anchor point is "Not at all, Rarely" and the 100 anchor point is "Very much so, Much of the time." The instructions at the top of the scale are "For each of the following statements, please mark an X at the point on the line that best describes the way you have felt *over the past 24 hours.* Although there may have been some change during that time, try to give a single summary rating for each item." Items for each of the subscales are then summed to provide the subscale score.

Item text	Subscale
Today my mood is changeable.	Perceived Conflict
Today I feel irritable.	Perceived Conflict
Today I feel like a capable person.	Well-Being
Today I feel like people are out to get me.	Perceived Conflict
Today I actually feel great inside.	Well-Being
Today I feel impulsive.	Activation
Today I feel depressed.	Depression Index
Today my thoughts are going fast.	Activation
Today it seems like nothing will ever work out for me.	Depression Index
Today I feel overactive.	Activation
Today I feel as if the world is against me.	Perceived Conflict
Today I feel "sped up" inside.	Activation
Today I feel restless.	Activation
Today I feel argumentative.	Perceived Conflict
Today I feel energized.	Well-Being

ISS SUBSCALES AS DISCRIMINATORS OF MOOD EPISODES

The Well-Being subscale used in conjunction with the Activation subscale is useful in discriminating between depressed, (hypo)manic, and subsyndromal/euthymic states. In this capacity, the ISS has proven valid by discriminant function analysis, although the exact cut-off scores may vary somewhat from site to site and therefore should be standardized by each investigator.

The revised algorithm for mood state discrimination (Bauer et al., 2000) is as follows:

Mood state	Activation subscale score	Well-being subscale score
(Hypo)mania	≥155	≥125
Mixed state	≥155	<125
Euthymia	<155	≥125
Depression	<155	<125

ISS SUBSCALES AS INDICATORS OF SYMPTOM SEVERITY

The Activation subscale correlates highly and specifically with clinician ratings of manic symptoms ($r = 0.60$ vs. Young Mania Rating Scale), and the Depression Index correlates highly and specifically with clinician ratings of depressive symptoms ($r = 0.84$ vs. Hamilton Depression Rating Scale). These are the two most useful subscales in tracking mood disorders.

The Perceived Conflict subscale correlates most highly with the Brief Psychiatric Rating Scale ($r = 0.56$), but also correlates significantly with the Hamilton Depression and Young Mania Rating Scales. Thus, it appears to serve as an index of global psychopathology. Preliminary evidence indicates that it is particularly high in individuals with psychotic symptoms.

ADDITIONAL NOTES

The ISS is in the public domain. However, the authors would appreciate information regarding who is using it and how. Correspondence should be sent to Mark S. Bauer, MD, at Mark_Bauer@brown.edu

- Spanish translation: Sheri Johnson, PhD (sjohnson@umiami.ir.miami.edu)
- French translation: Jean Michel Aubry, MD (jaubry@worldcom.ch)
- German translation: Thomas Meyer, MD (th.meyer@uni-teubingen.de)

Note that a Likert-scaled version can also be used without loss of precision. In this format, 11 circles are used, with the first and eleventh corresponding to the anchor points, and no intervening anchors. The major advantage of Likert over visual analogue scoring is that the Likert can be scored by optical scanning, which is much faster than measuring and summing the underlined items.

FUNCTIONAL OUTCOME

Functional outcome measures include measures of occupational and social function and health-related quality of life. Note that these types of measures do not identify the cause of the change in functional status. That is, functional status may improve because disease processes are under better control due to improved medication management, or because of psychotherapeutic interventions aimed specifically at improving functional outcome, or because of some other unidentified factor. Most typically, improvements in functional status are due to combinations of these factors.

Two single-item therapist-completed instruments assess occupational status and degree of living structure required (Exhibit 32). These have been adapted from instruments developed by Dion and coworkers (1988). These indices are expected to change slowly as individuals, improve vocational status and become more independent in living. In some individuals, these indices may not change at all, because their functional limitations may be more severe and their goals more modest, or because they already function within the highest measurable levels. In addition, some changes that are clinically important, such as improved relations with coworkers or spouse, or increased productivity, will not be reflected in changes in these measures. These aspects of functional status are difficult to measure with instruments that are sufficiently brief to be used in clinical practice. These issues are partially addressed in the choice of quality-of-life instruments.

There are several instruments available for measuring health-related quality of life, an area that has been reviewed extensively elsewhere (e.g., Feinstein, Josephy, & Wells, 1986; Goldman, Skodol, & Lave, 1992; Stewart & Ware, 1992; Wallace, 1986; Weissman et al., 1981). We have had good success in this population with the widely used Health Status Questionnaire (SF-36; Stuart & Ware, 1992; Wells et al., 1989), the shorter SF-12 (Ware et al., 1996), or the very simple EuroQol thermometer (EuroQol Group, 1990). We have used the shorter SF-12 and EuroQol thermometer instruments successfully in individuals with manic-depressive disorder in various mood states, including mania (Vojta et al., 2001).

There are three additional aspects of functional outcome or quality of life that may be of particular interest to therapists using the Life Goals Program: social supports, life stresses, and self-esteem. The two instruments that

EXHIBIT 32   Functional Outcome Measures

OCCUPATIONAL STATUS

Circle the number for the category which best describes the subject's usual employment status during the past interval. Rate the predominant category for the interval.

1. Full-time gainful employment
2. Part-time gainful employment (anything 30 hours or less a week)
3. Unemployed but expected to work by self or others (e.g., laid off due to economic factors)
4. Unemployed but not expected to work by self or others (e.g., disabled due to physical or mental disorder)
5. Retired
6. Homemaker
7. Student (includes part time)
8. Leave of absence due to medical reasons (holding job, plans to return)
9. Volunteer work, full time
10. Volunteer work, part time
11. Other (specify)_____

LIVING STRUCTURE

Circle the number that best describes the subject's living situation over the past interval.

1 Head of household, or independent spouse
2 Lives alone, or with peer in platonic relationship
3 Lives with family, with minimal supervision
4 Cooperative apartment, or unsupervised boarding house
5 Halfway house, supervised boarding house, or lives with family with high supervision
6 Nursing home
7 Hospitalized continually

(Adapted from Dion, G., Tohen, M., Anthony, W., & Waternaux, C. (1988). Symptoms and functioning of patients with bipolar disorder six months after hospitalization. *Hospital and Community Psychiatry, 39,* 652–657.)

measure social support and life stress were developed as part of the Epidemiological Catchment Area study (see chapter 2) and are found in the article by Landerman and coworkers (Landerman, George, Campbell, & Blaser, 1989). One particular benefit of these scales is that they include measures of the person's perception of his or her supports and stresses, which may be at least as important as the more "objective" supports and stressors that an observer may identify. The Index of Self-Esteem (Hudson, 1982) has been used to measure this aspect of quality of life, which is one of the areas that the Life Goals Program is likely to affect.

ILLNESS COSTS

Monitoring illness costs can be quite a complex endeavor, requiring the assessment of both direct treatment costs and indirect costs of illness. There is continued debate in the research literature regarding the most valid and reliable ways to make these measurements. However, the assessment of the component of costs that is usually most relevant to mental health clinical program management, utilization of mental health services, is fairly straightforward. We have found that even in a moderately to severely impaired manic-depressive population individuals can accurately recall the number of ambulatory treatment contacts and hospitalizations over the prior months (Bauer et al., 1997b). Thus, querying for number of visits and recording them in a standardized fashion on a quarterly basis, then supplementing with information regarding number of hospital days and other interventions, should give a reasonably valid picture of service utilization. If one has access to computer-based records, as in the Department of Veterans Affairs medical centers or in one of the several large health maintenance organizations, the task is even easier. Nonetheless, it should be ascertained that the computer records are indeed accurate. In addition, individuals must still be queried for service use outside the health care plan, which may not appear in the central database.

We have found the form in Exhibit 33 useful to guide service utilization inquiries and track data. In implementing the Life Goals Program, one would expect ambulatory contacts to increase, particularly group contacts; there may be some increase in scheduled care with prescribers as well, if the group members become more active managers of their illness. The test of the success of the program in improving this aspect of outcome is in whether indices of chaotic service utilization, particularly emergency service utilization and hospitalizations, decrease.

EXHIBIT 33   Treatment Contacts

Name: _____

Date Range Covered: _____   Date Completed: _____

#/WK	#/WK	#/WK	#/WK
1 _____	_____	_____	_____
2 _____	_____	_____	_____
3 _____	_____	_____	_____
4 _____	_____	_____	_____
5 _____	_____	_____	_____
6 _____	_____	_____	_____
7 _____	_____	_____	_____
8 _____	_____	_____	_____
9 _____	_____	_____	_____
10 _____	_____	_____	_____
11 _____	_____	_____	_____

#/WK	#/WK	#/WK	#/WK
1 _____	_____	_____	_____
2 _____	_____	_____	_____
3 _____	_____	_____	_____
4 _____	_____	_____	_____
5 _____	_____	_____	_____
6 _____	_____	_____	_____
7 _____	_____	_____	_____
8 _____	_____	_____	_____
9 _____	_____	_____	_____
10 _____	_____	_____	_____
11 _____	_____	_____	_____

#/WK	#/WK	#/WK	#/WK
1 _____	_____	_____	_____
2 _____	_____	_____	_____
3 _____	_____	_____	_____
4 _____	_____	_____	_____
5 _____	_____	_____	_____
6 _____	_____	_____	_____
7 _____	_____	_____	_____
8 _____	_____	_____	_____
9 _____	_____	_____	_____
10 _____	_____	_____	_____
11 _____	_____	_____	_____

1. Medication session
2. Group psychotherapy
3. Individual psychotherapy
4. Couples/family psychotherapy
5. Day treatment program
6. Day hospital
7. Outpatient substance rehabilitation
8. Self-help groups
9. Emergency/triage visit (including overnight holds in Emergency Service)
10. Hospitalization
11. Other (specify)

References

Abraham, K. (1927). Notes on the psycho-analytical investigation and treatment of manic-depressive insanity and allied conditions (1911). In D. Bryan & A. Strachey (Trans.), *Selected papers of Karl Abraham, M.D.* (pp. 137–156). London: Hogarth Press.

Abramson, L., Seligman, M., & Teasdale, J. (1978). Learned helplessness in humans: Critique and reformulation. *Journal of Abnormal Psychology, 87,* 49–74.

Adler, N., Boyce, W. T., Chesney, M., Folkman, S., & Syme, L. (1993). Socioeconomic inequalities in health: No easy solution. *Journal of the American Medical Association, 269,* 3149–3145.

Agency for Health Care Policy and Research (AHCPR). (1993). Depression panel guideline report. Washington, DC: U.S. Government Printing Office.

Akiskal, H., Djenderedjian, A., Rosenthal, R. H., & Khani, M. K. (1977). Cyclothymic disorder: Validating criteria for inclusion in the bipolar affective group. *American Journal of Psychiatry, 134,* 1227–1233.

Akiskal, H. S. (1981). Subaffective disorders: Dysthymic, cyclothymic and bipolar II disorders in the "borderline" realm. *Psychiatric Clinics of North America, 4,* 25–46.

Akiskal, H. S., & Akiskal, K. (1988). Reassessing the prevalence of bipolar disorders: Clinical significance and artistic creativity. *Psychiatric Psychobiology, 3,* 29s–36s.

Ali, O. S., Denicoff, K. D., Altshuler, L. L., Hauser, P., Li, X., Conrad, A. J., Mirsky, A. F., Smith-Jackson, J. J., & Post, R. M. (2000). A preliminary study of the relation of neuropsychological performance to neuroanatomic structures in bipolar disorder. *Neuropsychiatry, Neuropsychology and Behavioral Neurology (NNBN), 13,* 20–28.

Altshuler, L., Cohen, L., Szuba, M., Burt, V., Gitlin, M., & Mintz, J. (1996). Pharmacologic management of psychiatric illness during pregnancy: Dilemmas and guidelines. *American Journal of Psychiatry, 153,* 592–606

Altshuler, L., Post, R., Leverich, G., Mikalauskas, K., Rosoff, A., & Ackerman, L. (1995). Antidepressant-induced mania and cycle acceleration: a controversy revisited. *American Journal of Psychiatry, 152,* 1130–1137.

Altshuler, L. L., Bartzokis, G., Grieder, T., Curran, J., Jimenez, T., Leight, K., Wilkins, J., Gerner, R., & Mintz, J. (2000). An MRI study of temporal lobe structures in men with bipolar disorder or schizophrenia. *Biological Psychiatry, 48*(2), 147–162.

Altshuler, L. A., Kiriakos, L., Calcagno, J., Goodman, R., Gitlin, M., Frey, M., & Mintz, J. (2001). The impact of antidepressant discontinuation vs. antidepressant continuation on 1-year risk for relapse of bipolar depression: A retrospective chart review. *Journal of Clinical Psychiatry, 63,* 612–616.

American College of Cardiology/American Heart Association (ACC/AHA). (1996). Task force on practice guidelines ACC/AHA guidelines for the management of patients with acute myocardial infarction. *Journal of the American College of Cardiology, 28,* 1328–1428.

American Psychiatric Association. (1980). *Diagnostic and statistical manual of mental disorders* (3rd ed.). Washington, DC: Author.

American Psychiatric Association. (1987). *Diagnostic and statistical manual of mental disorders* (3rd ed., rev.). Washington, DC: Author.

American Psychiatric Association. (1994a). *Diagnostic and statistical manual of mental disorders* (4th ed.). Washington, DC: Author.

American Psychiatric Association. (1994b). Practice guideline for the treatment of persons with bipolar disorder. *American Journal of Psychiatry, 151*(Suppl), 1–36.

American Psychiatric Association. (2000). *Diagnostic and statistical manual of mental disorders* (4th ed., rev.). Washington, DC: Author.

Amsterdam, J. D., Winokur, A., Lucki, I, Caroff, S., Snyder, P., & Rickels, K. (1983). A neuroendocrine test battery in bipolar patients and health subjects. *Archives of General Psychiatry, 40,* 515–521.

Andrews, G., Sanderson, K., & Beard, J. (1998). Burden of disease: Methods of calculating disability from mental disorder. *British Journal of Psychiatry, 173,* 123–131.

Angst, J. (1978). The course of affective disorders: 2. Typology of bipolar manic-depressive illness. *Archive for Psychiatrie und Nervenkrankheiten, 226,* 65–73.

Angst, J. (1981). Course of affective disorders. In H. M. van Praag (Ed.), *Handbook of biological psychiatry* (pp. 225–242). New York: Marcel Dekker.

Arana, G. W. (1988). An overview of side effects caused by typical antipsychotics. *Journal of Clinical Psychiatry, 61*(Suppl 8), 5–11.

Arana, G. W., & Forbes, R. A. (1991). Dexamethasone for the treatment of depression: A preliminary report. *Journal Clinical Psychiatry, 52*(7), 304–306.

Ascher-Svanum, H. A. (1989). A psychoeducational intervention for schizo-phrenic patients. *Patient Education and Counseling, 14,* 81–87.

Baastrup, P. C., Poulsen, J. C., Schou, M., Thomsen, K, & Amdisen, A. (1970). Prophylactic lithium: Double blind discontinuation in manic-depressive and recurrent-depressive disorders. *Lancet, 2,* 326–330.

Ballenger, J. C., & Post, R. M. (1978). Therapeutic effects of carbamazepine in affective illness: A preliminary report. *Communications in Psycho-pharmacology, 2,* 159–175.

Ballenger, J. C., & Post, R. M. (1980). Carbamazepine in manic-depressive illness: A new treatment. *American Journal of Psychiatry, 137,* 782–790.

Banks, R., Aiton, J., Cramb, G., & Naylor, G. J. (1990). Incorporation of inositol into the phosphoinositides of lymphoblastoid cell lines established from bipolar manic-depressive patients. *Journal of Affective Disorders, 19*(1), 1–8.

Barbini, B., Scherillo, P., Benedetti, F., Crespi, G., Colombo, C., & Smeraldi, E. (1997). Response to clozapine in acute mania is more rapid than that of chlorpromazine. *International Clinical Psychopharmacology, 12,* 109–112.

Baron, M. (1977). Linkage between an X-chrosome marker (deutan color blindness) and bipolar affective illness. *Archives of General Psychiatry, 34,* 721–725.

Baron, M., Gershon, E. S., Rudy, V., Jonas, W. Z., & Buchsbaum, M. (1975). Lithium carbonate response in depression. *Archives of General Psychiatry, 32,* 1107–1111.

Basco, M., & Rush, A. J. (1996). *Cognitive-behavioral therapy for bipolar disorder.* New York: Guilford.

Bauer, M., & Whybrow, P. (1990). Rapid cycling bipolar affective disorder: II Treatment of refractory rapid cycling with high-dose levothyroxine. *Archives of General Psychiatry, 47,* 435–440.

Bauer, M., & Whybrow, P. C. (2001). Thyroid hormone, neural tissue and mood modulation. *World Journal of Biological Psychiatry, 2,* 59–69.

Bauer, M. S. (1993). Summertime bright-light treatment of bipolar major depressive episodes. *Biological Psychiatry, 33,* 663–665.

Bauer, M. S. (1994). Rapid cycling. In R. Joffe & J. Calabrese (Eds.), *Anticonvulsants in psychiatry* (pp. 1–26). New York: Marcel Dekker.

Bauer, M. S. (2001a). The collaborative practice model for bipolar disorder: Design and implementation in a multi-site randomized controlled trial. *Bipolar Disorders, 3,* 233–244.

Bauer, M. S. (2001b). An evidence-based review of psychosocial treatments for bipolar disorder. *Psychopharmacology Bulletin, 35*(3), 109–134.

Bauer, M. S. (2003). *The field guide to psychiatric assessment and treatment.* Philadelphia: Lippincott, Williams, & Wilkins.

Bauer, M. S., Calabrese, J., Dunner, D., Post, R., Whybrow, P., Gyulai, L., Tay, L., Younkin, S., Bynum, D., Lavori, P., & Price, R. A. (1994a).

Multi-site data reanalysis: Rapid cycling as a modifier for bipolar disorder in DSM-IV. *American Journal of Psychiatry, 151,* 506–515.

Bauer, M. S., Callahan, A., Jampala, C., Petty, F., Sajatovic, M., Schaefer, V., Wittlin, B., & Powell, B. (1999). Clinical practice guidelines for bipolar disorder from the Department of Veterans Affairs. *Journal of Clinical Psychiatry, 60,* 9–21.

Bauer M. S., Crits-Christoph, P., Ball, W., Dewees, E., McAllister, T., Alahi, P., Cacciola, J., & Whybrow, P. (1991). Independent assessment of manic and depressive symptoms by self-rating scale: Characteristics and implications for the study of mania. *Archives of General Psychiatry, 48,* 807–812.

Bauer, M. S, Crits-Christoph, P., & Whybrow, P. (1993a). What is the core symptom of mania? (Letter). *Archives of General Psychiatry, 50,* 71–72.

Bauer, M. S., & Dunner, D. L. (1993). Validity of seasonal pattern as a modifier for recurrent mood disorders for DSM-IV. *Comprehensive Psychiatry, 34,* 159–170.

Bauer, M. S., & Frazer, A. (1994). Mood disorders. In P. Molinoff, A. Frazer, & A. Winokur (Eds.), *Biology of normal and abnormal brain function* (pp. 301–323). New York: Raven.

Bauer, M. S, Gyulai, L., Yeh, H-S., Gonnel, J., & Whybrow, P. (1994c). Testing definitions of dysphoric mania and hypomania: Prevalence, clinical characteristics, and inter-episode stability. *Journal of Affective Disorders, 32* 201–204.

Bauer, M. S., Kirk, G., Gavin, C., & Williford, W. (2001a). Correlates of functional and economic outcome in bipolar disorder. A prospective study. *Journal of Affective Disorders, 65,* 231–241.

Bauer, M. S., Kurtz, J. W., Rubin, L. B., & Marcus, J. G. (1994). Mood and behavioral effects of four-week light treatment in winter depressives and controls. *Journal of Psychiatric Research, 28,* 135–145.

Bauer, M. S., & McBride, L. (1996). *Structured group psychotherapy for bipolar disorder: The Life Goals Program* (1st ed.). New York: Springer.

Bauer, M. S., & McBride, L. (1997). Psychoeducation: Conceptual framework and practical considerations. *Journal of Practical Psychiatry and Behavioral Health, 3,* 18–27.

Bauer, M. S., McBride, L., Chase, C., Sachs, G., & Shea, N. (1998). Manual-based group psychotherapy for bipolar disorder: A feasibility study. *Journal of Clinical Psychiatry, 59,* 449–455.

Bauer, M. S., McBride, L., Shea, N., Gavin, C., Holden, F., & Kendall, S. (1997). Impact of an easy-access clinic-based program for bipolar disorder: Quantitative analysis of a demonstration project. *Psychiatric Services, 48,* 491–496.

Bauer, M. S., Shea, N., McBride, L., & Gavin, C. (1997c). Predictors of service utilization in veterans with bipolar disorder: A prospective study. *Journal of Affective Disorders, 44,* 159–168

Bauer, M. S., Vojta, C., Kinosian, B., Altshuler, L., & Glick, H. (2000). The Internal State Scale: Replication of its discriminating abilities in a multi-site, public sector sample. *Bipolar Disorders, 2,* 340–346.

Bauer, M. S., & Whybrow, P. (1990). Rapid cycling bipolar affective disorder: 2: Adjuvant treatment of refractory rapid cycling with high dose thyroxine. *Archives of General Psychiatry, 47,* 435–440.

Bauer, M. S., & Whybrow, P. C. (1991). Rapid cycling bipolar disorder: Clinical features, treatment, and etiology. In J. D. Amsterdam (Ed.), *Advances in neuropsychiatry and psychopharmacology* (Vol. 2, pp. 191–208). New York: Raven Press.

Bauer, M. S., & Whybrow, P. (1993). Validity of rapid cycling as a modifier for bipolar disorder in DSM-IV. *Depression, 1,* 11–19.

Bauer, M. S, Williford, W., Dawson, E., Akiskal, H., Altshuler, L., Fye, C., Gelenberg, A., Glick, H., Kinosian, B., & Sajatovic, M. (2001b). Principles of effectiveness trials and their implementation in VA Cooperative Study #430, "Reducing the Efficacy-Effectiveness Gap in Bipolar Disorder." *Journal of Affective Disorders, 67,* 61–78.

Bauwens, F., Tracy, A., Pardoen, D., Vander Elst, M., & Mendlewicz, J. (1991). Social adjustment of remitted bipolar and unipolar out-patients: A comparison with age- and sex-matched controls. *British Journal of Psychiatry, 151,* 239–244.

Baxter, L. R., Jr., Phelps, M. E., Mazziotta, J. C., Schwartz, J. M., Gerner, R. H., Selin, C. E., & Sumida, R. M. (1985). Cerebral metabolic rates for glucose in mood disorders: Studies with positron emission tomography and fluorodeoxyglucose F 18. *Archives of General Psychiatry, 42,* 441–447.

Beahrs, J. O., & Gutheil, T. (2001). Informed consent in psychotherapy. *American Journal of Psychiatry, 158,* 4–10.

Beck, A. T., Rush, A. J., Shaw, B., & Emery, G. (1979). *Cognitive therapy of depression.* New York: Guilford Press.

Bellack, A. S., Morrison, R. L., Mueser, K. T., & Wade, J. (1989). Social competence in schizoaffective disorder, bipolar disorder, and negative and non-negative schizophrenia. *Schizophrenia Research, 2,* 391–401.

Bellack, A., & Musser, T. (1993). Psychosocial treatment for schizophrenia. *Schizophrenia Bulletin, 19,* 317–335.

Benazzi, F. (2001a). The clinical picture of bipolar II outpatient depression in private practice. *Psychopathology, 34,* 81–84.

Benazzi, F. (2001b). Course and outcome of bipolar II disorder: A retrospective study. *Psychiatry and Clinical Neuroscience, 55,* 67–70.

Benes, F. M., & Berretta, S. (2001). GABAergic interneurons: Implications for understanding schizophrenia and bipolar disorder. *Neuropsychopharmacology, 25*(1), 1–27.

Benson, R. (1975). The forgotten treatment modality in bipolar illness: Psychotherapy. *Diseases of the Nervous System, 36,* 634–638.

Berk, M. (1999a). Lamotrigine and the treatment of mania in bipolar disorder. *European Neuropsychopharmacology, 9*(S4), S119–S123.

Berk, M., Ichim, L., & Brook, S. (1999b). Olanzapine compared to lithium in mania: A double-blind randomized controlled trial. *International Clinical Psychopharmacology, 14,* 339–343.

Berrios, G., & Hauser, R. (1988). The early development of Kraepelin's ideas on classification: A conceptual history. *Psychological Medicine, 18,* 813–821.

Bertelsen, A. (1979). A Danish twin study of manic-depressive disorders. In M. Schou & E. Stromgren (Eds.), *Origin prevention and treatment of affective disorders* (pp. 227–239). London: Academic Press.

Blacker, D., & Tsuang, M. (1992). Contested boundaries of bipolar disorder and the limits of categorical diagnosis in psychiatry. *American Journal of Psychiatry, 149,* 1473–1483.

Blackwell, B. (1995). Noncompliance with treatment. In H. Kaplan & B. Sadock (Eds.), *Comprehensive textbook of psychiatry* (6th ed., pp. 1611–1614). Baltimore: Williams and Wilkins.

Bleuler, E. (1924). *Textbook of psychiatry* (4th ed.), A. A. Brill (trans). New York: Macmillan.

Bocchetta, A., Bernardi, F., Burrai, C., Pedditzi, M., & Del Zompo, M. (1993). A double-blind study of L-sulpiride versus amitriptyline in lithium-maintained bipolar depressives. *Acta Psychiatrica Scandinavica, 88,* 434–439.

Botts, S. R., & Raskind, J. (1999). Gabapentin and lamotrigine in bipolar disorder. *American Journal of Health—Systems Pharmacology, 56,* 1939–1944.

Bowden, C., Brugger, A., Swann, A., Calabrese, J., Janicak, P., Petty, F., Dilsaver, S., Davis, J., Rush, J., Small, J., Trevino, E., Risch, C., Goodnick, P., & Morris, D. (1994). Efficacy of divalproex vs lithium and placebo in treatment of mania. *Journal of the American Medical Association, 271,* 918–924.

Bowden, C. L., Calabrese, J. R., McElroy, S. L., Gyulai, L., Wassef, A., Petty, F., Pope, H. G., Chou, J. C. Y., Keck, P. E., Rhodes, L. J., Swann, A. C., Hirschfeld, R. M. A., & Wozniak, P. J. (2000). A randomized, placebo-controlled 12 month trial of divalproex and lithium in treatment of outpatients with bipolar I disorder. *Archives of General Psychiatry, 57,* 481–489.

Bowden, C. L., Calabrese, J. R., McElroy, S. L., Rhodes, L. J., Keck, P. E., Cookson, J., Anderson, J., Bolden-Watson, C., Ascher, J., Monaghan, E., & Shou, J. (1999). The efficacy of lamotrigine in rapid cycling and non-rapid cycling patients with bipolar disorder. *Society of Biological Psychiatry, 45,* 953–958.

Bradley, C., & Zarkin, G. (1996). In-patient stays for patients diagnosed with severe psychiatric disorders and substance abuse. *Health Services Research, 31,* 387–409.

Bradwejn, J., Shriqui, C., Koszycki, D., Meterissian, G. (1990). Double-blind comparison of the effects of clonazepam and lorazepam in acute mania. *Journal of Clinical Psychopharmacol, 10,* 403–408.

Brambilla, P., Harenski, K., Nicoletti, M., Mallinger, A. G., Frank, E., Kupfer, D. J., Keshavan, M. S., & Soares, J. C. (2001). MRI study of posterior fossa structures and brain ventricles in bipolar patients. *Journal of Psychiatric Research, 35*(6), 313–322.

Bratfos, O., & Haug, J. O. (1968). The course of manic-depressive psychosis: A follow-up investigation of 215 patients. *Acta Psychiatrica et Neurologica Scandinavica, 44,* 89–112.

Broadhead, W. E., Blazer, D., George, L., & Tse, C. K. (1990). Depression, disability days, and days lost from work in a prospective epidemiologic survey. *Journal of the American Medical Association, 264,* 2524–2528.

Brown, A., Mallinger, A., & Renbaum, L. (1993). Elevated platelet membrane phosphatidylinositol-4, 5-bisphosphate in bipolar mania. *American Journal of Psychiatry, 150,* 1252–1254.

Brown, D., Silverstone, T., & Cookson, J. (1989). Carbamazepine compared to haloperidol in acute mania. *International Clinical Psychopharmacology, 4,* 229–238.

Brown, G. (1989). Life events and measurement. In G. Brown & T. Harris (Eds.), *Life events and stress* (pp. 3–45). New York: Guilford Press.

Brown, G., Harris, T., & Copeland, J. (1977). Depression and loss. *British Journal of Psychiatry, 130,* 1–18.

Brunet, G., Verlich, B., Robert, P., Dumas, S., Souetre, E., & Darcourt, G. (1990). Open trial of a calcium antagonist, nimodipine, in acute mania. *Clinics in Neuropharmacology, 13,* 224–228.

Buchsbaum, M. S., Wu, J., DeLisi, L. E., Holcoomb, H., Kessler, R., Johnson, J., King, A. C., Hazlett, E., Langston, K., & Post, R. M. (1986). Frontal cortex and basal ganglia metabolic rates assessed by positron emission tomography with [^{18}F]2-deoxyglucose in affective illness. *Journal of Affective Disorders, 10,* 137–152.

Bunney, W. E., Goodwin, F.K., Davis, J. M., & Fawcett, J. A. (1968). A behavioral-biochemical study of lithium treatment. *American Journal of Psychiatry, 125,* 91–104.

Bunney, W. E. Jr., Goodwin, F. K., & Murphy, D. L. (1972). The "switch process" in manic-depressive illness: 3. Theoretical implications. *Archives of General Psychiatry, 27,* 312–317.

Bunney, W. E. Jr., Goodwin, F. K., Murphy, D. L., House, K. M., & Gordon, E. K. (1972). The "switch process" in manic-depressive illness: 2. Relationship to catecholamines, REM sleep, and drugs. *Archives of General Psychiatry, 27,* 304–309.

Bunney, W. E. Jr., Murphy, D., Goodwin, F. K., & Borge, G. F. (1972). The "switch process" in manic-depressive illness: 1. A systematic study of sequential behavior change. *Archives of General Psychiatry, 27,* 295–302.

Calabrese, J. R., Bowden, C. L., McElroy, S. L., Cookson, J., Andersen, J., Keck, P. E., Rhodes, L., Bolden-Watson, C., Shou, J., & Ascher, J. A. (1999a). Spectrum of activity of lamotrigine in treatment-refractory bipolar disorder. *American Journal of Psychiatry, 156*, 1019–1023.

Calabrese, J. R., Bowden, C. L., Sach, G. S., Ascher, J. A., Monaghan, E., & Rudd, G. D. (1999b). A double-blind placebo-controlled study of lamotrigine monotherapy in outpatients with bipolar I. *Depression, 60*, 79–88.

Calabrese, J. R., Kimmel, S. E., Woyshville, M. J., Rapport, D. J., Faust, C. J., Thompson, P. A., & Meltzer, H. Y. (1996). Clozapine for treatment-refractory mania. *American Journal of Psychiatry, 153*, 759–764.

Calabrese, J. R., Suppes, T., Bowden, C.L., Sachs, G. S., Swann, A. C., McElroy, S. L., Kusumakar, V., Ascher, J.A., Earl, N. L., Greene, P. L., & Monaghan, E. T. (2000). A double-blind, placebo-controlled prophylaxis study of lamotrigine in rapid-cycling bipolar disorder. *Journal of Clinical Psychiatry, 61*, 841–850.

Calabrese, J., Woyshville, M., Kimmel, S., & Rapport, D. (1993). Predictors of valproate response in bipolar rapid cycling. *Journal of Clinical Psychopharmacology, 13*, 280–283.

Callahan, A., Fava, M., & Rosenbaum, J. (1993). Drug interactions in psychopharmacology. *Psychiatric Clinics of North America, 16*, 647–671.

Carlson, G. A., & Kashani, J. H. (1988). Phenomenology of major depression from childhood through adulthood: Analysis of three studies. *American Journal of Psychiatry, 145*, 1222–1225.

Carlson, G., Kotin, J., Davenport, Y., & Adland, M. (1974). Follow-up of 53 bipolar manic-depressive patients. *British Journal of Psychiatry, 124*, 134–149.

Carney, P. A., Fitzgerald, C. T., & Monaghan, C. E. (1988). Influence of climate on the prevalence of mania. I>British Journal of Psychiatry, 152, 820–823.

Carr-Hill, R. (1989). Background material for the workshop on QUALYs: Assumptions of the QUALY procedure. *Social Science and Medicine, 29*, 469–477.

Carver, C. S., & Scheier, M. F. (2001). Optimism, pessimism, and self-regulation. In E. C. Chang (Ed.), *Optimism and pessimism: Implications for theory, research, and practice* (pp. 31–51). Washington, DC: American psychological Association.

Casey, D. (1984). Tardivd dyskinesia and affective disorders. In G. Gardos & D. Casey (Eds.), *Tardive dyskinesia and affective disorders* (pp 2–19). Washington, DC: American Psychiatric Association Press.

Cerbone, M., Mayo, J., Cuthbertsone, B., & O'Connell, R. (1992). Group therapy as an adjunct to medication in the management of bipolar disorder. *Group, 16*, 174–187.

Chalmers, I. (1993). The Cochrane Collaboration: Preparing, maintaining, and disseminating systematic reviews of the effects of health care. *Annals of the New York Academy of Sciences, 703,* 156–163.

Chengappa, K. N., Gershon, S., & Levine, J. (2001). The evolving role of topiramate among other mood stabliizers in the management of bipolar disorder. *Bipolar Disorder, 3,* 215–232.

Chengappa, K. N. R., Levine, J., Gershon, S., Mallinger, A. G., Hardan, A., Vagnucci, A., Pollock, B., Luther, J., Butterfield, J., Verfaille, S., Kupfer, D. J. (2000). Inositol as an add-on treatment for bipolar disorder. *Bipolar Disorders, 2,* 47–55.

Chouinard, G., Young, S. N., & Annable, L. (1983). Antimanic effect of clonazepam. *Biological Psychiatry, 18,* 451–466.

Ciechanowski, P. S., Katon, W. J., Russo, J. E., & Walker, E. A. (2001). The patient-provider relationship: Attachment theory and adherence to treatment in diabetes. *American Journal of Psychiatry, 158,* 29–35.

Clark, H. M., Berk, M., & Brook, S. (1997). A randomized controlled single blind study of the efficacy of clonazepam and lithium in the treatment of acute mania. *Human Psychopharmacology, 12,* 325–328.

Clarkin, J. F., Carpenter, D., Hull, J., Wilner, P., & Glick, I. (1998). Effects of psychoeducational intervention for married patients with bipolar disorder and their spouses. *Psychiatric Services, 49,* 531–533.

Clarkin, J. F., Glick, I., Haas, G., Spencer, J., Lewis, A., Peyser, J., DeMane, N., Good-Ellis, M., Harris, E., & Lestell, V. (1990). A randomized clinical trial of inpatient family intervention: 5. Results for affective disorder. *Journal of Affective Disorders, 18,* 17–28.

Clayton, P. J. (1981). The epidemiology of bipolar affective disorder. *Comprehensive Psychiatry, 22,* 31–43.

Cochran, S. (1984). Preventing medical noncompliance in the outpatient treatment of bipolar affective disorders. *Journal of Consulting and Clinical Psychology, 52,* 873–878.

Cohen, L., Friedman, J., Jefferson, J., Johnson, E. M., & Weiner, M. (1994). A re-evaluation of the risk of in utero exposure to lithium. *Journal of the American Medical Association, 271,* 146–150.

Cohen, M. B., Baker, G., Cohen, R. A., Fromm-Reichmann, F., & Weigert, E. V. An intensive study of twelve cases of manic-depressive psychosis. 17, 103–137.

Cohn, J. B., Collins, G., Ashbrook, E., & Wernicke, J. F. (1989). A comparison of fluoxetine imipramine and placebo in patients with bipolar depressive disorder. *Clinical Psychopharmacology, 4,* 313–322.

Collen, M., & Goodman, C. (1985). Cost-effectiveness and cost-benefit analyses. In Institute of Medicine (Eds.), *Assessing medical technologies* (pp. 136–145). Washington, DC: National Academy Press.

Colligan, R., Offord, K., Malinchoc, M., Schulman, P., & Seligman, M. (1994). CAVEing the MMPI for an Optimism-Pessimism Scale: Seligman's attributional model and the assessment of explanatory style. *Journal of Clinical Psychology, 50,* 71–95.

Cookson, J. C., Silverstone, T., & Wells, B. (1979). A double-blind controlled study of pimozide vs chlorpromazine in mania. *Neuropharmacology, 18,* 1011–1013

Cooper, A. (1985). Will neurobiology influence psychoanalysis? *American Journal of Psychiatry, 142,* 1395–1402.

Coppen, A., Noguera, R., & Bailey, J. (1971) Prophylactic lithium in affective disorders controlled trial. *Lancet, 2,* 275–279.

Coppen, A., Prange, A. J. Jr., Whybrow, P. C., & Noguera, R. F. (1972). Abnormalities of indoleamines in affective disorders. *Archives of General Psychiatry, 26,* 474–478.

Coryell, W., Endicott, J., Andreasen, N., & Keller, M. (1985). Bipolar I, bipolar II, and nonbipolar major depression among the relatives of affectively ill probands. *American Journal of Psychiatry, 142,* 817–821.

Coryell, W., Endicott, J., Keller, M., Andreasen, N., Grove, W., Hirschfeld, R. M. A., & Scheftner, W. (1989). Bipolar affective disorder and high achievement: A familial Association. *American Journal of Psychiatry, 146,* 983–988.

Coryell, W., Keller, M., Endicott, J., Andreasen, N., Clayton, P., & Hirschfeld, R. (1989). Bipolar II illness: Course and outcome over a five-year period. *Psychological Medicine, 19,* 129–141.

Coryell, W., Endicott, J., & Keller, M. (1992). Rapidly cycling affective disorders: demographics, diagnosis, family history, and course. *Archives of General Psychiatry, 49,* 126–131.

Coryell, W., Scheftner, W., Keller, M., Endicott, J., Maser, J., & Klerman, J. (1993). The enduring psychosocial consequences of mania and depression. *American Journal of Psychiatry, 150,* 720–727.

Coxhead, N., Silverstone, T., & Cookson, J. (1992). Carbamazepine versus lithium in the prophylaxis of bipolar affective disorder. *Acta Psychiatrica Scandinavica, 85,* 114–118.

Coyne, J., & Gotlib, I. (1986). Studying the role of cognition in depression: Well-trodden paths and cul-de-sacs. *Cognitive Therapy and Research, 10,* 695–705.

Cozza, K. L., & Armstrong, S. C. (2001). *Concise guide to the cytochrome P450 system: Drug interactions for medical practitioners.* Washington, DC: American Psychiatric Press.

Craddock, N., & Jones, I. (1999). Genetics of bipolar disorder. *Journal of Medical Genetics, 36,* 585–594.

Craighead, W. E., & Miklowitz, D. J. (2000). Psychosocial interventions for bipolar disorder. *Journal of Clinical Psychiatry, 61*(13), 58–64.

Craighead, W. E., Miklowitz, D. J., Vajc, F. C., Frank, E. (2000). Psychosocial interventions for bipolar disorder. *Journal of Clinical Psychiatry, 61*(13), 58–64.

Cramer J., & Spilker, B. (Eds.). (1994). *Patient compliance in medical practice and clinical trials.* New York: Raven.

Crane, G. (1957). Iproniazid phospate (Marsilid): A therapeutic agent for mental disorders and debilitating diseases. *Psychiatric Research Reports, 8,* 142–152.

Crow, T., & Deakin, J. (1981). Affective change and the mechanisms of reward and punishment: A neurochemical hypothesis. In C. Perris, G. Struwe, & B. Jansson (Eds.), *Biological psychiatry* (pp. 536–541). Amsterdam: Elsevier.

Cundall, R. L., Brooks, P. W., & Murray, L. G. (1972). A controlled evaluation of lithium prophylaxis in affective disorders. *Psychological Medicine, 2,* 308–311.

Davenport, Y., Ebert, M., Adland, M., & Goodwin, F. (1977). Couples group therapy as an adjunct to lithium maintenance of the manic patient. *American Journal of Orthopsychiatry, 47,* 495–502.

DeCarolis, V., Gilberti, F., Roccatagliata, G., Rossi, R., & Venutti, G. (1964). Imipramine and electroshock in the treatment of depression: A clinical statistical analysis of 437 cases. *Sistema Nervosa, 16,* 29–42.

Deicken, R. F., Calabrese, G., Merrin, E. L., Vinogradov, S., Fein, G., & Weiner, M. W. (1995). Asymmetry of temporal lobe phosphorous metabolism in schizophrenia: A 31phosphorous magnetic resonance spectroscopic imaging study. *Biological Psychiatry, 38*(5), 279–286.

Delgado Escueta. A., & Janz. D. (1992). Consensus guidelines: Pre-conception counselling, management and care of the pregnant woman with epilepsy. *Neurology, 42*(Suppl), 149–160.

Deltito, J., Moline, M., Pollak, C., Martin, L., & Maremmami, I. (1991). Effects of phototherapy on non-seasonal unipolar and bipolar depressive spectrum disorders. *Journal of Affective Disorders, 23,* 231–237.

Denicoff, K. D., Smith-Jackson, E. E., Bryan, A. L., Ali, S. O., & Post, R. M. (1997a). Valproate prophylaxis in a prospective clinical trial of refractory bipolar disorder. *American Journal of Psychiatry, 154,* 1456–1458.

Denicoff, K., Smith-Jackson, E., Disney, E., Ali, S., Leverich, G., & Post, R. (1997b). Comparative prophylactic efficacy of lithium, carbamazepine, and the combination in bipolar disorder. Journal of Clinical Psychiatry, 58, 470–478.

DePaolo, J. R., Simpson, S. G., Folstein, S., & Folstein, M. (1989). The new genetics of bipolar affective disorder: Clinical implications. *Clinical Chemistry, 35/7*(B), B28–B32.

Department of Health, Education, and Welfare Medical Practice Project. (1979). *A state-of-the-science report for the Office of the Assistant Secretary of the U.S. Department of Health, Education, and Welfare.* Baltimore: Policy Research.

Depression Guideline Panel. (1993). *Depression in primary care: 2. Treatment of major depression clinical practice guideline.* (No. 5. AHCPR Publication No. 93-0551). Rockville, MD: Department of Health and Human Services, Public Health Service, Agency for Health Care Policy and Research.

Depue, R., & Iacono, W. (1989). Neurobiological aspects of affective disorders. *Annual Review of Psychology, 40,* 457–492.

Depue, R., Kleinman, R., Davis, P., Hutchinson, M., & Kraus, S. (1985). The behavioral high-risk paradigm and bipolar disorder, 8: Serum-free cortisol in nonpatient cyclothymic subjects selected by the GBI. *American Journal of Psychiatry, 142,* 175–181.

Dion, G., Tohen, M., Anthony, W., & Waternaux, C. (1988). Symptoms and functioning of patients with bipolar disorder six months after hospitalization. *Hospital and Community Psychiatry, 39,* 652–657.

Dooley, L. (1921). A psychoanalytic study of manic depressive psychoses. *Psychoanalytic Review, 8,* 144–167.

Dowrick, C., Dunn, G., Ayuso-Mateos, J. L., Dalgard, O. S., Page, H., Lehtinen,V., Casey, P., Wilkinson, C., Vazquez,-Barquero, J. L., Wilkinson, G, and the Outcomes Depression International Network (ODIN) Group. (2000). Problem solving treatment and group psychoeducation for depression: Multicentre randomized controlled trial. *British Medical Journal, 321,* 1–6.

Drevets, W. C., Frank, E., Price, J. C., Kupfer, D. J., Holt, D., Greer, P. J., Huang, Y., Gautier, C., & Mathis, C. (1999). PET imaging of serotonin 1A receptor binding in depression. *Biological Psychiatry, 46*(10), 1375–1387.

Dubovsky, S. L., Franks, R. D., Allen, S., & Murphy, J. Calcium antagonists in mania: A double-blind study of verapamil. *Psychiatry Research, 18,* 309–320.

Dunner, D. L. (1993). A review of the diagnostic status of "bipolar II" for the DSM-IV work group on mood disorders. *Depression, 1,* 2–10.

Dunner, D. L., & Fieve, R. R. (1974). Clinical factors in lithium prophylaxis failure. *Archives of General Psychiatry, 30,* 229–233.

Dunner, D. L., Stallone, F., & Fieve, R. R. (1976). Lithium carbonate and affective disorders. *Archives of General Psychiatry, 33,* 117–120.

Edlund, M., & Craig, T. (1984). Antipsychotic drug use and birth defects: An epidemiologic reassessment. *Comprehensive Psychiatry, 25,* 32–37.

Edwards, R., Stephenson, U., & Flewett, T. (1991). Clonazepam in acute mania: A double blind trial. *Australian and New Zealand Journal of Psychiatry, 25,* 238–242.

Ehlers, C., Frank, E., & Kupfer, D. (1988). Social zeitgebers and biological rhythms. *Archives of General Psychiatry, 45,* 948–952.

Eidelson, J. (1985). Cognitive group therapy for depression: "Why and what." *International Journal of Mental Health, 13,* 54–66.

Ellenberg, J., Salamon, I., & Meaney, C. (1980). A lithium clinic in a community mental health center. *Hospital and Community Psychiatry, 12,* 834–836.

Ellicott, A., Hammen, C., Gitlin, M., Brown, G., & Jamison, K. (1990). Life events and the course of bipolar disorder, *American Journal of Psychiatry, 147*(9), 1194–1198.

el-Mallakh, R., & Li, R. (1993). Is the Na(+)-K(+)-ATPase the link between phosphoinositide metabolism and bipolar disorder? *Journal of Neuropsychiatry and Clinical Neurosciences, 5*(4), 361–368.

Ellsworth, A. J., Witt, D. M., Dugdale, D. C., & Oliver, L. M. (2001). *Mosby's 2001–02 medical drug reference.* St. Louis: Mosby.

Emrich, H. M., von Zerssen, D. V., Kissling, W., Moller, H. J., & Windorfer, A. (1980). Effect of sodium valproate on mania: The GABA-hypothesis of affective disorders. Archives of Psychiatry and Nervenkrankheiten, 229, 1–16.

Endicott, J., Nee, J., Andreasen, N., Clayton, P., Keller, M., & Coryell, W. (1985). Bipolar II: Combine or keep separate? *Journal of Affective Disorders, 8,* 17–28.

Engel, G. L. (1977). The need for a new medical model: A challenge for biomedicine. *Science, 196,* 129–136.

Erfurth, A., Kammerer, C., Grunze, H., Narmann, C., & Walden, J. (1998). An open label study of gabapentin in the treatment of acute mania. *Journal of Psychiatric Research, 32,* 261–264.

Esparon, J. (1986). Comparison of the prophylatictic action of flupenthixol with placebo in lithium treated manic-depressive patients. *British Journal of Psychiatry, 148,* 723–785.

EuroQol Group. (1990). EuroQol—a new facility for the measurement of health-related quality of life. *Health Policy, 16,* 199–208.

Evidence-Based Working Group (EBWG). (1992). A new approach to teaching the practice of medicine. *Journal of the American Medical Association, 268,* 2420–2425.

Faedda, G. L., Tondo, L., Baldessarni, R. J., Suppes, T., & Tohen, M. (1993). Outcome after rapid vs. gradual discontinuation of lithium treatment in bipolar disorders. *Archives of General Psychiatry, 50,* 448–455.

Farkas, T., Dunner, D. L., & Rieve, R. R. (1976). L-Tryptophan in depression. *Biological Psychiatry, 11,* 295–302.

Feighner, J. P., Robins, E., Guze, S. B., Woodruff, R. A., Winokor, G., & Munoz, R. (1972). Diagnostic criteria for use in psychiatric research. *Archives of General Psychiatry, 26,* 57–63.

Fein, R. (1958). *Economics of mental illness.* New York: Basic Books.

Feinstein, A., Josephy, B., & Wells, C. (1986). Scientific and clinical indexes of functional disability. *Annals of Internal Medicine, 105,* 413–420.

Fenichel, O. (1945). The psychoanalytic theory of neuroses. New York: Norton.

Ferguson, J. M. (2001). The effects of antidepressants on sexual functioning in depressed patients: A review. *Journal of Clinical Psychiatry, 62*(Suppl 3), 22–34.

Ferster, C. (1974). Behavioral approaches to depression. In R. Friedman, & M. Katz (Eds.), *The psychology of depression: Contemporary theory and research* (pp. 29–53). New York: Wiley.

Fieve, R. R. (1975). The Lithium clinic: A new model for the delivery of psychiatric services. *American Journal of Psychiatry, 132*(10), 1018–1022.

Fieve, R. R., Kumbaraci, R., & Dunner, D. L. (1976). Lithium prophylaxis of depression in bipolar I, bipolar II, and unipolar patients. *American Journal of Psychiatry, 133*, 925–929.

Fieve, R. R., Platman, S. R., & Plutchik, R. R. (1968a). The use of lithium in affective disorders I: Acute endogenous depression. *American Journal of Psychiatry, 125*, 487–491.

Fieve, R. R., Platman, S. R., & Plutchik, R. R. (1968b). The use of lithium in affective disorders: II. prophylaxis of depression in chronic recurrent affective disorder. *American Journal of Psychiatry, 125*, 492–498.

Fitzgerald, R. G. (1972). Treatment with family therapy and lithium carbonate. *American Journal of Psychotherapy, 26*, 547–553.

Foelker, G. A. Jr., Molinari, V., Marmion, J. J., & Chacko, R. C. (1986). Lithium groups and elderly bipolar outpatients. *Clinical Gerontology, 5*(3/4), 297–307.

Frank, E., Swartz, H., & Kupfer, D. (2000). Interpersonal and social rhythm therapy: Managing the chaos of bipolar disorder. *Biological Psychiatry, 48*, 593–604.

Frank, E., Swartz, H., Mallinger, A. G., Thase, M. E., Weaver, E. V., & Kupfer, D. J. (1999). Adjunctive psychotherapy for bipolar disorder: Effects of changing treatment modality. *Journal of Abnormal Psychology, 108*, 579–587.

Freeman, T., Clothier, J., Pazzaglia, P., Lesem, M., & Swann, A. (1992). A double-blind comparison of valporate and lithium in the treatment of acute mania. *American Journal of Psychiatry, 149*, 108–111.

Fremming, K. H. (1951). The expectation of mental infirmity in a sample of the danish population (Occasional Papers in Eugenics No. 7). London: Cassell.

Freud, S. (1924). *Mourning and melancholia* (Collected Papers, Vol. 4). London: Hogarth Press.

Freud, S. (1933). New introductory lectures on psychoanalysis. In E. Mosbacher & J. Strachey (Trans.), *Standard edition* (vol. 22, pp. 3–182). New York: Basic Books.

Fromm-Reichmann, F. (1949). Intensive psychotherapy of manic-depressive. *Confinia Neurologica, 9,* 158–165.

Fromm-Reichmann, F. (1950). *Principles of intensive psychotherapy.* Chicago: University of Chicago Press.

Frye, M., Altshuler, L., Szuba, M., Finch, N., & Mintz, J. (1996). The relationship between antimanic agent for treatment of classic or dysphoric mania and length of hospital stay. *Journal of Clinical Psychiatry, 51,* 17–21.

Frye, M. A., Ketter, T. A., Kimbrell, T. A., Dunn, R. T., Speer, A. M., Osuch, E. A., Luckenbaugh, D. A., Cora-Ocatelli, G., Leverich, G. S., & Post, R. M. (2000). A placebo-controlled study of lamotrigine and gabapentin monotherapy in refractory mood disorders. *Journal of Clinical Psychopharmacology 2000, 20,* 607–614

Gareri, P., Falconi, U., DeFazio, P., & DeSarro, G. (2000). Conventional and new antidepressant drugs in the elderly. *Progressive Neurobiology, 61,* 353–396.

Garfinkel, P. E., Stancer, H. C., & Persad, E. (1980). A comparison of haloperdol, lithium carbonate and their combination in the treatment of mania. *Journal of Affective Disorders, 2,* 279–288.

Garza-Trevino, E., Overall, J., & Hollister, L. (1992). Verapamil versus lithium in acute mania. *American Journal of Psychiatry, 149,* 121–122.

Gelenberg, A., Kane, J., Keller, M., Lavori, P., Rosenbaum, J., Cole, K., & Lavelle, J. (1989). Comparison of standard and low serum levels of lithium for maintenance treatment of bipolar disorder. *New England Journal of Medicine, 321,* 1489–1493.

Geller, B., Bolhofner, K., Craney, J. L., Williams, M., DelBello, M. P., & Gunderson, K. (2000). Psychosocial functioning in a prepubertal and early adolescent bipolar disorder phenotype. *Journal of the Americam Academy of Child and Adolescent Psychiatry, 39,* 1543–1548.

Gershon, E. S., Hamovit, J., Guroff, J. J., Dibble, E., Leckman, J. F., Sceery, W., Targum, S. D., Nurnberger, J. I., Jr., Goldin, L. R., & Bunney, W. E. (1982). A family study of schizoaffective, bipolar I, bipolar II, unipolar, and normal control probands. *Archives of General Psychiatry, 39,* 1157–1167.

Gershon, E. S., Hamovit, J. H., Guroff, J. J., & Nurnberger, J. I. (1987). Birth-cohort changes in manic and depressive disorders in relatives of bipolar and schizopaffective patients. *Archives of General Psychiatry, 44,* 314–319.

Giannini, A. J., Houser, W. L., Loiselle, R. H., Giannini, M. C., & Price, W. A. (1984). Antimanic effects of verapamil. *American Journal of Psychiatry, 141,* 1602–1603.

Giannini, A. J., Nakoneczie, A. M., Melemis, S. M., Ventresco, J., Condon, M. (2000). Magnesium oxide augmentation of verapamil maintenance therapy in mania. *Psychiatric Research, 93,* 83–87.

Gilbert, D., Altshuler, K., Rago, W., Shon, S., Crismon, M. L., Toprac, M., & Rush, A. J. (1998). Texas Medication Algorithm Project: Definitions, rationale, and methods to develop medication algorithms. *Journal of Clinical Psychiatry, 59,* 345–351.

Gitlin, M., Cochran, S., & Jamison, K. (1989). Maintenance lithium treatment: Side effects and compliance. *Journal of Clinical Psychiatry, 50,* 127–131.

Gitlin, M. J., & Jamison, K. R. (1984). Lithium clinics: Theory and practice, *Hospital and Community Psychiatry, 35*(4), 363–368.

Gitlin, M. J., & Jamison, K. R. (1984). Lithium clinics theory and practice. *Hospital and Community Psychiatry, 35,* 363–368.

Glanz, K., Lewis, R. M., & Rimer, B. K. (1997). *Health behavior and health education: Theory, research, and practice* (2nd ed.). San Francisco: Jossey-Bass.

Glynn, S., & Mueser, K. (1986). Social learning for chronic mental inpatients. *Schizophrenia Bulletin, 12,* 648–667.

Gold, M. R., Siegel, J. E., Russell, L. B., & Weinstein, M. C. (1996). *Cost-effectiveness in health and medicine.* New York and Oxford: Oxford University Press.

Goldman, H., Skodol, A., & Lave, T. (1992). Revising Axis V for DSM-IV: A review of measures of functioning. *American Journal of Psychiatry, 149,* 1148–1156.

Goodwin, F. K., & Jamison, K. (1990). *Manic-depressive illness* (pp. 541–574). New York: Oxford University Press.

Goodwin, F. K., Murphy, D. L., & Bunney, W. F. Jr. (1969). Lithium carbonate treatment in depression and mania: A longitudinal double-blind study. *Archives of General Psychiatry, 21,* 486–496.

Goodwin, F. K., Murphy, D. L., Dunner, D. L., & Bunney, W. E., Jr. (1972). Lithium response in unipolar versus bipolar depression. *American Journal of Psychiatry, 129,* 44–47.

Goodwin, F. K., & Sack, R. L. (1974). Behavioral effects of a new dopamine-beta-hydroxylase inhibitor (dusaric acid) in man. *Journal of Psychiatric Research, 11,* 211–217.

Gottschalk, A., Bauer, M., & Whybrow, P. (1995). Evidence for chaotic mood variation in bipolar disorder. *Archives of General Psychiatry, 53,* 947–959.

Gouliaev, F., Licht, R. W., Vestergaard, P., Merinder, L., Lund, H., & Bjerre, L. (1996). Treatment of manic episodes: Zuclopenthixol and clonazepam versus lithium and clonazepam. *Acta Psychiatrica Scandinavica, 93,* 119–124.

Green, A. I., Tohen, M., Patel, J. K., Banov, M., DuRand, C., Berman, I., Chang, H., Zarate, C., Posener, J., Lee, H., & Dawson, R. (2000). Clozapine in the treatment of refractory psychotic mania. *American Journal of Psychiatry, 157,* 982–986.

Greenberg, P. E., Stiglin, L. E., Finkelstein, S. N., & Berndt, E. R. (1990). The economic burden of depression in 1990. *Journal of Clinical Psychiatry, 54,* 405–418.

Greenberger, D., & Padesky, C. A. (1995). *Mind over mood.* New York: Guilford Press.

Greenblatt, M., Grosser, G. H., & Wechsler, H. (1964). A comparative study of selected antidepressant medications and EST. *American Journal of Psychiatry, 120,* 144–153.

Greene, B. L., Lee, R. R., & Lustig, N. (1975). Treatment of marital disharmony where one spouse has a primary affective disorder (manic depressive illness): 1. General overview—100 Couples. *Journal of Marriage and Family Counseling, 1,* 39–50.

Greil, W., Steber, R., & vanCalker, D. (1991). The agonist-stimulated accumulation of inositol phosphates is attenuated in neutrophils from male patients under chronic lithium therapy. *Biological Psychiatry, 30*(5), 443–451.

Grunze, H., Erfurth, A., Marcuse, A., Amann, B., Normann, C., & Walden, J. (1999). Tiagabine appears not to be efficacious in the treatment of acute mania. *Journal of Clinical Psychiatry, 60,* 759–762.

Halaris, A. (Ed). (1987). *Chronobiology and psychiatric disorders.* New York: Elsevier.

Hall, K., Dunner, D., & Zeller, G., & Fieve, R. (1977). Bipolar illness: A prospective study of life events. *Comprehensive Psychiatry, 18,* 497–502.

Harmon, R., & Tratnack, S. Teaching hospitalized patients with serious, persistent mental illness. *Journal of Psychosocial Nursing, 30,* 33–36.

Harrow, M., Goldberg, J., Grossman, L., & Meltzer, H. (1990). Outcome in manic disorders: A naturalistic follow-up study. *Archives of General Psychiatry, 47,* 665–671.

Hartmann, C. E. (2002). Life as death: Hope regained with ECT. *Psychiatric Services, 53,* 413-414.

Harvey, N. S., & Peet, M. (1991). Lithium maintenance, 2: Effects of personality and attitude on health information acquisition and compliance. *British Journal of Psychiatry, 158,* 200–204.

Haslam, D., Kennedy, S., Kusumakar, V., Kutcher, S., Matte, R., Parikh, S., Sharma, V., Silverstone, P., & Yatham, L. (1997). The treatment of bipolar disorder: Review of the literature, guidelines, and options. *Canadian Journal of Psychiatry, 42,* 67S–99S.

Hastings, D. (1958). Follow-up results in psychiatric illness. *American Journal of Psychiatry, 114,* 1057–1066.

Hastings, D. (1989). Self-management in bipolar affective disorder. *Canadian Journal of Nursing, 30,* 20–22.

Hauser, P., Matochik, J., Altshuler, L. L., Denicoff, K. D., Conrad, A., Li, X., & Post, R. M. (2000). MRI-based measurements of temporal lobe and ventricular structures in patients with bipolar I and bipolar II disorders. *Journal of Affective Disorders, 60*(1), 25–32

Haykal, R., & Akiskal, H. (1990). Bupropion as a promising approach to persons with rapid cycling bipolar II disorder. *Journal of Clinical Psychiatry, 51,* 450–455.

Haynes, R. B., Taylor, D. W., & Sacket, D. C. (Eds.). (1979). *Compliance in health care.* Baltimore: Johns Hopkins University Press.

Helgason, T. (1979). Epidemiological investigations concerning affective disorders. In M. Schou & E. Stromgren (Eds.), *Origin, prevention and treatment of affective disorders* (pp. 241–255). London: Academic Press.

Heninger, G., & Charney, D. (1987). Mechanism of action of antidepressant treatments: Implications for the etiology and treatment of depressive disorders. In H. Y. Meltzer, (Ed.), *Psychopharmacology: The third generation of progress* (pp. 535–544). New York: Raven Press.

Himmelhoch, J., Mulla, D., Neil, J. F., Detre, T. P., & Kupfer, D. J. (1976). Incidence and significance of mixed affective states in a bipolar population. *Archives of General Psychiatry, 33,* 1062–1066.

Himmelhoch, J., Thase, M., Mallinger, A., & Fuchs, C. Z. (1991). Tranylcypromine versus imipramine in anergic bipolar depression. *American Journal of Psychiatry, 148,* 910–915.

Himmelhoch, J., Thase, M., Mallinger, A., & Houck, P. (1991). Tranylcypromine versus imipramine in anergic bipolar depression. *American Journal of Psychiatry, 148,* 910–916.

Hlastala, S. A., Frank, E., Mallinger, A. G., Thase, M. E., Ritenour, A. M., & Kupfer, D. J. (1997). Bipolar depression: An underestimated treatment challenge. *Depression and Anxiety, 5,* 73–83.

Hogue, M., & McLoughlin, K. (1991). Group psychotherapy in acute treatment settings: Theory and technique. *Hospital and Community Psychiatry, 42,* 153–158.

Honig, A., Hofman, A., Rozendaal, N., & Dingemans, P. (1997). Psychoeducation in bipolar disorder: Effect on expressed emotion. *Psychiatry Research, 72,* 17–22.

Hoschl, C., & Kozeny, J. (1989). Verapamil in affective disorders: A controlled, double-blind study. *Biological Psychiatry, 25,* 128–140.

Hudson, W. W. (1982). *The clinical measurement package: A field manual.* Chicago: Dorsey Press.

Hume, A. J. A., Barker, P. J., Robertson, W., & Swan, J. (1988). Manic-depressive psychosis: An alternative therapeutic model of nursing. *Journal of Advanced Nursing, 13,* 93–98.

Hunt, N., Bruce-Jones, W., & Silverstone, T. (1992). Life events and relapse in bipolar affective disorder. *Journal of Affective Disorders, 25,* 13–20.

Hutchinson, S. A. (1992). People with bipolar disorders quest for equanimity: Doing grounded theory. In P. Munhall & C. Boyd (Eds.), *Nursing research: A qualitative perspective.* New York: NLN Press.

Hyman, S. E., Arana, J. W., & Rosenbaum, J. F. (1995). *Handbook of psychiatric drug therapy* (3rd ed.). Boston: Little, Brown.

Ichim, L., Berk, M., & Brook, S. (2000). Lamotrigine compared with lithium in mania: A double-blind randomized controlled trial. *Annals of Clinical Psychiatry, 12,* 5–10.

Institute of Medicine (IOM). (1985). *Assessing medical technologies.* Washington, DC: National Academy Press.

Iqbal, M. M. (1999). Effects of antidepressants during pregnancy and lactation. *Annals of Clinical Psychiatry, 11,* 237–256.

Irwig, L., Tosteson, A. N., Gatsonis, C., Lau, J., Colditz, G., Chalmers, T. C., & Mosteller, F. (1994) Guidelines for meta-analyses evaluating diagnostic tests. *Annals of Internal Medicine, 120,* 667–676.

Jacobson, N. S., Dobson, K. S., Truax, P. A., Addis, M. E., Koerner, K., Gollan, J. K., Gortner, E., & Prince, S. E. (1996). A component analysis of cognitive-behavioral treatment for depression. *Journal of Consulting and Clinical Psychology, 64,* 295–304.

Jackson, M .(1993). Manic-depressive psychosis: Psychopathology and individual psychotherapy within a psychodynamic milieu. *Psychoanalytic Psychotherapy, 7,* 103–133.

James, N. M., & Chapman, C. J. (1975). A genetic study of bipolar affective disorder. *British Journal of Psychiatry, 126,* 449–456.

Jamison, K. R., & Akiskal, H. S. (1983). Medication compliance in patients with bipolar disorder. *Psychiatric Clinics of North America, 6,* 175–192.

Jamison, K. R., Gerner, R. H., & Goodwin, F. K. (1979). Patient and physician attitudes toward lithium: Relationship to compliance. *Archives of General Psychiatry, 36,* 866–869.

Janicak, P. G., Bresnahan, D. B., Sharma, R., Davis, J. M., Comaty, J. E., & Malinick, C. (1988). A comparison of thiothixene with chlorpromazine in the treatment of mania. *Journal of Clinical Psychopharmacology, 8,* 33–37.

Janicak, P. G., Sharma, R. P., Pandey, G., & Davis, J. M. (1998). Verapamil for the treatment of acute mania: A double-blind, placebo-controlled trial. *American Journal of Psychiatry, 155,* 972–973.

Janowsky, D. S., El-Yousef, M. K., Davis, J. M., et al. (1973). Parasympathetic suppression of manic symptoms by physostigmine. *Archives of General Psychiatry, 28,* 542–547.

Joffe, R., Singer, W., Levitt, A., & MacDonald, C. (1993). A placebo-controlled comparison of lithium and triiodothyronine augmentation of tricyclic antidepressant in unipolar refractory affective depression. *Archives of General Psychiatry, 50,* 387–393.

Johnson, G., Gershon, S., Burdock, E. I., Floyd, A., & Hekimian, L. (1971). Comparative effects of lithium and chlorpromazine in the treatment of acute manic states. *British Journal of Psychiatry, 119,* 267–276.

Johnson, G., Gershon, S., & Hekimian, L. J. (1968). Controlled evaluation of lithium and clorpromzine in the treatment of manic states: An interim report. *Comprehensive Psychiatry, 9,* 563–573.

Johnson, S., & Roberts, J. R. (1995). Life events and bipolar disorder: Implications from biological theories. *Psychology Bulletin, 117,* 434–449.

Johnson, S., Greenhouse, W., & Bauer, M. (1999). Psychosocial approaches to the treatment of bipolar disorder. *Current Opinion in Psychiatry, 13,* 69–72.

Johnson, S. L., & Kizer, A. (2002). Bipolar and unipolar depression: A comparison of clinical phenomenology and psychosocial predictors. In I. Gotlib & C. Hammen (Eds.), *Handbook of depression and its treatment.* New York: Guilford Press.

Jurjus, G. J., Nasrallah, H. A., Brogan, M., & Olson, S. C. (1993). Developmental brain anomalies in schizophrenia and bipolar disorder: A controlled MRI study. *Journal of Neuropsychiatry and Clinical Neurosciences, 5,* 375–378.

Jurjus, G., Nasrallah, H., Olson, S., et al. (1993). Cavum septum pellucidum in schizophrenia, affective disorders, and healthy controls: A magnetic resonance imaging study. *Psychological Medicine, 23,* 319–322.

Kahn, D. A. (1993). The use of psychodynamic psychotherapy in manic-depressive illness. *Journal of American Academy of Psychoanalysis, 21*(3), 441–455.

Kahn, D., Docherty, J., Carpenter, D., & Frances, A. (1997). Consensus methods in practice guideline development: A review and description of a new method. *Psychopharmacology Bulletin, 33,* 631–639.

Kamen-Seigel, L., Rodin, J., Seligman, M., & Dwyer, J. (1991). Explanatory style and cell-mediated immunity in elderly men and women. *Health Psychology, 10,* 229–235.

Kamo, J., Shin-ichiro, T., Susumu, N., et al. (1993). Season and mania. *Japanese Journal of Psychiatry and Neurology, 47*(2), 473–474.

Kane, J., Hongfeld, G., Singer, J., & Meltzer, H. Clozapine for the treatment-resistant schizophrenic. *Archives of General Psychiatry, 45,* 789–796.

Kane, J. M., Quitkin, F., Rifkin, A., Ramos-Lorenzi, J., Nayak, D., & Howard, A. (1982). Lithium carbonate and imipramine in the prophylaxis of unipolar and bipolar II illness. *Archives of General Psychiatry, 39,* 1065–1069.

Kaplan, S. H., Greenfield, S., & Ware, J. E. (1989). Assessing the effects of physician-patient interactions on the outcomes of chronic disease. *Medical Care, 27,* S110–127, 679.

Kapur, S., & Mann, J. J. (1992). Role of the dopaminergic system in depression. *Biological Psychiatry, 32,* 1–17.

Kato, T., Takahashi, S., Shioiri, T., Murashita, J., Hamakawa, H., Inubushi, T. (1994). Reduction of brain phospphocreatinine in bipolar II disorder detected by phosphorus-31 magnetic resonance spectroscopy. *Journal of Affective Disorders, 31,* 125–133.

Kay, D. S. G., Naylor, G. H., Smith, A. H. W., & Greenwood, C. (1984). The therapeutic effect of ascorbic acid and EDTA in manic-depressive psychosis: Double-blind comparisons with standard treatments. *Psychological Medicine, 14,* 533–539.

Keck, P. E., McElroy, S. L., & Bennett, J. A. (1994). Pharmacology and pharmacokinetics of valproic acid. In R. T. Joffe & J. R. Calabrese (Eds.), *Anticonvulsants in mood disorders* (pp. 27–42). New York: Marcel Dekker.

Keck, P., McElroy, S., Strakowski, S., Balistreri, T., Kizer, D., & West, S. (1996). Factors associated with maintenance antipsychotic treatment of patients with bipolar disorder. *Journal of Clinical Psychiatry, 57,* 147–151.

Keck, P., McElroy, S., Strakowski, S., Bourne, M., & West, S. (1997). Compliance with maintenance treatment in bipolar disorder. *Psychopharmacology Bulletin, 33,* 87–91.

Keck, P. E., Jr., McElroy, S. L., Strakowski, S. M., West, S. A., Sax, K. W., Hawkins, J. M., Bourne, M. L., & Haggard, P. (1998). 12-Month outcome of patients with bipolar disorder following hospitalization for a manic or mixed episode. *American Journal of Psychiatry, 155,* 646–652.

Keller, M. B., & Boland, R. J. (1997). Antidepressants. In A. M. Tasman, J. Kay, & J. A. Lieberman (Eds.), *Psychiatry* (pp. 1606–1639). Philadelphia: Saunders.

Keller, M., Lavori, P., Coryell, W., Andreasen, N., Endicott, J., Clayton, P., Klerman, G., & Hirschfeld, R. (1986). Differential outcome of episodes of illness in bipolar patients: Pure manic, mixed/cycling, and pure depressive. *Journal of the American Medical Association, 255,* 3138–3142.

Kelly, G., Mamos, J., & Scott, J. (1987). Utility of the health belief model in examining medication compliance among psychiatric outpatients. *Social Sciences and Medicine, 25,* 1205–1211.

Kennedy, S., Thompson, R., Stancer, H. C., Roy, A., & Persad, E. (1983). Life events precipitating mania. *British Journal of Psychiatry, 142,* 398–403.

Kessler, R. C., Crum, R. M., Warner, L. A., Nelson, C. B., Schulenberg, J., & Anthony, J. C. (1997). Lifetime co-occurrence of DSM-III-R alcohol abuse and dependence with other psychiatric disorders in the national comorbidity survey. *Archives of General Psychiatry, 54,* 313–321

Ketter, T. A., & Post, R. M. (1994). Clinical pharmacology and pharmacokinetics of carbamazepine. In R. T. Joffe & J. R. Calabrese (Eds.), *Anticonvulsants in mood disorders* (pp. 147–188). New York: Marcel Dekker.

Kimmel, S., Calabrese, J., Woyshville, M., & Meltzer, H. (1994). Clozapine in treatment-refractory mood disorders. *Journal of Clinical Psychiatry, 55,* 91–93.

Kirov, G., Murphy, K. C., Arranz, M. J., Jones, I., McCandles, F., Kunugi, H., Murray, R. M., McGuffin, P., Collier, D. A., Owen, M. J., &

Craddock, N. (1998). Low activity allele of catechol-o-methyltransferase gene associated with rapid cycling bipolar disorder. *Moldecular Psychiatry, 3*(4), 342–345.

Klerman, G. L., Dimascio, A., Weissman, M., Prusoff, B., & Paykel, E. S. (1974). Treatment of depression by drugs and psychotherapy. *American Journal of Psychiatry, 131,* 186–191.

Klerman, G., Olfson, M., Leon, A., & Weissman, M. (1992). Measuring the need for mental health care. *Health Affairs, 11,* 23–33.

Klerman, G., Weissman, M., Rounsaville, B., & Chesron, E. (1984). *Interpersonal psychotherapy of depression.* New York, Basic Books.

Kraepelin, E. (1921). *Manic-depressive insanity and paranoia.* (R. M. Barclay, Trans., G. M. Robertson (Ed.). Edinburgh: E&D Livingstone. (Reprinted Birmingham, AL: Classics of Psychiatry and Behavioral Science, (1989)

Kramlinger, K., & Post, R. (1989a). The addition of lithium to carbamazepine. *Archives of General Psychiatry, 46,* 794–800.

Kramlinger, K. G., & Post, R. M. (1989b). Adding lithium carbonate to carbamazepine: Antimanic efficacy in treatment-resistant mania. *Acta Psychiatrica Scandinavica, 79,* 378–385.

Kreen, M. J., & Koob, G. F. (1998). Drug dependence: Stress and dysregulation of brain reward pathways. *Drug and Alcohol Dependence, 51,* 23–47.

Kripke, D. F., & Robinson, D. (1985). Ten years with a lithium group. *McLean Hospital Journal, 10,* 1–11.

Kufferle, B. (1988). Group dynamics as emotional turmoil precipitating psychotic manifestations. *Psychopathology, 21,* 111–115.

Kuhn, R. (1958). The treatment of depressive states with G22355 (imipramine hydrochloride). *American Journal of Psychiatry, 115,* 459–464.

Lachman, H. M., Morrow, B., Shprintzen, R., Veit, S., Parsia, S. S., Faedda, G., Goldberg, R., Kucherlapati, R., & Papolos, D. F. (1996). Association of codon 108/158 catechol-o-methyltranferase gene polymorphism with the psychiatric manifestations of velocardia-facial syndrome. *American Journal of Medical Genetics, 67*(5), 468–472.

Lam, D. H., Bright, J., Jones, S., Hayward, P., Schuck, N., Chisolm, D., & Sham, P. (2000). Cognitive therapy for bipolar illness—a pilot study of relapse prevention. *Cognitive Therapy Research, 24,* 503–520.

Landerman, R., George, L. K., Campbell, R. T., & Blaser, D. G. (1989). Alternative models of the stress buffering hypothesis. *American Journal of Community Psychology, 17,* 625–642.

Leaf, A. (1993). Preventive medicine for our ailing health care system. *Journal of the American Medical Association, 269,* 616–618.

Lee, S., Wing, Y. K., & Wong, K. C. (1992). Knowledge and compliance towards lithium therapy among Chinese psychiatric patients in Hong Kong. *Australia and New Zealand Psychiatry, 26,* 444–448.

Lehman, H., & Hanrahan, G. (1954). Chlorpromazine: New inhibiting agent for psychomotor excitement and manic states. *Archieves of Neurological Psychiatry, 71,* 227–237.

Lenox, R., & Watson, D. (1994). Lithium and the brain: A psychopharmacological strategy to a molecular basis for manic-depressive illness. *Clinical Chemistry, 40*(2), L309–314.

Lenox, R. H., Newhouse, P. A., Creelman, W. L., & Whitaker, T. M. (1992). Adjunctive treatment of manic agitation with lorazepam versus haloperidol: A double-blind study. *Journal of Clinical Psychiatry, 53,* 47–52.

Lenzi, A., Lazzerini, F., Marazziti, D., Raffaelli, S., Rossi, G., & Cassano, G. B. (1993). Social class and mood disorders: Clinical features. *Social Psychiatry Psychiatric Epidemiology, 28,* 56–59.

Leonhard, K. (1979). *The classification of endogenous psychoses* (5th ed.), Trans. R. Berman. New York: Irvington.

Lerer, B., Moore, N., Meyendorff, E., Cho, S. R., & Gershon, S. (1987). Carbamazepine versus lithium in mania: A double-blind study. *Journal of Clinical Psychiatry, 48,* 89–93.

Leverich, M. (1990). Factors associated with relapse during maintenance treatment of affective disorders. *International Journal of Clinical Psychopharmacology, 5,* 135–156.

Levinstein, S., Klein, D., & Pollack, M. (1966). Follow-up study of formerly hospitalized voluntary psychiatric patients: The first two years. *American Journal of Psychiatry, 122,* 1102–1109.

Levitt, J., & Tsuang, M. (1988). The heterogeneity of schizoaffective disorders: Implications for treatment. *American Journal of Psychiatry, 145,* 926–936.

Lewinsohn, P. (1974). A behavioral approach to depression. In R. Friedman & M. Katz (Eds.), *The psychology of depression: Contemporary theory and research* (pp. 157–185). New York: Wiley.

Lewy, A., Nurnberger, J., Wehr, T., Pack, D., Becker, L., Powell, R., & Newsome, D. (1985). Supersensitivity to light: Possible trait marker for manic depressive illness. *American Journal of Psychiatry, 142,* 725–727.

Lewy, A., Wehr, T., Goodwin, F., Newsome, D., & Markey, S. (1980). Light suppresses melatonin secretion in humans. *Science, 210,* 1267–1269.

Li, T., Vallada, H. P., Liu, X., Xie, T., Tang, X., Zhao, J., O'Donovan, M. C., Murray, R.M., Sham, P. C., & Collier, D. A. (1998). Analysis of CAG/CTG repeat size in Chinese subjects with schizophrenia and bipolar affective disorder using the repeat expansion detection method. *Biological Psychiatry, 44,* 1160–1165.

Liebenluft, E. (1999). *Gender differences in mood and anxiety disorders: From bench to bedside.* Washington, DC: American Psychiatric Press.

Liebenluft, E., & Suppes, T. (1999). Treating bipolar illness: Focus on treatment algorithms and management of the sleep–wake cycle. *American Journal of Psychiatry, 156,* 976–981.

Lindblad, K., Bylander, P. O., Zander, C., Yuan, Q. P., Stahle, L., Engstrom, C., Balciuniene, J., Pettersson, U., Breschel, T., McInnis, M., Ross, C. A., Adolfsson, R., & Schalling, M. (1998). Two commonly expanded CAG/CTG repeat loci: Involvement in affective disorders? *Molecular Psychiatry, 3*(5), 405–410.

Lish, J., Dime-Meenan, S., Whybrow, P., Price, R. A., & Hirschfeld, R. (1994). The national depressive and manic depressive (DMDA) survey of bipolar members. *Journal of Affective Disorders, 31,* 281–294.

Loomer, H., Saunders, J., & Kline, N. (1957). A clinical and pharmacodynamic evaluation of iproniazid as a psychic energizer. *Psychiatric Research Reports, 8,* 129–141.

Lorig, K., Gonzalez, V., & Laurent, D. (1999). *The chronic disease self-management workshop: Leaders manual.* Stanford, CA: Stanford Patient Education Research Center.

Lorig, K., Holman, H., Sobel, D., Laurent, D., Gonzalez, V., & Minor, M. (1994). *Living a healthy life with chronic conditions.* Palo Alto, CA: Bull.

Ludman, E. J., Simon, G. E., Rutter, C. J., Bauer, M. S., & Unutzer, J. (2002). Adaptation of a measure for assewsing patient perception of provider support for self-management of bipolar disorder. *Bipolar Disorders, 4,* 249–253.

Lundquist, G. (1945). Prognosis and course in manic-depressive psychosis. *Acta Psychiatrica et Neurologica Scandinavica, 35*(Suppl), 1–96.

Lusznat, R., Murphy, D., & Nunn, C. (1988). Carbamazepine vs. lithium in the treatment and prophylaxis of mania. *British Journal of Psychiatry, 153,* 198–204.

Maggs, R. (1963). Treatment of manic illness with lithium carbonate. *British Journal of Psychiatry, 109,* 56–65.

Maj, M., Pirozzi, R., & Starace, F. (1989). Previous pattern of course of the illness as a predictor of response to lithium prophylaxis in bipolar illness. *Journal of Affective Disorders, 17,* 237–241.

Malhotra, A., Litman, R., & Pickar, D. (1993). Adverse effects of antipsychotic drugs. *Drug Safety, 9,* 429–436.

Manji, H. K., & Lenox, R. H. (2000). Signaling: Cellular insights into the pathophysiology of bipolar disorder. *Biological Psychiatry, 15, 48*(6), 518–530.

Markar, H., & Mander, A. (1989). Efficacy of lithium prophylaxis in clinical practice. *British Journal of Psychiatry, 155,* 496–500.

Markowitz, J., Weissman, M., Oulette, R., Lish, J., & Klerman, G. (1989). Quality of life in panic disorder. *Archives of General Psychiatry, 46,* 984–992.

Martinez-Áran, A., Vieta, E., Colom, F., Reinares, M., & Benabarre, A. (2000). Cognitive dysfunctions in bipolar disorder: Evidence of neuropsychological disturbances. *Psychotherapy and Psychosomatics, 69,* 2–18.

Mason, J. (1975). Emotion as reflected in patterns of endocrine integration. In L. Levi (Ed.), *Emotions—their parameters and measurement* (pp. 143–181). New York: Raven Press.

Massion, A., Warshaw, M., & Keller, M. (1993). Quality of life and psychiatric morbidity in panic disorder and generalized anxiety disorder. *American Journal of Psychiatry, 150,* 600–607.

Maynard, A. (1990). The design of future cost-benefit studies. *American Heart Journal, 119,* 761–765.

McCay, E. A. (1984). Schizophrenia and the effect of patient education. *Nursing Papers, 16,* 55–68.

McElroy, S. L., Altshuler, L. L., Suppes, T., Keck, P. E., Frye, M. A., Denicoff, K. D., Nolen, W. A., Kupka, R. W., Leverich, G. S., Rochussen, J., Rush, A. J., & Post, R. M. (2001). Axis I psychiatric comorbidity and its relationship to historical illness variables in 288 patients with bipolar disorder. *American Journal of Psychiatry, 158,* 420–426.

McElroy, S., Keck, P., Pope, H., Hudson, J. I., Faedda, G. L., & Swann, A. C. (1992). Clinical and research implications of the diagnosis of dysphoric or mixed mania or hypomania. *American Journal of Psychiatry, 149,* 1633–1644.

McGuire, T. (1991). Measuring the economic costs of schizophrenia. *Schizophrenia Bulletin, 17,* 375–388.

McInnis, M. G., McMahon, F. J., Chase, G. A., Simpson, S. O., Ross, C. A., & DePaula, J. R., Jr. (1993). Anticipation in bipolar affective disorder. *American Journal of Human Genetics, 53,* 385–390.

McLellan, A. T., Childress, A. R., & Woody, G. E. (1985). Drug abuse and psychiatric disorders: Role of drug choice. In A. I. Alterman (Ed.), *Substance abuse and psychopathology* (pp. 137–172). New York: Plenum Press.

Meehan, K., Shang, F., David, S., Tohen, M., Janicak, P., Small, J., Koch, K., Rizk, R., Walker, D., Tran, P, & Breier, A. (2001). A double-blind randomized comparison of the efficacy and safety of intramuscular injections of olanzapine lorazepam or placebo in treating acutely agitated patients diagnosed with bipolar mania. *Journal of Clinical Psychopharmacology, 21,* 389–397.

Mendels, J. (1976). Lithium in the treatment of depression. *American Journal of Psychiatry, 133,* 373–378.

Mendlewicz, J., & Rainer, J. D. (1977). Adoption study supporting genetic transmission in manic-depressive illness. *Nature, 268,* 327–329.

Mendlewicz, J., & Youdim, M. B. H. (1980). Antidepressant potentiation of 5-hydroxytryptophan by L-deprenil in affective illness. *Journal of Affective Disorders, 2,* 137–146.

Miklowitz, D. J., & Goldstein, M. J. (1988). Family factors and the course of bipolar affective disorder. *Archives of General Psychiatry, 45,* 225–231.

Miklowitz, D. J., & Goldstein, M. J. (1990). Behavioral family treatment for patients with bipolar affective disorder. *Behavior Modification, 14,* 457–489.

Miklowitz, D. J., & Goldstein, M. J. (1997). *Bipolar disorder: A family-focused treatment approach.* New York: Guilford.

Miklowitz, D. J., Simoneau, T. L., George, E. L., Richards, J. A., Kalbag, A., Sachs-Ericsson, N., & Suddath, R. (2000). Family-focused treatment of bipolar disorder: One-year effects of a psychoeducational program in conjunction with pharmacotherapy. *Biological Psychiatry, 48,* 582–592.

Miller, W. R., & Rollnick, S. (2002). *Motivational interviewing. Preparing people for change* (2nd ed.). New York: Guilford.

Mishory, A., Yaroslavsky, Y., Bersudsky, Y., & Belmaker, R. H. (2000). Phenytoin as an antimanic anticonvulsant: A controlled study. *American Journal of Psychiatry, 157,* 463–465.

Moller, H. J., Kissling, W., Riehl, T., Bauml, J., Binz, U., & Wendt, G. (1989). Double-blind evaluation of the antimanic properties of carbamazepine as a comedication to haloperidol. *Progress in Neuropsychopharmacology and Biological Psychiatry, 13,* 127–136.

Moller, H. J., von Zerssen, D., Emrich, H. M., Kissling, W., Cording, C., Schietsch, H. J., Riedel, E. (1979). Action of d-pro9pranolol in manic psychosis. *Archives of Psychiatry and Nervenkrankheiten, 227,* 301–317.

Moller, M., & Wer, J. (1989). Simultaneous patient/family education regarding schizophrenia. Archives of Psychiatric Nursing, 3, 332–337.

Montgomery, S. A. (1998). Efficacy and safety of the selective serotonin reuptake inhibitors in treating depression in the elderly patients. *International Clinical Psychopharmacology, 13*(Suppl 5), S49–54.

Muller-Oerlinghausen, B., Retzow, A., Henn, F. A. Giedeke, H., & Walden, J. (2000). Valproate as an adjunct to neuroleptic medication for the treatment of acute episodes of mania: A prospective, randomized, double-blind, placebo-controlled multicenter study. *Journal of Clinical Psychopharmacology, 20,* 195–203.

Mundo, E., Walker, M., Cate, T., Macciardi, F., & Kennedy, J. L. (2001). The role of serotonin transporter protein gene in antidepressant-induced mania in bipolar disorder: Preliminary findings. *Archives of General Psychiatry, 58*(6), 539–544.

Murray, C. J. L., & Lopez, A. D. (Eds.). (1996). *The global burden of disease: A comprehensive assessment of mortality and disability from diseases, injuries, and risk factors in 1990 and projected to 2020.* Cambridge, MA: Harvard University Press.

Mynors-Wallis, L. M., Gath, D. H., Day, A. & Baker, F. (2000). Randomized controlled trial of problem solving treatment, antidepressant medication, and combined treatment for major depression in primary care. *British Medical Journal, 320,* 26–30.

Nasrallah, H., Coffman, J., & Olson, S. (1989). Structural brain imaging findings in affective disorders: An overview. *Journal of Neuropsychiatry and Clinical Neuroscience, 1,* 21–26.

National Advisory Mental Health Council (NAMC). (1993). Health care reform for Americans with severe mental illness: Report of the National Advisory Mental Health Council. *American Journal of Psychiatry, 150,* 1445–1465.

National Institute of Mental Health (NIMH) National Advisory Mental Health Council. (1991). *Caring for people with severe mental disorders: A national plan of research to improve services.* USDHHS Pub. No. (ADM)91-1762). Washington, DC: U.S. Government Printing Office.

National Institute of Mental Health (NIMH) National Advisory Mental Health Council. (1993). Health care reform for Americans with severe mental illness: Report of the National Advisory Mental Health Council. *American Journal of Psychiatry, 150,* 1445–1465.

Naylor, G. J., Martin, B., Hopwood, S. E., & Watson, Y. (1986). A two-year double-blind crossover trial of the prophylactic effect of methylene blue in manic-depressive psychosis. *Biological Psychiatry, 21,* 915–920.

Naylor, G. J., & Smith, A. H. W. (1981). Vanadium: A possible aetiological factor in manic depressive illness. *Psychological Medicine, 11,* 249–256.

Nemeroff, C. B., Evans, D. L., Gyulai, L., Sachs, G. S., Bowden, C. L., Gergel, I. P., Oakes, R., Pitts, C. D. (2001). Double-blind, placebo-controlled comparison of imipramine and paroxetine in the treatment of bipolar depression. *American Journal of Psychiatry, 158,* 906–203.

Nilsson, A., & Axelsson, R. (1989). Psychopathology during long-term lithium treatment of patients with major affective disorders: A prospective study. *Acta Psychiatrica Scandinavica, 80,* 375–388.

Nurnberger, J., Berrettini, W., Tamarkin, L., Hamovit, J., Norton, J., & Gershon, E. S. (1989). Supersensitivity to melatonin suppression by light in young people at high risk for affective disorder: A preliminary report. *Neuropsychopharmacology, 1,* 217–223.

O'Connell, R. A., Mayo, J. A., Eng, L. K., Jones, J. S., & Gabel, R. H. (1985). Social support and long term lithium outcome. *British Journal of Psychiatry, 147,* 272–275.

O'Connell, R., Mayo, J., Flatow, L., Cuthbertson, B., & O'Brien, B. (1991). Outcome of bipolar disorder on long-term treatment with lithium. *British Journal of Psychiatry, 159,* 123–129.

Okuma, T., Inanaga, K., Otsuki, S., Sarai, K., Takahashi, R., Hazama, H., Mori A., & Watanabe, M. (1979). Comparison of the antimatic efficacy of carbamazepine and chlorpromazine: A double-blind controlled study. *Psychopharmacology, 66,* 211–217.

Okuma, T., Inanaga, K., Otsuki, S., Sarai, K., Takahashi, R., Hazama, H., Mori, A, & Watanabe, S. (1981). A preliminary double-blind study on the efficacy of carbamazepine in prophylaxis of manic-depressive illness. *Psychopharmacology, 73,* 95–96.

Okuma, T., Yamashita, I., Takahashi, R., Itoh, H., Otsuki, S., Watanabe, S., Sarai, K., Hazama, H., & Inanaga, K. (1990). Comparison of the antimanic efficacy of carbamazepine and lithium carbonate by double-blind controlled study. *Pharmacopsychiatry, 23,* 143–150.

Orlando, I. J. (1961). *The dynamic nurse–patient relationship: Function, process and principles.* New York: Putnam.

Padesky, C. A., & Greenberger, D. (1995). *Clinician's guide to mind over mood.* New York: Guilford Press.

Palmer, A. G., & Williams, H. (1995). CBT in a group format for bi-polar affective disorder. *Behavioral and Cognitive Psychotherapy, 23,* 153–168.

Pande, A. C., Crockett, J. G., Janney, C. A., Werth, J. L., & Tsaroucha, G. (2000). Gabapentin in bipolar disorder: A placebo-controlled trial of adjunctive therapy. *Bipolar Disorder, 2,* 249–255.

Papolos, D. F., Veit, S., Faedda, G. L., Saito, T., & Lachman, H. M. (1998). Ultra-rapid cycling bipolar disorder is associated with low activity catecholamine-o-methyltransferase allele. *Molecular Psychiatry, 3*(4), 346–349.

Parsons, P. L. (1965). Mental health of Swansea's old folk. *British Journal of Preventive and Social Medicine, 19,* 43–47.

Paykel, E., & Cooper, Z. (1992). Life events and social stress. In E. Paykel (Ed.), *Handbook of affective disorders* (pp. 149–170). New York: Guilford.

Payton, O. D., & Ivy, A. E. (1981). The role of psychoeducation in allied health practice and education. *Journal of Allied Health, 10,* 91–100.

Pazzaglia, P. J., Post, R. M., Ketter, T. A., Callahan, A. M., Marangeli, L. B., Frye, M. A., George, M. S., Kimbrell, T. A., Leverich, G. S., Cora-Locatelli, G., & Luckenbaugh, D. (1998). Nimodipine monotherapy and carbamazepine augmentation in patients with refractory recurrent affective illness. *Journal of Clinical Psychopharmacology, 18,* 404–413.

Pazzaglia, P. J., Post, R. M., Ketter, T. A., George, M. S., & Marangell, L. B. (1993). Preliminary controlled trial of nimodipine in ultra-rapid cycling affective dy. *Psychiatry Research, 49,* 257–272.

Peet, M., & Harvey, N. S. (1991). Lithium maintenance: 1. A standard education programme for patients. *British Journal of Psychiatry, 158,* 197–200.

Perlick, D., Clarkin, J. F., Sirey, J., Raue, P., Greenfield, S., Struening, E., & Rosenheck, R. (1999). Burden experienced by care-givers of persons with bipolar affective disorder. *British Journal of Psychiatry, 175,* 56–62.

Perris, H. (1984a). Life events and depression: 1. Effect of sex, age and civil status. *Journal of Affective Disorders, 7,* 11–24.

Perris, H. (1984b). Life events and depression: 2. Results in diagnostic subgroups and in relation to the recurrence of depression. *Journal of Affective Disorders, 7,* 25–36.

Perry, A., Tarrier, N., Morriss, R., McCarthy, E., & Limb, K. (1999). Randomised controlled trial of efficacy of teaching patients with bipolar disorder to identify early symptoms of relapse and obtain treatment. *British Medical Journal, 318,* 149–153.

Peterson, C., & Seligman, M. (1984). Causal explanations as a risk factor for depression: Theory and evidence. *Psychological Review, 91,* 347–374.

Peterson, C., & Seligman, M. (1987). Explanatory style and illness: Personality and physical health. *Journal of Personality, 55,* 237–265.

Petronis, A., & Kennedy, J. (1995). Unstable genes—unstable mind? *American Journal of Psychiatry, 152,* 164–172.

Petterson, U. (1977). Manic-depressive illness: A clinical, social, and genetic study. *Acta Psychiatrica Scandinavica,* (Suppl), 269.

Petty, F., Kramer, G. L., Fulton, M., Moeller, F. G., & Rush, A. J. (1993). Low plasma GABA is a trait-like marker for bipolar illness. *Neuropsychopharmacology, 9,* 125–132.

Petty, F., Rush, J., Davis, J., Calabrese, J., Kimmel, S., Kramer, G., Small, J., Miller, M., Swann, A., Orsulak, P., Blake, M., & Bowden, C. (1996). Plasma GABA predicts acute response to divalproex in mania. *Biological Psychiatry, 39,* 278–284.

Platman, S. (1970). A comparison of lithium carbonate and chlorpromazine in mania. *American Journal of Psychiatry, 127,* 351–353.

Plumlee, A. A. (1986). Biological rhythms and affective illness. *Journal of psychosocial Nursing, 24,* 12–17.

Pollack, L. E. (1990). Improving relationships: Groups for inpatients with bipolar disorder. *Journal of Psychosocial Nursing and Mental Health Services, 28,* 17–22.

Pollack, L. E. (1993). Content analysis of groups for inpatients with bipolar disorder. *Applied Nursing Research, 6,* 19–27.

Pope, H., McElroy, S., Keck, P., & Hudson, J. (1991). Valproate in the treatment of acute mania. *Archives of General Psychiatry, 48,* 62–68.

Post, R. M. (1992). Transduction of psychosocial stress into the neurobiology of recurrent affective disorder. *American Journal of Psychiatry, 149,* 999–1010.

Post, R. M., Gerner, R. H., Carman, J. S., Gillin, J. C., Jimerson, D. C., Goodwin, F. K., & Bunney, W. E. (1978). Effects of a dopamine agonist piribedil in depressed patients. *Archives of General Psychiatry, 35,* 609–615.

Post, R. M., Kotin, J., & Goodwin, F. K. (1976). Effects of sleep depreivation on mood and central amine metabolism in depressed patients. *Archives of General Psychiatry, 33,* 627–632.

Post, R., DeLisi, L., Holcomb, H., Uhde, T., Cohen, R., & Buchsbaum, M. (1987). Glucose utilization in the temporal cortex of affectively ill patients: Positron emission tomography. *Biological Psychiatry, 22,* 545–553.

Post, R. M., Leverich, G. S., Altshuler, L., & Mikalavskas, K. (1992). Lithium-discontinuation-induced refractoriness: Preliminary observations. *American Journal of Psychiatry, 149,* 1727–1729.

Post, R., Rubinow, D., Ballenger, J. (1985). Conditioning, sensitization, and kindling: Implications for the course of affective illness. In R. Post & J. Ballenger (Eds.), *Neurobiology of mood disorders* (pp. 432–466). Baltimore: Williams & Wilkins.

Post, R. M., Uhde, T. W., Rubinow, D. R., & Weiss, S. (1986). Anti-manic effects of carbamazepine: Mechanisms of action and implications for the biochemistry of manic-depressive illness. In A. Swann (Ed.), *Mania: New research and treatment* (pp. 95–176). Washington, DC: American Psychiatric Press.

Potash, J. B., & DePaulo, J. R. (2000). Searching high and Low: A review of the genetics of bipolar disorder. *Bipolar Disorders, 2,* 8–26.

Powell, B. J., Othmer, E., Sinkhorn, C. (1977). Pharmacological aftercare for homogeneous groups of patients. *Hospital and Community Psychiatry, 28,* 125–127.

Prange, A. J. (1964). The pharmacology and biochemistry of depression. *Disorders of the Nervous System, 25,* 217–221.

Prien, R. (1972). Comparison of lithium carbonate and chlorpromazine in the treatment of mania. *Archives of General Psychiatry, 26,* 146–153.

Prien, R. (1973). Prophylactic efficacy of lithium carbonate in manic-depressive illness. *Archives of General Psychiatry, 28,* 337–341.

Prien, R., Caffey, E., & Klett, C. J. (1972). A comparison of lithium carbonate and chlorpromazine in the treatment of excited schizo-affectives. *Archives of General Psychiatry, 27,* 182–189.

Prien, R., & Gelenberg, A. (1989). Alternatives to lithium for the preventive treatment of bipolar disorder. *American Journal of Psychiatry, 146,* 840–848.

Prien, R., Klett, C. J., & Caffey, E. (1973b). Lithium carbonate and imipramine in prevention of affective episodes. *Archives of General Psychiatry, 29,* 420–425.

Prien, R. F., Kupfer, D. H., Mansky, P. A., Small, J. G., Tuason, V. B., Voss, C. B., & Johnson, W. E. (1984). Drug therapy in the prevention of recurrences in unipolar and bipolar affective disorders. *Archives of General Psychiatry, 41,* 1096–1104.

Prochaska, J., & DiClemente, C. (1984). *The transtheoretical approach: Crossing traditional boundaries of therapy.* Homewood, IL: Dow Jones-Irwin.

Quitkin, F. M., Kane, J., Rifkin, A., Ramos-lorenzi, J. R., & Nayak, D. V.

(1981). Prophylactic lithium carbonate with and without imipramine for fipolar 1 patients. *Archives of General Psychiatry, 38,* 902–907.

Regier, D., Farmer, M., Rae, D., Locke, B., Keith, S., Judd, L., & Goodwin, F. (1990). Comorbidity of mental disorders with alcohol and other drugs: Results from the Epidemiological Catchment Area (ECA) study. *Journal of the American Medical Association, 264,* 2511–2518.

Rehm, L. (1985). A self-management therapy program for depression. *International Journal of Mental Health, 13,* 34–53.

Reich, T., Clayton, P., & Winokur, G. (1969). Family hostory studies: 5. The genetics of mania. *American Journal of Psychiatry, 125,* 1358–1369.

Reilly-Harrington, N. A., Alloy, L. B., Fresco, D. M., & Whitehouse, W. G. (1999). Cognitive styles and life events interact to predict bipolar and unipolar symptomatology. *Journal of Abnormal Psychology, 108*(4), 567–578.

Retzer, A., Simon, F. B., Weber, G., Stierlin, H., & Schmidt, G. (1991). A follow-up study of manic-depressive and schizoaffective psychoses after systemic family therapy. *Family Process, 30,* 139–153.

Rice, D., Kelman, S., Miller, I.., & Dunmeyer, S. (1990). *The economic costs of alcohol and drug abuse and mental illness: 1985.* DHHS Publication No, ADM90-1694). Rockville, MD: National Institute of Mental Health.

Richelson, E. (1993). Treatment of acute depression. *Psychiatric Clinics of North America, 16,* 461–478.

Riefman, A., & Wyatt, R. J. (1980). Lithium: A brake in the rising cost of mental illness. *Archives of General Psychiatry, 37,* 385–388.

Robins, E., & Guze, S. B. (1970). Establishment of diagnostic validity in psychiatric illness: Its application to schizophrenia. *American Journal of Psychiatry, 126,* 983–987.

Robins, L., & Regier, D. (1990). *Psychiatric disorders in America. The Epidemiologic Catchment Area study.* New York: The Free Press.

Romans, S. G., & McPherson, H. M. (1992). The social networks of bipolar affective disorder patients. *Journal of Affective Disorders, 25,* 221–228.

Rotter, J. (1966). Generalized expectancies for internal versus external control of reinforcement. *Psychiatric Monographs, 80,* 1–28.

Roy-Byrne, P., Post, R., Uhde, T., Porcu, T., & Davis, D. (1985). The longitudinal course of recurrent affective illness: Life chart data from research patients at the NIMH. *Acta Psychiatrica Scandinavica, 71*(Suppl 317), 3–34.

Rudorfer, M., Manji, H., & Potter, W. (1994). Comparative tolerability profiles of the newer versus older antidepressants. *Drug Safety, 10,* 18–46.

Rush, A. G., Rago, W. V., Crismon, M. L., Toprac, M. G., Shon, S. P., Suppes, T., Miller, A. L., Trivedi, M. H., Swann, A. C., Biggs, M. M., Shores-Wilson, K., Kashner, T. M., Pigott, T., Chiles, J. A., Gilbert, D. M., &

Altshuler, K. Z. (1999). Medication treatment for the severely and persistently mentally ill: The Texas Medication Algorithm Project. *Journal of Clinical Psychiatry, 60*, 284–291.

Rush, A. J., & Hollon, S. (1991). Depression. In B. Beitman & G. Klerman (Eds.), *Integrating pharmacotherapy and psychotherapy* (pp. 121–142). Washington, DC: American Psychiatric Press.

Sachs, G., Lafer, B., Stoll, A., Banov, M., Thibault, A., Tohen, M., & Rosenbaum, J. (1994). A double-blind trial of bupropion vs. desipramine for bipolar depression. *Journal of Clinical Psychiatry, 55*, 391–393.

Sachs, G., Lafer, B., Truman, C., Noeth, M., & Thibault, A. (1994). Lithium: Miracle, myth, and misunderstanding. *Psychiatric Annals, 24*, 299–306.

Sachs, G., Printz, D. J., Kahn, D. A., Carpenter, D., & Docherty, J. P. (2000). *Medication treatment of bipolar disorder 2000.* Minneapolis: McGraw-Hill Healthcare Information Programs.

Sackeim, H. A., Decina, P., Kanzler, M., Kerr, B., & Malitz, S. (1987). Effects of electrode placement on the efficacy of titrated, low-dose ECT. *American Journal of Psychiatry, 144*, 1449–1455.

Sackeim, H. A., Prudic, J., Devanand, D. P., Kiersky, J. E., Fitzsimmons, L., Moody, B. J., McElhiney, M. C., Coleman, E. A., & Settembrino, J. M. (1993). Effects of stimulus intensity and electrode placement on the efficacy and cognitive effects of electroconvulsive therapy. *New England Journal of Medicine, 328*, 839–846.

Sackeim, H. A., Prudic, J., Devanand, D. P., Nobler, M. S., Lisanby, S. H., Peyser, S., Fitzsimmons, L., Moody, B. J., & Clark, J. (2000). A prospective, randomized, double-blind comparison of bilateral and right unilateral electroconvulsive therapy at different stimulus intensities. *Archives of General Psychiatry, 57*, 425–434.

Sassi, R. B., & Soares, J. C. (2002). Neural circuitry and signaling in bipolar disorder. In G. B. Kaplan & R. P. Hammer (Eds.), *Brain circuitry in psychiatry: Basic science and clinical implications* (pp. 179–200). Washington, DC: American Psychiatric Press.

Savard, R. J., Rey, A. C., & Post, R. M. (1980). Halstead-Reitan category test in bipolar and unipolar affective disorders. *Journal of Nervous and Mental Diseases, 168*, 297–304.

Scanlon, P. (1982). Fee and missed appointments as transference issues. *Social Casework, 63*, 540–546.

Schatzberg, A. F., Cole, J. O., & DeBattista, C. (1997). *Manual of clinical psychopharmacology* (3rd ed.). Washington, DC: American Psychiatric Press.

Schildkraut, J. (1965). The catecholamine hypothesis of affective disorder: A review of supporting evidence. *American Journal of Psychiatry, 122*, 509–522.

Schnur, D. B., Mukherjee, S., Sackiem, H. A., Lee, C., & Roth, S. D. (1992).

Symptomatic predictors of ECT response in medication nonresponsive manic patients. *Journal of Clinical Psychiatry, 53,* 63–66.

Schou, M., Goldfield, M., Weinstein, M., & Villeneuve, A. (1973). Lithium and pregnancy, 1: Report from the Register of Lithium Babies. *British Medical Journal, 2,* 135–136.

Schwartz, D. (1961). Some suggestions for a unitary formulation of manic-depressive reactions. *Psychiatry, 24,* 238–245.

Sclare, P., & Creed, F. (1990). Life events and the onset of mania. *British Journal of Psychiatry, 156,* 508–514.

Scott, J. (1996a). Cognitive therapy for clients with bipolar disorder. *Behavioral and Cognitive Psychotherapy, 3,* 29–51.

Scott, J. (1996b). The role of cognitive behavior therapy in bipolar disorder. *Behavioral and Cognitive Psychotherapy, 24,* 195–208.

Seeger, P. A., Stern, S. L., & Dennert, J. W. (1989). A combined group and individual approach to outpatient lithium treatment. *Ohio Medicine, 85,* 300–302.

Segal, J., Berk, M., & Brook, S. (1998). Risperidone compared with both lithium and haloperidol in mania: A double-blind randomized controlled trial. *Clinical Neuropharmacology, 21,* 176–180.

Segal, Z., & Shaw, B. (1986). When cul-de-sacs are more mentality than reality: A rejoinder to Coyne and Gotlib. *Cognitive Therapy and Research, 10,* 707–714.

Seligman, M. (1975). *Helplessness: On depression, development and death.* San Francisco: Freeman.

Seligman, M. E., Abramson, L. Y., Semmel, A., & von Baeyer, C. (1979). Depressive attributional style. *Journal of Abnormal Psychology, 88*(3), 242–247.

Seligman, M., Nolen-Hoeksema, S., Thronton, N., & Thornton, K. (1990). Explanatory style as a mechanism of disappointing athletic performance. *Psychological Science, 1,* 143–146.

Shakir, S., Volkmar, F. R., Bacon, S., & Pfefferbaum, A. (1979). Group psychotherapy as an adjunct to lithium maintenance. *American Journal of Psychiatry, 136,* 455–456.

Shea, N., McBride, L., Gavin, C., & Bauer, M. (1995). *Effects of a high intensity ambulatory collaborative practice model on process and outcome of care for bipolar disorder.* Unpublished manuscript.

Shea, N., McBride, L., Gavin, C., Bauer, M. (1997). Effects of an ambulatory collaborative practice model on process and outcome of care for bipolar disorder. *Journal of the American Psychiatric Nurses Association, 3,* 49–57.

Shelley, E., & Fieve, R. (1974). The use of nonphysicians in a health maintenance program for affective disorders. *Hospital and Community Psychiatry, 25,* 303–305.

Shopsin, B. (1983). Bupropion's prophylactic efficacy in bipolar affective illness. *Journal of Clinical Psychiatry, 44*(Suppl 5), 163–169.

Shopsin, B., Gershon, S., Thompson, H., & Collins, P. (1975). Psychoactive drugs in mania. *Archives of General Psychiatry, 32,* 34–42.

Shulman, K., Walker, S., MacKenzie, S., & Knowles, S. (1989). Dietary restriction, tyramine, and the use of monoamine oxidase inhibitors. *Journal of Clinical Psychopharmacology, 9,* 397–402.

Silverstone, T., Moclobemide Biopolar Study Group. (2001). Moclobemide vs. imipramine in bipolar depression: A multicentre double-blind clinical trial. *Acta Psychiatrica Scandinavica,104,* 104–109.

Simhandl, C., Denk, E., & Thau, K. (1993). The comparative efficacy of carbanazepine low and high serum level and lithium carbonate in the prophylaxix of affective disorders. *Journal of Affective Disorders, 28,* 221–231.

Simon, G. E., Ludman, E. J., Unutzer, J., & Bauer, M. S. (2002a). Design and implementation of a randomized trial evaluating systematic care for bipolar disorder. *Bipolar Disorders, 4,* 226–236.

Simon, G. E., Ludman, E., Unutzer, J., & Bauer, M. S. (2002b). *Population-based treatment for bipolar disorders.* National Institute of Mental Health Services Research Meeting, Washington, DC.

Simon, G. E., & Unutzer, J. (1999). Health care utilization and costs among patients treated for bipolar disorder in an insured population. *Psychiatric Services, 50,* 1303–1308.

Simoneau, T. L., Miklowitz, D. J., Richards, J. A., & Saleem, R. (1998). Expressed emotion and interactional patterns in the families of bipolar patients. *Journal of Abnormal Psychology, 107,* 497–507.

Simoneau, T. L., Miklowitz, D. J., Richards, J. A., Saleem, R., & George, E. L. (2000). Bipolar disorder and family communication: Effects of a psychoeducational treatment program. *Journal of Abnormal Psychology, 108,* 588–597.

Simpson, S. G., Folstein, S. E., Meyers, D. A., McMahon, F. J., Brusco, D. M., & DePaulo, J. R., Jr. (1993). Bipolar II: The most common bipolar phenotype? *American Journal of Psychiatry, 150,* 901–903.

Small, J. G., Klapper, M. H., Milstein, V., Kellams, J., Miller, M. J., Marhenke, J. D., & Small, I. F. (1991). Carbamazepine compared with lithium in the treatment of mania. *Archives of General Psychiatry, 48,* 915–921.

Soares, J. C., Chen, G., Dippold, C. S., Wells, K. F., Frank, E., Kupfer, D. J., Manji, H. K., & Mallinger, A. G. (2000). Concurrent measures of protein kinase C and phosphoinositides in lithium-treated bipolar patients and healthy individuals: A preliminary study. *Psychiatry Research, 95*(2), 109–118.

Solomon, D., Ryan, C., Keitner, G., Miller, I., Shea, T., Kazim, A, & Keller, M. (1997). A pilot study of lithium carbonate plus divalproex sodium for the continuation and maintenance treatment of patients with bipolar I disorder. *Journal of Clinical Psychiatry, 58,* 95–99.

Spitzer, R. L., Endicott, J., & Bobins, E. (1978). Research diagnostic criteria: Rationale and reliability. *Archives of General Psychiatry, 35,* 773–782.

Spring, G., Schweid, D., Gray, C., Steinberg, J., & Horwitz, M. (1970). A double-blind comparison of lithium and chlorpromazine in the treatment of manic states. *American Journal of Psychiatry, 126,* 1306–1309 or Supp 140–143.

Stahl, S. M. (2000). *Essential psychopharmacology* (2nd ed.). Cambridge: University Press.

Stallone, F., Shelley, E., Mendlewizc, J., & Fieve, R. R. (1973). The use of lithium in affective disorders III: A double-blind study of prophylaxis in bipolar illness. *American Journal of Psychiatry, 130,* 1006–1010.

Stancer, H. C., & Persad, E. (1982). Treatment of intractable rapid-cycling manic-depressive disorder with levothyroxine: Clinical observations. *Archives of General Psychiatry, 39*(3), 311–312.

Stanniland, C., & Taylor, D. (2000). Tolerability of atypical antipsychotics. *Drug Safety, 22,* 195–214.

Starkstein, S. E., Boston, J. D., & Robinson, R. G. G. (1988). Mechanisms of mania after brain injury: Twelve case reports and review of the literature. *Journal of Nervous and Mental Disorders, 176,* 87–100.

Stewart, A., Greenfield, S., Hays, R., Wells, K., Rogers, W., Berry, S., McGlynn, E., & Ware, J. (1989). Functional status and well-being of patients with chronic conditions. *Journal of the American Medical Association, 262,* 907–913.

Stewart, A., & Ware, J. (1992). *Measuring functioning and well-being: The medical outcomes study approach.* Durham, NC: Duke University Press.

Stokes, P. E., Stoll, P. M., Shamoian, C. A., & Patton, M. J. (1971). Efficacy of lithium as acute treatment of manic-depressive illness. *Lancet,* 1319–1325.

Stoll, A. L., Serverus, E., Freeman, M. P., Rueter, S., Zboyan, H. A., Diamond, E., Cress, K. K., & Marangell, L. B. (1999). Omega 3 fatty acids in bipolar disorder. *Archives of General Psychiatry, 56,* 407–412.

Stoudemire, A., Frank, R., Hedemark, N., Kamlet, M., & Blazer, D. (1986). The economic burden of depression. *General Hospital Psychiatry, 8,* 387–394.

Strakowski, S. M., Keck, P. E., Jr., McElroy, S. L., West, S. A., Sax, K. W., Hawkins, J. M., Kmetz, G. F., Upadhyaya, V. H., Tugrul, K. C., & Bourne, M. L. (1998). Twelve-month outcome after a first hospitalization for affective psychosis. *Archives of General Psychiatry, 55,* 49–55.

Strakowski, S. M., Tohen, M., Stoll, A. L., Faedda, G. L., & Goodwin, D. C. (1992). Comorbidity in mania at first hospitalization). *American Journal of Psychiatry, 149,* 554–556.

Strakowski, S. M., Shelton, R. C., & Kolbrener, M. L. (1993). The effects of race and comorbidity on clinical diagnosis in patients with psychosis. *Journal of Clinical Psychiatry, 54,* 96–102.

Strakowski, S. M., Wilson, D. R., Tohen, M., et al. (1993). Structural brain abnormalities in first-episode mania. *Biological Psychiatry, 33,* 602–609.

Strakowski, S. M., Woods, B. T., & Tohen, M. (1993). MRI subcortical signal hyperintensities in mania at first hospitalization. *Biological Psychiatry, 33,* 204–206.

Strip, E. (2000). Novel antipsychotics: Issues and controversies—typicality of atypical antipsychotics. *Journal of Psychiatry and Neuroscience, 25,* 137–153.

Suppes, T., Baldessarini, R. J., Faedda, G. L., Jondo, L., & Tohen, M. (1993). Discontinuation of maintenance treatment in bipolar disorder: Risks and implications. *Harvard Review of Psychiatry, 1,* 131–144.

Sussman, N. (1994). The potential benefits of serotonin receptor-specific agents. *Journal of Clinical Psychiatry, 55*(Suppl), 45–51.

Swann, A. C. (2001). Major system toxicities and side effects of anticonvulsants. *Journal of Clinical Psychiatry, 62*(Suppl 14), 16–21.

Swann, A. C., Secunda, S. K., Katz, M. M., Koslow, S. H., Maas, J. W., chang, S., & Robins, E. (1986). Lithium treatment of mania: Clinical characteristics, specificity of symptom change, and outcome. *Psychiatric Research, 18,* 127–141.

Takahashi, R., Sakuma, A., Itoh, K., Itoh, H., Kurihara, M., Saito, M., & Watanabe, M. (1975). Comparison of efficacy of lithium carbonate and chlorpromazine in mania. *Archives of General Psychiatry, 32,* 1310–1318.

Taylor, D. M., & McAskill, R. (2000). Atypical antipsychotics and weight gain—a systematic review. *Acta Psychiatrica Scandinavica, 101,* 416–432.

Taylor, M. A., Abrams, R., & Hayman, M. A. (1980). The classification of affective disorders: A reassessment of the bipolar-unipolar dichotomy: A clinical, laboratory and family study. *Journal of Affective Disorders, 2,* 95–109.

Terman, M., Terman, J., Quitkin, F., McGrath, P. J., Stewart, J. W., & Rafferty, B. (1989). Light therapy for seasonal affective disorder: A review of efficacy. *Neuropsychopharmacology, 2,* 1–22.

Thase, M., Mallinger, A., McKnight, D., & Himmelhoch, J. M. (1992). Treatment of imipramine-resistant recurrent depression: 4. A double-blind crossover study of tranylcypromine for anergic bipolar depression. *American Journal of Psychiatry, 149,* 195–198.

Thase, M. E., & Sachs, G. S. (2000). Bipolar depression: Pharmacotherapy and related therapeutic strategies. *Biological Psychiatry, 48,* 558–572.

Tohen, M., Baker, R. W., Altshuler, L. L., Zarate, C. A., Suppes, T., Ketter, T. A., Milton, D. R., Risser, R., Gilmore, J. A., Breier, A., & Tollefson, G. A. (2002). Olanzapine versus divalproex in the treatment of acute mania. *American Journal of Psychiatry, 159,* 1011–1017.

Tohen, M., Jacobs, T. G., Grundy, S. L., McElroy, S. L., Banov, M. C., Janicak, P. G., Sanger, T., Risser, R., Shang, F., Toma, V., Francis, J., Tollefson, G. D., & Breier, A. (2000). Efficacy of olanzapine in acute bipolar mania: A double-blind placebo-controlled study. *Archives of General Psychiatry, 57,* 841–849.

Tohen, M., Sanger, T. M., McElroy, S. L., Tollefson, G. D., Chengappa, R., Daniel, D. G., Petty, F., Centorrino, F., Wang, R., Grundy, S. L., Greaney, M. G., Jacobs, T. G., David, S. R., Toma, V., and the Olanzapine HGEH Study Group. (1999). Olanzapine versus placebo in the treatment of acute mania. *American Journal of Psychiatry, 156,* 702–709.

Tohen, M., Waternaux, C., & Tsuang, M. (1999). Outcome in mania: A 4-year prospective follow-up of 75 patients utilizing survival analysis. *Archives of General Psychiatry, 47,* 1106–1111.

Torrance, G. (1987). Utility approach to measuring health-related quality of life. *Journal of Chronic Disease, 40,* 593–600.

Tsai, S. M., Chen, C., Kuo, C., Lee, J., Lee, H., & Strakowski, S. M. (2001). Fifteen-year outcome of treated bipolar disorder. *Journal of Affective Disorders, 63,* 215–220.

Tsuang, M., Woolson, R., & Fleming, J. (1979). Long-term outcome of major psychoses. *Archives of General Psychiatry, 36,* 1295–1301.

van Berkestijn, H., van der Meulen, L., Flentge, F., Dols, L., & van den Hoofdakker. (1990). RS 86 in manic disorder. *Biological Psychiatry, 27,* 109–112.

Van Gent, E., Vida, S., & Zwart, F. (1988). Group therapy in addition to lithium therapy in patients with bipolar disorders. *Acta Psychiatrica Belgica, 88,* 405–418.

Van Gent, E., & Zwart, F. (1991). Psychoeducation of partners of bipolar-manic patients. *Journal of Affective Disorders, 21,* 15–18.

Van Gent, E. M., & Zwart, F. M. (1993). Five-year follow-up after educational group therapy added to lithium prophylaxis: Five years after group added to lithium. *Depression, 1,* 225–226.

Vasudev, K., Goswami, U., & Kohli, K. (2000). Carbamazepine and valproate monotherapy: Feasibility, relative safety and efficacy and therapeutic drug monitoring in manic Disorder. *Psychopharmacology, 150,* 15–23.

Vaughan, C. E., & Leff, J. P. (1976). The influences of family and social factors on the course of psychiatric illness. *British Journal of Psychiatry, 129,* 125–137.

Veterans Health Administration (VHA). (1997). *Clinical guidelines for management of persons with psychoses.* Washington, DC: Office of Performance Management, VHA.

Vojta, C., Kinosian, B., Glick, H., Altshuler, L., & Bauer, M. (2001). Self-reported quality of life across mood states in bipolar disorder. *Comprehensive Psychiatry, 42,* 190–195.

Volkmar, F., Shakir, S., Bacon, S., & Pfefferbaum, A. (1981). Group therapy in the management of manic-depressive illness. *American Journal of Psychotherapy, 35,* 226–234.

Von Korff, M., Gruman, J., Schaefer, J., Curry, S. J., & Wagner, E. H. (1997). Collaborative management of chroinc illness. *Annals of Internal Medicine, 127,* 1097–1102.

Wagner, E. H., Austin, B. T., & Von Korff, M. (1996). Organizing care for patients with chronic illness. *Milbank Quarterly, 74,* 511–544.

Walden, J., Schaerer, L., Schloesser, S., & Grunze, H. (2000). An open longitudinal study of patients with bipolar rapid cycling treated with lithium or lamotrigine for mood stablization. *Bipolar Disorder, 2,* 336–339.

Wallace, C. (1986). Functional assessment in rehabilitation. *Schizophrenia Bulletin, 12,* 604–630.

Walton, S. A., Berk, M., & Brook, S. (1996). Superiority of lithium over verapamil in mania: A randomized, controlled, single-blind trial. *Journal of Clinical Psychiatry, 57,* 543–546.

Ware, J., Jr., Kosinski, M., & Keller, S. D. (1996). A 12-item short-form health survey: Construction of scales and preliminary tests of reliability and validity. *Medical Care, 34,* 220–233.

Wehr, T., & Goodwin, F. (1979). Rapid cycling in manic-depressives induced by tricyclic antidepressants. *Archives of General Psychiatry, 36,* 555–559.

Wehr, T., Goodwin, F., Wirz-Justice, A., Breitmeier, J., & Craig, C. (1982). Forty-eight-hour sleep–wake cycles in manic-depressive illness: Naturalistic observations and sleep deprivation experiments. *Archives of General Psychiatry, 39,* 559–565.

Wehr, T., Murdock, R., & Coryell, W. (1993). Can antidepressants induce rapid cycling? [Letters to the Editor]) *Archives of General Psychiatry, 50,* 495–498.

Wehr, T. A., Sack, D. A., & Rosenthal, N. E. (1987). Sleep reduction as a final common pathway in the genesis of mania. *American Journal of Psychiatry, 144,* 201–204.

Weinstein, M., & Stason, W. (1977). Foundations of cost-effectiveness analysis for health and medical practices. *New England Journal of Medicine, 296,* 71–21.

Weiss, R. D., Griffin, M. L., Greenfield, S. F., Najavits, L. M., Wyner, D., Soto, J. A., & Hennen, J. A. (2000). Group therapy for patients with bipolar disorder and substance dependence: Results of a pilot study. *Journal of Clinical Psychiatry, 61,* 361–367.

Weiss, R. D., Mirin, S. M., Griffin, M. L., & Michael, J. L. (1988). Psychopathology in cocaine abusers: Changing trends. *Journal of Nervous Mental Disorders, 176,* 719–725.

Weissman, M., & Klerman, G. (1991). Interpersonal psychotherapy for depression. In B. Beitman & G. Klerman (Eds.), *Integrating pharma-*

cotherapy and psychotherapy (pp. 379–394). Washington, DC: American Psychiatric Press.

Weissman, M. M., Leaf, P. J., Tischler, G. L., Blazer, D. G., Karno, M., Bruce, M. L., & Florio, L. P. (1988). Affective disorders in five United States communities. *Psychological Medicine, 18,* 141–153.

Weissman, M., Sholomskas, D., & John, K. (1981). The assessment of social adjustment: An update. *Archives of General Psychiatry, 38,* 1250–1258.

Weissman, M. M., & Myers, J. K. (1978). Affective disorders in a U.S. urban community: The use of research diagnostic criteria in an epidemiological survey. *Archives of General Psychiatry, 35,* 1304–1311.

Wells, K., Stewart, A., Hays, R., Burnam, M. A., Rogers, W., Daniels, M., Berry, S., Greenfield, S., & Ware, J. (1989). The functioning and well-being of depressed patients: Results from the Medical Outcomes Study. *Journal of the American Medical Association, 262,* 914–919.

Welner, A., Welner, Z., & Leonard, A. (1977). Bipolar manic-depressive disorder: A reassessment of course and outcome. *Comprehensive Psychiatry, 18,* 327–332.

Widiger, T., & Frances, A. (Eds.). *Sourcebook for DSM-IV.* Washington DC: American Psychiatric Press.

Wilcox, D. R. C., Gillan, R., & Hare, E. H. (1965). Do psychiatric patients take their drugs? *British Medical Journal, 2,* 790–792.

Wilkinson, L. (1991). A collaborative model: Ambulatory pharmacotherapy for chronic psychiatric patients. *Journal of Psychosocial Nursing, 29*(12), 26–29.

Williams, P., & McGlashan, T. (1987). Schizoaffective psychosis: 1. Comparative long-term outcome. *Archives of General Psychiatry, 44,* 130–137.

Winokur, G., Clayton, P. J., & Reich, T. (1969). *Manic depressive illness.* St. Louis: Mosby.

Winsberg, M. E. DeGolia,S. G., Strong, C. M., & Ketter, T. A. (2001). Divalproex therapy in medication—Naïve bipolar II depression. *Journal of Affective Disorders, 67,* 207–211.

World Health Organization. (1977). *Manual of the international statistical classification of diseases, injuries, and causes of death* (9th ed., Vol. 1). Geneva: Author.

Wyatt, R. J., & Hentner, I. (1995). An economic evaluation of manic-depressive illness—1991. *Social Psychiatry and Psychiatric Epidemiology, 30,* 213–219.

Yalom, I. D. (1975). *The theory and practice of group psychotherapy.* New York: Basic Books.

Yildiz, A., Sachs, G. S., Dorer, D. J., & Renshaw, P. F. (2001). 31P nuclear magnetic resonance spectroscopy findings in bipolar illness: A meta-analysis. *Psychiatry Research, 106*(3), 181–191.

Young, L. T., Joffe, R. T., Robb, J. C., MacQueen, G. M., Marriott, M., & Patelis-Siotis, I. (2000). Double-blind comparison of addition of a

second mood stablizer versus an antidepressant to an initial mood sta-
blizer for treatment of patients with bipolar depression. *American Journal of Psychiatry, 157,* 124–126.

Zarate, C. A. (2000). Antipsychotic drug side effect issues in bipolar manic patients. *Journal of Clinical Psychiatry, 61*(Suppl 8), 52–61.

Zaretsky, A. E., Segal, Z. V., & Gemar, M. (1999). Cognitive therapy for bipolar depression: A pilot study. *Canadian Journal of Psychiatry, 44,* 491–494.

Zarin, D. A., & Pass, T. M. (1987). Lithium and the single episode: When to begin long-term prophylaxis for bipolar disorder. *Medical Care, 25*(12), S76–S84.

Zornberg, G. L., & Pope, H. G. (1993). Treatment of depression in bipolar disorder: New directions for research. *Journal of Clinical Psychopharmacology, 13,* 397–408.

Zubieta, J. K., Huguelet, P., O'Neil, R. L., & Giordani, B. J. (2001). Cognitive function in euthymic bipolar I disorder. *Psychiatry Research, 102,* 9–20.

Zullow, H., Oettingen, G., Peterson, C., & Seligman, M. (1988). Pessimistic explanatory style in the historical record: CAVing LBJ, presidential candidates, and East versus West Berlin. *American Psychologist, 43,* 673–682.

Zullow, H., & Seligman M. (1990). Pessimistic rumination predicts defeat of presidential candidates, (1900 to 1984). *Psychological Inquiry, 1,* 52–61.

Index